THE NEGRO
IN AMERICA

BY

ARNOLD ROSE

WITH A FOREWORD

BY GUNNAR MYRDAL

THE BEACON PRESS   BOSTON

CONTENTS

Chapter 18. *The Negro Community*   293

Chapter 19. *America at the Crossroads*   312

FOREWORD

By Gunnar Myrdal

This book is a condensed version of *An American Dilemma,* published in 1944 as the final report of a comprehensive study of the American Negro problem, sponsored by the Carnegie Corporation of New York. The size of the original publication—1024 large pages of text in 45 chapters and 526 pages of introductions, footnotes, appendices and bibliography—is not deterring many who are not scholars and specialists from reading it, in whole or in part. Up until December 31st, 1947, it has sold over 30,000 copies. But it is obviously not a convenient book for the general reader. The present small volume, produced by one of my two friends and trusted collaborators in the preparation of the original volume, Dr. Arnold Rose, meets this demand for an easily accessible short text which should ensure it the widest possible circulation. In this work Dr. Rose has been assisted by his wife, Mrs. Caroline Baer Rose, who has contributed not only her time but also her loyalty to the *Dilemma,* for she assisted in doing research for the book at the end of the project.

It is no surprise at all but nevertheless most gratifying for me to realize, that the present volume is a faithful condensation, expertly done and true to the spirit of the whole undertaking. The cutting process has provided, in a palatable form, the gist of the knowledge and the thought that has gone into the larger study. So far as I can judge, no significant point of view, body of facts, or main conclusion is left out. Naturally, the supporting evidence is not here. The condensation is also more definitely focused on the Negro problem as such and contains relatively less of the foreigner's curiosity about American civilization as a whole. Naturally, also, the content of the ten appendices had to be omitted entirely, though the three first of them constitute the methodological justification for the study and indicate the ways in which it represents a major departure from previous social science studies. But without omissions there would be no condensation, and the curious or questioning reader will have to refer to the parent volume.

In another respect, this book is more than a condensation. Since the finishing touch was given to the *Dilemma* in January, 1943, many things have happened in the field of its subject matter. Dr. Rose has had to bring many facts up to date and to describe several new trends. The points of view and the organization are the same. In the last chapter Dr. Rose has, however, chosen to write in his own name, as an American to his fellow Americans, and even if the main ideas agree with those of the corresponding chapter of the *Dilemma,* this last chapter should stand as his own responsibility.

A few paragraphs should be given to the history of *An American Dilemma* (the full story is given in Mr. Keppel's foreword and my own preface to that book). The idea originated with Newton D. Baker, Secretary of War in Wilson's Cabinet, of having the Carnegie Corporation, one of the two largest philanthropic foundations, sponsor a comprehensive study of the Negro in the United States. It fell to the late Frederick P. Keppel, then President of the Carnegie Corporation, to give reality to this idea. According to his plans, the study of the American Negro should "be undertaken in a wholly objective and dispassionate way as a social phenomenon." To head up the study he looked for a social scientist from a foreign "non-imperialistic country, and with no background of domination of one race over another, who could approach this task with a fresh mind, uninfluenced by traditional attitudes or by earlier conclusions. It was understood that he should be free to appoint and organize a staff of his own selection in the United States and that he should draw upon the experience of other scholars and experts in less formal fashion, but that the report as finally drawn up and presented to the public should represent and portray his own decisions, alike in the selection of data and in the conclusions as to their relative importance."

Upon this basis I was approached, and I accepted the invitation. In September, 1938, I arrived in the United States and set to work. Richard Sterner, then of the Royal Social Board of Sweden, was with me from the beginning. I, and also Sterner, made extensive field trips all over the country. In drawing up the detailed plan for the study I had the advantage of criticism and suggestions from practically the whole range of the American specialists in the various fields related to the Negro problem and from many scholars, administrators and leaders outside that circle. When my plans matured, I followed up the program already referred to, that a number of American experts should be asked to collaborate by preparing research monographs for the study. There were 6 top staff members, 31 independent workers outside the staff, 36 assistants to the staff members and outside collaborators, and a corps of secretaries and typists. The first phase of the study was considered to be the preparation of monographs on the full range of subjects connected with the Negro problem, according to a detailed plan. Forty-four monographs were produced of which nine were published in four volumes, and the rest, together with my own successive plans for the entire study, made available for the public at the Schonburg Collection of the New York Public Library. When the Germans invaded Denmark and Norway, in April, 1940, I felt it was my duty to return to Sweden. From then until September, 1940, the entire project was directed by Samuel A. Stouffer, then Professor of Sociology at the University of Chicago. It was due to Stouffer's untiring efforts that the monographs, more than 15,000 typewritten pages of manuscripts, were completed by the deadline of September 1940.

The second stage of the study began when I returned to America in early March, 1941. After intensive library work during the spring and summer of 1941, I set out to write *An American Dilemma*. The unprinted manuscripts, prepared for the study during its first stage, were utilized in the same manner as printed literature and referred to as source material accordingly. The vast printed literature was, of course, depended upon to an even greater extent than upon the specially prepared monographs. I also drew upon my personal observations of conditions and attitudes in various parts of the country and upon the observations of my collaborators. From the collaboration in the first stage of the study—which embraced in friendship and concerted effort, white and Negro men and women of different specialities, ages and previous accomplishments—I learned much more, in an informal way, even about the specific problems of race relations which we studied together, than I could duly account for by references to the prepared manuscripts.

In September, 1941, I was joined by Richard Sterner and Arnold Rose (the former had been my associate on the study throughout its first stage, and the latter had been one of two "shock troops" brought in by Stouffer during the summer of 1940 to help complete the monographs, but I had never met him until May, 1941). Their names appear rightly on the title page of *An American Dilemma* as assistants. Since Rose now has undertaken to produce the condensed version, it should be made clear that he is deeply and intimately identified with the original volume. On his role in preparing it, I want to quote two paragraphs from my Preface:

"Arnold Rose has prepared drafts for Chapters 5, 6, 7, and 8 on problems connected with race and population, Chapter 22 on the present political scene, Chapter 29 on the patterns of discrimination, Chapters 41 and 42 on church and education, and Appendices 4, 7 and 8. He has also prepared drafts for many sections of other chapters. For still other chapters he has assembled and filled in gaps. For the final formulation of the main methodological analysis in Appendix 2 on facts and values in social science, his contribution has been of great importance. He has read the manuscripts of all parts and edited them. His editing work has included much more than polishing the English. It has, rather, been a most conscientious checking of basic data as well as of inferences, and a critical consideration of arrangement, viewpoints and conclusions. Both his criticisms and suggestions have, with few exceptions, led to changes in the final manuscript, and many of these changes are important. His wide knowledge of the social science literature and his sound judgment on methodological problems have, in this critical work, been significant. When I delivered the manuscript and departed from America, there was still a great deal of checking to be done and gaps to be filled in for which he was responsible, as well as for the proof reading. He also had to write Chapters 43 and 44, on the Negro community and culture, and Sections 1 and 4 of Appendix 10. For the present form of these two chapters and the appendix, Rose is himself responsible.

"About the contribution of both Sterner and Rose I want to add the following. The size of the book, and still more the scope of the problems involved, will make it understandable even to the reader who is not himself familiar with many of the specific fields, that the work done has been immense. We have had to dig deep into primary sources in many fields of social science and a major part of this digging has been done by them. The collaboration, which stretched ruthlessly over evenings and weekends, has been a sheer pleasure to me, as I have felt more than I have ever experienced before the stimulation of an ideal cooperation where we not only added together the results of our labor but imagined that we in our concerted endeavors sometimes reached higher than an arithmetical sum. A similar outlook on the methodological problems of social science and a mutually shared scientific curiosity in seeing our structure of hypothesis, data, and conclusions rise, have given to our collaboration a spirit of intellectual exploration which I will not soon forget."

The Negro problem was not "solved" in the study, as it is not solved in American society. The soul-searching process continues after the war, and this condensation appears primarily as one response to the need of Americans to find out what they are doing to Negroes and, as a consequence, to themselves. I do not believe that those white and Negro Americans, who are striving to give more of reality to the democratic creed of the American civilization in its application to the crucial Negro problem, need to feel discouraged. The long trend in American history is, in spite of temporary periods of reaction, a continuous development towards liberalism and democracy. Let me end by quoting again from the Preface to the *Dilemma*:

"If this book gives a more complete record than is up to now available of American shortcomings in this field, I hope, however, that it also accounts more completely for the unstability in relations, the hope for great improvements in the near future and, particularly, the dominant role of ideals in the social dynamics of America. When looking back over the long manuscript, one main conclusion—which should be stressed here since it cannot be reiterated through the whole book— is this: that not since Reconstruction has there been more reason to anticipate fundamental changes in American race relations, changes which will involve a development toward the American ideals."

Geneva, April, 1948
United Nations
Palais des Nations

Introduction to the Beacon Paperback Edition

What is the present state of the Negro problem and of civil rights in the United States? There is no practical answer to this question because change in the area is so rapid that any description, no matter how thorough, is out of date by the time it is brought into print. The history and sociology of any given aspect of human life are crowded at certain times, and relatively sparse at other times. For the Negro problem, these are unusually crowded times. There are more opportunities to study various aspects of race relations in the United States right now than there are social scientists studying them. Yet change is so rapid that these opportunities will have disappeared in a short while—probably happily from the standpoint of our social values.

Work on *An American Dilemma* (by Gunnar Myrdal, with the assistance of Richard Sterner and Arnold Rose) was completed in January 1943. It was published a year later, and even then the war was drastically changing the facts that the book recorded. I prepared a condensation in 1947, which was published as *The Negro in America* in 1948, and it brought the more selected facts up to date. Yet that volume, which is herewith republished without change, also—*in a sense*—rapidly became out of date. The only way to keep factually up to date on the Negro problem is to read such periodicals as *The Southern School News* and the *Race Relations Law Reporter*. But these deal only with changes in the schools and the law in the South, and there is little comparable reporting in the manifold other areas of the problem. And if there were, the conscientious reader of all of them would have to spend all his time reading on this problem alone, and would probably lose sight of the forest for the trees. The fact is that there is no book that is up to date on the Negro problem in the United States, nor can there now be, nor would it do anyone much good if it did exist because of its length and detail.

In another sense, *An American Dilemma* and *The Negro in America* come close to being adequate descriptions and analyses of the Negro problem today. They attempt to present the problem, in all its manifest forms, and then analyze the dynamics of social change affecting the problem. The reader is offered a sketch of all the varied aspects of the problem—as, say, of the year 1942—and then provided the tools with which to make a prediction of the future. While several criticisms were offered when these volumes were published in 1944 and 1948, respectively, the dynamic analysis has proved remarkably prescient of changes that occurred up to 1956. Neither those who insisted that changes would occur extremely slowly (or not at all), nor those who held that rapid change would occur if—and only if—Negroes joined white workers in class warfare, have received corroboration by the actual course of events since 1944. The facts are that social change in the area of race relations in the United States has been rapid within the framework of our democratic, modified-capitalistic system, and this is how our book sized up the situation.

What are the important factors to be considered in an analysis of the dynamic forces operating during the summer of 1956? Some of those who held with our theses up through the school-segregation decisions of the Supreme Court in 1954 and 1955 have now come to doubt that changes will continue rapidly toward equalization of opportunity for the Negro in American life. They have been impressed, if shocked, by the reaction of certain elements in the white South to these decisions, and now believe that the dominant group in the white South has put an end to change or is even beginning to revert to a more rigid caste system. This I doubt; I hold to the prognosis of this book that change toward equalization is likely to continue at about the same rate. Two types of events could change this prognosis: (1) catastrophe in other parts of the social structure, as a result of war, totalitarian revolution, or great depression; (2) a strong movement in the North among articulate people to "let the South solve its own problem" and to "forget about the Negro." I can neither predict, nor deny, the possibility of either of these developments.

The remainder of this Foreword consists of an analysis of the dynamic forces operating in the present situation. Any analysis inevitably involves the selection of what is most significant from the complexity of current reality. The need to make this presentation brief prevents me from offering a full exposition of the bases of selection and a statement of all my assumptions. Let it suffice to say that I give greatest weight to forces involving social power, both political and economic; secondary weight to changes in ideologies; and tertiary weight to factors usually singled out as "psychological" (although it seems to me that a better socio-psychological analysis would not separate the psychological factors from factors involving social power and ideologies).

The major forces causing the rapid change in race relations in the United States since 1940 seem to have been economic prosperity, continuous industrialization and technological advance, the high level of mobility among the American people, an increased American awareness of world opinion, the organization and political education of minority groups, a fairly consistent support for civil rights on the part of the Supreme Court, and the propaganda and educational effort for more equal civil rights. Some of these forces are likely to continue as they are; others are likely to change, and new forces are likely to have increasing influence.

It would be hazardous indeed to predict continued economic prosperity. But it is unlikely that our nation, in the present state of world affairs, would tolerate extensive unemployment; minority groups would be most affected by such unemployment, because of their relatively marginal role in the economy and because of prejudice on the part of individual employers. A continued high level of employment will see minority persons acquiring stronger roots in the economic structure of the society; a continued high level of income will permit the purchase of goods and services that will provide increased opportunities and advantages in other spheres of life (education, for example). A high level of employment generally will also tend to prevent the accumulating frustrations in the dominant group that lead to scapegoating.

Industrialization is proceeding at a more rapid pace than ever. In fact, the prospects for automation and the use of nuclear energy are such as to promise a new industrial revolution. While this will involve higher productivity and hence a higher standard of living, it will also involve a disruption for manual workers. Occupational training and retraining will be crucial; if minority workers get the new job training they will be better off than before, as they will no longer be behind the already skilled workers of the majority group. The new technology has also been invading the farms, reducing their number and sending minority farmers to the cities at a rapid rate. With increased productivity in farming and manufacturing, sales and the services will be relatively more in demand, and minority groups concentrated in those occupations (such as Jews and Orientals) will be relatively better off.

Technological change will assure a continuing high level of residential and occupational mobility among the American people. Mobility has worked in at least two ways to improve the position of minorities: First, it has provided a measure of flexibility and impersonality to the whole social structure, and reduced the number of communities in which there is cohesive and fixed sentiment against minorities. Second, for Negroes particularly, it has involved their moving out of areas where they experience most discrimination into areas where they have considerable civil rights. Only a little over half of the Negroes still live in the South, whereas fifty years ago nine-tenths lived there.

Americans have been becoming more sensitive to world opinion regarding mistreatment of minorities, and the central position of the United States in world affairs as well as the increased international travel of Americans will tend to make them even more sensitive. It is unlikely that this country will once more go isolationist.

Minority groups are raising their average levels of education, as better schools open to them and as they move farther away from immigrant status. Whether this will continue to mean increasing political and organizational sophistication, it is difficult to say. The membership of minority defense and improvement associations has been rising, but probably the mitigation of some of the discriminations will ultimately reduce interest in these organizations.

Since 1915 and especially since 1944, the United States Supreme Court has stated clearly, in a series of unanimous decisions, that the Fifth, Fourteenth, and Fifteenth Amendments to the Constitution specify that no branch of government may show discrimination to any citizen. The last shred of doubt on this subject was removed by the decision of May 17, 1954, in which even segregation—because forced and invidious—was held to be discrimination, and hence illegal. The Court can go no further along this line, except to implement in specific ways the principles already enunciated, for all legal support to discrimination has now been removed. The Court as presently constituted can hardly reverse itself; only amendment to the Constitution or tampering with the Court could change the principles now stated to be the law. Some individuals advocate doing either or both of these things, but no specific action has yet been taken.

Finally, it is to be noted that the deliberate education of the American people, minority and majority, in school and out, for fuller civil rights continues apace. There is little immediate prospect that it will shrink, and there is some possibility that the techniques of this education will improve. The program has run into difficulties in some communities as the whole liberal movement suffered the effects of mass anxiety over communism and treason. But the anxiety has abated, and there is a tendency to distinguish between civil rights and civil liberties—even on the part of the leaders in the attack on civil liberties.

This brief survey of the dominant forces affecting the status of civil rights in the United States during the past decade thus seems, on the whole, to promise a continuation of the effect of these forces during at least the coming decade. It was necessary to examine these broad social forces before turning to the analysis of the immediate situation in the South and in the North and specify some of the new forces that are now entering the balance. Too often, the war is lost sight of during a battle, and one is hard put to see change from day to day when one is in the midst of one of the most pervasive social changes in the history of mankind.

The position of the Negro in the Southern states reached its low point around 1900. It was then that segregation was most complete, violence outside the courts and mistreatment within the courts the most extreme, the vote for Negroes almost non-existent, occupational restrictions most stringent, public facilities least available, the minority group most leaderless and voiceless. In 1901 the first modern voice of Negro protest arose;[1] in 1905 the forerunner of the NAACP came into existence; in 1915 the Supreme Court announced its first decision in favor of Negro rights, and Negroes began to move northward in significant numbers. Progress was slow until about 1942, but then it took the upward spurt that we have already noted. Then—after a half century of progress and about a decade of really rapid change—the white people of the South first expressed concerted antagonism to the changes in 1954. It was not until almost the very apex[2] of the Southern caste system had been threatened that the alarm was sounded. A large number of very fundamental changes were made in race relations before anyone expressed any apprehension. Why is this and what does it mean for the future?

As mentioned above, segregation is not very old in the South, historically speaking. But it has been used to justify and buttress the whole system of race relations. Race relations have changed, but the old justification remains. We are dealing with a peculiar phenomenon well known among mankind: ideologies remain, long after the behavior which they justify disappears. It is like a man whose health has been running down for years unnoticed. Then someone—perhaps a doctor—says to him that his body is weak and that he is no longer capable of heavy physical exertion. The man then cries out in anguish; he suddenly realizes what has been true for years. His body has been changing gradually, but his conception of himself has changed suddenly. So it is with the South: suddenly, since 1954, it has been changing its conception of itself as a region. It is rapidly becoming aware that it can no longer think of itself as a region of romantic old plantations, with lots of old-fashioned courage but no modern tools or weapons, an ancient antagonist of the materialistic North which has always been thought of as exploiting the South. A very large number of Southerners have suddenly come to realize that their region

[1] In 1901 Monroe Trotter and George Forbes founded the first of the modern type of protesting Negro newspaper, the Boston *Guardian*.

[2] Myrdal hypothesized a hierarchy of requirements in the Southern caste system; he considered the sexual taboo as the topmost demand, with social segregation, especially of youth, being next to it. This hypothesis is developed in the first chapter of this book.

is becoming quite like the North, industrially and culturally. Those who loved the old romantic myth are now howling; they are shouting that they will defend to the death—what? Something that no longer exists. They are defending a memory, not a living institution.

Can it last? Men have been known to put their memories ahead of reality and adhere to this state indefinitely; but such men are mad and let their current affairs go to pot. This does not seem to me to be what is happening in the South today. There are many sane men in the South today who are unwilling to forgo their current prosperity and cultural progress merely to salvage the regional memory. While not particularly fond of Negroes, they feel that it is about time for the South to stop "fighting the War Between the States and join the rest of the world." Although these people are perhaps in a minority among older people, they are supported by a majority of the younger ones; and they provide much of the leadership in business, in the unions, and even in politics. Some lower-income Southerners grumble about their leaders that, because of their wealth, *they* don't have to associate with Negroes as poorer white folk do. The main source of opposition to racial equality lies in the working class, and part of their opposition lies in the fact that with equality they will lose their one basis for feeling superior. Those who heavily rely on racial inequality for psychological satisfaction will strongly resist desegregation for quite some time.

Some of the traditional leaders of Southern society—the wealthy, the educated, the politicians, the clergymen—are adhering to the principle that leaders should not move too far away from their followers. But their own interests and their clearer perception of social reality are encouraging these traditional leaders to urge the South slowly toward racial equality. In a few communities, they have shown some hesitancy about assuming leadership of the White Citizens' Council movement, and a new leadership has grown up spontaneously out of the mass. It is this latter leadership, capitalizing on an opportunity hitherto unavailable, that seeks to go to extremes. In the larger number of communities where the traditional leaders are active in the White Citizens' Councils, their influence is exerted against violence and against drastic action, even while they seek to maintain subordination of the Negro.

Violence is something to be expected when social change is rapid. There is much disturbance of usual habits, feelings of insecurity are stirred up, fears of the unknown are aroused—and all of these permit people to behave in ways they would not usually think of doing. A demagogue may come along under these circumstances and get money out of people by churning up their anxieties; violence is an incidental—and usually short-lived—consequence. Bryant Bowles, with his National Association for the Advancement of White People, operating in Delaware in 1955, was an example of this. If the leadership remains local and indigenous, it may be the non-traditional leaders who provoke violence, as they have no other claim to anything exceptional. The leader of the riot at the University of Alabama last winter was a 20-year-old, previously undistinguished student. The traditional leaders, who have a vested interest in keeping things on an even keel, tend in the long run to pull the community back to normalcy. Violence directed against Negroes can easily spread to white-owned property and other institutions, and so the traditional leaders work to quench the excitement.

Another force limiting violence in the South is the attitude of the Negroes. They are increasingly well-organized and politically sophisticated. The Montgomery bus strike showed Negroes all over the South one way to attain immediate goals by concerted action. Negroes have been victims of considerable violence in the South for quite some time: the usual pattern has been for an individual white man or a small group of white men to beat up an unresisting individual Negro. If the Negro resisted, he—or some other Negro—would be killed by a white mob. This pattern is now beginning to change. Negroes are beginning to organize to resist violence, whether started by an individual white man or by a white mob, and to offer violence in return. In Florida in early 1956, when a white employer shot a Negro worker in the leg for doing something wrong—a typical occurrence in the South—the new result was that a group of some thirty Negroes quickly collected and beat up the white man. There are two general consequences of the Negroes' new resistance: (1) Violence is now likely to take a two-way form, and therefore to be more extreme and more spectacular when it does occur. (2) Some white people are going to think twice before starting violence, as there is now a good chance that there will be unpleasant consequences for themselves; hence there will be less violence. The fact is that there is much less violence involving Negroes in the South today than there was fifty years ago, or even twenty years ago. But such violence as there is, is more likely to be mentioned in Northern newspapers because it is more spectacular and because there is greater interest in it.

A final important thing to be said about the South is that there are great variations within the region. Mississippi and South Carolina are the only states where Negroes constitute more than a third of the population; these two states, with parts of Georgia and Alabama, are the only areas that are vocally and vociferously resisting desegregation completely. The border states of Missouri, Kentucky, West Virginia, Maryland, and Delaware seem to be moving rapidly through the processes of change; already they do not differ much from Northern states. The remaining states are somewhere between these two extremes. In Tennessee, Arkansas, Oklahoma, North Carolina, Texas, Louisiana, Virginia, and Florida, there have been desegregation in some communities and strong resistance to desegregation in other communities; there have been strong voices urging violence and strong voices speaking out for law and order.

Northern opinion has always played a major role in the South. When Northern opinion was dominated by the theme of "let's forget the South" in the 1880's and thereafter, the South moved quickly toward a much more rigid caste system. The stories about Negro lynching in the Northern newspapers after about 1910 helped to reduce that extreme form of violence. The white South naturally does not like unfavorable publicity, insisting that "we'll work out the Negro problem if the North will leave us alone." Yet the South has always moved more rapidly toward better race relations when prodded by the North; this has been most apparent in the last ten years. Thus it is important for an analysis of the South to predict what Northern opinion will be regarding the South.

Some articulate and respected white Southerners have started a propaganda campaign that may alarm the North—we note the menacing phrases of the ex-governor Byrnes, the novelist Faulkner, the newspaper editor Waring. These men promise violence and even imply civil war. They are having a considerable influence on a certain type of Northern liberal, who is now coming to preach "moderation." The argument makes the reasonable-sounding statement that both kinds of extremists are dangerous, as though there were any significant number of extremists among the Negroes (except in a relative sense). The argument fails to distinguish between means, which must consider strategy, and ends or ultimate goals, which must be clear and inviolable. The argument is full of myth-making, for example, about Autherine Lucy's driving to register at the University of Alabama in a Cadillac, when actually she arrived in the Pontiac of some friends. The argument makes direful predictions which cannot possibly come to pass, about the South starting up the Civil War again and about the entire South leaving the Democratic Party. In view of the historical role which Northern opinion has played in the South, I would say that the most important immediate force which might prevent the early solution of the Southern race problem is the opinion of a certain type of Northern liberal, who may succeed in persuading the entire North once more to lose interest in the Southern Negro. All that is asked of the Northerner is moral support, but if that is not forthcoming the South may revert.

A word needs to be said to explain this central role accorded to Northern public opinion. First, Northern public opinion influences powerful political and economic forces. Few Northern congressmen would support "civil rights" if Northern white voters sympathized with the majority of white Southerners. Some Northern businessmen who have important business relations with the South are influenced by their general social ideology as well as by their dollars-and-cents concern for social stability. Second, Northern public opinion works on the divided conscience of the South. The white South has never been wholeheartedly anti-Negro, and is less so today than it has been for many decades. Respectable Southerners do not like to have their region described in Northern newspapers as one of racial lynchings and exploitation. Many white Southerners want to be part of the modern United States and the modern world, in the opinion of outsiders. Third, and perhaps most important in the immediate situation, Northern public opinion supports the Supreme Court decision of 1954, and this pressure of "the law" is very important in the dynamics of the Southern racial situation. As Rayford Logan has so well demonstrated, the *Plessy v. Ferguson* decision of 1896 could be enunciated and maintained only because there was no significant element of white opinion to challenge it. And so the present Court cannot be expected to stand by, and follow up on, its present decisions unless there is at least a strong and articulate minority of the American people to support the decisions. In speaking of Northern public opinion, we of course refer to articulate voices, which in the area of race relations have been predominantly those of liberals in recent years. The expressed opinions of Northern liberals have been important thus far in improving the status of the Negro in the South; if these opinions change significantly, they may also be important in the future in discouraging further improvement.

Still, there is a dilemma for some Northern liberals, and this can be illustrated by the situation of organized labor. The national leaders of organized labor are now being told by Southern labor leaders that the relatively few unions in the South may revolt from the AFL-CIO and set up an independent organization. These Southern leaders are on the spot, as they are receiving opposing pressures from their own members and from the national organization. If it is expedient for them to keep quiet on race matters right now, that is not the case for the national leaders. Most of the Southern unions are very weak, and would soon come under company domination if they split off from the national AFL-CIO. Would Southern white workers long be happy to sacrifice much of their prosperity to glorify the regional myth? A few might do it, but they would soon be back in the labor movement. If the national labor leaders were to soft-pedal their support for civil rights, they would lose the possibility of developing a strong and unified labor movement in the South, and lose the respect of foreign labor leaders.

In the North civil rights have not moved so rapidly as in the South, perhaps mainly because they never reached such a low point to move away from. Still, the North has seen a remarkable movement in the past dozen years toward the passage of Fair Employment Practice laws reducing job discrimination in most Northern areas where there are large minority groups, toward the lessening of residential restriction, toward the weakening of hate groups, and toward the lessening of group violence. Both formal and informal segregation have also declined somewhat in the North, although there is still considerable segregation in interpersonal relations, and members of majority and minority groups seldom know each other as close friends. Law is stronger in the North, and Northern politicians have been sensible of the key role of the minority vote. Perhaps almost half of the majority group *feel* they shouldn't discriminate even if in fact most of them do. Good sense and firmness are needed in the North in the handling of a host of minor incidents involving intergroup relations. The consequences of failure in these matters is indicated by the frightening sequence of near-riots in Chicago during the past decade.

New kinds of problems arise on the forefront of progress in the North, problems for which the old terms, such as "discrimination" and "prejudice," do not apply. One of these might be called the "tradition of backwardness" among lower-class Negroes. Because they have no particular occupational skills and families do not encourage children to prepare themselves for good jobs, many Negroes are not able to take advantage of all the good job opportunities that are available. Another problem is that Negroes and whites do not know how to associate with each other; they are excessively formal and sensitive in interpersonal relations. A third problem is the age-old one of immigrants who don't know how to make an adjustment to big-city life; this probably is most serious for Indians right now, but it is also a problem for Negro migrants from the Deep South.

In this analysis, I have given little attention to psychological factors, as I believe they are of secondary importance in comparison to power relations and ideologies, and because they are less flexible and mobile. But some aspects of the psychological situation deserve attention. Some Southern whites are sincerely terrified by the thought of social equality; the unconscious symbolic meanings of the Negro and of social equality present an irrational but nevertheless real enough danger to these people. A redefinition of the situation is needed, and a frank uncovering of symbolism is necessary. This is extremely touchy, and propagandists here would do well to get the advice of psychiatrists. A redefinition of the situation, which is already coming about through events, can smooth the pain of transition and possibly even hasten it. Intercultural education for youth can also do with a continual readjustment of means to ends; the techniques that were psychologically successful at one stage of change may be fairly useless at later stages. We need constant testing and evaluation of approaches and techniques of education and propaganda. We also need to change our stress on different psychological components: I would guess that the period of McCarthyism drew most of the so-called "authoritarian personalities" away from race prejudice and discrimination into other activities, perhaps equally vicious but different. My impression is that there are about as many "authoritarian personalities" today among the fighters against discrimination as among the fighters for it. If these observations are correct, we need a new psychological analysis.

We are living at a time at which we can get rid of the social disease of racism which has darkened the pages of American history and weakened this country both internally and in its relations with other nations. Whether we like it or not, the struggle against racism within this country has become identified with the world struggle of the darker peoples against colonialism. The colored peoples, both at home and abroad, so identify themselves, and America's whole position in the world is being affected by the domestic changes and events. What is most necessary in the current situation is to extend our perspectives both in time and space.

ARNOLD M. ROSE

University of Minnesota
July 1956

CHAPTER I

The Negro Problem

and Its American Setting

1. Unity of Ideals and Differences in Culture in America

It has become commonplace to point out that America is a land of great differences and rapid changes. Still there is strong unity in this nation. Americans of all national origins, classes, regions, creeds, and colors have something in common: a set of beliefs, a political creed. This "American Creed" is the cement in the diversified structure of this great nation.

America, compared to every other country in Western civilization, large or small, has the most definite and clearly expressed system of ideals in reference to human relations. This body of ideals is more widely understood and appreciated than similar ideals are anywhere else. To be sure, the political creed of America is frequently not put into effect; but as a principle which *ought* to rule, the Creed has been made conscious to everyone in American society. These principles of social ethics have been hammered into easily remembered formulas. All means are used to stamp them into everybody's mind. The schools teach them, the churches preach them. The courts pronounce decisions in their terms.

The Negro people in America are no exception to the national pattern. A Negro political scientist, Ralph Bunche, observes:

Every man in the street, white, black, red or yellow, knows that this is "the land of the free," the "land of opportunity," the "cradle of liberty," the "home of democracy," that the American flag symbolizes the "equality of all men" and guarantees to us all "the protection of life, liberty and property," freedom of speech, freedom of religion and racial tolerance.[1]

The American Negroes know they are an oppressed group experiencing, more than anybody else in the nation, the consequences of the fact that the Creed is not lived up to in America. Yet their faith in the Creed is not simply a means of pleading for their rights. They, like the whites, believe, with one part of themselves, that the Creed is ruling America.

These ideals of the essential dignity of the individual, of the basic equality of all men and of certain inalienable rights to freedom, justice, and fair opportunity, represent to the American people the meaning of the nation's early struggle for independence. These principles were written into the Declaration of Independence, the Preamble to the Constitution, the Bill of Rights, and into the constitutions of the states. The ideals of the American Creed have thus become the highest law of the land. The Supreme Court pays its reverence to these principles when it declares what is constitutional and what is not. They have been elaborated upon by all national leaders, thinkers and statesmen. Throughout its history, America has had a continuous discussion of the principles. In all wars, including the last one, the American Creed has been the foundation of national morale.

2. SOME HISTORICAL REFLECTIONS

It is remarkable that a vast democracy with so many cultural differences has been able not only to reach agreement on its ideals, but also to make them supreme. There are more things to be wondered about. The differences in national origin, language, religion and culture, during the long period of mass immigration into the United States, have been closely related to income differences and social class distinctions. "Old Americans" have owned the country and held political power; they have often despised and exploited "the foreigners." To this extent, conditions in America were favorable to the formation of a rigid class society; but this did not happen.

Historians point out that the free land and boundless natural resources, for one thing, allowed ambitious and energetic men to rise. For another, the settlers on the new Western land were always the spearhead of the democratic movements which, from time to time, swept over America. And always the rallying cry of these movements was the ideals of the American Creed.

[1] "Conceptions and Ideologies of the Negro Problem," unpublished manuscript prepared for *An American Dilemma* (1940).

For long periods in American history, property interests triumphed and blocked the will of the people. And there are today large geographical regions and fields of human life which, particularly when measured by the high goals of the American Creed, are conspicuously lagging. But taking a broad historical view, the American Creed has triumphed. It has given the main direction to change in this country. America has had gifted conservative statesmen and national leaders, but, with few exceptions, only the liberals have gone down in history as major national heroes. America is, as we shall point out, conservative in fundamental principles, but *the principles conserved are liberal* and some, indeed, are radical. The Creed, once set forth and spread among the American people, became so strongly imbedded in their hearts, and the circumstances have since then been so relatively favorable, that it has succeeded in keeping itself very much alive for more than a century and a half.

3. THE HISTORICAL ROOTS OF THE AMERICAN CREED

The American Creed stems partly from the liberalism of the eighteenth century Enlightenment. The main norms of the American Creed are centered in the belief in equality and in the right to liberty. In the Declaration of Independence, equality was given the supreme rank and the right to liberty stems from equality. This was clearly expressed in Jefferson's first version of the Declaration of Independence: "All men are created equal *and from that equal creation* they derive rights inherent and unalienable, among which are the preservation of life and liberty and the pursuit of happiness."

In society, liberty for one may mean the suppression of liberty for others. Against this, the equalitarianism in the Creed has been persistently revolting. The reason why American liberty was not more dangerous to equality was, of course, the open frontier and the free land. When opportunity became bounded in the last generation, the conflict between equality and liberty flared up. Equality is slowly winning. The New Deal during the thirties was a landslide in that direction.

If the European philosophy of Enlightenment was one of the roots of the American Creed, another equally important one was Christianity, particularly as it took the form in the colonies of various Protestant sects, split off from the Anglican Church.

Although we now realize that many of the early settlers did not come to America to seek religious freedom and that many of the early colonial churches were themselves authoritarian, the *idea* that America is a haven for the religiously oppressed has been important in American history. Religion in America took on a spirit of fight for liberty. Moreover, the basic teaching of Protestant Christianity is democratic: we are all poor sinners and have the same Heavenly Father.

Ministers have sometimes been reactionaries in America. They have on occasion tried to stifle free speech; they have organized persecutions of unpopular dissenters and have even, in some regions, been active as the organizers of the Ku Klux Klan and similar "un-American" (in terms of the American Creed) movements. But, on the whole, church and religion in America strengthen the American Creed. The mere fact that there are many competing denominations forces American churches to a greater tolerance and to a greater interest in social problems than the people in the churches might otherwise call for. American churches have also contributed something essential to the Creed. Competent and sympathetic foreign observers have always noted the generosity and helpfulness of Americans. This and the equally conspicuous formal democracy in human contacts are partly a result of the predominantly lower-class origin of the American people and the many opportunities to rise. But it also seems to be true that the Christian neighborliness of the common American reflects the influence of the churches.

The third main influence behind the American Creed is English law. The concept of a government "of laws and not of men" contained ideas of both equality and liberty.

4. AMERICAN CONSERVATISM

These forces of Christian religion and English law also explain why America has so doggedly stuck to its high ideals: why it has been so conservative in keeping to liberalism as a national creed, even if not as its actual way of life. This conservatism has, to a great extent, been perverted into a nearly fanatic worship of the Constitution. The worship of the Constitution is a flagrant violation of the American Creed, which, as far as realizing the will of the people is concerned, is strongly opposed to stiff formulas.

On the other hand, the common American does not think of the difference in spirit between the Constitution and the Declaration of Independence. When he worships the Constitution, he is, more than likely, thinking in terms of the American Creed. The Old Americans adhere to the Creed as the faith of their ancestors. The others—the Negroes, the new immigrants, the Jews, and other disadvantaged and unpopular groups—could not possibly have invented a system of political ideals which better corresponded to their interests. So it has developed that the rich and secure, out of pride and conservatism, and the poor and insecure, out of dire need, have come to believe in the same social ideals. Behind it all is the historical reality that makes it possible for a president to appeal to all in the nation in this way: "Let us not forget that we are all descendants of revolutionaries and immigrants."

5. THE AMERICAN CONCEPTION OF LAW AND ORDER

While the Creed is important and is enacted into law, it is not lived up to in practice. To understand this we shall have to examine American attitudes toward law.

Americans are accustomed to write their ideals into laws, ranging from their national Constitution to their local traffic rules. American law, thus, often contains rules which are not enforceable but which merely express the legislators' hopes, desires, advice, or dreams. Legislating ideals has the "function" not only of giving them high publicity and prestige, but also of dedicating the nation to the task of gradually approaching them.

Another cultural trait of Americans is a relatively low degree of respect for law and order. This trait, as well as the one just mentioned, is of great importance for the Negro problem as will be shown in some detail in later chapters. There is a relation between high ideals in some laws and low respect for all laws, but this relation is complicated.

One most relevant attitude toward law in America is expressed in the common belief that there is a "higher law" behind and above the specific laws contained in constitutions, statutes, and other regulations. This idea of a "natural law" has long been part of the Western legal tradition. When representative bodies, among them the English Parliament, emerged as political institutions, they did not conceive of themselves as "legislatures" in the modern sense, but pretended only to state the law that already "existed." In America the Revolution gave a tremendous spread to this idea of "natural law," since natural law had to be appealed to when the king's laws were violated. The idea fixed itself upon the entire American state structure. The role given to the Supreme Court to refer to the higher principles back of the Constitution strengthened still more the grip of this old idea on the minds of the Americans. Undoubtedly the idea that American law is an expression of natural law strengthens the rule of law in America.

On the other hand, laws become debatable on moral grounds. Each law is judged by the common citizen in terms of his conception of the higher natural law. He decides whether it is "just" or "unjust" and has the dangerous attitude that, if it is unjust, he may feel free to disobey it. The stress on individual rights and the almost complete silence on the citizen's duties in the American Creed make this reaction natural. The Jeffersonian distrust of government—"that government is best which governs least"—soon took the form, particularly on the Western frontier, of distrust of and disrespect for the enacted laws.

But the frontier was not, in this respect, fundamentally different from the old colonies. Without stepping outside the American tradition, Garrison could pronounce even the Constitution to be a "compact with Hell" on the slavery issue. This, by itself, would not have been dangerous to democracy if he had meant to argue only for a change of the Constitution. But he and many more Northerners found it a moral obligation not to obey the fugitive slave laws. Here the citizen does not stop to criticize the laws and the judicial system and demand a change in them, but sets his own conception of the higher law above the existing laws in society and feels it is right to disobey them. It is against this background that we shall have to study the amazing disrespect for law and order which even today characterizes the Southern states in America and constitutes such a large part of the Negro problem.

This anarchistic tendency in America's legal culture becomes even more dangerous because of a desire to regulate human behavior tyrannically by means of formal laws. This is a heritage from early American puritanism, which was sometimes fanatical and dogmatic and always had a strong inclination to mind other people's business. So this American, who announces that he will not obey laws other than those which are "good" and "just," as soon as the discussion turns to something which in his opinion is bad and unjust, will emphatically state that "there ought to be a law against . . ." America has thus become a country where exceedingly much is permitted in practice but at the same time exceedingly much is forbidden in law. This conflict occurs in all angles of the Negro problem.

A low degree of law observance had become habitual and nationally cherished in colonial times when the British Parliament and Crown, increasingly looked upon as a foreign ruler by Americans, insisted upon passing laws which the Americans considered unwise, impractical, or unjust. The free life on the frontier also strained legal bonds. The mass immigration and the resulting cultural differences were other factors hampering the establishment of a firm legal order in America. The presence of states within the nation with different sets of laws and the high mobility between states were contributing factors. The jurisdictional friction between the states and the federal government, the difficulty of changing the federal Constitution, the great complexity of the American legal system, and the mass of legal fiction and plain trickery also are important. For example, it cannot be conducive to the highest respect for the legal system that the federal government is forced to carry out important social legislation under the fiction that it is regulating "interstate commerce," or that gangsters are punished for income tax evasion rather than for the capital crimes they have committed.

Under the influence of all these and many other factors the common American citizen has acquired a low degree of personal identification with the state and legal machinery. When Theodore Roosevelt exclaimed, "Damn the law! I want the canal built," he spoke the language of his contemporary business world and of the ordinary American.

The American nation has, further, experienced severe disappointments in its attempts to legislate social change. One of the disappointments was the Reconstruction legislation, which attempted to give Negroes civil rights in the South; another was antitrust legislation; a third was the Prohibition Amendment.

6. Pessimism

Against this background, and remembering the tendency in America to make all sorts of laws directed at symptoms and not at causes, it is understandable that Americans have developed a pessimistic attitude toward the possibility of producing social change by means of legislation. This tendency affects many aspects of the Negro problem.

The pessimism is often phrased as "laws cannot change folkways." This theory obviously cannot be true, since in other parts of the world similar changes are produced by legislation, and it has been done even in America, particularly in recent years. The explanation of why some laws have been more successful than others in America is that they have been better prepared and better administered. This means that, among the explanations for the general disrepute and deficiency of law and order in America, there are two other factors: the habit of passing laws without careful investigation and the relatively low standard of American administration of laws. If Americans are brought to be a law-abiding people, and if they, at the same time, succeed in keeping alive not only their conservatism in fundamental principles and their pride and devotion to their national political institutions, but also some of their puritan eagerness and courage in attempting to reform themselves and the world, this great nation may become the master builder of a stable but progressive commonwealth.

The popular explanation of the conflict in America between ideals and actual behavior is that Americans do not have the slightest intention of living up to their ideals. This explanation is too superficial. To begin with, the true hypocrite sins in secret. The American, on the contrary, is strongly and sincerely "against sin," even, and not least, against his own sins. If all the world is well informed about the political corruption, organized crime, and the faltering system of justice in America, it is primarily due to America's publicity about its own faults. America's handling of the Negro problem has been criticized emphatically by white Americans since long before the Revolution, and the criticism has steadily gone on and will not stop until America has completely reformed itself.

In a great nation there is, of course, division of labor. Some Americans do most of the sinning, but most do some of it. Some specialize in muckraking, preaching, and lamentations; but there is a little of the muckraker and preacher in all Americans. On the other hand, superficially viewed, Americans often appear cynical. As a matter of fact, this young nation is the least cynical of all nations. It labors persistently with its moral problems. It is taking its Creed very seriously indeed. The cultural unity of the nation is this sharing in both consciousness of sins and devotion to high ideals.

7. VALUE PREMISES IN THIS STUDY

For the study of a national problem which cuts so sharply through the whole body politic as does the Negro problem, no other set of values could serve as adequately as value premises as the American Creed. No other standard could compete in authority over people's minds. The American Creed represents the national conscience. The Negro is a "problem" to the average American partly because of a conflict between the place awarded him in American society and those ideals.

The American Creed, just because it is a living reality in a developing democracy, is not a fixed and clear-cut dogma. It is still growing. It is now discovering its ideals in the social and economic spheres and in the field of international organization. While this is going on, there are great differences in opinion even on fundamentals in these new fields. In any other social problem, these differences would make it difficult to use the Creed as a set of specified and definite value premises for research. This is not true, however, with the Negro problem. The Creed is clear and explicit in practically all respects for the

Negro problem. Most of the value premises with which we shall be concerned have actually been incorporated for a long time in the national Constitution and in the constitutions and laws of the states.

One reason for this is that the position of the Negro in America represents a long lag of public morals. In principle the Negro problem was settled long ago; but the Negro in America has not yet been given the basic civil and political rights of democracy, including a fair opportunity to earn his living, upon which there was general agreement when the American Creed was first taking form. This lag constitutes the "problem" both to Negroes and to whites.

Finally, in order to avoid possible misunderstanding, it should be explained that we have called this Creed "American" in the sense that Americans believe in it. But, of course, with minor variations, the American Creed is the common democratic creed. "American ideals" are just humane ideals as they have grown up in our common Western civilization upon the foundation of Judaism and Christianity and under the influence of the economic, scientific, and political development over a number of centuries. The American Creed is older and wider than America itself.

8. THE NEGRO PROBLEM ON THE MINDS OF THE WHITES

There is a "Negro problem" in the United States and most Americans are aware of it, although it assumes varying forms and intensity in different regions of the country and among diverse groups of the American people. Americans have to react to it, politically as citizens and, when there are Negroes present in the community, privately as neighbors.

To begin with, the Negro is a problem to himself. The contented Negro, whose mind is at peace on the race issue, is rare. The Negro protest has been rising for a long time and the recent war has caused an even more rapid increase in the discontent and protest.

The white man worries about the Negro problem, too, and not least when he wants to convince himself and others that it is settled for all time. The problem has varying degrees of importance in different regions, depending partly on their historical backgrounds and partly on the number of Negroes in the area. However, even in those Northern states with few Negroes, the Negro problem is always present, though there is little excitement around it. Nearly everybody in America is prepared to discuss the issue, and almost nobody is without opinions on it. Opinions vary. They may be vague and hesitating or even questioning, or they may be hardened and articulate. But few Americans are unaware of the Negro problem.

The American Negro problem is a problem in the heart of the

American. It is there that the decisive struggle goes on. This is the central viewpoint of this study. Though our study includes economic, social, and political race relations, at bottom the problem is the moral dilemma of the white American—the conflict between his moral values. The American dilemma is the ever-raging conflict between, on the one hand, the values which we shall call the "American Creed," where the American thinks, talks, and acts under the influence of high national and Christian morals, and, on the other hand, the values of individual and group living, where personal and local interests; economic, social, and sexual jealousies; considerations of community prestige and conformity; group prejudice against particular persons or types of people; and all sorts of miscellaneous wants, impulses, and habits dominate his outlook.

9. VALUES AND BELIEFS

The Negro problem in America would be different, and easier to understand, if the moral conflict raged only between values held by different groups of people. The essence of the moral situation is, however, that conflicting values are also held by the same person. The moral struggle goes on within people and not only between them. When people's values are conflicting, behavior becomes a moral compromise.

The unity of a culture consists in the fact that all values are shared in some degree. Even a poor and uneducated white person in some isolated and backward rural region in the Deep South, who is violently prejudiced against the Negro and intent upon depriving him of civic rights and human independence, has also a compartment in his mind housing the entire American Creed of liberty, equality, justice, and fair opportunity for everybody. And, to some extent, these ideals shape his behavior.

In America, as everywhere else, people agree that the more universal values—those which refer to man as such and not to any particular group or temporary situation—are morally higher. These values are given the approval of religion and national legislation. They are incorporated into the American Creed. The other values— which refer to various smaller groups of mankind or to particular occasions—are commonly referred to as "irrational" or "prejudiced," sometimes even by people who express them. They are defended in terms of tradition, expediency, or utility.

Trying to defend their behavior to others, and primarily to themselves, people will attempt to conceal the conflict between their different values by keeping some values away from consciousness and by focusing attention on others. For the same purpose, people will twist and mutilate their beliefs of how reality actually is. There are whole systems of popular beliefs concerning the Negro which are bluntly false and which can only be understood when it is remembered what purposes they serve. These "popular theories," because of the rationalizing function they serve, are heavily loaded with emotions. But people also want to be rational. Science and education are slowly correcting the beliefs and thereby also influencing the values.

The task of this study is to ascertain social reality as it is. Material facts are in large measure the product of what people think, feel, and believe. The actual conditions, from this point of view, indicate great differences between the whites' and Negroes' aspirations and realizations. The interrelations between the material facts and people's values and beliefs about these facts are precisely what make the Negro a social problem.

When the Negro problem is viewed as primarily a moral issue, this is in line with popular thinking. It is as a moral issue that this problem presents itself in the daily life of ordinary people. This study, therefore, will constantly take its starting point in the ordinary man's own ideas, doctrines, theories, and mental constructs.

In approaching the Negro problem as primarily a moral issue of conflicting values, it is not implied, of course, that we shall pronounce which values are "right" and which are "wrong." In so far as we make our own judgments of value, they will be based on clearly stated value premises selected from among those values actually observed as existing in the minds of the white and Negro Americans. Our value judgments thus have no greater validity than the value premises from which they are derived.

10. To the Negroes Themselves

To the Negro himself, the Negro problem is all-important. A Negro probably seldom talks to a white man, and still less to a white woman, without consciousness of this problem. Even in a mixed white and Negro group of closest friends in Northern intellectual circles, and probably even in an all-Negro group, the Negro problem constantly looms in the background. It steers the jokes and allusions if it is not one of the dominant topics of conversation.

The Negro leader, the Negro social scientist, the Negro man of arts and letters is likely to view all social, economic, political, indeed, even aesthetic and philosophical issues from the Negro angle. What is more, he is expected to do so. He would seem entirely out of place if he spoke simply as a member of a community, a citizen of America, or as a man of the world. In the existing American civilization he can attain some degree of distinction, but always as a representative of "his people," not as an ordinary American. He can criticize, but only as a Negro defending Negro interests. Even if he had originally had the interests and aptitudes for wider knowledge and a broader career, the pressure from society conditions his personality and forces him willy-nilly into the role of Negro champion. The Negro genius is imprisoned in the Negro problem.

The difference in this respect between the Negro and other minorities—the Jews, for example—is notable. A Jewish economist is not expected to be a specialist on Jewish labor. A Jewish sociologist is not assumed to confine himself to studying the ghetto. A Jewish singer is not doomed eternally to perform Jewish folk songs. The Jew is discriminated against in America but there is a quantitative difference between this and the discrimination against the Negro which is so great that it becomes qualitative.

So far, we have been commenting on the fate of those rare persons with extraordinary talents. The ordinary members of the Negro upper and middle class—the preachers, teachers, professionals, and businessmen—have to build their whole economic and social existence on the basis of segregation of their people in response to the dictates of white society. To state the situation bluntly: these upper-class Negroes are left free to earn their living and their reputation in the backwater of discrimination, but they are not free to go into the main current of the river itself.

The masses of the Negro people are hampered and enclosed behind the walls of segregation and discrimination even more. They, too, are imprisoned in the Negro problem. The late James Weldon Johnson sums up the situation of the Negro people in the following way:

And this is the dwarfing, warping, distorting influence which operates upon each and every coloured man in the United States. He is forced to take his outlook on all things, not from the view-point of a citizen, or a man, or even a human being, but from the view-point of a *coloured* man. It is wonderful to me that the race has progressed so broadly as it has, since most of its thought and all of its activity must run through the narrow neck of this one funnel.[2]

11. Explaining the Problem Away

White Americans can, of course, keep the Negro problem out of their minds to a greater extent and, in addition, they have good

[2] *The Autobiography of an Ex-Coloured Man* (Boston: Sherman, French and Company, 1927; first edition, 1912), p. 21.

selfish reasons for keeping it below the level of consciousness. To be sure, the investigator is frequently told that there is "no Negro problem" in America. Everything is quiet on the racial front. Negroes are all right in their place; and they, for their part, do not want things changed. In fact, they are the happiest lot on earth. Just look at them: how they laugh and enjoy themselves; how they sing and praise the Lord.

This attitude is met most frequently and expressed most emphatically in the Deep South. But it is not true. The contrary statement, that the white South is constantly concerned with the Negro problem, that it has allowed the Negro problem to rule its politics and its business, fetter its intelligence and human liberties, and hamper its progress in all directions, would be nearer the truth. In the South, statements that there is "no Negro problem" cover doubt, disagreement, concern and anxiety, moral tension, and a need for escape and defense. To furnish such a covering is, from a psychological point of view, the "function" of such statements.

The usefulness of this escape has a limit, however. The limit is reached when open interracial struggles appear. The notion of "no Negro problem" is then suddenly transformed into an alarming awareness that the contrary is so. A white Southerner will, for instance, defend the suppression of the Negroes by saying that they are satisfied with their status and lack any desire for change. Without any other remark, he will then explain that suppression is necessary and that Negroes must be kept down by all means. Attempts to draw attention to the contradiction seldom succeed.

12. Explorations in Escape

The following experiences show how the carefully constructed agreement that there is no Negro problem will crash if pushed from the outside:

In a big city in the Deep South I was once taken by a friend to an upper-class club for a luncheon party. The conversation turned around world affairs, the business trend, art, literature and some personal gossiping; the tone was congenial and free. Near the intended end of the party, my friend announced the reason for my being in America at the time and invited the company to tell me their frank opinions on the Negro problem.

For a moment a somewhat awkward silence descended upon our party. I was marked off as the stranger peeping in on them and their secret, the Negro problem. The situation most urgently had to be redefined. The responsibility was shouldered by an elderly, very distinguished doctor. He made a short speech (the discussion had suddenly turned very formal) to the effect that in the South there was "no Negro problem."

The doctor finished. Everybody agreed, and there was really nothing in the issue to discuss. The few moments' stress was eased and a measure of congeniality again restored. I then reflected that the South was, as I was finding out, now on the way to giving the Negroes a real chance in education. As more and more Negro youths received a better education, it might make it difficult to keep the Negro in his place. It might, for instance, make it much less easy to hold him disfranchised.

After this remark, I did not need to say anything more for the next hour or two but could lean back and listen to one of the most revealing and ably performed, though sometimes heated, intellectual debates on the Negro problem in America I had, up till then, heard. At the end I had the opportunity to restore good feeling between the debaters in a roar of understanding laughter when I closed my thanks for Southern hospitality with the observation that apparently they seemed to have a most disturbing Negro problem on their minds down in the Old South.

A situation in the Negro world parallel to this experience shows how the problem burns under the cover of a placid stereotype. A Negro leader prominent in banking and insurance arranged for me a gathering in his office of a group of about thirty Negro gentlemen of upper-class status, representing business, church, university, and professions. One of his subordinates had been given the task of relating statistics on the progress of Negro business in America. He fulfilled his task with much ability and eloquence. The lecture ended in a cheerful and challenging mood.

This spirit prevailed until I happened to touch off some of the unfortunate realities so carefully concealed within the statistical house of cards that had just been erected. I referred to the facts, that one of the white companies alone had more Negro insurance business than all the Negro companies together, that Negro banking had a rather serious record of bankruptcies, and to other similar facts.

My remarks were formulated as questions, and I was hoping for some discussion. But I had never expected the tumultuous and agitated controversy that broke loose. The comforting agreement of a few minutes before broke suddenly into the full range of American Negro ideologies bearing not only on business but on all other aspects of life as well.

I once visited an art exhibition in one of the cultural centers of the Old South. Among other exhibits was a man-sized sculpture in terra cotta called "Soldier in the Rain," representing a Negro man lynched by hanging. The piece was forcefully done; I thought it a masterpiece.

Quite unintentionally I happened to refer to the sculpture as representing a lynching. My hostesses immediately reacted as to a shock and explained eagerly that I was totally mistaken. The sculpture represented a soldier being hanged, probably behind the front for some offense, "just any soldier." It had nothing to do with the Negro problem. They were bent on convincing me that I was wrong. I answered that soldiers were never anywhere executed by hanging and in the popular conception, which is the important thing for an artist, hanging is usually associated with the English custom of hanging petty thieves and American lynching parties. I even pointed out that the sculptor had given the hanged man the long limbs and facial characteristics commonly ascribed to the Negro race. But no arguments had any weight. The visit ended with some mutually felt embarrassment.

As my curiosity was awakened I went to see the sculptor. He is an immigrant from one of the republics of Latin America and is of nearly pure Indian descent. I was told later that because of his slightly dark color, he sometimes had met some difficulties when he was not personally recognized. His first answer was that his sculpture represented a soldier being hanged, "any soldier." I finally yielded to exasperation and said, "If you, the artist, do not know what you have created, I know it as an art spectator. You have depicted a lynching, and, more particularly, a lynching of a Negro." The sculptor suddenly became intimate and open and said: "I believe you are right. And I have intended it all the time." I asked, "Don't you think everybody must know it?" He said, "Yes, in a way, but they don't want to know it." I asked again, "Why have you spent your time in producing this piece? You understand as well as I that, even if it is admirable and is also being greatly admired by the public, nobody is actually going to buy it." He answered, "I know. I suppose that I have made this for myself. I am going to keep it in a closet. This is the 'American Skeleton in the Closet.' That would be the right name for my sculpture. 'Soldier in the Rain' is only a fake, a deception between me and the public down here."

13. THE ETIQUETTE OF DISCUSSION

Generally the form of a matter becomes important when the matter itself is touchy. Explosives must be handled with care. Educators, reformers, and journalists with liberal leanings in the South have a standard text which they recite to please one another and the visitor. Everything can be said in the South if it is said "in the right way." Criticisms and even factual statements should be phrased in such a manner that they do not "offend" or create "embarrassment." Someone will brag because he was able to "get by" in saying something in an indirect way or because he was able to "put over" something on the public by camouflaging it.

A whole system of moral escape has become polite form in the South. It renders the spoken or written word less effective. It hampers raising issues and facing problems. At the same time as it purposely opens a means of escape it ties everything to the problem suppressed —the Negro problem on their minds.

When talking about the Negro problem, everybody tries to locate race prejudice outside himself. "Public opinion" or "community feel-ings" are held responsible. The whites practically never discuss the issue in terms of "I" or "we" but always in terms of "they," "people in the South," "people in this community," or "folks down here will not stand for . . ." this or that.

In the more formal life of the community the Negro problem and the Negro himself are almost completely avoided. The subject is seldom referred to in the church. In the school it will be avoided, like sex. The press, with a few exceptions, ignores the Negroes, except for their crimes. The public affairs of the states and cities are ordi-narily discussed as if Negroes were not part of the population. The strange unreality of this situation becomes clear when one realizes that for generations hardly any public issue has been free of the race issue, and that the entire culture of the region—its religion, literature, art, music, dance, its politics and education, its language and cooking —are partly to be explained by positive or negative influences from the Negro.

If the Negro is a shunned topic in formal conversation, he enters all informal life to a great extent. He is the standard joke. It is in-teresting to note the great pleasure white people in all classes take in these stereotyped jokes and in indulging in discussions about the Negro and what he does, says, and thinks. The stories and the jokes give release to a troubled people. When people are up against great inconsistencies in their creed and behavior, which they cannot or do not want to account for rationally, humor is a way out. To the whites, the Negro jokes serve the function of "proving" the inferiority of the Negro. To the Negroes, the antiwhite jokes put the whites in a ridiculous light.

In this situation the minds of people are likely to show signs of deep-seated conflict of attitudes. White Southerners like individual Negroes and sometimes Negroes in general; they apparently also hate them. What applies to the emotional level may also be found on the intellectual level. From a single person one can hear both a condemnation of recalcitrant Negro youth as compared to the "good old Negroes" and praise for what education is doing for Ne-groes. Sometimes contradictions are elaborated into theories and find their way into learned studies and documents of state policy. There are plenty of people in the South who will tell you, honestly and sincerely, that Negroes have equal educational opportunities with whites. They probably believe it—for a moment, in a way, and with a part of their minds. Their conviction rests on two contradictory principles between which they shift.

These inconsistencies and contradictions should not be taken as indicating personal insincerity. They are, rather, symptoms of much deeper, unsettled conflicts of values. The absorbing interest in the form of a matter; the indirectness of approach to a person, a subject, or a policy; the training to circumvent sore points—which we consider as symptoms of escape—have developed into a pattern of thinking and behavior which molds the entire personality. People become trained to sacrifice truth, realism, and accuracy for the sake of keeping harmony in every situation.

This escape mechanism works, however, only to a point. When that point is reached, it can be suddenly thrown out of gear. Then grace and chivalry, in fact, all decent form, are forgotten; criticism becomes bitter; disagreement can turn into physical conflict. Then it is no longer a question of escape. The conflict is raging in the open.

14. THE CONVENIENCE OF IGNORANCE

In this connection, the remarkable lack of correct information about the Negroes and their living conditions should at least be touched upon. One need not be a trained student of the race problem to learn a lot in a couple of days about the Negroes in a community which is not known by even otherwise enlightened white residents. To an extent, this ignorance is part of the escape reaction.

Not only the man in the street, but also the professional man in the South, shows ignorance in his own field of work. One meets physicians who hold absurd ideas about the anatomical characteristics of the Negro people or about the frequency of disease among the Negroes in their own community; educators who have succeeded in keeping wholly unaware of the results of modern intelligence research; lawyers who believe that practically all lynchings are caused by rape. In the North, knowledge may be no greater, but the number of erroneous conceptions seems much smaller. The important thing, and the reason for suspecting this ignorance to be part of the escape mechanism, is that knowledge is constantly *twisted in one direction —toward classifying the Negro low and the white high.*

The ignorance about the Negro is not, it must be stressed, just lack of interest and knowledge. It is a tense and high-strung restriction and distortion of knowledge, and it indicates much deeper dislocations within the minds of Southern whites. These dislocations are clearly visible in stereotyped opinions. The stereotypes[3] are ideas

[3] By stereotype is meant a false and oversimplified idea of a group. For instance, if one thinks Negro women are like the "mammy" on the Aunt Jemima Pancake box or that Negro men are like Stepin Fetchit, he is thinking in stereotypes. There are many

which are agreed on and permitted. They express a belief that "all niggers" are thus and so. They block accurate observation. It is amazing to see the stern look on even educated people when they repeat these trite and worn stupidities, inherited through the generations, as if they were something new and tremendously important and also to watch their confusion when one tries to disturb their ways of thinking by "outlandish" questions.

15. NEGRO AND WHITE VOICES

What is at the bottom of this elaborated escape psychology? Has the Negro scholar W. E. B. Du Bois struck a vein of truth when he remarks:

Nor does the paradox and danger of this situation fail to interest and perplex the best conscience of the South. Deeply religious and intensely democratic as are the mass of the whites, they feel acutely the false position in which the Negro problems place them.[4]

Booker T. Washington said the same thing:

. . . [white people] are moved by a bad conscience. If they really believe there is danger from the Negro it must be because they do not intend to give him justice. Injustice always breeds fear.[5]

James Weldon Johnson, a third Negro leader, pointed out:

. . . the main difficulty of the race question does not lie so much in the actual condition of the black as it does in the mental attitude of the whites.[6]

And again:

The race question involves the saving of black America's body and white America's soul.[7]

White people have seen the same thing. Ray Stannard Baker wrote:

It keeps coming to me that this is more a white man's problem than it is a Negro problem.[8]

---

other Negro stereotypes called up by the phrases "Negroes like flashy clothes," "All Negroes are good singers," and so on.

[4] *The Souls of Black Folk* (Chicago: A. C. McClurg & Company, 1924; first edition, 1903), p. 186.

[5] *The Story of the Negro,* Vol. 1 (Garden City, N. Y.: Doubleday, Page & Company, 1909), p. 180.

[6] *The Autobiography of an Ex-Coloured Man, op. cit.,* p. 166.

[7] James Weldon Johnson, *Along This Way* (New York: Viking Press, 1933), p. 318.

[8] *Following the Color Line* (Garden City, N.Y.: Doubleday Page & Company, 1908), p. 65.

A Southerner, Thomas P. Bailey, said:

The real problem is not the negro but the white man's attitude toward the negro.

and

Yes, we Southerners need a freedom from suspicion, fear, anxiety, doubt, unrest, hate, contempt, disgust, and all the rest of the race-feeling begotten brood of viperous emotions.[9]

And so the conflict in the troubled white man's soul goes on.

16. The North and the South

In the North, the observer finds a different mental situation in regard to the Negro problem. The South is different from the rest of the country not only in having the bulk of the Negro population within its region but also in other ways, all, as we shall find, directly or indirectly connected with the Negro problem.

There has been less social change in the South. The South is poorer on the average, but the tradition of aristocracy is much stronger there. Because of this tradition and because of the lack of much industrialization, a main way to get and remain rich in the South has been to exploit the Negroes and other weaker people, rather than to work diligently, make oneself indispensable, or have brilliant ideas.

The mere existence of a more rapid tempo of life in the North, the constant changes, and the feeling of progress push the Negro problem into the background. The Negro problem has nowhere the importance in the North that it has in the South. There are few Negroes living in most of the North, especially in the rural regions. In the big cities, where the greater part of the Northern Negro population lives, the whites are protected from getting the Negro problem too much on their minds by the anonymity of life and the spatial segregation of racial groups.

The Northern whites have also been able to console themselves by comparing the favorable treatment of Negroes in the North relative to that of the South. This "passing the buck" is, of course, a device of Northerners to quiet their consciences. It is prominently displayed by Southerners also. The latter get satisfaction out of every indication that Negroes are not well treated in the North and, indeed, that groups other than Negroes are living in distress in the North. Such things help quiet their consciences. While each of the two guilty regions points

[9] *Race Orthodoxy in the South* (New York: Neale Publishing Company, 1914), pp. 37 and 347.

to the other's sins, the object of this maltreatment, namely, the Negro in both South and North, is the loser.

The Northerners want to hear as little as possible about the Negroes, both in the South and in the North. The result is an astonishing ignorance about the Negro on the part of the white public in the North. There are many educated Northerners who are well informed about poverty in foreign countries but almost absolutely ignorant about Negro conditions both in their own city and in the nation as a whole.

This has great practical importance for the Negro people. Many Northerners, perhaps the majority, are shocked and shaken in their consciences when they learn the facts. The average Northerner does not understand the effects of the discriminations in which he himself takes part every day. Nor are the Southerners entirely different on this point from the Northerners. It is quite possible that a majority, even of Southerners, especially in the younger generations, would be prepared for much more justice to the Negro if they were really brought to know the situation. To get publicity is, thus, of the highest importance to the Negro people. The simple fact is that an educational offensive against racial intolerance, going deeper than the reiteration of the "glittering generalities" in the nation's political creed, has never seriously been attempted in America.

17. AMERICAN MINORITY PROBLEMS

For some time there has been a tendency to include the American Negro problem in the broader American minority problem. In the United States the minority groups—except the Indians and the Negroes—are relatively recent immigrants, who were, for a long time, welcomed into the country. The newcomers were bent upon giving up their languages and other cultural traits and acquiring the ways and attitudes of the new nation.

The immigrants experienced personal misery and social pressure of all kinds. America has seen strong feeling against Germans, Irish, Jews, Scandinavians, Poles, Italians, and Mexicans. While there has been prejudice and discrimination against the immigrants, the outside observer is always amazed when he sees that the children and grandchildren of these unassimilated foreigners are well-adjusted Americans.

While race prejudice and discrimination persist, so does the American Creed. In trying to reconcile these conflicting values; the ordinary American believes that, as generations pass, the remaining minority groups—with certain exceptions which will be discussed later—will be assimilated into the nation. They see obstacles; they emphasize the religious and "racial" differences; they believe it will take a long time. But they assume that it is going to happen, and do not have, on the whole, strong objections to it—provided it is located in a distant future.

18. THE ANTI-AMALGAMATION DOCTRINE

The Negroes, on the other hand, are commonly assumed to be unassimilable and this is the reason why the Negro problem is different from the ordinary minority problem in America. The Negroes are set apart, together with other colored peoples, principally the Chinese and Japanese. While all other groups are urged to become Americanized as quickly and completely as possible, the colored peoples are excluded from assimilation.

Among the groups commonly considered unassimilable, the Negro people is by far the largest. The Negroes do not, like the Japanese and the Chinese, have a political organization and an accepted culture of their own outside of America to fall back upon. Unlike the Oriental, there attaches to the Negro an historical memory of slavery and inferiority. It is more difficult for them to answer prejudice with prejudice and, as the Orientals frequently do, consider themselves and their history superior to white Americans and their recent cultural achievements.

To the ordinary white American, the caste line between whites and Negroes is based upon, and defended by, the anti-amalgamation doctrine. This doctrine, more than anything else, is at the heart of the Negro problem. When the Negro people is characterized as unassimilable, it is not, of course, meant that amalgamation is not biologically possible. But crossbreeding is considered undesirable. Sometimes the view is expressed that the offspring of crossbreeding is inferior to both parent stocks. Usually it is stated that he is inferior to the "pure" white stock, and the assumption then is that the Negro stock is "inferior" to the white stock. On the inherited inferiority of the Negro people there exists among white Americans a folklore, which is remarkably similar throughout the country. Whether the idea of the inferiority of the Negro is basic to the anti-amalgamation doctrine or only a rationalization of it can, for the moment, be left open. The two notions, at any rate, appear together.

A remarkable peculiarity of this American doctrine is that it is applied differently to lawful and unlawful matings. As far as lawful marriage is concerned, the racial doctrine is laden with emotion. Even in the Northern states, where, for the most part, intermarriage is not barred by law, mixed couples are punished by nearly complete social ostracism. On the other hand, in many regions, especially in the South, where intermarriage is strictly forbidden by law, illicit relations are widespread. Cohabitation with a Negro woman is, apparently, considered a less serious breach of sexual morals than illicit intercourse with a white woman. The illicit relations freely allowed or only frowned upon, are, however, restricted to those between white men and Negro women. A white woman's relation with a Negro man is met by the full fury of the anti-amalgamation penalties.

White people, when arguing against interracial sex relations, appeal to the Negroes' "race pride" and their interest in keeping their own blood "pure." But this is a white, not a Negro argument. The Negro is amused at the idea of keeping his blood pure, owing to the fact that the large majority of American Negroes already have white and Indian ancestry as well as African Negro blood. In general, they are aware of this fact.

Although the idea of race pride has been growing with the Negro, this is due to the common white opinion of the racial inferiority of the Negro people and the whites' intense dislike of intermarriage. The fact that a large amount of exploitative sexual intercourse between white men and Negro women has always been a part of interracial relations, coupled with the further fact that the Negroes feel the disgrace of their women who are not accepted into matrimony, and the inferior status of their mixed offspring, is a strong practical reason for the Negro's preaching race pride in his own group. But it is almost certainly not based on any fundamental feeling condemning miscegenation on racial or biological grounds. On this central point, as on so many others, the whites' attitudes are primary and decisive; the Negroes' are in the nature of accommodation or protest.

19. The White Man's Theory of Color Caste

It is rare to meet a white American who will confess that he has no strong objection to intermarriage. The intensity of this attitude seems to be markedly stronger in the South than in the North. It is less strong the higher the economic, social, and educational status of the individual. It is strong even in most of the noncolored minority groups. But even a liberal-minded Northerner will, in nine cases out of ten, express a definite feeling against amalgamation. He will not usually be willing to hinder intermarriage by law. Individual liberty is to him a higher principle. But he will regret the exceptional cases that occur. He may sometimes feel that in centuries to come amalgamation is bound to happen and might become a solution.[10]

This attitude of refusing to consider amalgamation is the complex center of the Negro problem. Almost unanimously white Americans have expressed the following ideas of race relations, which we shall call the "white man's theory of color caste."

(1) The concern for "race purity" is basic in the whole issue. The primary idea is to prevent amalgamation; the whites are determined to use every means to this end.

(2) Rejection of "social equality" is to be understood as a precaution to hinder intermarriage.

(3) The danger of intermarriage is so tremendous that segregation and discrimination must be extended to nearly all spheres of life —recreation, religion, education, politics, law, housing, and breadwinning.

This popular theory is, of course, a rationalization of other motives, among them economic interests; sexual urges, inhibitions, and jealousies; social fears; and cravings for prestige and security. As the reader goes on, he will get a clearer idea of how this rationalization works, and why, for instance, this biological doctrine refers to legal marriage and to relations between Negro men and white women, but not to extramarital sex relations between white men and Negro women. He will also be able to understand the emotion attached to the Negro problem. In Western civilization, particularly in America, sex and social status are for most individuals the danger points where they fear sinister onslaughts on their personal security. Anything connected with these two problems is likely to be pushed deep down into the subconscious and become laden with emotions. The American puritan tradition gives everything connected with sex a high emotional charge. Social climbing has been so easy in America that competition for social position has become absorbing. In a manner and to a degree most uncomfortable for the Negro people in America, both these sexual and social problems have become related to the Negro problem.

[10] The response is likely to be anything but pleasant if one jokingly argues that a small fraction of Negro blood in the American people, if it were blended well with all the other good stock brought over to the new continent, might create a race of unsurpassed excellence; a people with just a little sunburn without extra trouble, even through the winter; with some curl in the hair without the cost of a permanent wave. Amalgamation is, to the ordinary American, not a proper subject for jokes at all, unless it can be pulled down to the level of dirty stories, where, however, it enjoys a favored place.

These problems are kept concealed most of the time. In occasional groups of persons and situations they break into the open. Even when not consciously seen or expressed, they ordinarily determine interracial behavior on the white side.

20. The "Rank Order of Discriminations"

When white Southerners are asked to rank, in order of importance, various types of discrimination, they consistently present a list in which these types of discrimination are ranked according to the degree of closeness of their relation to the anti-amalgamation doctrine. The "white man's rank order of discriminations," held nearly unanimously, is the following:

Rank 1. Highest in this order stands the bar against intermarriage and sexual intercourse involving white women.

Rank 2. Next come the etiquette and discrimination which concern behavior in personal relations. (These are the barriers against dancing, bathing, eating, drinking together, and social intercourse generally; peculiar rules as to handshaking, hat lifting, use of titles, house entrance to be used, social forms when meeting on the streets and in work, and so forth. These patterns are sometimes referred to as the denial of "social equality" in the narrow meaning of the term.)

Rank 3. Thereafter follow segregation and discrimination in use of public facilities such as schools, churches, and means of conveyance.

Rank 4. Next comes political disfranchisement.

Rank 5. Thereafter comes discrimination in law courts, by the police, and by other public servants.

Rank 6. Finally comes discrimination in securing land, credit, jobs, or other means of earning a living, and discrimination in public relief and other social welfare activities.

Next in importance to the fact of the white man's rank order of discriminations is the fact that the Negro's own rank order is parallel, but opposite, to that of the white man. The Negro resists least discrimination on the ranks placed highest in the white man's scale and resents most any discrimination on the lowest level. This is in accord with the Negro's immediate interests. Negroes are most in need of jobs and bread. Justice in the courts and the vote are more urgent than better schools and playgrounds. Such facilities are more important than civil courtesies. The marriage matter, finally, is of distant and doubtful interest.

If the white man is honestly prepared to carry out in practice his rank order theory, this opposite relationship between the Negro's and the white man's rank orders becomes of great importance in the practical and political sphere of the Negro problem. Such a relationship, or such a minimum moral demand on the ordinary white man, has often been the basis of attempts to compromise and come to a better understanding between leaders of the two groups. It has been the basis for interracial policy and also for most of the practical work carried out by Negro betterment organizations. Followed to its logical end, it should fundamentally change the race situation in America.

It has thus always been necessary for every Negro leader—who wishes to get a hearing from the white majority group—to support the anti-amalgamation doctrine and avoid expressing any desire on the part of the Negro people to intermarry with the whites. The request for intermarriage is easy for the Negro leader to give up. It is not practical as long as nearly all white individuals are against it, since marriage is an individual matter. Also, as a defense reaction, a strong attitude against intermarriage has developed among the Negro people itself.

At the same time, no Negro leader ever accepts the common white premise of racial inferiority of the Negro stock. Du Bois points out:

> . . . a woman may say, I do not want to marry this black man, or this red man, or this white man. . . . But the impudent and vicious demand that all colored folk shall write themselves down as brutes by a general assertion of their unfitness to marry other decent folk is a nightmare.[11]

Another deviation among the Negroes from the anti-amalgamation doctrine is the stress they lay on condemning exploitative illicit amalgamation. Here they have a strong point, and they know how to press it.[12] A third qualification in the Negro's acceptance of the anti-amalgamation doctrine is that intermarriage should not be barred by law. Respect for individual liberty is one argument, but, in addition, it is pointed out that this barrier, by releasing the white man from the consequences of intimacy with a Negro woman, has the effect of increasing miscegenation.

Even with all these qualifications, the anti-amalgamation doctrine is difficult for intellectual Negroes to accept. Negroes have always pointed out that the white man cannot be very certain of his woman's interest if he feels compelled to build up such formidable fences to prevent her marrying a Negro. With these reservations, both Negro

[11] Editorial, *The Crisis* (January, 1920), p. 106.

[12] "The rape which your gentlemen have done against helpless black women in defiance of your own laws is written on the foreheads of two millions of mulattoes, and written in ineffaceable blood." W. E. B. Du Bois, *The Souls of Black Folk* (Chicago; A. C. McClurg & Company, 1924; first edition, 1903), p. 106.

leadership and the Negro masses acquiesce in the white anti-amalgamation doctrine.

Whereas the Negro spokesman finds it possible to assent to the first rank of discrimination—miscegenation—it is more difficult for him to give his approval to the white man's refusal to extend the ordinary courtesies to Negroes in daily life. In the upper classes of Negroes there is a demand to have white men call them by the titles of Mr., Mrs., and Miss; to be able to enter a white man's house by the front door, and so on. The modern Negro leader usually states that no Negroes want to intrude upon white people's private lives. But Southern white opinion asks for a general order according to which *all* Negroes are placed under *all* white people and are excluded not only from the white man's society but also from the ordinary symbols of respect. Negroes resent this, but it is not in the forefront of their expressed criticism of white treatment.

At the next lower level of the rank order—that of the Jim Crow practices, the segregation in schools, disfranchisement, and discrimination in employment—increasingly larger groups of white people are prepared to take a stand against these discriminations. Also, Negro spokesmen are increasingly firm in their opposition to discrimination on these lower levels. It is principally on these lower levels of the white man's rank order of discriminations that the race struggle goes on.

Less discrimination in the North than in the South is apparently related to a weaker basic prejudice. In the North the Negroes have justice and are not disfranchised; they are not Jim-Crowed in public means of conveyance; educational institutions are less segregated. The interesting thing is that the decrease of discrimination does *not* regularly follow the white man's rank order. Thus intermarriage is legally permitted in all but one of the Northern states east of the Mississippi, and racial etiquette is practically absent from the North. On the other hand, employment discrimination is, at times, equally severe or more so in some Northern communities than in the South.

21. Relationships Between Lower-Class Groups

This country is a "white man's country," but, in addition, it is a country belonging primarily to the elderly, male, upper-class, Protestant Northerner. Viewed in this setting, the Negro problem in America is but one local and temporary aspect of that eternal problem of world dimensions—how to regulate the conflicting interests of groups in the best interest of justice and fairness.

We believe that in a society where a feeling of class is not too strong, where there are ethnic or religious splits in the lower income groups, these lower-class groups will, to a great extent, take care of keeping each other subdued, thus relieving, to that extent, the upper income group of this otherwise painful task necessary to safeguard its power and advantages. Our belief is similar to the view taken by an older group of Negro writers and by most white writers who have touched this crucial question: that the Negro's greatest enemy is the lower class of white people, the people without economic or social security who are competing with Negroes.

That part of the country where the Negro is dealt with most severely, the South, is also a disadvantaged and, in most respects, the most backward region in the nation. The Negro lives there in the midst of other relatively subordinated groups. The masses of white Southerners are poor and there is an obvious tendency for lower class groups to struggle against each other.

On the other hand, internal struggle in the lower classes is only one social force among many. Other forces are making for solidarity in the lower classes—tradition, fear, leadership, brute force, propaganda, as well as economic and social security and a planned program of civic education. In this connection the influence of liberal ideas must not be forgotten. Persons who are inclined to favor measures to help the underdog are also usually inclined to give the Negro a lift.

In general, however, poor people are not radical and not even liberal, even though such political opinions would often be to their interests. The South, furthermore, compared to the other regions of America, is most conservative. The South's conservatism is manifested not only with respect to the Negro problem but also with respect to all other important problems of the last decades. There are relatively few liberals in the South and practically no radicals.

The recent flood of social reforms thrust upon the South by the federal government and the fact that the rate of industrialization in the South is higher than in the rest of the nation are, however, causing an upheaval in the South's entire opinion structure. The importance of this for the Negro problem is considerable.

22. The Theory of the Vicious Circle

Throughout this inquiry there will be an assumption of an interdependence among all the factors in the Negro problem. White prejudice and discrimination keep the Negro low in standards of living, health, education, manners, and morals. This, in its turn, gives support to white prejudice. White prejudice and Negro standards thus mutually "cause" each other. If things remain as they are, this means that the two forces happen to balance each other. This is, however, entirely accidental. If either of the factors changes, this will cause a change in the other factor, too, and start a process of interaction where the change in one factor will continuously be supported by the reaction of the other factor. The whole system will be moving in the direction of the primary change, but much further.

If, for some reason, white prejudice could be decreased and discrimination lessened, this is likely to cause a rise in Negro standards, which may decrease white prejudice still a little more, which would again allow Negro standards to rise, and so on. If, instead, discrimination should be increased, the vicious circle would spiral downward. The original change can as easily be a change of Negro standards upward or downward.

The same principle holds true if we split prejudice and discrimination, on the one hand, or Negro standards, on the other, into their various parts. A rise in Negro employment, for instance, will raise family incomes, standards of nutrition, housing and health, the possibilities of giving the Negro youth more education, and so forth, and all these effects of the first change will, in their turn, improve the Negroes' possibilities of getting employment and earning a living. The original push could have been some factor other than employment, for example, an improvement of health or educational facilities for Negroes. Much the same thing holds true of the development of white prejudice. Even assuming no changes in Negro standards, white prejudice can change, for example, as a result of an increased general knowledge about biology, removing some of the false beliefs among whites concerning Negro racial inferiority. This system of interlocking causes is commonly called the "vicious circle" because it is generally, but falsely, assumed to work in only a bad direction.

One result of the vicious circle is practical. In the field of politics any push upward directed on any one of the factors moves all other factors in the same direction and has, through them, an increasing effect upon general Negro status. However, if one wishes to do something about the Negro problem on the basis of the vicious circle theory, it is necessary to understand how all the factors are interrelated: what effect a primary change upon each factor will have on all other factors. If only one factor is changed suddenly and with great force, it would probably throw the entire system out of gear or else prove to be wasteful, as the same effort by being spread over various factors and a period of time might have much greater end results.

23. A Theory of Democracy

Looking at race prejudice as it appears in American daily life, one finds it difficult to avoid the reflection that it seems much easier to increase than to decrease race prejudice. It is a common observation that the white Northerner who settles in the South will rapidly take on the stronger race prejudice of the new surroundings; while the Southerner going North is not only likely to keep his race prejudice unchanged but also, frequently, communicates it to those he meets. The Northerner in the South will find the whole community intent upon his conforming to local patterns. The Southerner in the North will feel, rather, that others are adjusting to him wherever he goes. If the local hotel in a New England town has accommodated a few Negro guests without much worry one way or the other, the appearance one evening of a single white guest who makes an angry protest against it might permanently change the policy of the hotel.

If a decrease in race prejudice is a goal, such a general tendency would be likely to force us to a pessimistic view. Why, then, in spite of all that has been noted, is discrimination, on the whole, not increasing, but decreasing? The first reason advanced in this study is the American Creed, the relation of which to the Negro problem will become clearer in later chapters. The Creed of progress, liberty, equality, and humanitarianism is not so uninfluential on everyday life as might sometimes appear.

The second point is the existence in society of huge institutional structures like the church, the school, the university, the foundation, the trade union, the association generally, and of course, the state. It is true that these institutions show an accommodation to local and temporary interests and prejudices. As institutions, they are, however, devoted to certain broad ideals. The school, in every community, is likely to be a degree more broad-minded than local opinion. So is the sermon in church. The national labor assembly is likely to decide slightly above the prejudice of the average member. When the man in the street acts through his orderly collective bodies, he acts more as an American, as a Christian, and as a humanitarian than if he were acting independently.

Through these huge institutional structures, a constant pressure is brought to bear on race prejudice, counteracting the natural tendency for it to spread and become more intense. The same people are acting in the institutions as when showing personal prejudice, but they

obey different moral values on different planes of life. Into their institutions they have placed their ideals of how the world ought to be.
The ideals thereby gain power and influence in society. This is a
theory of social self-healing that is present in the type of society we
call democracy.

CHAPTER II

Race: Beliefs and Facts

1. SOME HISTORICAL NOTES ON RACIAL BELIEFS

Before the eighteenth century, the upper classes in England and France, as everywhere else, developed a vague theory that the "lower classes" were inferior by nature.[1] It was against this convenient belief that the philosophers of the Enlightenment reacted. Their main interest was, however, not biological, but moral. When transferred to America, the equality doctrine became even more bent toward the moral. There is thus no doubt that the declaration that all men were "created equal" and, therefore, endowed with natural rights has to be understood in the moral sense that they were born equal as to human rights. Nevertheless, the moral equality doctrine carried with it, even in America, a belief in biological equality.

When the Negro was first enslaved, his slavery was not justified in terms of his biological inferiority. The imported Negroes—and the captured Indians—were originally treated in the same way as were the indentured white servants. When the Negroes were gradually pushed down into chattel slavery, while the white servants were allowed to work off their bond, the need was felt, in this Christian country, for some kind of justification of this other than economic expediency or the might of the strong. The arguments were broadly these: that the Negro was a heathen and a barbarian, an outcast among the peoples of the earth, a descendant of Noah's son Ham,

---

[1] Not only is the controversy over the relative importance of heredity *vs.* environment a very old one, but opinions on this question indicate more than anything else where each of us stands on the scale between extreme conservatism and radicalism. The liberal is inclined to believe that it is the occasion that makes the thief, while the conservative usually holds that the thief is likely to create the occasion. The liberal believes that the individual and society can be improved through education and social reform, while the conservative thinks that it is "human nature" and not environment that makes individuals and society what they are.

cursed by God Himself and doomed to be a servant forever on account of an ancient sin. Later these arguments were easily merged into the dogma of biological inequality.

There was, in the Revolutionary period and for several decades afterwards, a strong antislavery movement. Not only many of the early Christian thinkers and preachers, particularly among the Quakers, but also many of the enlightened slaveholders opposed slavery. Both Jefferson and Washington saw clearly the inconsistency between American democracy and Negro slavery, and looked forward to the rapid abolition of slavery. Even in terms of economic usefulness, slavery seemed for a time to be a decaying institution. In the first two decades of the nineteenth century, the Abolitionist movement was as strong in the South as in the North, if not stronger.

A most important economic factor had, however, entered into the historical development and it profoundly changed the issue. Several inventions in the process of cotton manufacture, principally Eli Whitney's cotton gin in 1794, transformed Southern agriculture. Increased cotton production and its profitability caused migration southward and westward from the old, liberal Upper South, and raised the prices of slaves, which had previously been declining.

Chiefly as a result of this, but also due to a general political reaction to the liberalism of the Revolution, the South developed, in the thirty years before the Civil War, not only a strong defense of slavery, but also a generally conservative political philosophy. More and more boldly as the conflict drew nearer, churchmen, writers, and statesmen of the South came out against the principle of equality as set forth in the Declaration of Independence. Here it should be recalled that Jefferson and his contemporaries, when they said that men were equal, had meant it primarily in the moral sense that they should have equal rights, the weaker not less than the stronger. This was what the South denied. As far as the Negroes were concerned, the South departed radically from the American Creed. Lincoln later made the matter plain when he observed that one section of the country thought that slavery was *right* while the other held it to be *wrong*.

In the proslavery thinking of the pre-Civil War period, the Southerners stuck to the American Creed as far as whites were concerned. In the situation where slavery showed increasingly greater prospects for profit, yet where the Southerners wanted to retain the democratic creed of the nation—the doctrine of biological inequality between whites and Negroes offered a convenient solution for the conflict in Southern minds. "All men are created equal" but Negroes were said not to be men.

2. THE COMPROMISE OF 1876

After the war and Emancipation, the race dogma was retained in the South as necessary to justify the caste system that succeeded slavery as the social organization of Negro-white relations. The North had never cleansed its own record in its dealing with the Negro even if it freed him and gave him permanent civil rights and the vote. In the North, however, race prejudice was never so deep and so widespread as in the South. A brief Reconstruction period was followed by the national compromise of the 1870's when the North allowed the South to have its own way with the Negroes in obvious contradiction to what a decade earlier had been declared to be the ideals of the victorious North and the policy of the nation. The North now also needed the race dogma to justify its course.

The fact that the same rationalizations[2] are used to defend slavery and caste is one of the connecting links between the two social institutions. In the South the connection is direct. Even today the average white Southerner uses the race dogma to defend, not only the present caste situation, but also slavery and, consequently, the righteousness of the Southern cause in the Civil War.

The partial exclusion of the Negro from American democracy has, however, in no way dethroned the American Creed. But the influences from the American Creed have a double direction. On the one hand, the Creed operates directly to suppress the dogma of the Negro's racial inferiority and to make people's thoughts more and more "independent of race, creed or color," as the American slogan runs. On the other hand, it indirectly calls forth the same dogma of inferiority to justify the exception of the Negro to the Creed. The need for race prejudice is, from this point of view, a need for defense on the part of the Americans against their own national Creed.

3. REFLECTIONS IN SCIENCE

This split in the American soul has been, and still is, reflected in scientific thought and in the literature on the Negro race and its characteristics. As the Civil War grew nearer, intellectuals were increasingly mobilized to serve the Southern cause and to satisfy the Southern needs for rationalization. After Reconstruction their theories were

[2] By rationalization is meant the use of "good," or moral-sounding, reasons instead of the real reason.

taken over by the whole nation. The numerous enemies of the Negro left a whole crop of unscientific writings in the libraries emphasizing racial differences. Without much change this situation continued into the twentieth century.

The last two or three decades, however, have seen a revolution in scientific thought on the racial characteristics of the Negro. This revolution embraces not only the whole race issue outside the Negro problem, but also the basic question of heredity versus environment. The social sciences in America, and particularly sociology, anthropology, and psychology, have increasingly found that environment, rather than heredity, is more important.

Social research has thus become extremely critical of earlier work.[3] It is constantly proving that apparent mental differences between Negroes and whites are not inborn, but are due to cultural and social differences. The popular race dogma is thus gradually exposed as false.

As creators of original scientific theories and as independent research workers in the field of social science, as in other fields, the Negroes came late and are even now rather exceptional. This is a consequence of the American caste system. But for a long time they have had gifted essayists well in touch with the trends in social sciences. From the beginning, Negro writers took the stand that the American dogma of racial inequality was a scientific fake. Kelly Miller said, for instance:

The Negro has never, during the whole course of history, been surrounded by those influences which tend to strengthen and develop the mind. To expect the Negroes of Georgia to produce a great general like Napoleon when they are not even allowed to carry arms, or to deride them for not producing scholars like those of the Renaissance when a few years ago they were forbidden the use of letters, verges closely upon the outer rim of absurdity. Do you look for great Negro statesmen in states where black men are not allowed to vote?[4]

[3] While much of the earlier work was merely naïve, some results were deliberately falsified. For instance, Robert B. Bean, a Southern student of Franklin P. Mall in the latter's laboratory at Johns Hopkins University, made a study showing that Negro skulls and brains were smaller than the skulls of white men, and the brains less convoluted and otherwise deficient. After Bean published his findings, Mall repeated the measurements on many of the same specimens and found that Bean had completely distorted his measurements and conclusions. (Franklin P. Mall, "On Several Anatomical Characters of the Human Brain, Said to Vary According to Race and Sex, With Especial Reference to the Weight of the Frontal Lobe," *American Journal of Anatomy*, 9 [February, 1909], 1–32.)

[4] *Race Adjustment—Essays on the Negro in America* (New York: The Neale Publishing Company, 1908), p. 40.

The Negro intellectuals' resistance to the white race dogma has been widely accepted among the Negro people, as it corresponds closely to Negro interests. Gradually the whites also are coming to believe that Negroes are not innately inferior, since modern science finds this to be the case. But the whites have been very slow to change their ideas, since the findings of modern science do not coincide with their interest in defending the caste order. However, it is now becoming difficult for even popular writers to express other views than the ones of racial equalitarianism and still retain intellectual respect. This is true even in the South. Research and education are bolstering the American Creed in its influence toward greater equalitarianism.

4. The Racial Beliefs of the Uneducated

In trying to understand how ordinary white people came to believe in the Negro's biological inferiority, it must be noted that there was shift from theological to biological thinking after the eighteenth century. As soon as the idea spread that man belongs to the biological universe, the conclusion that the Negro was *biologically* inferior was natural to the unsophisticated white man. It is obvious to the ordinary unsophisticated white man, from his everyday experience, that the Negro is inferior. And seemingly inferior the Negro really is; so he shows up even under scientific study. His body is more often deformed; his health is bad and his death rate higher; his intelligence performance, manners, and morals are lower. The *correct* observation that the Negro is inferior was tied up to the *correct* belief that man belongs to the biological universe and, by twisting logic, the *incorrect* deduction was made that the inferiority was biological in nature.

Race is a simple idea which easily becomes connected with certain outside visible signs such as skin color. Explanations in terms of environment, on the contrary, tax knowledge and imagination heavily. It is difficult for the ordinary man to understand clearly how malnutrition, bad housing, and lack of schooling can deform the body and soul. It is even more difficult to understand the subtle influences of the denial of outlets for ambition, social disparagement, cultural isolation, and the early conditioning of the Negro child's mind by the caste situation. The white man is, therefore, speaking in good faith when he says that he sincerely believes the Negro to be racially inferior, not merely because he has an interest in this belief, but simply because he has seen it. He "knows" it.

Tradition strengthens this honest belief. Originally the imported Negro slaves had hardly a trace of Western culture. The tremendous cultural differences between whites and Negroes were maintained and, perhaps, increased by the Negroes' being kept first in slavery and, later, in a subordinate caste, while American white culture changed apace. In addition, the Negroes showed obvious differences in physical appearance. Darker color, woolly hair, and other conspicuous physical Negro characteristics became steadily associated with servile status, backward culture, low intelligence performance, and lack of morals. All unfavorable reactions to Negroes became thus easily attributed to *every* Negro as a Negro, that is, to the *race,* and to the individual only secondarily as a member of the race.

However, the concept of race is not clear in the popular mind. The Negro race (in the popular theory) is said to be several hundreds or thousands of years behind the white man in "development." Culture is then assumed to be something *in the race*. A definite biological ceiling is usually provided: the mind of the Negro race cannot be improved beyond a given level. This odd theory is repeated through more than a century of literature. It is met everywhere in contemporary white America.

Closely related to this popular theory is the historical and cultural demonstration of Negro inferiority already referred to. It is constantly pointed out as a proof of his racial backwardness that the Negro was never able to achieve a culture of his own. Civilization is alleged to be the accomplishment of the white race.

Without doubt, there is also in the white man's concept of the Negro "race" an irrational element which cannot be grasped in terms of either biological or cultural differences. It is what is meant when using the word "blood" in describing ancestry. The ordinary man means something beyond rational understanding when he refers to "blood." In this magical sphere of the white man's mind, the Negro is inferior, totally independent of scientific proofs or disproofs. There is fear of the unknown in this feeling, which is "superstition" in the literal sense.

As a result, the Negro is segregated, and one deep idea behind segregation is that of quarantining what is evil, shameful, and feared in society. When one speaks about "Americans" or "Southerners," the Negro is not counted in. When the "public" is invited, he is not expected.

5. Beliefs with a Purpose

The Negro's situation being what it is and the unsophisticated white man's mind working as it does, the white man can honestly think and say that his beliefs are founded upon close personal experience and hard facts. He is not deliberately deceiving himself; but the beliefs are useful.

While the ordinary white American does not consciously concoct his prejudices for a purpose, unscrupulous demagogues appeal to prejudice with great profit. Many other white individuals occasionally find it to their private interest to stretch their biased beliefs a little more in a direction unfavorable to the Negro. Practically no white people examine their beliefs critically. And so through the generations, strengthened by tradition and community agreement, a public opinion among whites is formed which is plainly useful to the interests of the majority group.

If white Americans can believe that Negro Americans belong to a lower biological species than they themselves, this provides a good reason for saying that the white race should be kept pure. The theory of the inborn inferiority of the Negro people is, accordingly, used as an argument for the anti-amalgamation doctrine. This doctrine, in its turn, has, as we have seen, a central position in the American system of color caste. The belief in biological inferiority is thus another basic support of the system of segregation and discrimination. White Americans have an interest in deprecating the Negro race in so far as they identify themselves with the prevailing system of color caste.

Those who need to rationalize and defend the caste system specify that the following statements shall be held true:

(1) The Negro people belongs to a separate race of mankind.

(2) The Negro race has an entirely different ancestry.

(3) The Negro race is inferior in as many capacities as possible.

(4) The Negro race has a place in biology somewhere between the white man and the anthropoid apes.

(5) The Negro race is so different both in ancestry and in characteristics that all white peoples in America, in distinction to the Negroes, can be considered as one race.

(6) The individuals in the Negro race are very similar to one another and all of them are definitely more akin to one another than to any white man.

The major observation is that the six points stated above not only represent the ordinary white American's theory on the Negro race, but also that this theory is *needed* to rationalize the American caste situation.

Such beliefs are stronger in the South than elsewhere. The strength of such beliefs decreases as education increases. The white upper-class person, since his social distance from the Negro is so great and so secure, will often be willing to recognize individual Negroes as exceptions and more likely to classify poor whites as an inferior stock and sometimes "just as bad as" the average Negro. The lower classes of whites seem to be much more careful to keep the race dogma straight on both these points.

In adhering to his biological rationalization, the white man meets difficulties. To begin with, many Negroes, in spite of the handicaps they meet, are much better than they ought to be, according to the popular theory. A whole defense system is used to lessen this disturbance of the race dogma, which insists that *all* Negroes are inferior. From one point of view, segregation is a part of this defense system. It is, of course, not consciously devised for this purpose, and it serves other purposes as well, but this does not make its defense function less important. Segregation isolates especially the middle- and upper-class Negroes, and thus permits the ordinary white man in America to avoid meeting an educated Negro. The systematic tendency to leave the Negro out when discussing public affairs and to avoid mentioning anything about Negroes in the press except their crimes also serves this purpose. The aggressive and derogatory attitude toward "uppity" Negroes and, in particular, the tendency to include all educated Negroes in this group also belongs to the defense system.[5]

Since he has a psychological need to believe the popular theory of Negro racial inferiority, it is understandable why the ordinary white man does not want to hear about good qualities or achievements of Negroes. "The merits of Negro soldiers should not be too warmly praised, especially in the presence of Americans" reads one of the advices which the French Military Mission, stationed with the American Expeditionary Army during the First World War, circulated, but later withdrew.[6]

Another difficulty has always been the mulatto.[7] White Americans want to keep biological distance from the out-race and will, therefore, be tempted to discount the proportion of mulattoes and believe

[5] The term "uppity" is a Southern white man's term for all Negroes who try to rise, or have risen, out of the lower classes.

[6] Quoted from Willis D. Weatherford and Charles S. Johnson, *Race Relations* (Boston: D. C. Heath and Company, 1934), p. 235.

[7] The term "mulatto" is, according to American custom, understood to include all Negroes of mixed ancestry, regardless of the amount of intermixture and the remoteness of its occurrence. The term includes, in addition to "true" mulattoes, also quadroons, octoroons, and all other types of crossbreeds. In America they are all grouped with the Negro race. It is of interest that Negroes do not like the use of these terms any more than whites are willing to recognize that most American Negroes are of mixed blood. This is partly a defense reaction on the part of the Negroes and partly a way of keeping unity among the diverse colors.

that a greater part of the Negro people is pure bred than is true. A sort of collective guilt on the part of the white people for the large-scale miscegenation, which has changed the racial character of the Negro people, increases this interest. The ordinary white American is disturbed when he hears scientific estimates that the great majority of American Negroes are not of pure African descent. He is similarly disturbed when he hears that Negroes sometimes pass for white.

But the mulatto is a disturbance to the popular race theory not only because of his numbers. The question is also raised: is the mulatto a deteriorated or an improved Negro? There has never been popular agreement among white Americans on this question. The former belief strengthens the anti-amalgamation doctrine. The second can serve to explain away Negro accomplishments by attributing them to white blood. Actually, often the same man may be heard to use both arguments.

6. Specific Rationalization Needs

Practically every type of white-Negro relation, every type of discriminatory behavior, every type of interracial policy, raises its own peculiar demands for justification. Each type of situation produces its own belief. All the beliefs to be mentioned have been scientifically disproved, as we shall find as we go on.

The beliefs that Negroes get sleepy when working with machines and that they lack mechanical aptitudes serve a need to justify their being kept out of industry. The beliefs of their unreliability, their inborn lack of aptitude for sustained mental activity, and particularly, their lower intelligence help to justify vocational segregation and to excuse the barriers against promotion of Negroes to skilled and supervisory positions. The beliefs that the Negro race is "childish," immature, undeveloped, servile, and lacking in initiative are used to justify the denial of full civic rights and suffrage to Negroes.

The Negro's presumed lower intelligence and the belief that the mind of the Negro cannot be improved beyond a given level have always been the main arguments for discrimination in education and, specifically, for directing Negro education toward developing his hands and not his brains. The beliefs that Negroes have a much smaller skull and lower brain weights, a less complicated brain structure, thicker skull bones, and an earlier closing of the cranial sutures explain and strengthen the beliefs in the lesser development of the Negro's higher brain centers and, consequently, his lower intelligence and reasoning power.

The beliefs in the Negro's alleged inborn laziness and thriftlessness, his happy-go-lucky nature, his lack of morals, his criminal tendencies, and so on, serve the purpose of easing the conscience of the good, upright, white citizen when he thinks of the physical and moral slum conditions that are allowed in the Negro sections of all communities in America. They also rationalize the demand for housing segregation and tend, on the whole, to picture the Negro as a menace to orderly society unless "kept in his place" by the caste system. The exaggerated beliefs of the Negro's higher susceptibility to various diseases explain, in a way less compromising for the larger community, the high mortality rates, and the bad health conditions among the Negro population. Until recently, these beliefs have discouraged all programs of health improvement among Negroes.

The belief in a peculiar odor of Negroes, like similar beliefs about other races, is useful to justify the denial of social intercourse and the use of public conveniences that would imply close contact, such as restaurants, theaters, and public conveyances. It is remarkable that it does not hinder the utilization of Negroes in even the most intimate household work and personal services.

There are many popular beliefs deprecating the mulatto: that they are more criminally disposed than even Negroes in general; that they tend to be sterile; that they—having parents of two distinct races— are not harmoniously proportioned, but have a trait of one parent side by side with a trait of the other parent, paired in such a way that the two cannot function together properly; that they are more susceptible to tuberculosis; that, because Negroes have relatively long, narrow heads, Negro women, who tend to have narrow pelvises, and their mulatto offspring are endangered when they bear children of white men whose heads are rounder, and so on. These beliefs are all of a nature to discourage miscegenation and to keep up biological distance even in regard to crossbreeds. The assertion, particularly common among Southerners, that there are unfailing signs to detect everyone with the slightest amount of Negro blood, which is so easy for any observer to disprove by experiment, is a reassuring belief with a similar function.

The belief that practically all Negro women lack virtue and sexual morals bolsters up a collective bad conscience for the many generations of miscegenation. At the same time, it is, occasionally, a wishful expression of sexual appetite on the part of white men. The belief in the strong sexual urge and the superior sexual skill and capacity of Negro women more obviously has this latter function. The belief that Negro males have extraordinarily large genitalia is to be taken as an expression of a similar sexual envy and, at the same time, as part of the social control to aid in preventing intercourse between Negro males and white females.

There are also popular beliefs which are friendly; for example, that the Negro is more gifted in music, the arts, dancing, and acting than white people; that he is better in handling animals or, sometimes, children; that he is loyal and reliable as a servant (often, however, the opposite is asserted); that he is, on the whole, a more happy and mentally balanced human being; that he has more emotional warmth; that he is more religious. All such favorable beliefs seem to have this in common, that they do not raise any question concerning the advisability or righteousness of keeping the Negro in his place in the caste order. They do not react against the major need for justification. Rather they make it natural that he shall remain subordinate.

7. CHANGING BELIEFS

The rationalization needs do not work in a vacuum. They must have raw material to shape into the desired form. This material consists of white people's experiences with Negroes, how they behave and what they are, from his point of view. They also consist of the numerous myths, legends, and stereotypes that exist in American culture.

Assuming as our value premise that we want to reduce the bias in white people's racial beliefs concerning Negroes, our first practical conclusion is that we can partly effect this result by improving the Negro status, Negro behavior, Negro characteristics. The difficulty with this is, of course, that white beliefs are active forces in keeping the Negroes low.

A second line of strategy must be, therefore, to rectify the ordinary white man's observations of Negro characteristics and to inform him of the mistake he is making in ascribing them wholesale to inborn racial traits. People want to be rational, to be honest and well informed. This want, if it is properly nourished, competes with the desire to build false rationalizations.

A third line of strategy is, naturally, to attack the values which the false beliefs support. This must mean strengthening the American Creed.

It should be clear by this time that it is the popular beliefs that are of primary importance in interracial relations. We have concluded further, from the actual power situation in America, that the beliefs held by white people rather than those held by Negroes are of primary importance. Our theory is that beliefs are useful in defending interests. The ordinary American's interests in the Negro problem should not be assumed to be simple and harmonious. They are, instead, complicated and conflicting. The conflicts are largely suppressed and only vaguely conscious. The further analysis of the racial beliefs will, therefore, reach down to the deeper seated conflicts of values.

8. The American Definition of "Negro"

The "Negro race" is defined in America by the white people. Everybody having a *known* trace of Negro blood—no matter how far back it was acquired—is classified as a Negro. No amount of white ancestry, except one hundred per cent, will permit entrance to the white race.

This definition of the Negro race in the United States is different from that held in the rest of the American continent. "In Latin America whoever is not black is white: in teutonic America whoever is not white is black."[8] In the British colonies and dominions, primarily South Africa, the hybrids (half-castes) are considered as a group distinct from both whites and Negroes. Even in the United States many persons with a mixture of Indian and white blood are regarded as whites (for example, former Vice President Curtis and Will Rogers).

This social definition of the Negro race, even if it does not change anything in the biological situation, increases the number of individuals included in the Negro race. It relegates a large number of individuals who look like white people, or almost so, to the Negro race. In the American white population the so-called Nordic type, which is popularly assumed to be the opposite extreme from the black Negro, is very rare. Even the "Old American stock" was mainly "non-Nordic." But a few American Negroes also have the clearest of white skin, the bluest of blue eyes, and many have the long and narrow head that happens to be both a Negro and a "Nordic" trait.

The definition of the "Negro race" is thus a social and conventional, not a biological, concept. In modern biological or ethnological research "race" as a scientific concept has lost sharpness of meaning, and the term is disappearing in sober writings. In something even remotely approaching its strict sense, it applies only to exceptionally isolated population groups, usually with a backward culture, which thus seems to be associated with "racial purity."

Thus *the scientific concept of race is totally inapplicable at the very spots where we recognize "race problems."* Only the ignorant talk about the "Swedish" or "Scandinavian race," not to speak of the

[8] James Bryce, *The American Commonwealth,* Vol. 2 (New York: The Macmillan Company, 1910; first edition, 1893), p. 555.

"Anglo-Saxon" or "German race." The "white American race" has gradually become merely a joke even among people of low education, except in the South. Besides the recognized differences among individuals in any one group, the differences among averages of groups tend to pale into insignificance. Scientists now stress the unity of mankind and are skeptical of differences until they are demonstrated.

The common belief that the races could be ordered as higher or lower in an evolutionary series, so that Negroids could be deemed more ape-like than Caucasoids, is entirely discredited. It is now commonly assumed by expert opinion that man—the species *Homo sapiens*—evolved only once, and that such average differences as now exist between men are due to living under different geographic conditions after having separated from the common place of origin. Independent of this hypothesis, which, of course, can hardly be checked, it is a fact that the Negro is no more akin to the apes than the white man is. Of the four most noticeable characteristics generally ascribed to the average or typical Negro—dark skin, broad nose, woolly hair, thick lips—only the first two make him slightly more similar to the apes. The white man's thin lips and straight hair are, on the other hand, much nearer to the traits of apes.

When all this is said, it does not follow that the race concept is unimportant in the Negro problem. In spite of all heterogeneity, the average white man's observation is that most Negroes in America have dark skin and woolly hair, and he is, of course, right.

He is also right in ascribing the occurrence of these characteristics to African ancestry. His conception of the Negro race may be ever so arbitrary and scientifically inaccurate; his ideas about racial mental and moral traits may be fantastic and untenable; but the fact is that "race" in his definition is the basis of the social caste system as it exists in America. Because of social visibility and of community knowledge of the parentage of individuals, "race" has tremendous cultural consequences.

From one viewpoint the entire Negro problem in America hinges upon this social definition of "race." Should America wake up one morning with all knowledge about the African ancestry of part of its population and all memories of color caste absolutely forgotten and find all the outward physical characteristics of the Negro people gone, but no change in their mental or moral characteristics, nothing that is known about this group and other population groups in America would lead one to believe that the American Negro would not rapidly come to fit in as a well-adjusted ordinary American. His poverty and general backwardness would mean a low starting point and cause a larger portion of this population group to remain in the lower social strata. But, having been relieved of the specific caste deprivations and hindrances, his relative preponderance in the disadvantaged classes would immediately begin to decrease.

The Negro's relative isolation in America through slavery and subordinate caste position would, for a time, endow him with remnants of some peculiar cultural and personality traits. But they would be negligible even in the beginning—if, as we assume, they are unrelated through social visibility to his caste status—compared with much more glaring and "non-American" peculiarities of various groups of recent immigrants.

But this is only a dream. The Negro has to be defined according to social usage. With the social definition comes the whole stock of valuations, beliefs, and expectations in the two groups, causing and constituting the order of color caste in America.

9. Ancestry

Part of the ancestry of the American Negro people is African. Historical and anthropological evidence seems to indicate that the great majority of slaves brought directly to the United States came from the West Coast of Africa and hence belonged mainly to that racial group known as the "true Negroes." Even if we ignore the fact that there has been an admixture of white and Indian blood into the American Negro population, there have been some changes in this population stock which make it different from those African tribes from which it has descended. Those who became slaves in America were only a selection of Africans, not a representative sample of them. They were probably made even less representative by the rigors of the displacement from Africa to America, which killed off a certain number of them. After the Negroes came to America, their biological composition was probably changed by differential reproductivity and possibly even by mutation.

The slaves imported from Africa by no means represented "pure Negro races." Of the original tribal stocks many had an admixture of Caucasoid genes from crosses with Mediterannean peoples. During the slave trade more white genes were added. The slave traders themselves were known frequently to have had promiscuous intercourse with their female merchandise. Negroes who came, either during slavery or later from the West Indies, also had an appreciable amount of white and Indian blood. In the United States miscegenation with Indians and whites occurred from the very beginning.

As the slavery and plantation systems became more firmly established in the early eighteenth century, a second stage was reached in Negro-white sex relations. Wirth gives a balanced statement on the "amount of miscegenation during the period of slavery" when he says:

The contemporary observers, on the whole, tend to leave an impression that no likely looking Negro, or more especially mulatto, girl was liable to be left unmolested by the white males; that very few of the young white men grew up "virtuously," and that their loss of virtue was scarcely to be attributed to cohabitation with white women. While such impressionistic statements lead to the inference that interracial sexual relations were normal experiences for at least the white men of well-to-do families, they reveal nothing concerning the proportion of Negro women and, what is of less importance, of Negro men, who entered into interracial unions. It is conceivable that the emphasis on the sexual activities of the white male has tended to obscure the extent to which large numbers of Negro women may have been free from any sexual experiences with white men.[9]

It should not be assumed that interracial sex relations were a pattern only of the Southern rural plantations. There is general agreement among the authors who have studied the question of interracial sexual relations of this period that such relations—measured in proportion to the number of Negro women in the population—were even more frequent in the Southern cities and in the North.

The third stage of Negro-white sex contact came with the Civil War and its aftermath. The Northern army left an unknown amount of Yankee genes in the Southern Negro people. When the Negro population gradually settled down in the caste status that had been substituted for slavery, sexual mores can be assumed to have been continued much along pre-Civil War lines.

It is more difficult to form even a conjectural judgment as to the amount of interracial sexual relations during the twentieth century and as to the present trend than it is to ascertain broadly the facts for earlier periods. There have been no scientific studies which suggest even tentatively the actual quantitative trend of interracial sexual relations. Most of the informants questioned on local trends in the course of this study—but by no means all—have agreed in the belief that sex relations between members of the two groups are decreasing. The same opinion is expressed in the literature. It should, however, be considered with the greatest reservation, as such an opinion is convenient for both the white and the Negro groups to have.

[9] Louis Wirth and Herbert Goldhamer, "The Hybrid and the Problem of Miscegenation," in: Otto Klineberg (editor), *Characteristics of the American Negro* (New York: Harper & Brothers, 1944), pp. 267-268.

But even if interracial sexual relations have not been decreasing, the offspring from intermixture may be decreasing. There is probably a decrease in the more stable types of sexual relationships—marriage and concubinage—and an increase in prostitution and casual sex relations. Prostitution is usually sterile and contraception is probably widely used in the latter type of relationships. The scanty quantitative evidence and general opinion seem to indicate that there has been a decline in the rate at which white genes are being added to the Negro population.

Because of the American caste rule of classifying all hybrids as Negroes, it might be thought that no Negro blood would ever get into the white population. However, some extremely light Negroes—usually having more white than Negro ancestry—leave the Negro caste and become "white." Passing, as it is called, may occur only for segmented areas of life—such as the occupational or recreational—or it may be complete; it may be temporary or permanent; it may be voluntary or involuntary. Usually the only kind that is important for the genetic composition of both the white and the Negro population is that which is complete and permanent. Since passing is usually concealed and census data and vital statistics are not accurate enough to permit of estimates within reasonable limits, it is difficult to determine the extent of passing. However, it is probable that there has been much more passing than the white public suspects.

10. PRESENT AND FUTURE GENETIC COMPOSITION TRENDS

Everything said so far about the racial character of the slaves originally imported, about miscegenation and passing in this country, and about the various general factors that have influenced the American Negro stock, has been highly conjectural and speculative. Summing up this unsatisfactory knowledge can hardly lead to anything more than an expectation that the American Negro people is a considerably mixed population group. It is the merit of Professor Melville J. Herskovits[10] that he has finally approached the problem directly and has tried to ascertain the actual composition of the group.

Herskovits' most significant finding was that 71.7 per cent of his presumably representative sample of 1,551 Negroes had knowledge of some white ancestry, and that 27.2 per cent knew of some Indian ancestry. It is likely that Herskovits' sample contains too many upper-class Negroes who are known to have a disproportionate amount of white ancestry. The fact that many Negroes may not know of white

[10] Melville J. Herskovits, *The Anthropometry of the American Negro* (New York: Columbia University Press, 1930).

ancestry of several generations back may, however, counterbalance the selective factor in Herskovits' sample and leave his figure of 71.7 per cent with white ancestry not too inaccurate. This figure must tend to increase with time, if for no other reason than that full-blooded Negroes intermarry with mixed bloods and their offspring become mixed bloods.

A forecast of the future trend of genetic changes must be highly conjectural. Even for the immediate future it can amount to little more than an enumeration of the relevant factors and a consideration of their interrelations.

Miscegenation between American Negroes and whites is commonly believed to be on the decrease. At least, children of white-Negro unions are becoming rarer because of increasing knowledge of and accessibility to contraceptive devices.

Passing is becoming easier in the more mobile and anonymous society of today and tomorrow. The increasing economic and social opportunities for the Negro upper class (to which most of the light-colored mulattoes belong) in the segregated Negro communities will tend to decrease the desire to pass. So also will the rising race pride. The effect of passing, whatever its extent, is to neutralize the effect of miscegenation on the genetic composition of the Negro people.[11] It is even possible to conceive of a temporary condition in which the rate of passing would exceed the rate of addition of new white blood into the Negro group so that there would be a tendency for the American Negro group to become more negroized.

Differential reproductivity is a factor which can be expected to have a continuing importance within the next decades. Present knowledge rather favors the forecast that present fertility differences between the various Negro groups are not going to decrease much for a long time. Infant mortality and, generally, mortality in the lower age groups may be expected, on the other hand, to become gradually more equalized. There are, further, no sure signs that light-colored people will not remain in the upper class; since, with increasing segregation, the Negro upper class is relatively growing, it can come to include a relatively greater number of black Negroes without losing many of its mulattoes.

Reproduction differences have, in the main, the same effect on the Negro group as passing, except that the effect is not so exclusively

[11] The effect of passing on the American *white* population can never become important because those who pass usually have more Caucasoid genes than Negroid, and because the numbers who pass are insignificant compared to the huge American white population.

concentrated on the extremely light-colored Negroes. This factor, therefore, enters into the balance between miscegenation and passing and makes it more probable that the effects of miscegenation can be fully, or more than fully, counterweighted.

Internal miscegenation within the Negro group between individuals with a varying degree of white ancestry is continually going on. The result is a tendency toward a slow but continuous equalization of Negro and white genes in the Negro people, decreasing the relative numbers at both black and white extremes and concentrating the individuals ever closer to the average.

Immigration of Negroes (and mixed bloods) from the West Indies and from South America will somewhat change the genetic composition of the Negro people in a direction depending upon the genetic composition of the newcomers.

If a more complete amalgamation between whites and Negroes does not occur within the surveyable future, the proportion of very light mulattoes who now, so to speak, form a bridge between the two population groups will decrease by passing and by marriage with darker Negroes. Finally, let the reader be reminded again that the concept of the American Negro is a social concept and not a biological one. Even considerable changes in the genetic composition of the Negro people may leave the social problems, around which this inquiry is centered, unchanged.

11. Physical Traits

In this summary discussion of "racial" characteristics, physical traits are separated from mental traits. We have had to rely upon studies mainly concerned with those traits in which the Negroes differ from whites, which, by itself, represents a biased statement of the problem, tending to exaggerate differences and minimize similarities. Most of the studies attempt only to get *average* differences, and fail to measure the wide amount of variation and overlapping. In addition, much of the data is so weak that even the differences cannot be said to be satisfactorily established.

Ascertaining the differences between Negroes and whites in respect to physical traits involves not only measurements of Negroes but also the establishment of a "standard" set of measurements of whites. No anthropometric measurements of the American population have ever been undertaken on such a large scale and with such methodological precautions that valid comparisons between one subgroup and the rest of the population are possible. There are, however, a large number of studies on small samples of American Negroes and various groups of whites. For the Negroes, Herskovits' study is by far the best available. During his investigations, Herskovits tried to determine the representativeness of his sample; the investigators of white samples have not even made efforts to get representativeness, particularly important because of the heterogeneous origin of the American population.

It is no exaggeration to say that no physical difference between the average American Negro and the average American white, not even difference in color, has yet been measured quantitatively by research methods which conform to the rigid standards of statistics. At the maximum, one is justified in drawing from available studies only rather qualitative statements concerning average differences, the actual quantities of which—as well as the actual spreads around these averages—are not known.

Compared to the average white man, the average Negro of the present day seems to exhibit the following physical traits: head slightly longer and narrower; cranial capacity slightly less; interpupillary distance greater; nose broader; lips thicker; external ear shorter; nasal depth greater; nose shorter; torso shorter; arms and legs longer; pelvis narrower and smaller; stature shorter; skin with greater amount of black pigment; hair wavy, curly, frizzly, or woolly; distribution of hair less thick; more sweat glands; prognathism[12] is greater, not because the brain case stops growing in early childhood, but because the upper jawbone continues to grow after the age at which that of the white man stops. A larger proportion of Negroes have brown eyes, black hair, and sacral pigment spots than do Old Americans. This summary contains all those physical traits reported by more than one anthropologist, that distinguish the American Negro from the Old Americans.[13]

The traits vary greatly among different groups of Negroes. Stature, cranial capacity, and perhaps other traits are also modifiable by environmental changes over time. In many of these traits Negroes differ only slightly from white men; in nearly all of them there is some overlapping between Negroes and whites. The average person is, for these reasons, not aware of some of these differences. Some of the traits are outstanding and easily visible in the average Negro—although nearly or entirely lacking in many individual members of the

[12] Prognathism: The projection of the jaws beyond the upper part of the face.

[13] Old Americans: The white population most often used for furnishing a standard set of measurements. This group is composed mainly of Americans whose ancestors came from Britain, Germany, and Scandinavia, and includes a disproportionate number of persons of high socioeconomic status. It is not at all representative of the general American population.

Negro group—such as dark skin, woolly hair, broad nose, thick lips, and prognathism. These are the basic traits that account for the Negro's "social visibility."

The white man might be aware of other differences but grossly exaggerates them in his imagination, not because he has observed the differences but because he has certain opportunistic beliefs which he fortifies by hearsay testimony and by such occasional experiences of his own as happen to confirm his beliefs. He also usually attaches an incorrect interpretation to them. An example is the slightly smaller cranial capacity of the average Negro, which the white man associates with alleged lower reasoning power of the Negro despite the fact that no connection has been proved between cranial capacity and mental capacity among humans.

Certain traits are found only in popular beliefs and have no foundation at all in fact. Such are the beliefs that the time of suture closure in the brain case of the Negro is earlier than that of the Caucasoid, that the Negro's hands and feet are larger, and that his forehead slopes more. To the same category belongs the belief that the Negro has different vocal chords. This is associated with the rather unique pronunciation and speech habits of a large proportion of the Negro population.

Certain common beliefs have as yet not been checked by scientific research. This is, for instance, true of the beliefs that all male Negroes have extraordinary large genitalia and all Negroes a peculiar odor.[14] Such beliefs are frequently used to justify discrimination and segregation.

Since measurements of the American Negro are intended to be those of the average individual, and since the majority of American Negroes are mulattoes, the traits measured are predominantly those of mulattoes. Little is known of the actual mechanism of inheritance of the various traits when races cross, except that it is far from being

[14] Klineberg refers to a suggestive experiment made by Lawrence, "who collected in test tubes a little of the perspiration of White and Colored students who had just been exercising violently in the gymnasium. These test tubes were then given to a number of White subjects with instructions to rank them in order of pleasantness. The results showed no consistent preference for the White samples: the test tube considered the most pleasant and the one considered most unpleasant were both taken from whites." (Otto Klineberg, *Race Differences* [New York: Harper & Brothers, 1935], pp. 130–131.) Such experiments should be repeated on larger and more representative groups of whites, and the question should be asked whether the Negro sweat is identifiable, rather than whether it is pleasant. Even if it were established that Negroes had a different odor, it would not explain why this odor is considered offensive. Likes and dislikes in smells of this sort are a matter of personal taste and cultural conditioning.

simple Mendelian inheritance. Anthropologists find changes in traits from those of the pure Negro type to be roughly proportional, on the whole, to the amount of admixture of white blood.

12. BIOLOGICAL SUSCEPTIBILITY TO DISEASE

There is one type of physical trait which, if proved, would have great practical importance. We refer to the possibility of a differential susceptibility to various diseases.

At one time it was believed that the differences in specific disease rates were due to differences in biological constitution. The great decline in the Negro death rate since the turn of the century forced investigators to recognize environmental factors. Even so, few investigators have realized fully that the whole mode of existence of Negroes—with their segregation, overcrowding, and ignorance—helps to create a higher disease rate as compared to whites; and that these factors cannot be completely held constant because there is no group exactly comparable in the white world.

Furthermore, we must observe that the reporting of vital statistics for Negroes is very poor, largely because Negroes are concentrated in those population groups for which reporting is least complete. In addition, the fact that certain beliefs are prevalent about Negro susceptibilities and that there is often a question as to what shall be reported as the "cause of death" make the official statistics an imperfect source for determining ethnic differences in disease. This is especially important in the case of those diseases to which Negroes are supposed to be relatively immune, such as scarlet fever and diabetes.

We shall consider those diseases which are important as causes of death and those for which the differences between Negroes and whites are large enough to indicate that they are due to real differences and not to errors in observation or sampling. This narrows the problem down to pellagra, syphilis, nephritis, tuberculosis, and pneumonia-influenza. No one seems to have advanced the claim that the Negro's higher death rates due to pellagra (caused by poor diet), syphilis (caused by close contact with one having this virus infection), or nephritis results from his biological constitution. The question of innate racial differences seems to have cropped up mainly with reference to tuberculosis and pneumonia-influenza. Enough facts are available to indicate that the main reasons for the discrepancy between Negroes and whites in the incidence of tuberculosis are environmental and not hereditary. There is not so much direct evidence that the higher pneumonia-influenza rate for Negroes is due to environmental causes. However, other studies of these allied diseases have not succeeded in finding a strong hereditary susceptibility, and there is indirect evidence that malnutrition, overcrowding, and poor nursing are contributory causes.

In trying to determine whether Negroes have any special susceptibility to *mental* disease there are even more difficulties than in the case of physical disease. The only information comes from hospitals, which vary greatly in their policy respecting admission. Studies have been made in Illinois and New York, and Negroes were found to have a higher rate of dementia praecox than did whites. But Negroes there are concentrated in cities, which have a rate twice as high as the rural areas for whites also. Too, Negroes were concentrated in those age and income groups with the highest rates of dementia praecox. New York Negroes seem to have a much higher rate of general paresis than do whites. The explanation is that New York Negroes have much more syphilis than do whites, and syphilis is the cause of paresis. No racial susceptibility to syphilis has been demonstrated. In view of all these complications, recent students of mental diseases have tended to avoid completely the question as to whether Negroes have any special susceptibilities to mental disease.

In general, we must conclude that no innate susceptibilities or immunities to specific diseases on the part of the Negro have yet been conclusively demonstrated. Even if differential susceptibility to a disease should someday be demonstrated, it should be remembered that susceptibility does not mean disease: for proper preventive efforts can reduce the ill-effects of any degree of susceptibility. The practical conclusion is, therefore, that there is no reason for the American public to feel complacent about the higher disease and death rates of Negroes on the ground that they have a greater innate susceptibility.

13. MENTAL TRAITS

The belief in the innate inferiority of the Negro in mental capacities and moral traits has been central in the race dogma from the beginning. It is one of the main rationalizations for segregation and discrimination. Obvious cultural inferiorities existing in the Negro population made it easy and opportune to assume innate mental inferiority. Earlier, not only the man in the street but also the scientists made this assumption. And, usually, even the scientists found what they were seeking.

In view of these biases, the startling thing is that psychological research has failed to prove what it set out to prove. Huxley and Haddon make the important remark that it is "not without insignificance that such an enormous mass of investigation [on innate mental differences between human groups] has failed to demonstrate what so many are eager to prove."[15] This fact is of some importance as it should increase our right to feel confident in the results of the scientific trend toward finding no mental differences between Negroes and whites.

In addition, psychologists are coming to realize that they are not, and never will be, measuring innate traits directly, but are, rather, measuring performance in a limited number of selected tasks, and that performance is determined—in a most complex fashion—by many influences besides innate capacity. Most of this work has concerned intelligence, as measured by the intelligence quotient (I.Q.). The results are, on the whole, negative as far as hereditary differences are concerned: it has not been possible to prove beyond doubt the existence of any differences at all in innate intelligence between American Negroes and whites; neither has it been possible to prove, on the other hand, that no differences exist.

What is here said about the general level of intelligence applies also to more specific mental traits. The suggestion that Negro children have superior memory is not proved. Nor is it made credible that there are fewer Negroes in the highest ranges of intelligence.[16] The belief that the intelligence of Negro youth ceases to develop at an earlier age does not stand criticism. Nothing is proved concerning differences between Negroes and whites in sensory powers. No conclusions in regard to innate differences in other personality traits can be considered valid.

These negative conclusions from many decades of the most painstaking scientific labor stand in glaring contrast to the ordinary white American's firm conviction that there are fundamental mental differences between Negroes and whites. The ordinary white American has assumed that the personality and mental differences he has observed in the Negroes with whom he has had contact were innate and a part of "nature." He has not been able to discern the influence

[15] Julian S. Huxley and A. C. Haddon, *We Europeans* (New York: Harper & Brothers, 1936), pp. 96–97.

[16] No one has sought a representative sample of either white or Negro children to determine what proportions were very superior, but the only investigators who have sought superior Negro children had no special trouble finding them. Witty and Jenkins studied 26 Negro children with I.Q.'s of 140 and above, who came from grades 3–8 in 7 Chicago public schools. (Paul A. Witty and Martin A. Jenkins, "The Educational Achievement of a Group of Gifted Negro Children," *The Journal of Educational Psychology*, 25 [November, 1934], 585–597). The same authors report on one nine-year-old Negro girl with a Stanford-Binet I.Q. of 200. ("The Case of 'B'—A Gifted Negro Girl," *The Journal of Social Psychology*, 6 [February, 1935], 117–124).

of gross environmental differences, much less the influence of subtle life experiences. Also, he has made many observational errors, because his observations have been limited and biased.

As long ago as 1930, on the other hand, a questionnaire circulated among "competent scholars in the field of racial differences" revealed that only 4 per cent of the respondents believed in race superiority and inferiority. It is doubtful whether the proportion would be as large today.

These conclusions of psychological research have probably been more revolutionary and practically important, with respect to the Negro's problem, than the conclusions from any other sphere of science. In view of the negative results of long years of careful study, it is highly improbable that there will ever be found innate mental differences, between American Negroes and whites, so large that they could justify a differential treatment in matters of public policy such as in education, suffrage, and entrance to various sections of the labor market.

CHAPTER III

Population and Migration

1. THE GROWTH OF THE NEGRO POPULATION

There were about 17 times as many Negroes in the United States in 1940 as there were in 1790, when the first census was taken, but in the same period the white population increased 37 times. Negroes were 19.3 per cent of the American population in 1790 but only 9.8 per cent in 1940. There is no doubt that the heavy immigration of whites from Europe accounts for the largest part of this great decline in the proportion of Negroes until recently.

From now on, however, as during the 1930's, there will probably be little net immigration of whites from Europe. One important exception to this is the continuing immigration of Mexicans and Canadians. These groups will continue to provide a small but steady addition to the white population. Both white and Negro population groups are, therefore, now changing and will continue to change—if the assumption of little immigration is correct—almost entirely in accord with their respective birth and death rates.

For a first observation of Negro and white natural increase—that is, the balance of births and deaths—one may turn to the *net reproduction rate*.[1] For 1940 the rates were 107 for nonwhites and 94 for whites, including Mexicans. For 1930 the comparable rates were 110 for nonwhites, 111 for whites.

Despite errors in the data, it is possible to derive the following tentative conclusions: (1) that Negroes, like whites, are not reproducing themselves as rapidly as they used to; (2) that probably their rate is now higher than that of the whites; (3) that this differential is a new

[1] The net reproduction rate is a combined measure of the birth and death rates, adjusted for an abnormal age distribution in the population. A net reproduction rate of 100 means that the population is just reproducing itself; if it is under 100, the population will decrease, and conversely, if it is over 100, the population is increasing.

phenomenon. If such a differential continues into the future and if it is not fully compensated for by immigration of whites, the proportion of Negroes in the American population may be expected to rise, though slowly.

Until 1930 it was only because Negroes were concentrated in the South and in rural areas, which always have higher birth rates in their population, that Negroes were reproducing themselves as rapidly as whites. During the 1930's, however, white rates dropped so much, that, even when corrected for rural and Southern residence, Negro rates were higher than white rates. Thus, a fourth conclusion is that: (4) Even within regions and rural-urban areas taken separately, Negroes are no longer reproducing themselves at a lower rate than whites. In fact, the figures suggest that they are reproducing themselves more—thus reversing the position they held in 1930 and earlier.

2. Births and Deaths

The Negro birth rate, like the white birth rate, has been falling at least since 1880 and perhaps longer. Since 1850 it has been consistently higher than the white birth rate. These important generalizations about the birth rate have held true in recent years; in 1928–1932 the corrected gross reproduction rate[2] was 136 for Negroes—as compared to 122 for whites (1930)—and by 1933–1937 the Negro rate had fallen to 130.

While there are proportionately more Negro than white infants born, significantly fewer of the Negro infants live. During 1940, 73 out of every 1,000 live Negro infants were recorded to have died before reaching their first birthday, as compared to 43 white babies out of every 1,000 born. If the official statistics were more accurate, they would undoubtedly reveal a much greater differential in infant mortality rates. The difference in death rates for children and mature adults is apparently even greater. If a Negro child is born alive, it has (in 1945), on the average, a life expectancy of roughly 57.8 years, while the average white newborn child can expect to reach the age of 67.0 years.[3] Corrected death rates would be 20.6 per thousand population for Negroes and 16.4 per thousand for whites. The actually registered death rates were, in 1930, 16.5 per thousand for Negroes and

[2] The gross reproduction rate is a refined birth rate. It is the number of girl babies born to the average woman throughout her reproductive period. Unfortunately these rates are unreliable, but comparisons are justified even if we cannot rely on the exact magnitudes.

[3] Metropolitan Life Insurance Company, *Statistical Bulletin,* 28 (April, 1947), Table 1, p. 3.

10.8 for whites. The lower actual rates are due not only to under-registration but also to the abnormal age structure; both Negroes and whites have a disproportionate number of young adults.

The data are so poor that they do not permit us to compare trends in the Negro and white death rates. If the death rates have been falling for both groups, it would seem that they were falling more rapidly for whites than for Negroes until 1930. In 1930 the death rate for the Negro population was higher than the rate for the white population in 1900—thirty years ago. It is likely that since 1930 the death rate has fallen more rapidly for Negroes than for whites. Of particular interest would be the effects of a large-scale disease-prevention campaign. Since Negro death rates are now considerably higher than white death rates, it is more possible to bring them down.

Migration will continue to be of great importance for future trends in Negro birth and death rates. Migration from rural to urban areas universally reduces the birth rate. It has been related to the reduction of both white and Negro fertility over the past seventy years. Also, migration has probably meant a somewhat reduced death rate for the Negroes, but the decline in death rate has not balanced the decline in birth rate. In 1940 the nonwhite net reproduction rate for rural-farm areas was 154, as compared to 76 for urban areas; for whites the comparable figures were 132 and 76, respectively.

Popular theories on the growth of the Negro population in America have been diverse. At times it has been claimed that Negroes "breed like rabbits" and that they will ultimately crowd out the whites if they are not deported or their procreation restricted. At other times it has been pronounced that they are a "dying race," bound to lose out in the "struggle for survival." In spite of the inadequacy of the statistics, it can be stated confidently that both these ideas are wrong. *In their reproduction American Negroes are like American whites and show the same sort of differentials by regions and groups.*

3. Ends and Means of Population Policy

Both whites and Negroes are agreed on both the desirability and the necessity of raising the quality of the American Negro population. It is implicit in the American Creed, with its stress on the value and dignity of the individual human being. It is true that the average white American does not want to sacrifice much himself in order to improve the living conditions of Negroes. But on this point the American Creed is quite clear and explicit, and we can proceed safely on the value premise that the medical and health facilities and, indeed, all public measures in the field of education, sanitation, housing, nutrition, hospitalization, and so forth, to improve the quality of the population and to advance individuals and groups physically, mentally, or morally should be made just as available for Negroes as for whites in similar circumstances and with similar needs. This value premise has, in fact, sanction in the Constitution of the United States.

4. CONTROLLING THE DEATH RATE

Since there is no evidence at present that certain diseases are genetically more characteristic or less characteristic of Negroes than of whites, it is not necessary to single out Negroes for special attention in any efforts to cure or prevent disease. If disease-prevention work is to be effective, it must be planned on a national basis without regard to the color of the inhabitants. In the South as well as in the North there is an increasing popular recognition among whites that "diseases cannot be segregated" and that high rates of death, sickness, and poor health among Negroes carry tremendous social costs, directly and indirectly, even if they cannot be calculated accurately in dollars and cents.

Medical knowledge has advanced beyond medical practice, and medical practice has advanced far beyond most people's opportunity to take advantage of it. A reduction in these lags would have tremendous consequences for the well-being and happiness of every person in the nation. Of special significance to the Negroes is the lag of opportunity for some people to obtain the advantages of medical practice available to other people. Area for area, class for class, Negroes cannot get the same advantages in the way of prevention and cure of disease that the whites can. There is discrimination against the Negro in the availability to him of medical facilities.

Discrimination increases Negro sickness and death both directly and indirectly and manifests itself both consciously and unconsciously. Discrimination is involved when hospitals will not take in Negro patients; or when—if they do permit Negro patients—they restrict their numbers, give them the poorest quarters, and refuse to hire Negro doctors and nurses to attend them. In 1928 (the latest figures) there was available in the United States one hospital bed for each 139 of the white population but only one hospital bed for each 1,941 of the colored population. This means that at that time each white inhabitant of the United States had 14 times as good a chance for proper hospital care as had the colored citizen. The facilities for Negroes are generally of a much poorer quality than for whites. In

1937 only about 35 per cent of Southern Negro babies were delivered by a physician, as compared to 90 per cent of Southern white babies and 98 per cent of Northern white and Negro babies. In the whole United States in 1940 there were only about 3,530 Negro doctors, 7,192 Negro nurses, and 1,471 Negro dentists, and most of these were employed in the North.[4] It is true, of course, that Negroes cannot afford doctors and hospitals to the same extent as whites can, but that does not eliminate the fact of discrimination.

Perhaps the greatest need of the Negroes, in the way of reducing sickness and death, is for knowledge of how to take care of the body in both its normal and its sick state. Other needs are indicated by the diseases for which the Negro rate is strikingly higher than the white rate. These include pellagra (a result of improper diet), syphilis (a function of inadequate information, on the one hand, and social disorganization, on the other), homicide (partly a result of cultural isolation of a subordinated people and lack of police protection in Negro communities), pneumonia and influenza (a function of inadequate care), and tuberculosis (a result, largely, of inadequate sanitation and poor diet). These diseases not only kill but also reduce the efficiency of Negroes to a much greater extent than that of whites. Pellagra, syphilis, and tuberculosis, at least, can easily be recognized as public problems—the removal of which is necessary to the health and efficiency of the entire nation.

The infant mortality rate as registered is 69 per cent higher among Negroes than among whites (1940); the actual difference is probably even greater. The discrepancy in maternal mortality rates between the two races is much higher—official figures indicate that the rate for Negro mothers is two and one-half times as high as the rate for white mothers (1940). Both infant mortality and maternal mortality among the Negroes have been declining in the past decade. But the fact that they are still much higher for Negroes indicates that much can yet be done to reduce these types of death among Negroes.

We can conclude from known facts and the stated value premises that what is needed in the way of special attention to Negroes is constant vigilance against popular and official prejudice in the application of a general medical and health program.

In view of the racial attitudes of the South, and in view of the generally greater needs and smaller resources of the South, it is almost necessary that national organizations, and specifically the federal government, take a firm lead in this work. A national policy, working

[4] *Sixteenth Census of the United States: 1940. Population,* Vol. III. *The Labor Force* (Washington: Government Printing Office, 1943), Table 62.

toward an improvement of health and a decline in disease, will increase the happiness and efficiency not only of those directly served, but also of the general population. It will also, if carried out with intelligence and fairness, be a major example of the democratic process.

5. THE CASE.FOR CONTROLLING THE NEGRO BIRTH RATE

Aside from any desire on the part of white people to check the growth of the Negro population, there are in the South a great number of Negroes—as of whites—who are so destitute that from a general social point of view it would be highly desirable that they did not reproduce. The same is true, though to a much lesser degree, about the North. Many of these people are so ignorant and poor that they are not desirable parents and cannot offer their children a reasonably good home. The chances of their children dying at an early age are much greater than those of other children.

Without going into the reasons for spreading birth control in any population, a few remarks on the special reasons for Negroes are in point. One of the obvious misfortunes which a reduced birth rate could relieve is the poverty of the Negro masses. It is particularly strong as long as the state leaves the rising costs of bearing and rearing children almost entirely to the individual families. Since Negro women are employed to a greater extent than are white women, the periods of pregnancy, confinement, and dependency are a relatively greater economic burden to Negro families. If pregnancies occur too frequently, the mother's health is endangered. Besides poverty, there are other conditions among Negroes which motivate birth control. One is the high disease rate, especially of venereal diseases. Children born of untreated syphilitic women, if they live, nearly always have some permanent defect. A third special problem is suggested by the extremely high illegitimacy rate among Negroes, in itself a result of the poverty and disorganization of family life among Negroes.

6. BIRTH CONTROL FACILITIES FOR NEGROES

Public opinion, as measured by polls, is increasingly in favor of birth control. The number of contraceptive clinics rose from 34 in 1930 to 803 in 1942. In seven states—North Carolina, South Carolina, Florida, Mississippi, Texas, Virginia, and Alabama—*public* health authorities have taken the lead in bringing birth control clinics to rural areas where they are most needed.[5]

[5] Letter from Mrs. Marie S. Key, field consultant, Planned Parenthood Federation of America, Inc., 501 Madison Avenue, New York 22, N.Y., March 20, 1947.

The activity of the birth control movement's workers, the Southern whites, and the Negro leaders—all with the same aim of spreading birth control among Negroes—promises a great development of the movement in the future. A serious difficulty is that of educating Southern Negroes to the advantages of birth control. An intensive educational program is needed, giving special recognition to the prejudices and ignorance of the people whom the campaign is to benefit. The use of Negro doctors and nurses is essential.

With the growing popular and legal acceptance of birth control, it would seem that a shift in emphasis is needed. The birth control organizations have, in the past, run into so many difficulties that they are wary of direct propaganda that might antagonize doctors and the "best people." They tell people to see a doctor and so do not get over the fact that there are more easily accessible (and quite as reliable) devices for birth control and venereal prophylaxis than the ones usually prescribed by physicians. None of the present activities should be cut out, but the time has come for more direct and more widespread educational work. So far contraception has been most successful on a mass basis among city people, who learn about simple methods from their friends, not from doctors. The birth control organizations can do this more effectively, more speedily, and more scientifically than can rumors and jokes.

The main reason for advocating this shift in emphasis is that mass instruction and propaganda can reach more people in less time and at lower cost than the clinics run by doctors and nurses. The need for birth control is widespread and is only slightly touched by present activities despite their high cost. Birth control is fundamentally a simple matter, and it calls for adult education before clinical consultation.

7. THE GENERAL PICTURE ON MIGRATION

Ever since they were brought to this country as slaves, Negroes have been concentrated in the South. The North had little use for slavery and soon abolished it. The South, on the other hand, came to regard slavery as necessary to its economy and brought Negroes in as long as it was legally possible, and after that, bred and smuggled them to increase the number of slaves. As a result, at the end of the Civil War the great masses of American Negroes were concentrated in the rural South.

Even after the Negro was legally free to move as he pleased, there was relatively little migration until World War I. Outside the local

FIGURE 1. THE PROPORTION OF NEGROES IN THE POPULATION, BY STATES: 1940

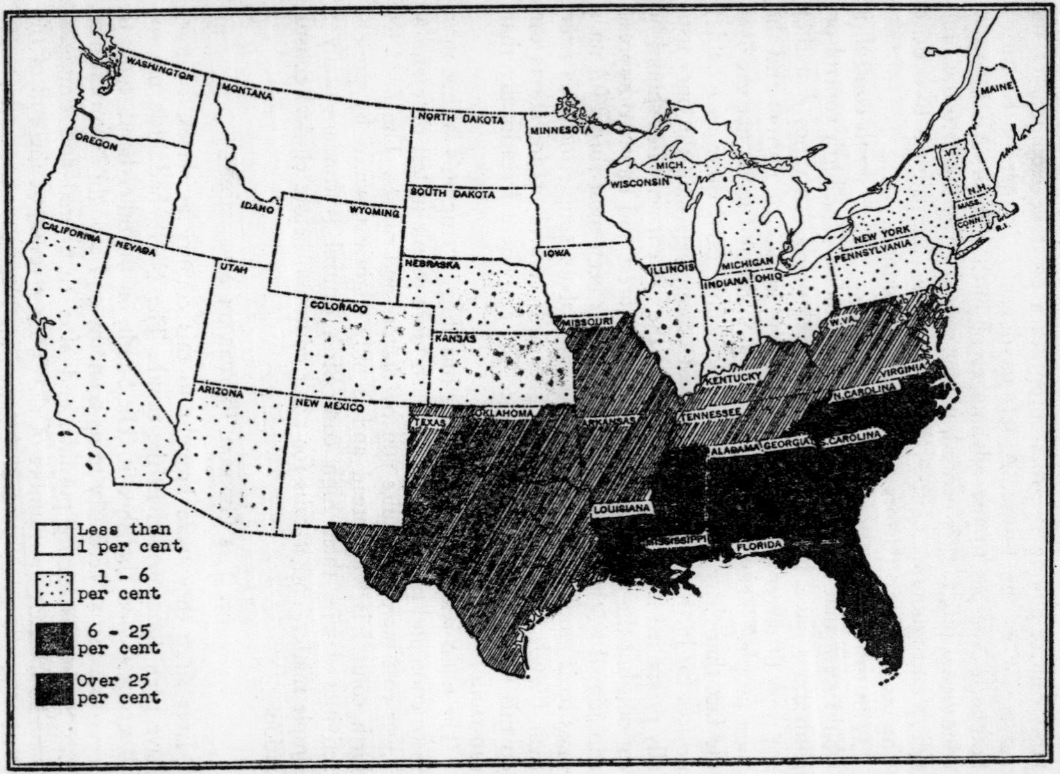

Less than 1 per cent

1 - 6 per cent

6 - 25 per cent

Over 25 per cent

Source: United States Census

migration, the only numerically important migration of Negroes between the Civil War and World War I was from rural areas to cities within the South.

The Great Migration, starting in 1915 and continuing in waves from then on, has brought changes in the distribution of Negroes in the United States. The proportion of all Negroes living in the North and West rose from 10.4 per cent in 1910 to 23.8 per cent in 1940, a net migration of about 1,750,000 from the South. However, because of the huge white population of the North, Negroes constituted only 3.7 per cent of the total Northern population in 1940. Practically all the migrants to the North went to the cities and almost all to the big cities. In the South, too, the proportion of the Negroes who lived in cities increased from 22.0 per cent to 37.3 per cent between 1910 and 1940.

In spite of these changes, in both North and South, during the past thirty years, the great majority of Negroes in the United States still live in the South (Figure 1). Why has the Negro not moved around more in America? And why have his moves—even in the past generation—been so restricted to a few main streams? A satisfactory answer cannot be given because of fragmentary knowledge. We can only review what facts there are.

After Emancipation there were four possible types of places where Negroes could move. First, they could leave the United States. Second, they could take part in the settlement of the frontier West. Third, they could move to the growing cities of the South or to other rural areas in the South. Finally, they could go North.

Colonization abroad had been attempted in the pre-Civil War South, but relatively few Negroes left. Some ten thousand Negroes went to Liberia and some thousands to Haiti before the Civil War, but after the war this emigration practically ceased.

Negroes did not participate in the settlement of the West. Most of the Negro migration to the West has occurred in the past fifteen years, a large part of it during the last years of World War II. The reasons why Negroes did not go west until recently are not clear. The primary explanation seems to be that in rural areas of the West white settlers in the early days after the Civil War decided that there were not to be any Negroes. The same seems to hold true in most rural areas of the Northeast and in most small towns of the entire North. But the Negroes also came to regard it as difficult to migrate to the West, and there was little by way of established Negro communities in the West to aid any newcomers. At any rate, it soon became a popular belief among Southern Negroes that the only outlet from the South was to the cities and preferably to the big cities, where Negro neighborhoods were already established. But there were cities in the West and a few of these grew rapidly. It is surprising that cities like San Francisco, Los Angeles, and Seattle did not attract a greater Negro population.

The South also had its western frontier, Oklahoma and western Texas. Negroes did not move to the areas, however, in any great numbers. Southern prejudice against the Negro seems to have been the most potent factor in keeping the Negro out of the new employment opportunities (oil and gas wells) in Texas and Oklahoma. In some towns, Negroes are not permitted to remain over twenty-four hours; everywhere the Negro is "kept in his place."

Negroes did go to the Southern cities but not so much as did the whites. The growth of the city represents the greatest economic change in the South that has occurred since the Civil War. The Industrial Revolution, with its progress and new opportunity, came to the South later than it did to the North. But Negroes were not allowed to share in many of its fruits. The tradition persisted that Negroes could not operate machines, or at least that was the argument used to keep them out of the new occupations. Negroes lost out in many of the skilled occupations they had formerly had. In the Southern city, the Negro is now mainly an unskilled laborer or a servant.

While Negroes have probably moved around locally in the South a great deal since 1860, the net result of this movement has been surprisingly small. Negroes have not been permitted to take advantage of new opportunities in rural areas any more than they have been in urban areas. Not only did the Negro not share in the expanding opportunities in the South, but also the areas in which the Negroes lived declined from an economic standpoint. Most important was the deterioration of cotton production in the Black Belt of the Southeast.

Thus, the Negro did not share much in the growth of either the West or of the South. For a long while—until the First World War —it did not seem that he would share in the even greater growth of the North. During and immediately after the First World War came the Great Migration, and ever since then Negroes have not stopped coming to the urban North.

8. The Great Migration to the Urban North

For the average Negro, living conditions in the North have always been more favorable than in the South. The North has—in spite of considerable discrimination—offered him more economic opportunities (in relief if not in employment), more security as a citizen, and greater freedom as a human being. Nevertheless, this great difference did not, by itself, cause more than a tiny stream of northward migration for two generations, until 1915.

What actually happened to a great number of Negroes at the start of the Great Migration must have been that they were unsettled, like everyone else, by the war and by all the changes occurring in the industrial system and the labor market. They found their chances in the South particularly bad. In addition, they heard about new openings in the North. Negroes already in the North wrote letters to relatives or friends in the South. Such letters were often passed around the community or their contents were passed on by word of mouth among the illiterates. To these means of communication were added those of the Negro press and the labor agents sent out by Northern industries.

A desire to improve oneself economically by going north was, of course, a chief motive for migration. Important was the general myth of Northern prosperity. Generally, however, the Negro was sought as an unskilled laborer and in such occupation, for the most part, he had to stay. The North, as well as the South, has been hesitant to mix the machine and the Negro; and yet, whether measured in terms of proportions in "desirable" occupations, average income, availability of unemployment relief or of other types of social security benefits, the Negro is considerably better off in the North than in the South.

Allied with the desire for economic improvement was a desire for social improvement. Like many other oppressed people, Negroes place a high premium on education. In the North, Negroes not only could go to more and better schools but they could more easily earn the money to go to them. Many Negroes also felt they could no longer tolerate their subordinate and restricted position. The general freedom, excitement, and anonymity of city life also attracted many rural Southern Negroes.

9. CONTINUED NORTHWARD MIGRATION

After the First World War, many of the same influences continued and Negroes kept up their migration northward. With the depression beginning in 1929, a new set of circumstances arose to determine the extent of the Negro's migration northward. There were no longer new jobs for Negroes in the North; in fact, Negroes were laid off by the thousands.

But a new form of livelihood arose to take the place of jobs. This was public assistance in its many forms. It was much harder for Negroes to get relief in the South than in the North. Hence, Negroes were again attracted northward—though not to the same extent as during the period of World War I and the 1920's. Many Northern states set up residence requirements—ranging up to five years—to keep out migrants seeking relief. These requirements were not rigorously enforced in the early days of the depression, but even when they were, Negroes felt it better to trust to luck for odd jobs or to their friends until residence requirements had been met rather than to meet almost sure starvation in the South.

Economic conditions had become relatively worse for Negroes in the South during the depression. Whites who had lost their small farms or their better jobs in the cities began to move in on the Negroes in the heavy unskilled occupations and even in the service occupations—the traditional jobs of the Southern Negro. Southern agriculture became worse, and the poorest owners and tenants—which included a disproportionate share of Negroes—were forced out. Most of these—including practically all the whites—went on relief, but many of the Negroes could not get relief and so moved north where practically no color distinction was made in the administration of public assistance.

The prosperity and full employment that accompanied World War II again had its effect on Negro migration. Negroes were more fully absorbed into war industries in World War II than in World War I for two reasons: (1) a much greater need for all kinds of labor; (2) a deliberate effort by the FEPC and other agencies to prevent discrimination. These greater economic opportunities attracted Negroes not only along the traditional paths of migration—from the South to the great Northern industrial cities, but also to other centers of wartime industry where there was a labor shortage: for example, the great shipbuilding centers of the South—Charleston, Hampton Roads, and Mobile; the new industries of the West in the Los Angeles area, the Portland-Vancouver area, the San Francisco Bay area, and the San Diego area.[6] There are not yet total figures for the amount of Negro migration during the war years, but close to 500,000 Negroes must have migrated to Northern and Western industrial centers, and another 500,000 to the cities of the South.

There were two factors that probably kept migration from becoming even greater: (1) drafted Negroes were in the age groups that most frequently migrate; (2) a special clause of the wartime manpower regulations allowed Southern farmers to hold farm laborers on the land as necessary to the war effort.

[6] U.S. Department of Commerce, Bureau of the Census, press release in Sunday papers, March 4, 1945. See, also, U.S. Department of Commerce, Bureau of the Census, *Resident Nonwhite Population for Ten Congested Production Areas, 1940 and 1944* (typescript).

10. The Future of Negro Migration

Taking the long historical view, the main observation to be made about Negro migration is that the Negro people have tended to stay where they were. Their movements between the regions of the country have been decidedly more restricted in amount and direction than those of the whites, except during periods of rapid economic changes such as in wars or in extreme depressions.

To forecast the future of Negro migration is, of course, difficult. It will be determined by social trends and by public policy. Certain of the main conditioning factors stand out rather clearly. The liberty of the individual to move freely in the country is a firmly entrenched principle of the American Creed. The future development will probably be to reinforce still more in practice the individual's freedom to migrate.

There seem to be good reasons to expect a continuation of the northward migration, in spite of depressions and booms. The pattern is now set and the lines of communication established. The general level of education and knowledge of the outside world is rising among Southern Negroes. In the South the continued crisis in cotton growing, which we foresee, and the concentration of its effects on the Negro farmers, will continue to act as a tremendous push. The psychological effects of World War II will encourage many of the younger Negroes to seek the greater freedom of the North. It may be that the increased racial tension of some of the Southern states will increase northward migration. On the other hand, some Southern states are becoming more liberal in their attitudes, which may increase opportunities for the Negro in the South.

In the North there are fair prospects of a somewhat decreased economic discrimination against Negro workers. This is largely the result of wartime developments: the FEPC, although no longer in existence, has taught many employers that Negroes can be good workers; six of the Northern states have state FEPCs. Many of the unions now have many Negro members, some in skilled jobs; to protect their membership they will have to continue to fight discrimination. In the North the large and varied labor force also keeps employment opportunities better.

There has now been established a new pattern—migration to the West. While this is strictly in the realm of prophecy, it may be that the growth of Negro settlements in the large Western cities may mean the establishment of a new path of migration—from the South to the West.

CHAPTER IV

The Economic Background

1. NEGRO POVERTY

Up to the late years of World War II the economic situation of the Negroes in America has been pathological. Except for a small minority enjoying upper- or middle-class status, the masses of American Negroes, in the rural South and in the segregated slum quarters in Southern and Northern cities, have been destitute. Even now, war and postwar prosperity have only pushed Negroes above the line of semistarvation or dependency. They own little property; even their household goods are usually inadequate and dilapidated. Their incomes are not only low, but irregular. Thus they live from day to day and have scant security for the future. Because of their economic situation, their individual interests and strivings must be narrow.

Why is such an extraordinarily large proportion of the Negro people so poor? One reason is that the Negroes are concentrated in the South, which is generally a poor and economically retarded region. A disproportionate number of them work in agriculture, which is a depressed occupation. Most rural Negroes are in Southern cotton agriculture, which is particularly overpopulated, backward in production methods, and hard hit by soil exhaustion, by the boll weevil, and by a long-time fall in international demand for American cotton. In addition, few Negro farmers own the land they work on, and the little land they do own is much poorer and less well equipped than average Southern farms. Most Negro farmers are concentrated in the lowest occupations in agriculture as sharecroppers or wage laborers.

Nonagricultural Negro workers are, for the most part, either in low-paid service occupations or have unskilled tasks in industry. Few are skilled workers. Most of the handicrafts and industries in the

South where they have a traditional foothold are declining. The majority of manufacturing industries gave jobs to Negroes only during World War II, when they had to because of manpower shortage and the presidential order that war contracts could be had only if there was no discrimination. Neither in the South nor in the North are Negroes in professional, business, or administrative positions except in rare instances and except when serving exclusively the Negro public—and even in this they are far from having a monopoly. Only recently have Negroes been allowed into white-collar jobs and the total number of them in these jobs is not high. And, most important, the unemployment risk of Negroes is very great.

One may ask: Why are Negroes in the poorest sections of the country, the backward industries, the lowest paid jobs? Why are they not skilled workers? Why do they not hold a fair proportion of well-paid middle-class positions? Why is their employment situation so precarious?

Part of the answer lies in the several factors of economic change. In most cases changes in the economic process seem to work against the Negroes. When modern techniques transform old handicrafts into machine production, Negroes lose jobs in the former but usually do not get into the new factories, at least not at the machines. Mechanization seems generally to displace Negro labor. When mechanized commercial laundries replace home laundries, Negro workers lose jobs. The same process occurs in tobacco manufacture, in the lumber industry, and in the turpentine industry. When tractors and motor trucks are introduced, new "white men's jobs" are created out of old "Negro jobs" on the farm and in transportation. Progress itself seems to work against the Negroes. When work becomes less heavy, less dirty, or less risky, Negroes are displaced. Old-fashioned, low-paying, inefficient enterprises, continually being driven out of competition, are often the only ones that employ much Negro labor.

It seems that the business cycles show something of the same tendency to work against Negroes as do technical changes. The Negro agricultural laborer is more likely to be forced out by depressions than is the white farmer and farm workers. In fact, in almost every given occupation Negroes tend to be "first fired" when depression comes. Even in the service and maintenance occupations, where Negroes are concentrated, Negroes are fired to give jobs to white workers. When prosperity returns, unless there is an extreme manpower shortage, the lost ground is never quite made up. The general level of unemployment, depression or no depression, is always higher for Negroes than for whites.

Likewise the organization of the labor market by trade unions has usually increased the difficulties for Negroes in getting and holding jobs. Even social legislation is not an undivided blessing to Negro workers. When the employer finds that he has to take measures to protect his workers' health and security and to pay them higher wages, he often substitutes white workers for Negroes. Sometimes sweatshop industries, existing only because of low-paid Negro labor, are driven out of business by legislation or union pressure, and the Negro is again the victim instead of the beneficiary of economic and social progress. Negroes have been willing—if it were allowed them—to take the jobs at the bottom. But until the war forced a demand for them their unemployment was growing relative to that of the whites.

2. THE VICIOUS CIRCLE

There is a tradition that white people exploit Negroes. In the beginning Negroes were owned as property. When slavery disappeared, caste remained. Within this framework of adverse tradition the average Negro in every generation has had a most disadvantageous start. Discrimination against Negroes is thus rooted in this tradition of economic exploitation. It is justified by the false racial beliefs we studied in Chapter 2. This belief in the inability of the Negro to become a good worker is bolstered by the low standards of efficiency, reliability, ambition, and morals actually displayed by the average Negro. This is what the white man "sees" and he exaggerates what he "sees." He "knows" that the Negro is not "capable" of handling a machine, running a business, or learning a profession. As we know that these deficiencies are not inborn in him, we must conclude that they are caused, directly or indirectly, by the very poverty we are trying to explain, and by other discriminations in legal protection, public health, housing, education, and in every other sphere of life. Poverty itself breeds the conditions that cause poverty to continue.

The vicious circle operates, of course, also in the case of whites. Few people have enough imagination to see clearly what a poor white tenant or common laborer in the South would look like if he had more opportunities at the start. Upper-class people in all countries are accustomed to look down upon poor people as born to be inferior. In the case of the Negroes, this belief is strengthened by the elaborate system of racial beliefs, and the discriminations are organized into a rigid caste system.

3. The Value Premise in the Economic Sphere

The system of social ideals, which we have called the American Creed, is not specific in the economic field. A major part of the ideological battle and of political divisions, in the past decade, has concerned a conflict of ideals in the economic sphere. "Equality of opportunity" has been battling "liberty to run one's business as one pleases."

The best way of determining our value premises for the economic part of this study is, perhaps, to start from the viewpoint of what the average American does *not* want. The ordinary American does not want, and probably will not want within the near future, equal income for everyone. Such an idea would be contrary to the basic individualism of American thinking. On the other hand, although there is a great deal of inequality of income and wealth in America, the American Creed has always been definitely opposed to class divisions and class inequalities. Americans are, indeed, hostile to the very idea of class. But this hostility is directed only against a rigid system of privileges in which the individual inherits his status, and not against differences in wealth as such. The American demand is for *fair opportunity and free scope for individual effort.*

In a new nation with rapid social climbing this way of reconciling liberty with equality is understandable. Great differences in culture within the nation and huge geographical space permitted some ignorance of distress. Because of the rapid tempo of economic progress and the rapidly growing market, economic adversities never did appear so final and hopeless. Land was abundant and practically free, and there was at least a national ideal of free education for everybody.

The principle of noninterference on the part of the state in economic life, therefore, did not seem incompatible with the principle of equality of opportunity. There have always been qualifications of this idea, however. In recent times the qualifications have been increasing in importance, slowly remolding this part of the American Creed. Probably most Americans are today prepared to accept a considerable amount of public control for the purpose of preserving natural resources. In the whole nation, a vivid realization has grown up of the waste and damage done to these national assets in reckless exploitation and speculation.

In regard to the personal resources of the nation, Americans are not as willing to have public control. But in the one field of education they have been the pioneering radicals of the world bent upon improving people by means of proper schooling. Within the past few decades this spirit has spread to other fields. Social legislation has been instituted to regulate children's and women's work, safety measures and other working conditions in industry, and—later—wages, hours, and labor organizations. A system of social insurance has gradually been taking form.

The mass unemployment during the depression of the thirties and the realization that whole regions and occupational groups can be brought to destitution through no fault of their own brought to full consciousness a sense of public responsibility for these things. For the first time America saw itself compelled to organize a large-scale system of public relief. For the first time, also, America made substantial exertions in the field of public housing. The school lunch program, the food stamp plan, and the distribution of surplus commodities represent other activities in the same direction, as do also the attempts to induce Southern farmers and sharecroppers to have year-round gardens. Public health programs were expanded, and the nation is gradually facing the task of organizing the care of the sick in a more socially protective way.

Behind this great movement is an unmistakable trend in social outlook and political values. An articulate opinion is gradually taking form that there is a minimum standard of living below which no group of people in the country should be permitted to fall. Neither the political conflicts raging around the proper means of providing help by public measures nor the widespread uncertainty and disagreement concerning the actual height of the minimum standard to be protected by those measures should conceal the important fact *that the American Creed is changing to include a decent living standard and a measure of economic security among the liberties and rights that are given this highest moral approval.*

At the same time, social welfare policy—by increasing stress upon the preventive instead of the merely curative aspects—is becoming integrated with economic policy. Social welfare policy is bound to become looked upon in terms of the economic criterion of what is to be got out of each investment of public wealth.

We shall, in our inquiry, assume that the following norms are generally and clearly held on the higher or national plane in the hearts of ordinary Americans.

1. There is nothing wrong with economic inequality by itself. The mere fact that the Negro people are poorer than other population groups does not in itself constitute a social problem.

2. No American population group shall be allowed to fall under a certain minimum level of living. This also assumes that Negroes and others can be poor. It insists only that poverty shall not go too far without being given public attention and help. It offers a means of evaluating the social effects of poverty and affords a motivation for social welfare policy. Even if the general principle of a minimum level of living must now be considered as established in national thinking, it is still undecided how high or low this minimum level should be.

3. Our third value premise is bound to be the most significant one for our inquiry and it brings out the principal chasm between American ideals and practices: that Negroes shall be awarded equal opportunities. In so far as Negro poverty is caused by discrimination, the American Creed is challenged in one of its most specific and longest established principles. Equality of opportunity, fair play, free competition—"independent of race, creed, or color"—is deeply imprinted in the nationally approved social morals of America.

Discrimination is, for this reason, the key term in such a study. This term is defined in relation to the norm of equality of opportunity in the American Creed.

4. The Conflict of Values

This listing of the value premises, and particularly the third one demanding fair play, again brings out the split in American personality and American social morals. The central problem is neither the exploitation of the Negro people nor the various effects of this exploitation on American society, but rather the moral conflict in the hearts of white Americans.

A few words may be said about some of the standard rationalizations by which the American white man tries to build a bridge of reason between his equalitarian creed and his nonequalitarian treatment of the Negroes. The prejudiced white man has to justify to himself and to others his discrimination against the Negro. It should be understood that the popular theories which follow are based upon what the ordinary white man *thinks* are his own observations and upon what he *believes* to be common knowledge. The folklore in the South will be taken up first.

Sometimes a mere reference to custom is advanced as a reason for economic discrimination against Negroes. A report on teachers' salaries prepared by a university in one of the Border states reads:

An additional argument in favor of the salary differential is the general tradition of the South that negroes and whites are not to be paid equivalent salaries for equivalent work. The attitude may be considered wrong from whatever angle it is viewed, but the fact remains that the custom is one that is almost universal and one that the practical school administrator must not ignore.[1]

For not a few, this logic that "what was and is, shall be and ought to be" seems sufficient.

Interestingly enough, only rarely will a white man in the South defend economic discrimination in terms of white people's interest to have cheap labor available. Nearest to such a motivation come statements like: "This is a white man's country"; or, more expressively: "We don't have money enough to pay our white workers decent wages"; or, in regard to discrimination in the school system: "The appropriations do not suffice even to give the white children good schools."

Such statements are common in the whole South. They are made even by intellectuals. Often there is a further rationalization behind such statements to the effect that "Negroes are the wards of the white people"; "Negroes couldn't live at all without the aid and guidance of the white people"; "What little they have, they have got from the whites." The Negroes' own sacrifices apparently do not count. Their poverty itself becomes, in fact, the basis of the rationalization: "The whites give them all the jobs"; "Actually, they live on us white people"; "They couldn't sustain themselves a day if we gave them up"; "The whites pay all the taxes anyway."

Then, too, economic inequality "has to" be maintained, for it is the barrier against "social equality": "You wouldn't let your sister or daughter marry a nigger." The sister or the daughter comes inevitably into even the economic discussion.

This is the ordinary Southerner explaining the matter in plain words to the questioning stranger. He is serious and, in a sense, honest. We must remember that the whole white Southern culture, generation after generation, is laboring to convince itself that there is no conflict between the equalitarianism in the American Creed and the economic discrimination against Negroes. And they can never get enough good reasons for their behavior. They pile arguments one on top of the other.

The most important intellectual bridge between the American Creed and actual practices in the economic sphere is, of course, the racial beliefs discussed in Chapter 2. Their effect in the economic

[1] *Bulletin of the Bureau of School Service, University of Kentucky,* "A Salary Study for the Lexington Public Schools" (March, 1935), p. 26.

sphere is that the Negro is looked upon as inherently inferior as a worker and as a consumer. God himself has made the Negro to be only a servant or a laborer employed for menial, dirty, heavy, and disagreeable work. And since practically all such work is badly paid, it is God's will that the Negro should have a low income. Also, any attempt to raise Negro incomes goes against the "laws of supply and demand," which are part of the order of nature. The Negro is a bad consumer, too. "If you give him more pay, he will stop working"; he will "drink it up and start a row"; "Higher wages will make the nigger lazy and morally degraded." This last belief, particularly, and also many of the others are strikingly similar to ideas about the laboring class developed by European writers in the seventeenth and eighteenth centuries.[2]

On the other hand, it is said that the Negro is accustomed to live on little. "It is a marvel how these niggers can get along on almost nothing." This would imply that the Negro is a careful consumer—but the conclusion is never expressed that way. This popular theory is presented in the following way:

. . . observation alone would suggest to the unbiased observer that the negro teacher will be able to purchase within her society a relatively higher standard of living than the white teacher will be able to secure with the same amount of money.[3]

Statistical investigations are referred to which seem to indicate the remarkable fact that Negro teachers with smaller salaries spend less money for various items than better paid white teachers.

Scientifically, this is nonsense, of course. That poor people get along on less has nothing to do with cost of living. They *must* get along on less, even when the cost of living is higher for them. Sometimes, an attempt is made to give the theory greater logic by inserting the idea that "Negroes don't have the same demands on life as white people"; "They are satisfied with less." This assumption of a racial difference in wants is, of course, entirely unfounded.

Others are heard expressing the theory of lower demands on life in the following way: "Their cost of living is obviously lower since

[2] The whole Southern system of bias displays a precapitalistic tendency. When white Southerners object to a rise in Negro levels of living, they act much like the upper classes in most European countries acted centuries ago when they frowned upon lower class people's rise to higher levels and even instituted regulations forbidding the humbler classes to have servants, to own certain types of dress, and so on. An American Negro in a luxurious car draws unfavorable comment, and so—in previous times—did a Swedish maid who "dressed like a lady."

[3] *Bulletin of the Bureau of School Service, University of Kentucky, op. cit.,* p. 25.

they have a lower standard of living." Lower wages and lower relief grants are generally justified in this way. The rationalizations
amount to this: since Negroes are poor and always have been poor,
they are inferior and should be kept inferior. It is seldom expressed
so bluntly. Expressions like "standard of living" and "cost of living"
are employed because they have a scientific flavor. They avoid hard
thinking. They enable one to stand for economic discrimination
without facing the fact that one is violating the American Creed.

In the North there exist practically none of these piled-up, criss-
crossing, elaborated theories. Most Northerners, even in parts of the
country where there are Negroes, know only vaguely about the
economic discriminations Negroes are meeting in their communities.
They are often uninformed of the real meaning of those discriminations which they themselves uphold.

It is generally held in the North that such discrimination is wrong.
The present writer believes that a large majority of Northerners
would come out for full economic equality if they had to vote on the
issue and did not think of their own occupations. Northern states
and municipalities, on the whole, hold to the principle of nondiscrimination in relief, and this probably is not only due to considerations of the Negro vote but is also in obedience to the American
Creed.

As will be shown in later chapters, however, there is plenty of economic discrimination in the North. The average Northerner will occasionally refer to the interest of himself and his group in keeping
away Negro competition—a thing which seldom or never happens
in the South. His rationalizations will seldom go much further than
presenting his beliefs in the Negroes' racial inferiority and the observation that he "just doesn't want to have Negroes around" or that
he "dislikes Negroes." Southern-born white people in the North usually keep more of the complete defense system and also spread it in
their new surroundings. Even in the North it happens occasionally,
when economic discrimination is discussed, that the "social equality"
issue and the marriage matter are brought up, though with much
less emotion.

A main difference in the two regions seems to be that the Southerners still think of Negroes as their former slaves, while the association with slavery is notably absent from the minds of Northerners.

5. Economic Exploitation

To the pre-Civil War South slavery was, of course, a tremendous
moral burden. Human slavery, in spite of all rationalization, was

absolutely contrary to the American Creed. The South had to stand before all the world as the land which, in modern times, had developed and perfected the evil old institution.

But, in a sense, exploitation of Negro labor was less embarrassing to the pre-Civil War planter than to the modern Southerner. Slavery then was lawful and regulated. Today exploitation is dependent upon extralegal devices, and the popular theories defending caste exploitation are not recognized as respectable even by most Southerners.

An examination of the actual practices, however, shows that the tradition of human exploitation—and now not only of Negroes—has remained from slavery as the most important factor in the South's economic life. A great number of fortunes are achieved by petty exploitation of the poor. As contrasted with the North, there is less investment, less market expansion, less inventiveness, and less risktaking. Sweatshop conditions are more common. Even the Southern middle class depends on exploitation of labor. The white workers, in their turn, often seek to defend themselves against the potential or actual competition from Negro labor by non-economic means. They themselves are often held in paternalistic economic and moral dependence by their employers. This pattern of common exploitation—where everyone is the oppressor of the one under him, where the Negroes are at the bottom, and where big landlords, merchants, and Northern capital are at the top—is obviously the extension into the present of a modified slavery system.

The South tries to blame its economic backwardness on the differential in freight rates, the national tariff system, and other economic irregularities, but these are minor matters. Nor does the destruction of material and human values during the Civil War explain the present situation. About three generations have elapsed since then and such wounds can be healed rapidly. The same is true of the head start in industrialization that the North had; it could have been overcome. To complain about the lack of capital is to beg the question. In modern economics, capital is considered the result rather than the prerequisite for production. The investment in the South of Northern capital has not been detrimental but, on the contrary, is a reason why the South is not more backward economically than it is.

The explanation for the economic backwardness of the South must be carried down to the rigid structure of the economic life of the region, which is derived from slavery and rooted in the minds of the people.

6. SLAVERY AND CASTE

It is often argued that the static, noncompetitive, and semifeudal slavery-plantation system did not fit into modern American capitalism. But in certain respects the surviving caste system shows even more resistance to change than did slavery. Under slavery, the employer really owned his labor. He had a vested interest in using it most profitably. He could move slaves where they could be put to the best use—into new Western lands, for example. After Emancipation the freedman as a group were blocked from entering new rural territory in the Southwest. Before Emancipation it was in the interest of slaveowners to use Negro slaves wherever it was profitable in handicraft and manufacture. After Emancipation, Negro laborers were squeezed out of skilled employment into "Negro jobs." Since slaves were expensive, the slaveowner had an interest in caring for their material welfare. The rise in sickness and death rates that seems to have occurred following the Civil War bears out the opinion that the first economic effect of freedom was a decreased level of living for the Negro people.

Important for the development of the new labor structure into which the freed Negro slaves were pressed was the fact that Emancipation was not related to any change of mind on the part of white people. The reform was thrust upon the South. The South did not —and still does not—want the Negro to be successful as a freedman. White Southerners are prepared to abstain from many liberties and sacrifice many advantages for the purpose of withholding them from the Negroes.

The temporary Negro vagrancy that followed the Civil War confirmed the Southerner's conviction that most Negroes will not work unless kept under severe discipline.[4] This was a convenient way out. It offered an escape from the difficult task of having to introduce a new pattern of dealing with labor. The plantation South was ruined through the war—ruined, it was felt, because of the

[4] In comparison with Southern whites, especially upper-class whites and white women of all classes, Negroes were probably never characterized by unusual laziness. It was only by comparison with the continuous labor under slavery, and aided by forced unemployment, that Negroes suddenly appeared lazy. If Negroes were ever unusually unwilling to work, it was only in the first year or two after the end of the Civil War. In so far as it did appear during this period of general disorganization, it was just plain human. The institution of slavery to a great extent had debased ordinary work in the appreciation of black and white alike. It was psychologically inescapable that slavery should backfire in this way, particularly during the initial period of freedom.

Negro. Under the circumstances it was likely that the South would try to build up a labor organization as similar as possible to slavery.

As the years passed, the old plantation system re-established itself. After some attempts with a wage system, sharecropping became the labor pattern into which the Negroes and, later, poor whites were pressed.

7. THE LAND PROBLEM

An economic reconstruction of the South which would have succeeded in opening the road to economic independence for the ex-slaves would have had to include, besides emancipation, suffrage and full civil liberties: rapid education of the freedmen, abandonment of discrimination, and land reform. There were some few statesmen who grasped the importance of such basic economic reform for the Reconstruction program. Thaddeus Stevens and Charles Sumner saw it. But their strivings came to practically nothing.

After the Civil War the overwhelming majority of Negroes were concentrated in Southern agriculture. Consequently, the greatest problem was what to do with these great masses of Southern Negroes, most of whom were former slaves. Successful reform of the Southern plantation economy must have included the following points:

1. Paying the slaveowners out of federal funds.

2. Breaking up the larger part of the plantations and paying the owners for them out of federal funds.

3. Distributing the land in small farms to those who wanted it, with long-time mortgages on the property.

4. Supervising the freedmen both to protect them and to educate them to their new responsibilities.

5. Introducing taxation to pay the former slave- and land-owners and to reduce repayments for the land by the new owners.

6. Helping Negroes to take part in the westward rural migration to relieve Negro population pressure in the South.

The cost of this reform would have been trifling compared with the actual cost of Reconstruction and Restoration, not to speak of the Civil War. What happened, however, was that the slaves were freed without any remuneration being paid their former owners; and, with few exceptions, the freedmen were not given access to land. In spite of the lack of land reform and against heavy odds in practically all respects, there was a slow rise of Negro small-scale landowner-ship in the South until about 1900. But the proportion of Negroes owning their own land has never been large, and it has been declining for the past thirty or forty years.

8. The Tenancy Problem

But even if land reform was not carried out, there should have been legal regulation of the tenancy system, aimed not only at protecting the tenants but also at preserving the soil and raising the economic efficiency of Southern agriculture. There were individuals who saw clearly what was at stake. The Freedmen's Bureau of the federal government tried without success to regulate labor and tenant contracts.

Today the legal organization of landlord-tenant relations in Southern states has no real parallel in other advanced parts of the Western world. There are a number of state laws—some of the most extravagant kind—to defend the planters' interests. There are a few laws, however, to defend the tenants' interests. The tenant does not have any right to permanency of tenure on the land he cultivates. He seldom has any right to be repaid for permanent improvements which he makes on the land. The tenant is not secured in his contractual rights.

Among the many laws to protect the planters' interests against the tenants are the various kinds of lien laws. They are sometimes strengthened by laws making a tenant a criminal when he is deemed negligent in his duties. During the thirties, federal agencies have been more active in stamping out debt peonage, but it still exists.

Another type is the vagrancy laws. Vagrants are made to choose between accepting the employment offered them or being sentenced by the court to forced labor in chain gangs. Another practice is for white employers to get Negro tenants or laborers by paying their fines at court. Or an employer pays a Negro's debt to a former employer or to a merchant and, by taking over the debt, also takes over the worker. The police and the courts have often been active in "creating" the debts by exacting fines for petty offenses or upon flimsy accusations. Sometimes a number of self-employed or unemployed Negroes are "rounded up" and given out for the price of the fines to interested employers who are short of labor. More often the police and the courts only act to enforce an existing situation of debt peonage.

The police and courts, as we shall show later, have traditionally been active as agents for white employers. Traditionally the planters and other whites have few scruples against taking the law into their own hands. Threats, whippings, and even more serious forms of violence have been customary to maintain a strict discipline over Negro labor but have seldom been employed against white labor. The few laws in favor of the Negro tenant have not been enforced against the white planter.

CHAPTER V

The Old Plantation Economy

and the New

1. OVERPOPULATION AND SOIL EROSION

The main facts of rural Southern poverty and the distress of the rural Negro people in the South are well known. The plantation-tenant system is one of America's "public scandals."

Rural farm areas in the United States in 1940 had a population of about 30,000,000. More than half of this population, over 16,000,000, was in the South; over one-fourth of the Southern farm population (around 4,500,000) was Negro. But the South had only 35 per cent of all land in farms in the country and the value of this farm land, as well as of the buildings on the land, the farm implements and machinery, was but 28 per cent of the national figure. Only 8 per cent of the Southern farm land was operated by Negro owners, tenants, and croppers, and their share in the value of Southern farms, buildings, implements, and machinery was equally small.

The meaning of these broad facts is important. They are behind all the rural poverty of the South. The agricultural South is over-populated, and the overpopulation has been steadily increasing. More-over, since slavery days the land has been uncared for and wasted. A study made in 1933 suggested that one-third of the Southern land was eroded and that at least half of all eroded land in the country was in the South. The soil is usually light, and there is heavy rainfall in most parts of the region. Concentration upon cash crops, such as cotton, deplete fertility, especially when planted without crop rotation or other preventive measures. The high rate of tenancy, leaving the immediate care of the land to people who are not only ignorant but also lack any incentive to maintain the productivity of the land (as the preceding chapter suggests), is another cause of soil erosion.

2. TENANCY, CREDIT, AND COTTON

The extent to which Southern cash-crop production is based on tenancy is indicated by the following figures. Almost three-fourths of all Southern cotton farms and more than half of the crop-specialty farms (tobacco, potatoes, peanuts, and so on) were, in 1929, operated by tenants. About two-thirds of all tenants in the South, and almost three-fourths of the croppers, worked on cotton farms. Of the full owners, on the other hand, less than one-third had farms where cotton accounted for 40 per cent or more of the gross income. Most of the other two-thirds owned farms which were crop specialty, general, or self-sufficing.

Negro farmers have always been dependent on the cotton economy to a much greater extent than have the white farmers in the South. By 1929 three out of four Negro farm operators, as against two out of five white farmers, received at least 40 per cent of their gross income from cotton. Although not more than about one-tenth of the Southern farm land was cultivated by Negro owners, tenants, and croppers, almost one-third of the total output in cotton was produced on this Negro-operated land. In addition, an unknown but probably considerable quantity of cotton was produced by Negro wage labor on holdings operated by white farmers. The importance of cotton growing for the Negro farmer can hardly be overestimated.

Cotton in most places is cultivated by a primitive and labor-consuming technique which has not changed much since slavery. Cotton is largely responsible for the fact that the Southeast alone had to pay more than half of the national bill for commercial fertilizers. Cotton growing invites child labor and causes retardation in schools. It favors large families.

The wide fluctuations in the price of cotton—due to wars, inflation, deflation, and competition from other countries—makes cotton a most risky crop. In spite of all this, the continued cultivation of cotton is called forth by the plantation and tenancy system because it is labor consuming, simple in technique, and easily supervised. Cotton production is also stimulated by overpopulation and tenancy, and—because cotton is a cash crop—by the dependence of Southern agriculture on short-term credit. The rural South has been dependent on outside credit both because of the low standards of income and savings in the region and because of the high requirements of operating capital for cotton growing. The fluctuation of cotton prices and farm incomes makes lending abnormally risky and consequently makes loans expensive. Also, from the point of view of business administration, the organization of banking and credit is most inadequate and it remains so because of the low plane of political life in the South.

As part of federal agricultural policy, great improvements have been made by the organization of new credit agencies. But credit is still expensive and difficult to get in the rural South. This is part of the explanation for the lack of investment in land and buildings and the slowness of mechanization. To the tenants, credit pressures mean usurious rates charged by planters and merchants for advances on food and farming necessities. For agriculture as a whole, credit pressures—themselves partly caused by dependence on cotton growing—mean a constant stimulus to keep the land in cotton.

3. THE BOLL WEEVIL

In this vicious system of economic poverty the boll weevil caused catastrophe. It advanced eastward, passing the Mississippi River about 1910. The destruction was terrible. In many places, farms and plantations were permanently abandoned.

But as one state was suffering, those west of it were recovering. Thus, the boll weevil helped Texas, Louisiana, Arkansas, and Oklahoma to increase their share in the national output of cotton until in 1929 they had about three-fifths of the total acreage in cotton. In these Southwestern states cotton cultivation is less dependent on Negro labor and is more mechanized. Therefore, concentration of cotton in these states tended to push Negro tenants off the land. The ravages of the boll weevil in the old Cotton Belt had the same effect.

In spite of all misfortunes, cotton was still king in 1929. More than half of the total acreage harvested in the South in 1929 was in farms for which 40 per cent or more of the gross income came from cotton. Also crop-specialty farms appeared much more important than in the nation as a whole. Self-sufficing farms, too, were more prevalent in the Southeast than elsewhere, which reflects a cashless, agricultural economy. Dairy farming, on the other hand, has been lagging in the South. In 1939 Southern agriculture accounted for only slightly more than one-tenth of the national value production of milk and dairy products.[1]

[1] *Sixteenth Census of the United States, Special Cotton Report* (Washington: Government Printing Office, 1943), Table 16, p. 186.

4. Main Agricultural Classes

The chances for small- and middle-sized ownership in the South have been more restricted than in most other American regions. Owner-operated land in 1940 had a lower acreage value in the South ($27.11 including buildings) than in the nation as a whole ($31.37); the fact that Southern land operated by croppers had a per unit value ($33.28) even higher than the latter figure, indicates that only in part is this caused by inferiority of Southern soil. Rather, the explanation is that most of the best land in the South was originally taken by the dominant plantation owners. The rest of the Southern farmers had to fight against heavy odds. They had to compete with slave labor and at the same time cultivate soil of lower quality. The Civil War failed to bring about any change in this condition. The owners of the plantations regained much of their political power. Their land was still superior in spite of being mistreated. And to compete with the plantations was still to compete with sweatshop labor.

In 1940 the total labor force in Southern agriculture—if we except the large group of unpaid family workers—was constituted as in the accompanying table. We see that there are many types of "farmers" in the South.

TABLE

Negro and White Agricultural Workers in the South, By Tenure: 1940

TENURE	NUMBER		PER CENT	
	Negro	White	Negro	White
Total*	1,187,569	2,892,599	100.0	100.0
Owners and managers	173,628	1,384,249	14.7	47.9
Cash tenants	64,684	189,667	5.4	6.6
Other tenants, except croppers	142,836	510,815	12.0	17.6
Croppers	299,118	242,173	25.3	8.4
Wage laborers	507,303	565,695	42.6	19.5

Source: Data on owners, tenants, and croppers are from the *Sixteenth Census of the United States: 1940 Agriculture*, Vol. III, *General Report*, Table 14. They include a small number of nonwhites other than Negroes. Data on wage laborers are from the *Sixteenth Census of the United States: 1940. Population*, Vol. III, *Labor Force*, Pt. 1, *U.S. Summary*, Table 63.
* Exclusive of unpaid family workers.

Highest of the nonowners are the renters and the cash tenants who rent their farms for a fixed sum of money. All other kinds of arrangements entitle the landlord to a certain share of the main crop. Tenants who receive one-half (or less) of the crop are the sharecroppers. The cash tenants usually furnish all the work, stock, feed, fertilizer, and tools themselves. The other groups furnish less and less of these things the lower their tenure status. Those lowest on the scale have little or nothing but their labor to offer. Sometimes their position tends to be even less independent than that of ordinary wage earners.

5. THE NEGRO LANDOWNER

There was a time when it looked as if the rural Negro had some chance of getting established on an ownership basis. By the year 1900, 193,000 Negro farm homes in the United States were owned by their occupants—about 25 per cent of all Negro farm homes. The increase continued for some time, but at a slower rate. In 1910 the number of colored farm owners in the South reached 220,000. After 1920 it declined, and dropped to 174,000 by 1940, even though white farm ownership increased in the South.

The existence of any small owner-operator in the South, white or Negro, is always marginal, but the Negro has had special handicaps. There is his background in slavery and the fact that he has scarcely ever been encouraged to show much initiative or been taught that it pays to look after oneself rather than to be dependent. He has been given to understand that his racial status provides an excuse for not being able to shift for himself, and that acceptance of a low position would rate a reward bigger than that offered for attempts to reach a higher position. In the rural South he has certainly not enjoyed much legal security, which is a necessary condition for successful enterprise; he has certainly had far less of it than whites with whom he has had to compete. His best security has been to become associated with a white person of some standing in the community; in most cases that has meant an employer-employee or landlord-tenant relationship. Since his earnings have usually been less than those of white workers he has had less chance to save for the purpose of buying land. The belief that he is racially inferior and the social isolation between the two castes have also affected the credit rating of even those Negroes who would have been excellent risks. His educational opportunities in the rural South have been extremely poor.

In addition, rural Negroes are concentrated in plantation areas where few small holdings are for sale. The Negro did not share in the development of the West, but even in Kansas, where Negro settlements were made, there were not more than a few hundred Negro owner-operators in 1940. Undoubtedly the attitudes of the white settlers constituted the main cause for this lack of success. In the overpopulated, white-dominated districts of the South these attitudes were still more pronounced.

The Negro has usually been at a disadvantage when competing with white buyers. Apart from economic and other factors already mentioned, he has had to overcome segregational and discriminatory attitudes of the rural white population. There has always been an active solidarity among white people to prevent Negroes from acquiring land in white neighborhoods. The intensity of these attitudes seems to have increased toward the turn of the century. There were even a few attempts at this time to pass laws blocking Negro ownership in white rural districts. It is noteworthy that the trend toward increase of Negro landownership stopped at about the same time.

The past fifteen years, finally, have brought a new advantage to the white owner. Government regulations have, no doubt, helped the Negro owner along with the white owner. The fact, however, that the local administration of the new government policies was entirely in the hands of white people could not fail to make the Negroes a relatively disfavored group.

6. TENANTS AND WAGE LABORERS

In 1880, 64 per cent of the Southern farms were operated by owners. The figure for 1900 had fallen to 53 per cent. By 1930 it was down to 44 per cent, but by 1940 it was up again to 51 per cent—undoubtedly the result of the strenuous efforts of the Farm Security Administration to increase farm ownership in the South. In 1930 a majority of the Southern farm operators were tenants and sharecroppers. There was a similar development in other parts of the country; but nowhere else did it go so far.

Almost two-thirds of the tenants are white. It does not follow, however, that white tenancy is more serious than Negro tenancy. Rather, it is the other way around. Negroes, more than whites, are concentrated in the lower tenure groups, and in each tenure group Negroes are economically much weaker than whites. Contrary to common belief, the majority of all tenants do not work on plantations but on small holdings. Most of those on small holdings are white, but the majority of the plantation tenants are Negro. There has been, however, a "white infiltration" into this mainstay of Negro tenancy.

The plight of the plantation tenant is the problem of an antiquated paternalistic labor institution in the midst of modern American capitalistic society. Most plantation tenants are just ordinary laborers; their work is usually supervised by the landlord or his representative. Sometimes they work by the clock and in gangs. Their wages, however, are not determined according to supply and demand in a free labor market. Wages are not fixed per hour, per week, or per year. Instead, the cropper gets a share of the product. The quantity of the product depends not only on the efforts of the workers but on the conditions of the soil and on the hazards of wind and weather; and it is not the quantity of the output alone but also its price that determines the final reward. While in other parts of our economic system it has been the accepted ideal that risk of investment should be directly correlated with the size of the investment, the share-cropper and the share tenant—although nothing but laborers from economic and social viewpoints—have to carry a considerable share of the risk. It is true that the share tenant shares in the benefit of a good crop and favorable market conditions with the landowner. It is true also that he does not have much capital of his own. If losses run so high that at the end of the year he finds himself indebted to the landlord, he may be able to get rid of this debt by moving to another plantation. But many times he may find that after investing a full season's work he has not received anything near the wages he would have earned had he been a wage laborer with full employ-ment. On such occasions he has to face long months of semistarva-tion for himself and his family. That certainly is a business risk. Should the tenant have livestock or other assets, the landlord is al-ways free to take them to cover possible debts. In nine cotton states "the landlord has the legal right to sell any and all property the tenant may have to secure payment of rent and furnishings."[2]

Any study of the system reveals that the sharecropper or share tenant usually has most of the disadvantages of being an independent farmer without the rights that ordinarily go with such a position. Seldom are his rights and obligations set down in a written con-tract. Usually he does not sell his own share of the cotton crop him-self. According to the crop lien laws in most states, he has no right to dispose of it until he has paid to the landlord all the rent due and the advances he has received during the season. Since he cannot do that until the crop has been sold and paid for, the landlord is legally entitled to handle all the marketing as he sees fit.

Worse, however, is the pattern of making account keeping a one-sided affair. The tenant usually has to take the landlord's word for what price has been obtained for the cotton, for the total amount of advances received from the landlord, and for what the interest on these advances is, and so on. An attempt of a Negro tenant to check the accounts against his own itemized account—if he should have

---

[2] Arthur Raper, "Race and Class Pressures," unpublished manuscript prepared for *An American Dilemma* (1940), p. 181.

kept any (which is rarely done)—will not accomplish much except possibly to infuriate the landlord.

The "advancing" of food, clothing, and other necessities of life is an important part of the system. Since the tenant is ordinarily without resources—otherwise he would not be a tenant—he cannot wait for his wages until the crop has been harvested and sold. He has, therefore, to live on a credit basis at least during a large part of the year. The interest rates charged for these advances are extremely high. A flat rate of 10 per cent is usual but, since the duration of the credit is only a few months, the annual rate is several times as high. According to Woofter's sample study in 1934, the annual interest rate was 37 per cent.

In addition, in stores owned by plantation owners where tenants must buy if they want credit, prices are often "marked up" to a considerable extent. When the advances are paid in cash, which sometimes happens, the tenant naturally has greater freedom to buy at ordinary market prices. The tenant usually ends the year in debt to his landlord: it is to the interest of the landlord that the tenant remain in debt so that he cannot leave the plantation.

The system doubtless has some positive sides. There are good landlords who try to take care of their tenants. They are the ones who get and hold the good tenants. Since the general standard is so low, it is not expensive to be an exceptionally good planter and have the best tenants. It is our impression that most Negro tenants feel they can get more or less out of the landlord depending upon what kind of landlord he is, and how he is approached. But they have not often been taught that they have definite rights and definite obligations and that it is up to them to make good. Several local Farm Security officials in the South have told us of how the paternalistic attitude on the part of the planters and the corresponding attitudes of dependence, carelessness, and lack of ambition on the part of the tenants constitute the toughest problem in their work. The plantation system, in summary, fails to meet American standards of economic efficiency and justice.

7. Agricultural Trends during the Thirties

Of all the calamities that struck the rural Negro people in the South—soil erosion, the infiltration of white tenants into plantation areas, the ravages of the boll weevil, the southwestern shift in cotton cultivation—none has had such grave effect as the combination of world agricultural trends and the federal agricultural policy of the thirties. They have already rooted out a considerable portion of the

Negro farmers and made the future of the rest extremely problematic.

It was during the thirties that the overproduction of cotton became serious. Demand declined sharply both at home and abroad due to the depression, to the growing competition from other countries, and to the increased use of substitutes. The cotton economy suffered much more from the depression, and recovered much less afterward, than did American agriculture in general. Southern tobacco and sugar cane also were losing out on the international market. Thus, even under favorable circumstances, it would not have been impossible to avoid widespread unemployment of agricultural labor. Although attempts were made to deal with the problem of structural change, the major New Deal efforts, as we shall find, did not fit into a constructive, long-range program for a reorganization of Southern agriculture. War has, of course, brought temporary relief by using up surplus production; but after the destruction in Europe and elsewhere has been overcome, American agriculture will again appear as overexpanded. The long-range employment prospects in Southern agriculture, on the whole, are rather dark.

8. The Disappearing Sharecropper

By 1940 it became apparent that tenancy was on the decline. In 1940 there was a somewhat larger number of white owners than in 1930, but a slightly lower number of Negro owners. There was a much lower number of Negro cash and share tenants, and of Negro and white croppers. The changes do not mean that the situation has been improved, but rather that it has deteriorated to such an extent that sharecroppers and tenants are being forced out. Many of the ex-tenants and ex-croppers may have stayed in agriculture. They have simply been reduced to wage laborers on the farms.

The main reason why the Negro lost out, probably, was the fact that he, much more than the white operator and worker, was dependent on the cotton economy, which was hit most severely by the depression and by the falling off of foreign markets. Yet, the depression by itself seems to have had more effect on income than on employment, for the decline in Negro tenancy before 1935 was limited compared with what was to come after that year. It seems, therefore, that the agricultural policies, particularly the Agricultural Adjustment program (AAA) which was begun in May, 1933, was the factor directly responsible for the drastic curtailment in number of Negro and white sharecroppers and Negro cash and share tenants. The AAA raised the income not only for planters and other owners but—to an extent—for those tenants and croppers who were allowed to stay in employment. But hundreds of thousands of them were pushed off the land, and the AAA hastened their going.

The fundamental objective of the AAA was to raise and stabilize farm income by:

(1) Limiting acreages given over to cash crops,
(2) Removing surpluses from regular markets to keep up prices,
(3) Paying direct subsidies to farmers,
(4) Encouraging conservation practices.

The cut in amount of land growing cotton was drastic, but improved methods of production kept up the output. So there had to be buying of surpluses by the government. Keeping up prices by removing surpluses from the market caused the United States to lose its foreign market to competing countries. Had it not been for the war, there could ultimately have been but two alternatives: either further drastic cuts in cotton acreage or collapse of the whole program. In either case, the Negro would have been hurt severely.

9. AAA AND THE NEGRO

Payments for reducing acreage obviously reduced the number of tenants. On the large plantations (where acreage could be and was most drastically reduced) the tenants were mainly Negro. There were other factors. At first, the landlords simply grabbed the benefit checks which they were supposed to forward, in part, to the tenants. The credit relations between landlord and tenant, the one-sided system of account keeping, and the legal impotence of the Negro tenants enabled the landlord to receive a larger share of the benefits than he was entitled to. After complaints, checks were paid directly to the tenants and the tenants received a larger share of the benefit. The later changes in favor of the tenants, however, gave the landlord a considerable economic interest in decreasing the number of tenants or lowering their status to wage laborers. This is what seems to have happened in the latter part of the thirties. The net result was that there were fewer tenants and croppers, but more farm laborers.

10. THE LOCAL ADMINISTRATION OF THE AAA

The local administration is in the hands of the Extension Service —that is, the County Farm Demonstration Agents—and the County Agricultural Conservation Committees representing local farmers. It is our impression, based upon a large number of interviews, that the county agents in the plantation South have attitudes on economic, social, and racial questions similar to those of the large landowners. Some of them are planters themselves. The committees, at least in plantation counties, have an overrepresentation of big estate owners.

It is true that the Negroes commonly voted in AAA referenda for certain decisions. But Negroes were seldom allowed to vote for committeemen. Not only Negro tenants and croppers, but Negro farm owners as well, were jeopardized by their lack of influence on the decisions of the local AAA administration. The allotment of cotton acreage and benefit payments was rather a complicated affair. The accuracy of the records and calculations depended on the good will, conscientiousness, and competence of those in charge of the local control. If they do not represent all local farm groups, it is likely that the rights and interests of underrepresented or unrepresented farmers and tenants will suffer. This is more likely if such groups, particularly Negroes, include a large proportion of more or less illiterate people who are unable to understand the intricate regulations well enough to find out whether or not they have been wronged.

11. Mechanization

Another factor that seems bound to influence displacement of Negro labor on Southern plantations is mechanization. Until now, mechanization has not been important. The low degree of mechanization is the reason why cotton growing requires so much labor and keeps this labor down to such low levels of living. At the same time, the cheap labor makes mechanization unprofitable.

In the past fifteen years, however, there has been a slight tendency toward mechanization in the Southeast. Considerable mechanization has already occurred in the two Southwestern states, Texas and Oklahoma. Hindrances to mechanization have been both the difficulty of getting credit and the high rate of interest. The New Deal reform in the organization of agricultural credit reduced this obstacle considerably. AAA benefit payments added to the supply of cash that planters could use for mechanization. The great profits of the war have undoubtedly added to the ready cash in the South. Undoubtedly, the main factor now holding back mechanization in the South is the inability to get new machinery. When demand falls in the next few years, manufacturers will certainly turn to creating and perfecting machinery for the special needs and new markets of the South.

The threat against employment opportunities in the South is very great. Machines are likely to be used on large holdings. Negroes are concentrated in those regions where holdings are large. They are also more dependent on the cash-crop culture. They are objects of prejudice, especially when it comes to handling machinery. To operate an expensive machine is to have a position of responsibility, which, even in the rural South, must draw "white man's pay." More and more the Negro will be reduced to a seasonal worker, and even this opportunity will dwindle if chopping and picking should become mechanized.

12. Labor Organizations

In view of the labor displacement during the thirties, one would have expected widespread unrest among sharecroppers. There was unrest among the sharecroppers. There was publicity about it. The federal government did make attempts to improve the conditions by its various Farm Security programs. But the organized attempts of the tenants and sharecroppers to fight for their needs were rather weak and scattered.

It should not surprise us that organizational efforts among Southern tenants and farm hands were practically absent before the New Deal and remained weak even during the latter part of the thirties. Everywhere the organization of agricultural labor has always been a hard task. Isolation, a low educational level, poverty, lack of cooperative habits, the tradition of paternalism and dependence, frequent moving, a weak legal order, and the split between the Negroes and whites further hampered organization in the South. The last factor is of special importance. There is intense competition between Negroes and whites. The whites could not possibly gain anything by organizing unions excluding Negroes. Whites and Negroes are exchangeable from the employers' point of view, and, except during war time, there exists a pressing labor surplus, particularly of Negro labor.

This is the general background against which the first labor movement among Southern farm workers should be viewed. The Southern Tenant Farmers' Union is the main organization in the field. In 1946 it claimed a membership of 20,000. Whites and Negroes have been organized together and, on the whole, successfully. About 50 per cent of the members are Negroes.[3]

The future of trade unionism in the plantation South is hard to predict. Economic pressure is likely to continue and become worse. The growth of unionism in industry in the South during the war means that legal protection for trade unions has been strengthened. The experience of unionism has also become more familiar. Negroes who have been in the Army may provide both leadership and a more

[3] Charles S. Johnson and Associates, *Into the Main Stream* (Chapel Hill: University of North Carolina Press, 1947), p. 99.

independent outlook. It may be that white veterans have less prejudice. At any rate, it seems likely that the present ferment in the
South will be fertile ground for at least attempts at greater unionization of the agricultural workers.

13. The Dilemma of Agricultural Policy

If the farm workers become organized in the South and if their
organizations are able to enter into successful collective bargaining
with the planters, any success in raising the earnings and living levels
of farm labor on Southern plantations will make plain the basic
overpopulation of Southern agriculture. Increased wages will increase costs and encourage mechanization, or will displace cotton
by other crops which do not need so much labor, or both. In the
long run this is desirable in terms of both economic efficiency and
human welfare. But the immediate effect, if vigorous measures to
remove surplus population from the cotton land are not taken,
would be increased unemployment; the Negroes would be hurt most.
This is the dilemma of agricultural policy in the South.

The dilemma is much more general. Whenever farming becomes
more productive and efficient, a lower number of acres and workers
is needed to satisfy the demand for farm products. The less efficient
are driven off the land and must be absorbed in other parts of the
economy. On the other hand, to make farmers go in for a system
of almost complete self-sufficiency can do but little to cure basic rural
overpopulation. It means dividing the farm population into parts
only one of which would be allowed to go in for specialization and
modern, efficient techniques. The other half would have to diversify
its efforts and use inefficient techniques to the extent where they
would be working hard and getting little in return, including practically nothing in the way of modern conveniences. This plan would
never provide what is understood to be "the American standard of
living." Too, it would require the permanent stifling of ambition
and an economic dictatorship to separate those kept in commercial
agriculture from those forced into a self-sufficient agriculture. Such a
solution on a large scale would not be acceptable to the American
people.

14. Economic Evaluation of the AAA

While the restriction of acreage and the resulting unemployment
did not occur during the war, there is no reason to believe that either
the difficulties inherent in the cash-crop system or the basic over-

population of the South have changed. They have merely been obscured by the great demand and high prices for cotton during the war. Even if the AAA program is not renewed, mechanization, specialization, and unemployment of Negroes is likely to go on; therefore, what we have to say of the effects of the AAA program on the Negro farmer applies equally well to the postwar situation.

From the point of view of efficiency, reduction of cotton acreage, the resulting dismissal of tenants, mechanization, or a rise in wages due to collective bargaining are desirable. But, employment must be found for the agricultural labor unemployed as a result of these changes. There is a need for more labor in American industry: houses need to be built; people need more and better furniture and other household equipment; large parts of the American population do not have enough health, educational, or recreational facilities. Obviously, the AAA policy should have included a large-scale effort to move part of the agricultural population to industry. This effort should be concentrated upon the younger generation, which needs vocational training to make it fit for industrial work. In regard to Negro education in the South, this policy will require a complete reform of the educational system and a reformulation of the aims of vocational education.

Unfortunately, the AAA was carried out during the depression. During the thirties even the experts doubted if there would be any place for more workers in American industry. The shortage of skilled labor during and after the war showed clearly how mistaken this idea was. Certainly, a policy designed to relieve agricultural overpopulation in the future will have to consider resettlement.

15. SOCIAL EVALUATION OF THE AAA

A primary aim of the AAA was to bring relief to the rural population, which had experienced a serious economic setback. Huge amounts have been spent for this purpose. The total appropriations for direct payments to farmers during the period 1934–1941 has been estimated to be over $5,300,000,000, or more than three-fourths of the total costs for all farm policies (including land utilization, soil erosion, rural electrification, farm security, and so on). In view of these high costs, one could have expected more results for those in great need. Yet, as we have shown, large numbers of those most in need of assistance lost rather than gained because of the AAA; the benefits were not distributed in relation to needs.

The total agricultural cash income for nine Southeastern states was twice as high in 1940 as in 1932. Nevertheless, it was still more than 20 per cent below the 1929 level. There is no way of telling how large a share in these income gains the Negroes have received. More Negroes than whites have been made to leave the land, and those who left, of course, got nothing of the increase of farm income or of AAA benefits. It can be argued that higher cotton prices and the AAA benefits allowed higher wages for those who stayed. Independent Negro farmers probably shared equally with white farmers of the same economic status. Negro tenants have increasingly received their share. However, the Negro's share was by no means proportionate to his numbers and still less to his greater needs. Every tenant and share-cropper had to let his landlord get part of the benefit payments for the land he was farming, and the wage laborer received no part of it at all. And there are more white landlords and fewer white wage laborers.

There is an even more basic problem involved: no consideration was taken of the fact that some groups needed aid much more than others. The manner of distribution of the AAA benefits, which were taxpayers' money being used for relief purposes, gave more to those who had more. A sample study of 246 Southern plantations shows that the planters' average cash income per plantation was $2,528 in 1934 and $3,590 in 1937. Out of these amounts not less than $979 and $833, respectively, came from AAA payments. The tenants on the same plantation, on the other hand, had a net cash income for these two years of $236 and $300, respectively, out of which but $11 and $27 were AAA payments. Thus, even in proportion to their higher "basic" income, the planters received more of this assistance than did their plantation tenants. A few large landlords may have received as much as $10,000 per year in AAA payments. It has now become apparent that the economic policy of the AAA only increased the problems of Southern agriculture.

In a few years we—as well as other countries—shall again face the same agricultural problems as before the war. Some of the problems will have been aggravated. One-third of the American Negro people in Southern agriculture are still in the bottom layer of the American economic system; they have tremendous interests at stake in the new agricultural policy of America. It is necessary for them that agricultural policy be planned with recognition of the serious overpopulation, of the necessity of large-scale movement of labor, and of the big income differences within the agricultural population. It is both desirable and necessary that international needs and competition be considered too.

16. CONSTRUCTIVE MEASURES

Besides the AAA, there are a number of more or less independent agricultural policies with more constructive long-range aims. Much less has been spent on those policies than on the AAA.

In some of the programs there is an emphasis on new sources of income—both agricultural and nonagricultural. The Tennessee Valley Authority (TVA) and the Rural Electrification program have encouraged nonagricultural, rural industries. There is an enormous number of other programs: soil conservation projects; farm and home demonstration work; 4-H clubs; reforms in the farm credit system; county planning; encouragement of agricultural co-operation; research and experimentation; and together with these programs, adult education.

Negroes are frequently not reached with these programs, although as a group they need them most. Co-operation is difficult where discussion or participation on an equal footing between whites and Negroes is taboo. Landlords have often objected to farm and home demonstration agents approaching families on their holdings. Moreover, by January 1, 1942, there were altogether only 558 Negro extension workers in the South, or about 1.2 per 10,000 Negro persons on the rural farms. The corresponding figure for the total rural farm population in the South by mid-1939 was more than twice as high, or 2.7.

One noteworthy accomplishment has been in the field of mortgage credit. The average interest rates for all short-term loans have decreased substantially. Yet they are still very high. The real expense even for government loans in 1937 was no less than 11.9 per cent. Negro owners and cash renters should have some chance of getting assistance through the government credit agencies. But it must be considered that Negro owners and cash tenants have much smaller and less valuable farms than white owners and cash tenants and cannot present much security. Therefore, their share in this new government credit must be far smaller than is the proportion of Negroes among even the more independent Southern farmers, who are mostly white.

Indeed, it is probably even more limited; the local administration of some of the most important credit agencies is in the hands of credit co-operatives such as the farm loan associations, for Federal Home Loan Bank loans, and the production credit associations, for production credit loans. These associations are dominated by white farmers. It can be taken for granted. in view of previous evidence on how white farmers have misused administrative power under other new economic programs, that the temptation to discriminate against the Negro is frequently too strong to resist.

17. FARM SECURITY PROGRAMS

There is a series of programs for the little man in the farm business known as the Farm Security programs (FSA). Hundreds of thousands of Southern farm families have received assistance under these programs. Negroes have received a good share in the FSA benefits—almost as much as would correspond to their population ratio in Southern farm areas. Even so, these efforts do not measure up to the size of the problems: $5,300,000,000 was appropriated for AAA policies during the period 1934–1941, but only one-fifth of this amount ($1,121,000,000) for Farm Security programs. And a large part of FSA assistance consisted of loans on which repayment could be expected. As for the Negro's share, it does not compare with his relative needs and it is much more difficult for a Negro than for a white farmer in similar circumstances to receive assistance in this form.

The explanation is simple. The poorer groups in Southern agriculture, and particularly the Negroes, have no political power. As a result, this program is more limited than is other farm aid and there is less assurance of its being continued. At the end of 1941 a congressional committee, headed by Senator Harry F. Byrd of Virginia, while wanting to maintain the AAA payments, proposed that all Farm Security activities be abolished in the interest of wartime economy. There are several reports that the Farm Bureau pushed similar demands. The result was a reduction in the budget of the FSA in 1942. In August, 1946, the functions of the Farm Security Administration were transferred to a new agency, the Farmers' Home Administration, where the work continues much as before. But these incidents indicate the attitude toward the Farm Security work among those who have power in the South. There seems to be a notion that since this kind of assistance is given to poor people it is "relief" and, consequently, bad, whereas the fact that the AAA payments are distributed to all farmers, so that those in higher income brackets receive a much larger share than others, makes them "business" and not "relief." Actually, both are forms of government assistance.

The differential treatment of the Negro can be explained on similar grounds. The local administration is not entirely in the hands of the officials of the FSA. Clients usually have to be passed on by committees of local farmers, over which Negroes have practically no influence. Under such circumstances it is surprising that Negroes have received as much as they have. The FSA has, from the beginning, been fighting courageously and persistently against differential treatment.

There are still other difficulties. The laws and law enforcement give the tenant little protection against the landlord. The FSA would have been more efficient under a strong and impartial legal system. To rehabilitate tenants or other impoverished farms, it is not enough to give them loans, and then to sit back, expecting them to pay it all back while improving their economic status. It is a major educational job, and the FSA has faced it.

It is a question of teaching farmers, who have known little but specialized cash- and feed-crop production, to diversify their efforts—to grow much of what they need for their own use. Farmers who have been nothing but dependent tenants have to become independent farmers. They have to learn that, from now on, they have definite rights and definite obligations, and that it usually pays to stay at the same place. Detailed farm and household plans are made for them—if they do not know how to do it themselves; and they are encouraged to stick to those plans as far as possible. They are taught to keep accounts. Some are illiterate; their children have to be taught how to help them. Many clients have difficulties because they are sick; a co-operative health program is organized for them. The idea behind FSA, which was begun in 1934 and completely organized in 1937, was that it would be far better to help needy rural families, who were competent and willing to work, to grow their own food and earn a little cash income on farms rather than to give them cash doles.

The rehabilitation program, which includes assistance of various kinds on an individual basis, takes up the major part of the work and the budget of FSA. By December, 1939, there were in the South 154,000 white and 45,000 Negro "standard rehabilitation borrowers." While more than one-fourth of the Southern rural farm population is Negro, the number of Negroes on the program was a somewhat smaller proportion (23 per cent) of the total number of clients. Compared with the total estimated number of white and colored farm families which were either on relief or had an income of less than $500, the participation in the program amounted to 22 per cent of the whites and 11 per cent of the Negroes. This suggests that a low-income white family had about twice the chance of a Negro family in the same circumstances of being accepted on the program. The average amount of loan advances was somewhat higher for white ($685) than for colored ($606) clients.

Although the Negroes' gross cash income during 1939 was 40 per cent lower than that of white clients in the South, their repayment record was a slightly better one. The net income of the Negro clients was rather low—less than $100 in cash and about $240 in home-use production—whereas the corresponding figures for white clients were about $200 and $275, respectively. Both groups of clients bettered their conditions to a great extent during the time they were on the program—Negroes relatively more than whites.

Nobody who has had any contact with those doing field work for the FSA can escape being impressed by these attempts to rehabilitate farm families by "helping the clients to help themselves." The Farm Security work, after this period of experimentation, has provided the kind of practical experience that would be needed for a major reform of land and tenure conditions.

Jobs Outside Agriculture

1. The Urbanization of the Negro People

It is necessary to remind the reader that only a part of the present farm population in the South has any future on the land. Few people realize that almost two-thirds of the Negroes now live in nonfarm areas, and that eventually most Negroes will have to enter the nonagricultural economy of America. There is a widespread attitude in cities that the Negro ought to stay where he belongs—on the Southern farm land. But, as we have seen, there are few opportunities on Southern farm lands except for those with large amounts of capital.

The attitude that Negroes should stay in the rural South will not be able to stop the gradual urbanization of the Negro people. As we saw in Chapter 3, migration to the cities has been going on for a long time, and since the First World War the Negro farm population has actually been declining because of migration. But the popular attitude that the Negroes had better stay where they are has given, and will probably continue to give, a basis for segregation and discrimination both in housing and in employment. It even increases the ignorance about Negroes by making everyone want to look the other way.

2. In the South

Slavery and the suppression of free Negroes gave to Southern Negroes a monopoly on labor for a few years after the Civil War. Unskilled work was considered inferior in the South, and fit only for Negroes. Negroes were the domestics and the laborers. Negroes were also, to a large extent, the craftsmen and the mechanics. They were

[1] The material in this and the following chapters covers the period up to 1940. The changes brought about by World War II are extremely important and will be discussed in Chapter 8.

carpenters, bricklayers, painters, blacksmiths, harness makers, tailors, and shoemakers. For even skilled labor was degraded, and whites had often been denied the opportunity of acquiring training since so many masters had preferred to work with slaves. The high price paid for skilled slaves had encouraged their training in the crafts. But the great majority of Negroes, even in the cities, were domestics and unskilled laborers. Skilled or unskilled, their protection was that their work was characterized as "Negro jobs" and usually badly paid.

From the beginning the Negroes' position in the Southern nonagricultural labor market has been influenced by two trends working in opposite directions. One is the general expansion of the Southern nonagricultural economy. This tends constantly to increase the employment opportunities for Negroes as well as for whites. The other force is the competition from white job seekers. This tends to exclude Negroes from employment and to press them downward in the occupational levels.

The result of this pressure is well known; Negroes have been driven out of one kind of job after another. The competition from the white workers, and the gradual loss of protection from the former master class, meant not only that the Negroes' share in many traditional "Negro occupations" became smaller, but also, in most cases, Negroes failed to get an appreciable share in new jobs. Negro workers, therefore, are likely to be found in backward industries and occupations, as the expanding ones are usually the new ones. Whenever work became less strenuous, less dirty, and generally more attractive, these occupations often became "white man's work" instead of "Negro jobs."

The increased use of white women in industry meant a new source of competition. It also raised a new block against employing Negroes because of the "social equality" issue. White women and Negroes cannot work together under the Southern code. The Jim Crow legislation, enacted in the 1890's, drew the color line even sharper and thus had great importance in the economic sphere. During this development, defensive beliefs were constantly growing among the whites in the South that the Negro was inefficient, unreliable, and incompetent to work with machines. It was true that fewer and fewer young Negroes could keep up with skills when they were not allowed to experience the better working conditions and the new techniques or get training.

How, then, have the rising numbers of urban Negroes earned their living? For one thing, there has been a growing number of upper- and middle-class white families in the cities who can employ domestic servants. It is traditional in the South that every family which can afford it, even down to the lower middle class, should have domestic help. The growing industries, furthermore, created a considerable number of laboring jobs for Negroes, even when they were excluded from the machines. And they did get into some industries.

During parts of the period up to the First World War the absolute gains in job opportunities for Negroes in the South, in spite of relative losses, were considerable. From 1890 to 1910 Negro male workers in nonagricultural pursuits increased by two-thirds, or by more than 400,000. This increase was due mainly to expansion in certain typical "Negro job" industries, such as saw and planing mills, coal mining, and maintenance-of-way work on railroads. Since 1910, however, there has been a drastic decline in the gains made by Negroes. From 1910 to 1930 Negro males engaged in nonagricultural pursuits in the South increased by less than one-third, or by less than 300,000.

During the thirties the Negro's losses in employment were extremely serious. It was during the thirties that large numbers of Negroes were driven out of agriculture at a rapid rate. Many of these went to the city, where there was at least varied opportunity for employment and where relief standards were more liberal. In spite of the increase in the Negro population of the cities, Negroes continued to lose in importance as an element in Southern urban labor. The general increase in unemployment made white workers try even more to "drive the Negroes out." There was little increase in industrial expansion in the South during this period and less opportunity in the North to induce migration. All these factors made the plight of the Southern urban Negro extremely difficult. The history of the Negro in skilled and unskilled labor in the South from 1865 to 1940 is one of steadily increasing hardship, at least relative to the position of whites. The war brought changes; these will be discussed in a later chapter.

3. In the North

At the close of the Civil War the Negro wage earner in the North had a different position than in the South. There were only a few Negroes in the North, so that no occupations could be considered "Negro jobs." Negroes were not protected in their jobs by the vested interests of a white master class. Competition from white workers was intense. The constant stream of European immigrants to the North provided cheap labor which competed with Negro labor for even the lower jobs such as servants and common laborers. The trade unions were concentrated in the crafts; most of the time they kept Negroes out of skilled work. They could do it as unions were stronger in the North than in the South and as the Northern Negroes did not have the handicraft training Southern Negroes got under slavery. These are the things that established the opinion that the Negro could earn a living easier in the South than in the North.

This is still told to the observer in the South today, when it certainly is an exaggeration. Even for earlier times the proposition sounds questionable. The tremendous industrial development in the North and the small number of Negroes compared to the total labor demand were factors that worked to the Negroes' advantage. If we look over the whole period from the Civil War up to 1940, the general picture is that, while the Negroes in the South have been gradually losing out in most lines of work where they had been firmly entrenched at the time of slavery and have been allowed to get a favorable position in but few of the new industries, Negroes in the North have made some fairly significant gains in some occupations which are new or where few if any Negroes were allowed to work before. Still Negroes are completely, or almost completely, kept out of many manufacturing lines in the North.

A combination of factors explains the Negroes' gains in the North: the scarcity of labor during the First World War and the boom of the twenties, and at the same time the decline of immigration; lack of deep race prejudice on the part of white workers at first; the use of Negroes by employers to prevent unionization or break strikes. Obviously none of these conditions gave Negroes a firm and permanent hold on the Northern labor market, although between 1910 and 1930 they did manage to gain a foothold in some industries.

Between 1910 and 1930 the number of male Negro workers in nonagricultural pursuits in the North increased by 480,000, that is, more than doubled. Even the absolute increase was much larger than that in the South (about 295,000). Most of the increase occurred in the nonmanufacturing groups: domestic and nondomestic service workers, helpers, delivery men, teamsters, truck drivers, and so on. Other increases occurred in the building industry, among longshoremen, in garages; large gains were made in the coal mines and in the iron, steel machinery, and vehicle industries. Also important were gains in the clothing industries and certain food industries, particularly slaughter and meat-packing houses. But most other Northern manufacturing industries failed to hire Negro workers in any appreciable numbers. Thus, even in the North, the Negro remained confined to certain jobs—either those where he had earlier acquired something of a traditional position or where he managed to gain a foothold during the labor market crisis of the First World War.

This should be emphasized: large employment gains for Negroes in the North—except for the war boom of the Second World War— occurred only during the short period from the First World War until the end of the twenties. During the thirties the upward trend in number of Negro workers was broken even more definitely than in the urban South—and this in spite of the fact that the Negro population in the large Northern cities increased by as much as 23 per cent between 1930 and 1940.

This is explainable on several grounds. The depression hit the North worse than the South. Nevertheless, Negroes continued to go north in great numbers, because of better social conditions and higher relief standards. The decline in employment opportunities in the North during the thirties was thus due in part to the fact that the North, in other respects, treated the Negro better than the South did. Still, the record of the North is not a good one. Labor unions discriminated and so did many employers, especially when it came to skilled work.

4. The Employment Hazards of Unskilled Work

The concentration of Negroes in unskilled work is a hazard to future employment prospects. It means that the Negro's chances not only of getting ahead but of keeping any employment at all are restricted. The expansion in unskilled occupations has been limited during recent decades compared with that in occupations above the unskilled class. There are those who think that Negroes are over-ambitious when they try to get out of their position as common laborers, but Negroes *must* become skilled workers since the demand for unskilled workers is declining. Wage increases tend to spur mechanization; it goes without saying that the Negroes are the main sufferers in such a development. Unemployment, also, falls first on the less essential, unskilled laborer.

5. The Size of the Negro Labor Force

Considering the limitations that Negroes face in every occupation, what proportion of Negroes have any jobs at all? In nonfarm areas of the United States in 1940, 47 per cent of all nonwhite persons, 14 years of age or over, were registered as having employment. The corresponding figure for the white population was slightly lower, or 45 per cent. This does not mean that employment figures were more favorable for Negroes than for whites. It is because Negro women to a great extent take on gainful work outside their homes. Of all non-white women, 36 per cent were employed; for white women the figure was 24 per cent. For men it was the other way around: non-white men had employment less often (59 per cent) than had white men (66 per cent). This difference was greater in the North. In many Northern centers only about one-half of the Negro men had any employment. About 25 per cent of the nonwhite male labor force in nonfarm areas was without any employment on the labor market in 1940; and 15 per cent did not even have any work relief assignments. The corresponding figures for white males (16 and 11 per cent, respectively) were significantly lower. There was a similar difference, although on a somewhat lower level, between white and nonwhite females.

These race differences in employment are the result of two opposing factors. One is that the extreme poverty of most Negro families forces Negro women as well as Negro boys and aged Negro men on the labor market to a much greater extent than among whites. On the other hand, among both men and women who "are in the labor market" the proportion of those who fail to get any jobs is much higher for Negroes than for whites. There is often a causal relation between these two factors. A Negro woman may take a job because her husband is without one. On the other hand, if the employment situation is discouraging, some of the workers, particularly if they have secured public assistance, and especially if they are getting old, will tend to leave the labor market permanently.

The total number of both employed and unemployed workers (the so-called "labor force") has traditionally been much larger, in proportion, among Negroes than among whites. Gradually, however, an equalization between white and Negro male workers has taken place. This equalization was probably due to large-scale public relief, particularly old-age assistance, assistance to dependent children, and so on. In addition, during the great unemployment among Negroes in the thirties, Negroes who had lost their jobs, more often than whites, were probably discouraged from offering their services, and, thus, ceased to belong to either the actual or the potential labor force.

We should not, however, be hasty in jumping to the conclusion that "relief has demoralized the Negro." While this may have happened in individual cases among both whites and Negroes, we must keep in mind that no appeal has been made to the Negro to better himself economically. On the contrary, white people, by means of the severe job restrictions they have imposed upon the Negro—and by denying him sufficient public health facilities—have forced him to accept public relief as one of his "major occupations." Therefore, if the Negro has become "demoralized," it is because white people have given him a smaller share of the steady and worth-while jobs than of the public assistance benefits.

It should be emphasized, further, that, in spite of the more liberal relief policies of the past decades, there were until 1940 a proportionately greater number of workers and job seekers in the Negro than in the white population. The decline has occurred mainly among aged persons, who should be allowed to retire, among youth, who need some additional education, and among women, who have their own homes and families to attend to.

In the future, however, this problem may become of increasing significance. There is still much discrimination against the Negro in the relief system. If the discriminatory practices should be removed, but if job restrictions are maintained, then there is a real danger that the Negro will become a burden on the national economy. This is the basic dilemma in the problem of the Negroes being accepted into American economic life. It must be faced squarely.

6. THE WHITE-COLLAR OCCUPATIONS

The position of the Negro in business, the professions, public service, and other white-collar jobs is far different from that of the Negro wage earner. As a wage earner, the Negro is kept out of many trades. He is commonly held down to the position of laborer and is kept out of skilled work. But there are always possibilities for him to enter these jobs, and he is always struggling to do so. In the white-collar jobs, however, exclusion is usually much more complete and "settled." This is because of "social" considerations as well as economic ones.

Most Negro workers serve the white-dominated economy, but most Negro businessmen, professionals, and Negro white-collar workers are either dependent on the segregated Negro community for their market or they serve in public institutions—like schools and hospitals —set up exclusively for the use of Negroes. (Some civil service employees are the only significant exceptions.)

This exclusion from the larger white economy means a severe restriction upon the opportunities for Negroes to reach an upper- or middle-class status. It is one of the main ways of keeping the Negro upper and middle classes small. It also means that there is practically no opportunity for some kinds of work: while the Negro community gives places for a fair number of Negro preachers, teachers, and neighborhood storekeepers, it does not offer much chance for engineers, architects, or managers of industry. The latter group have to work in the white economy, which does not want Negroes in such positions.

The poverty of the Negro people also limits the opportunity for Negro businessmen and professionals. Since they are excluded from the white market, it becomes important for them to hold the Negro market as a monopoly. The monopoly over the Negro market of teachers, preachers, undertakers, beauticians, and others is generally respected. The Negro storekeeper, on the other hand, is in severe competition with the white storekeeper. To a lesser extent this is true also of the Negro doctor. The Negro lawyer has an even worse competitive position. The Negro journalist does not have to compete with whites in the Negro press, but, to some extent, the Negro press has to compete with the white press. All Negro businessmen and professionals have to try to make as much use as possible of racial solidarity as a selling point. This means that the entire Negro middle and upper class is caught in a dilemma. On the one hand, they find that the caste wall blocks their economic and social opportunities. On the other hand, they have a vested interest in racial segregation, since it gives them what opportunity they have.

7. The Negro in Business

In 1939 there were not quite 30,000 Negro retail stores, giving employment to a total of 43,000 persons. The total sales in 1939 were less than $2/10$ of 1 per cent of the national total.

The Negro's showing in business appears particularly poor when compared with that of certain other "alien" groups. The foreign-born are underrepresented in most white-collar jobs, but they are a larger proportion of the retail dealers than corresponds to their proportion in the population. This high proportion may be caused, of course, by their having greater difficulties than native Americans in getting employment in many other occupations. At the same time, it indicates a certain resourcefulness in the struggle against unemployment. Particularly interesting is the great number of stores and restaurants operated by Chinese and Japanese.

It is a problem to explain why the Chinese have been able to build up a prosperous restaurant business with white patronage, whereas Negro-owned eating places have but few white customers. It is true that the Chinese restaurant profits from the special appeal that a foreign culture always seems to have to the American. But Southern cooking has a similar reputation outside the South. Since the servants of the Southern aristocracy have usually been Negroes, well-trained Negro cooks and waiters have not been lacking, and one would have expected that the Negro-owned restaurant would have had a good chance to succeed. There are many reports about Negro restaurants having been popular among the white upper class in earlier times.

Already in the 1890's, however, the Negro caterer was losing out. Part of the explanation is probably the change in the character of the upper-class restaurant business. It became necessary to invest large capital in restaurants intended for the wealthy. The Negro caterer failed to modernize his business and be efficient generally. There have been, of course, social and political pressures as well as economic ones against Negro caterers.

The famous old Negro barbershops went the same way as the Negro restaurants. Laundry work is a similar example. It was the whites and the Chinese who started the commercial laundries, which have taken hundreds of thousands of job opportunities away from the Negro home laundresses. Not only his experience as a worker, but also his self-interest should have encouraged the Negro to go into this kind of business as an independent owner. Yet he failed to do so.

The fact that the Negro failed to establish himself in ordinary manufacturing industries is less surprising. In most manufacturing lines he has not even been able to become a skilled worker, much less a foreman, engineer, or office worker. The chances of acquiring managerial skills, under such circumstances, were scant. In addition, he had little chance of acquiring credit.

A recent development which may have some influence on the Negro's position in business is the "don't buy where you can't work" campaign that started almost twenty years ago. The direct purpose of the movement is to increase the number of Negroes employed in white-owned stores, movie theaters, and other establishments in Negro districts. One of the important results may be that a number of Negroes receive practical training in effectively managed businesses— a training that is badly needed but for which there has been little opportunity so far. We should not, however, forget the limitations of this strategy. Even if all jobs in white stores in Negro sections were given to Negroes (and Negroes are demanding only that *some* jobs be given to Negroes in these stores), it would be a drop in the bucket compared with the number of jobs Negroes need. The Negro's main concern must be to break down job segregation and job discrimination in the white economy. The very fact, however, that one of the

Negro's most spectacular fights for economic improvement has been directed on such rather limited objectives is an indication of how desperate his situation really is.

8. NEGRO FINANCE

Since the credit situation has been one of the major obstacles barring the way for the Negro businessman, it is possible that the chances for the Negro in trade might have been better had he been able to gain a position in the field of finance. But the Negro has been, and still is, almost completely insignificant as a banker. There were not even 1,000 Negro proprietors and managers of financial, real estate, and insurance establishments in 1940, or much less than 1 per cent of white workers in such occupations.[2] The story of the Negro in banking is a story about a handful of fairly successful small institutions—and a somewhat larger number of failures.

The Negro has made more progress in the field of insurance, due to several factors. For one thing, in the 1880's some white insurance companies started to apply higher premium schedules for Negroes than for whites and others decided not to take any Negro business at all. The underlying reason, of course, is that mortality rates are much higher for Negroes than for whites. This, however, is a social and economic rather than a racial phenomenon, and most Negroes in the upper and middle classes must consider the practice as highly discriminatory. Even when this treatment is economically wise from the point of view of the life insurance companies, it is only natural that it must be resented by all Negroes, and that they will be inclined to get around it by founding their own insurance companies.

Despite limited success, it is difficult to see a real future for a segregated Negro financial system. It is nothing but a poor substitute for what the Negroes really need: employment of Negroes in white-dominated institutions, where they can learn skills and eventually become competitors, and more consideration for them as insurance or credit seekers.

9. NEGRO PROFESSIONALS

In 1940 almost 7 per cent of all males in nonagricultural pursuits and 14 per cent of the female nonfarm workers were professionals, that is, teachers, clergymen, physicians, dentists, trained nurses, musicians, artists, and other professional workers. The figures for Negroes were much lower: 2.8 and 4.7 per cent, respectively.[3] Thus the

[2] *Sixteenth Census of the United States: 1940. Population*, Vol. III, *The Labor Force.* Pt. 1, *U.S. Summary* (Washington: Government Printing Office, 1943), Table 62.
[3] *Ibid.*

Negro's chance of getting a job as a professional was only one-third that of the white. Still, compared with the Negro's chances in other "higher" occupations, this is a relatively good record.

Teaching is the principal Negro profession. In the public school system in the South, only Negro teachers are allowed to teach Negro children. Yet Negroes had only about half the representation in the teaching profession as in the total population.

Clergymen are the second largest group among Negro "professional" workers. The ministry is the only profession in which Negroes have more representatives than they have in the general population. There are several possible reasons for this: that Negroes are more divided in their religious interests than are whites; that fewer opportunities in other desirable fields encourage a large number of Negroes to become preachers; that more Negroes attend church than do whites.

In 1940 there were about 3,500 Negro physicians and surgeons, or only about 2.2 per cent of the total number of physicians and surgeons in the whole country. That is, there were more than 45 times as many white as Negro doctors.[4] There are several reasons for the limitations in the opportunities for the Negro doctor. Most whites would not ordinarily turn to a Negro physician—partly because of race prejudice, partly because they would not trust his ability. Often Negroes prefer white doctors. Another reason is that most public health services in the South are poorer, in relation to the need, for Negroes than for whites. Even when there are facilities for Negro patients, it does not always mean that they offer any work opportunities for the Negro doctor. White professionals take care of the patients in both the white section and the "colored wing" of a typical Southern hospital. There are only a few hospitals in the United States, such as Harlem Hospital and the Sydenham Hospital in New York City, where Negro and white doctors work together in absolute equality.

The prospects of the Negro physician are becoming increasingly uncertain because of the growth of all kinds of public health facilities. This trend cannot fail to take the low-income clientele away from the private practitioner, and this, of course, means that the Negro doctor may lose nearly all his patients unless he is given a place in the new public health system.

The Negro doctor has such small opportunities for hospital training and specialized work so that there is some justification for the belief that the Negro is less well trained than the white physician or sur-

[4] *Ibid.*

geon. Their basic education is adequate. Only a small minority of Negro doctors are trained at white schools. About four-fifths of them get their education at two Negro medical schools: Meharry in Nashville, Tenn., and Howard in Washington, D.C. The percentage of failures at state board examinations is about the same for graduates of Negro schools as for graduates of white schools. It is obvious, however, that these institutions cannot offer any wide range of opportunities for specialized work.

The Negro dentist and nurse have a position much like that of the Negro physician. There were only 7,192 Negro nurses in 1940, constituting less than 2 per cent of the total number of nurses in the United States.[5] It would seem inconsistent with Southern ideas to let white women care for Negro male patients. But a solution to this delicate problem has been found other than that of letting the Negro nurse monopolize the work in the colored hospital wings. White nurses may treat Negro patients but they are assisted by Negro maids who do most of the dirty work.

Potentially, there should be great opportunities for Negro lawyers. So often is the Negro wronged—in the South at least—and so little do most white people understand his plight that there should be a tremendous need for Negro attorneys to assist Negro clients. Actually the legal insecurity of the Negro is such that the Negro lawyer has but little chance before a Southern court. Protection by a "respectable" white person usually counts more in the South for a Negro client than would even the best representation on the part of a Negro lawyer. In 1940 much less than 1 per cent of all lawyers were Negroes. Two-thirds of the 1,063 Negro lawyers resided outside the South.[6]

Many of the professionals discussed above are employed by federal, state, or county agencies; the largest of the remaining occupations is postal service, which had almost 18,000 Negro workers in 1940. In other public services (the armed forces are discussed later) about 3 per cent of the total were Negroes. There were fewer than 2,000 Negro policemen, sheriffs, and detectives.[7]

The Negro is often praised for his artistic talents, frequently in such a way as to imply that this is the only domain in which he is capable of achievements. Many white persons know the names of some outstanding Negro singers and jazz-band leaders, and believe that this is the one professional field in which the Negro has been able to make good. He has succeeded in this field to a certain extent,

[5] Ibid.
[6] Ibid.
[7] Ibid. and Table 76.

but even here his representation is not so great as in the total population. In the 1940 census there were about 12,000 Negroes registered as musicians, teachers of music, artists, teachers of art, actors, showmen, and showgirls, and this figure is only about 5 per cent of the national total.[8] It is probable that it includes a great number of persons who were not competent, and that many made part of their income in other occupations.

10. SHADY OCCUPATIONS

In the cities, particularly in the big cities, there is a Negro "underworld." To it belong not only petty thieves and racketeers, prostitutes and pimps, bootleggers, dope addicts, and so on, but also a number of "big shots" organizing and controlling crime, vice, and racketeering, as well as other more innocent forms of illegal activity such as gambling—particularly the "policy," or "numbers," game.

There are several reasons why it is to be expected that the Negro community should be extreme in sheltering a big underworld. One reason is the great restriction of economic and social opportunities for young Negroes in ordinary lines of work. The crowdedness in the Negro ghettos, the poverty and economic insecurity, and the lack of wholesome recreation are the other factors which foster antisocial tendencies.

In addition, much of the vice in the Negro community is there not for Negroes, but for whites; it is carried on in the Negro sections because they are disorganized, without adequate police protection, but with police and politicians looking for graft. Elaborate and expensive brothels, for instance, cater to whites and are largely owned by whites. The peddling of dope, obscene pictures, and other appurtenances of vice, like prostitution, are parts of organized vice rings usually owned by whites.

[8] *Ibid.*

CHAPTER VII

What the Negro Gets Out
of the Economy

1. THE PUBLIC BUDGET

In the preceding two chapters we have seen how the Negro tries to sell his labor and other services in the economic market and what difficulties he meets in competition with the whites. We shall now proceed to study the income he earns and what he is able to get for himself and his family on the basis of his income.

One of the first things to consider is what share the Negro gets from the public budget. To the public budgets—ranging from the budget of the local municipalities to the budget of the federal government—everyone contributes by paying various indirect and direct taxes. And everyone consumes some of the goods and services financed by these public budgets.

Public budgets, especially that of the federal government, are assuming new importance in America, as elsewhere. Public services are more and more being made available to all citizens who care to make use of them or are being distributed equally according to "needs" as defined in law. This centralization and extension of public budgets is a long-time trend and not a new development in our history. Free schools, for example, were once for the poor only. Today they are for everybody. We can expect that in the future public benefits will not only be increased for the needy but, in many respects, made available to everybody.

In regard to the distribution of public benefits one principle has been settled for a long time, and is the main basis for any democracy: the principle that the individual citizens have equal duties and rights in relation to the public household. In America this principle is embodied in the Constitution and becomes the value premise in this chapter: the Negro should partake of the burdens (taxes) and the benefits of the public economy like other citizens in similar circumstances.

2. Discrimination in Public Service

There is no evidence that there is any direct racial discrimination in regard to taxation, although the whites in the South certainly have the power to assess Negro-owned property differently than they assess white-owned property. In regard to public benefits, on the other hand, widespread discrimination exists in the entire South. In the North there is little if any direct discrimination. What inequality there is in the Negro's consumption of public services in the North is due mostly to poverty, lack of education, and other disabilities which he shares with other lower-class persons in the region.

In the South all the laws are written upon the principles of equality. They require services to be "separate but equal." The actual practice, however, is quite different. It is more difficult for Negroes than for whites in similar economic circumstances to get on the relief rolls, and relief grants are often lower for Negroes than for whites. There is an amazing discrimination against Negroes in the segregated school system of the South. Hospitals, libraries, parks, and other recreational facilities are much poorer for Negroes than they are for whites. The streets are not kept up in Negro sections of Southern cities the way they are in white sections, nor is garbage disposal as efficient. Public utility equipment is often less complete in Negro than in white neighborhoods. Police and judicial protection in the South is organized not so much for Negroes as against them. The Negro's representation on public payrolls is almost everywhere—and particularly in regard to high-paid jobs—much smaller than that of whites. As we have seen, there is discrimination against Negroes in agricultural policy. Under the New Deal discrimination in the South was decreased. The fight between Washington and the Southern state and county administrations goes on continually, yet much discrimination remains.

The observer is frequently told by white Southerners that, since Negroes are so poor and pay virtually no taxes, they are not entitled to get more public services than the whites care to give them. Negroes are here considered as an "out-group" not on a par with white citizens. Otherwise the same argument would hold true in regard to poor whites, which is usually not intended.

This popular theory is, of course, contrary to the American Creed and to the Constitution. The discrimination that exists, therefore, has to be carried out against the laws. Rights, in our Western legal order, are given not to a group or to a race but to individuals. An individual's right to receive public services is not related to the actual amount he has paid in taxes. The poor man should share equally in public consumption with the rich, though his taxes are lower.

Furthermore, there are some Negroes who pay quite high taxes, but they, nevertheless, meet discrimination in getting public service. There are whole Negro communities which actually pay more in taxes than is expended upon the particular public services supported by the taxes. Too, there is plain stealing in giving Negroes public services: for example, counties receive state or federal grants on the basis of the school population and misappropriate the funds in favor of the white schools.

Federal agencies or other groups who want to give the Negro his rightful share sometimes propose that Negroes and whites share in the benefits from the public economy in proportion to their numbers. This is in conflict with the Constitution, since it refers to the Negro *group* and does not guarantee *individuals* their rights, but it is a useful measure in the fight against discrimination.

3. EDUCATION

In the North it is taken for granted that schools should have equal standards whether a school is all white, all Negro, or mixed. It is mainly the Negroes' poverty that keeps them from utilizing educational facilities as much as do whites. Negroes migrating from the South to the North settle in the slum areas of Northern cities. Schools in needy districts tend to be somewhat older, less well equipped, and more overcrowded than those in better districts, but the differentials are seldom large.

In the South not only are school facilities in general much poorer, but racial discrimination in the apportionment of school facilities in the South is as spectacular as it is well known. The current expense per pupil in daily attendance per year in elementary and secondary schools in 10 Southern states in 1935–1936 was $17.04 for Negroes and almost three times as much, or $49.30, for white children. In Mississippi and Georgia only about $9 was spent on every Negro school child, but five times more on the average white pupil. Delaware,

Missouri, Oklahoma, and the District of Columbia did not discriminate to such a degree.

This great difference in expenditure per pupil in Negro and white schools comes out in various ways. The most important one has been the great differential in teachers' salaries. According to Johnson, the average annual salary for the Negro public school teacher in the 17 states with compulsory segregation laws was $601 in 1940. The corresponding figure for white teachers was $1,046. Johnson points out, however, that by 1943,

Salary discrimination had been practically wiped out in Maryland and Oklahoma, Kentucky and North Carolina had adopted state-wide equalization programs to wipe out these differentials within the next few years; and Negro teachers had won equalization of salary suits in six Southern states, Virginia, Florida (in four cities), Louisiana, Kentucky, Tennessee, and Texas. Before the year was out, Tennessee and Texas had also adopted state-wide equalization programs and were at work on them.[1]

The only logical argument for these differentials is that Negro teachers are not so well trained as white teachers. Not only are the salary differentials larger than the differences in competence—and they exist even when there is no difference in training—but the argument has the character of a vicious circle. By keeping down all appropriations for all kinds of Negro schools, including teachers' colleges, one can, of course, perpetuate the inferiority of training. Frequently Southern school authorities have gone so far as to hire Negro teachers without teaching certificates because they could have them at substandard salaries.

A second way in which difference in expenditure comes out is in the difference in number of pupils per teacher. In 13 Southern states and the District of Columbia there were 37.7 Negro pupils for every teacher in 1939–1940 as against 29.2 in schools for white children. Third, the per pupil expenditure on teachers' salaries was $13.35 for Negroes, $35.86 for whites. Fourth, the average school term in Negro schools was 156.3 days, and 170.8 days in white schools.[2]

The same discrimination may be noted in whatever item in the school budget is considered. In rural areas there is still a great number of Negro one-teacher and two-teacher schools whereas the consolidation movement has proceeded far in white schools. The value of Negro school property per child in 10 Southern states was scarcely

[1] Reprinted from *Into the Main Stream* (p. 137) by Charles S. Johnson and Associates, by permission of University of North Carolina Press. Copyright, 1947, by University of North Carolina Press.
[2] *Ibid.*

one-fifth of the corresponding figure for whites (1935–1936). This was so in spite of the fact that as much as one-third of the total value of Negro school property was in buildings partly financed by the Rosenwald Fund.[3] Additional savings are made on Negro education because only few Negroes go to high school and still fewer attend public colleges. Southern Negroes who want a decent education and can afford it go to private colleges.

Particularly remarkable is the fact that the differential in school expenditures is often greatest in states which have the highest proportion of Negroes. There is a similar tendency in counties within each state. The explanation is simple. State appropriations for education are usually given on a per capita basis. Counties with a high proportion of Negro children have, consequently, a bigger opportunity to deprive Negro schools of money intended for them and to use it for white schools. If, for instance, there are twice as many Negroes as white children, every dollar per pupil taken from the Negro groups means two dollars per pupil added to the appropriation for the white group.

It is generally said that school segregation increases the cost of the educational system. This is true if the two systems are really "equal" in standards. If the objective is not to have equal standards but one good and one poor system, then segregation becomes a means of economizing.

The whole system of discrimination in education in the South is not only tremendously harmful to the Negroes but is flagrantly illegal. The main organization for guarding civil liberties for Negroes, the National Association for the Advancement of Colored People (N.A.A.C.P.), has recently selected a few areas for attack: equalization of teachers' salaries and the admittance of graduate students to Southern universities. In these fields it is exerting considerable pressure upon Southern authorities. The federal government also is aiding the education of Negroes to a certain extent.

4. Public Health

In spite of the Negroes' greater need for public health services and the interest of the whole society that this need be filled, the pattern of public hospitalization is about the same as that for public instruction. The general level is comparatively high in the North, and

---

[3] Among ordinary white people in the South it is not well known that Northern philanthropic organizations have much of the credit for the fact that Negro education is not lower than it is, and still less is it known that Negro communities often contribute to building their own schools.

Negroes are seldom discriminated against. The general standard of public hospitalization in the South is much lower and there is discrimination against Negroes. Hospitals built with federal or philanthropic money usually do not discriminate, but there are few of these and only in the cities. Rural hospital facilities are totally inadequate almost everywhere in the South, especially for Negroes. There seems to be less discrimination against Negroes—and in many cases none at all—in the so-called out-patient services of public health institutions.

5. RECREATIONAL FACILITIES

The need for wholesome recreation for youth in cities, especially where housing conditions are crowded and unsanitary, incomes low, family life disorganized, and many mothers employed away from home, is very great. This means that, on the average, Negroes have greater need for public recreational facilities than have whites.

In the North there is occasional segregation and discrimination as, for instance, in public swimming pools. In the South segregation and discrimination are the general rule for all recreational facilities. Everywhere in the South beaches, playgrounds, and public parks are often entirely closed to Negroes. Often no substitutes at all, or very inferior ones, are offered the Negroes.

Damaging, from both cultural and recreational viewpoints, are the restrictions of public library facilities for Negroes. In 1939 it was found that of 774 public libraries in 13 Southern states only 99, or less than one-seventh, served Negroes. Of the 99 libraries, 59 were concentrated in four states.

6. PUBLIC HOUSING POLICIES

Recent housing policies have two main aspects: making credit available for private housing (the most important agency for this being the Federal Housing Administration—FHA) and providing public housing for low-income groups. Under the latter program the Negro has received a large share of the benefits, but compared to his need, the program has been only a drop in the bucket.

Certain policies of the FHA, however, have been extremely dangerous to the Negro. Private investors, under the FHA plan, make long-term, low-interest loans for buying or building homes, standards of structure and locations for which are subject to FHA control. Until January 1, 1947, property valuators of the FHA were specifically urged to consider whether the area or property to be insured was protected from "adverse influences," which included "prevention of the infiltration of ... inharmonious racial groups." This and several other antiminority group phrases have now been removed from the FHA *Underwriter's Manual*. It remains to be seen whether the change in instructions will carry over into the day-by-day work.

This matter is a serious one for the Negro. It is one thing when private tenants, property owners, and financial institutions maintain and extend patterns of racial segregation in housing. It is quite another matter when a federal agency sides with the segregationists. It seems probable that the FHA has brought about a greatly increased use of all sorts of restrictive covenants and deed restrictions. It is not only a matter of keeping Negroes and whites apart, but one of keeping the Negro out. Nothing has been done to give the Negro additional new living space which he so badly needs. The urban Negro population is bound to increase, and the present Negro ghettos will not suffice. The Negro will invade new urban territories. Unless these changes are properly planned, they will occur in the same haphazard and friction-causing manner with which we have been only too well acquainted in the past. This, for one thing, will jeopardize the objective of keeping the character of white neighborhoods intact.

7. FAMILY INCOME[4]

The typical Southern Negro farm family has an income of but a few hundred dollars a year. It is considerably lower than that of the average white farm family. This is due, in part, to the fact that Negroes are more concentrated at the bottom of the "agricultural ladder" than are whites. This is not the whole explanation, however, for the income of the average Negro family at any given level of ownership or tenancy is always much lower than is the income of the corresponding average white family. Extremely low, also, are the incomes of most Negro families in the villages and small cities in the South, according to a study made in 1935–1936. Income was higher in the middle-sized and large cities of the South. Nevertheless, half the "normal" Negro families in Atlanta had less than $632 a year and half the broken Negro families had less than $332. White families had more than twice and, in some cities, more than three times as much. Northern cities showed a substantially higher income level for Negroes. In New York City the median income for normal Negro families was $980 and in Chicago it was $726. Moreover, the differ-

---

[4] Substantiation for the facts in this and the next two sections can be found not only in Chapter 16 of *An American Dilemma* but also in Richard Sterner and Associates, *The Negro's Share* (New York: Harper & Brothers, 1943).

ence between whites and Negroes was less than in the South. The
reason for this is that—contrary to common belief—the white urban
population in the North does not have any significantly higher median
incomes than has the white urban population in the South.

It goes without saying that the majority of Negro families are
economically unable to live in a way compatible with any modern
concepts of a "minimum health standard." Although rising wages
have undoubtedly raised the amount of income Negro families now
receive, it is likely that they are worse off in relation to price increases
and no better off in relation to white incomes, except that there is
little unemployment.

Another factor is that Negroes have a greater proportion of large
families than have whites. Yet family income did not show any consistent tendency to be higher when the number of children under 16
in the family was greater. Sometimes it was even lower when there
were more children in the family.

8. The Family Budget

The Negro is generally believed to be an inefficient consumer. The
incomes of most Negroes are not only low but also insecure, which,
of course, makes budgeting and planning discouraging. Many of
them work in hotels, restaurants, and Pullmans where white people
do not always display habits of thrift. Every observer knows that
there is some conspicuous consumption and reckless spending even
among poor Negroes. The answer to such conditions, of course, is
more education and better jobs, not moral indignation.

While Negroes may be ignorant spenders, that can be said of most
of us. One excellent study on the subject, however, finds that Negroes
consistently balance their budgets better than do whites in the same
income groups. While one study, even though carefully done, is not
the final answer, it seems true that the general notions about Negro
improvidence are exaggerated. The Negro population includes a substantial number of families which know how to balance their family
budgets better than the average white family of the same means. To
a greater extent than among comparable white families, Negroes do
their laundry at home rather than send it to a commercial laundry.
Rarely do they hire domestic help; more often do they bake their
own bread; less often do they buy processed foods. They have fewer
cars, washing machines, and vacuum cleaners than have white families in similar economic circumstances—partly, perhaps, because it is
more difficult for them to obtain installment credit. Most of these

things mean that there is more work for Negro women to do in their own homes. Yet they take on gainful work outside their homes to a much greater extent than do white women.

9. HOUSING

Nothing is so obvious about the Negroes' level of living as the fact that most of them suffer from poor housing conditions. The South, generally, has the poorest housing conditions in the country, and in it the Negro farmer is, in every respect, worse off than the white farmer. The Consumer Purchases Study shows that half the white and four out of five of the Negro farm homes in 11 Southern states had foundations in poor condition, and about an equal number had roofs and interior walls and ceilings in poor condition. More than three-fourths of the Negro farm homes were unscreened, and only 3 per cent of all Negro homes—as against 24 per cent of the white homes—had screens which were in good condition. Ten per cent of Negro farm families and over 2 per cent of the white farm families were without any toilet or privy of any kind. This situation has probably improved, however, since federal agencies have, during recent years, built a great number of farm privies in the South.

In Southern villages race differentials in housing are enormous. For example, more than three-fourths of the Negro village families in one study were without any indoor water supply; the proportion of such families in the white group was 15 per cent.

Southern cities, just like Southern rural areas, have, in general, much worse housing conditions than other sections of the country. Negroes are worse off than are whites in both Northern and Southern cities. The National Health Survey shows that in one group of Northern cities studied (Chicago, Cleveland, Detroit, and St. Louis) 27 per cent of the Negro relief households and 21 per cent of the Negro nonrelief families were living in residences where there was no private toilet for each dwelling. The corresponding figures for white relief families and for white nonrelief families with an income of less than $1,000 were 13 and 11 per cent, respectively.

The racial differential in housing accommodations for all income groups combined is great. Let us take just a few examples from recent Real Property Inventories. In Detroit 34 per cent of the Negro-occupied dwelling units were considered to be either unfit for use or in need of major repairs; the same proportion for white-occupied dwelling units was 6 per cent. The corresponding figures for Harrisburg, Pa., were 73 per cent and 14 per cent, respectively; for Norfolk, Va., 25 and 5 per cent and for Savannah, Ga., 55 and 11 per cent. In fact, in cities where there is any appreciable Negro population, the slum problem is largely a Negro problem.

Urban Negro housing is poorer than even the low income of the Negroes would enable them to buy. There is general complaint among Negroes that they have to pay higher rents than do whites for equal housing accommodations; and most housing experts and real estate experts agree. The real reason for this is housing segregation. Particularly when the Negro population is increasing in a city, it is hard to see how this factor can fail to make Negro rents increase more than would be so if the Negroes had been free to seek accommodations wherever in the city they could afford to pay the rent.

After the war, the housing shortage was critical for whites, too, but Negroes fared even worse. For example, a report from the Chicago Mayor's Commission on Human Relations for 1946 said, in regard to Negro housing in Chicago:

. . . Chicago was worse off at the end of 1946 than at the end of 1945. The city had actually lost more dwelling units through fire, simple decay and disintegration than it put up during the year.[5]

[5] New York *Times* (Aug. 10, 1947), p. 15.

Economic Discrimination

and How It Works

1. The Practical Problem of Economic Discrimination

The main practical problem is how to open up new possibilities for Negroes to earn a living. Southern agriculture offers no such new opportunities. On the contrary, it is likely that Southern rural Negroes will continue to be pushed off the land. In Northern agriculture, too, the main trend will be a lessened demand for labor. The segregated Negro economy will never provide any great number of jobs. It is on the ordinary, nonfarm labor market that Negroes will have to look for new opportunities.

In the nonagricultural pursuits, Negro job limitations, as we have found, are of four different types:

(1) Negroes are kept out of certain industries, North as well as South.

(2) In industries where Negroes are working, they are often confined to certain establishments.

(3) In practically all industries where Negroes are accepted, they are confined to unskilled occupations and to such semiskilled and skilled occupations as are unattractive to white workers. Recent gains made during World War II, due to an extreme shortage of labor and the activities of the FEPC, are exceptions.

(4) Finally, there is geographical segregation. Negroes in the North and West are concentrated in a few large cities. Small cities in these regions have few Negroes, and rural areas have practically none.

Race prejudice and discrimination in the economic sphere operate principally in three different ways:

(1) Many white workers, even if they think that Negroes should have a fair share in the job opportunities in this country, are opposed to Negro competition in the localities, industries, occupations, and establishments where they themselves work.

(2) Some customers object to being served by Negroes unless the Negro has an apparently menial position.

(3) Many employers believe that Negroes are inferior as workers, except for dirty, heavy, hot, or otherwise unattractive work. Perhaps even more important is the fact that they pay much attention to the anti-Negro attitudes of both white customers and white workers.

Another general condition behind the Negro's economic plight is the fact that most white people are ignorant about what they have done to the Negro in the economic field. This, of course, is not a "primary cause." It only explains how white people have been able to do what they have done without a bad conscience. We frankly do not believe that the Negro's economic status would have been nearly so bad if white people realized how all specific economic discriminations add up, and how effectively they bar the way for the Negro when he attempts to better himself.

2. THE IGNORANCE AND LACK OF CONCERN OF NORTHERN WHITES

Even in the North the Negro is generally believed to be inferior as a worker. White employees are often against having any Negro coworkers. Yet these attitudes are less widespread and held less strongly in the North than in the South. Many, perhaps even most, Northerners are rather uncertain on such matters. The ideals of equality in the American Creed dominate people's opinions in the North. People in the North are "against" economic discrimination in general. If the white Northerners had to vote on the issue, a large majority would probably come out for full equality of opportunity on the labor market. They would be in favor of making employment opportunities "independent of race, creed, or color." Actual discrimination is, however, as we have seen, the rule and not the exception.

To understand this contradiction, we shall have to remember, first, that slight causes, when they cumulate, may have big effects; second, that the whole issue is enveloped in ignorance and indifference on the part of the whites.[1] The practical conclusion is that Northern

---

[1] The following experiences may serve as illustrations:

"A Negro lad in Minneapolis, Minnesota, had successfully prepared himself in the excellent vocational school of this Midwestern city to become an electrician. As he

whites need more specific education on the effects of their individual discriminations.

There has always been such education, but much of it was general and not specific, although during the war and recently there have been intensive nation-wide efforts to explain the problem to the American people. There are several reasons for thinking that such an educational campaign would be successful in the economic field. For one thing, the ordinary white American is prejudiced mainly when the matter is individual and personal. When he acts as a citizen, he is much more under the control of the American Creed. The labor market, through unionization and social legislation, is increasingly coming under formal regulation. This means that the problem will be one for the citizen rather than for the individual. For another thing, the problem is nation-wide in scope. The white Northerner can feel that the Negroes ought to be in the South. The white urban workers can feel that the Negroes should be in the country, and the white farmer that they should not compete for land. An individual employer or a local trade union may bar Negroes from a particular shop and claim that Negroes should be somewhere else. But on a national scale there is no "somewhere else." Getting employment for Negroes is a concern not only for them but for the nation. The alternative is to let them become public charges. A definite policy becomes a necessity.

---

had been told before he had started to take these courses, he encountered difficulties in getting apprenticeship training and employment in spite of the best personal recommendations and in spite of assistance from the local Urban League. Most of the contractors declared that they themselves had nothing against engaging him. They were not prejudiced, they explained, but they had to abstain on account of occasional customers who were prejudiced.

"I made some inquiries and found that most housewives I questioned did not mind. A few stated that they felt that they rather wanted to have white workers around in the house when something was to be repaired. They did not realize how their slight and unmotivated bias had the cumulated effect of closing employment opportunities to great numbers of Negro youths. They were actually shocked when informed of what they were doing. One young lady announced that she was immediately going to take up the matter in the church club.

"The incident from Minneapolis could be duplicated in any similar Northern city. In Minneapolis at the time of my visit (Christmas, 1939) the majority of Negro workers was unemployed. The total Negro population was estimated to be only four or five thousand in a total population of half a million. The local Urban League worked hard to find employment outlets but with scant success. The white people I met were all well informed about the criminality and viciousness in the Negro slum quarters but, on the whole, totally ignorant about Negro unemployment. They had given practically no thought to the possible causal relations between economic distress and morals."

Also, on a national scale, there is no possibility that Negroes will take over all industrial jobs. An individual employer or the individual group of white workers can always point out that they have to discriminate because everybody else does; otherwise, that particular employer or group would be swamped with Negroes denied opportunity elsewhere. But there is no such excuse in national employment policies. There are 10 per cent Negroes in the population and a little more in the total labor force. White workers will never be overwhelmed. By attacking the color bars everywhere, little change would be needed in any individual establishment to integrate the Negro completely into the economic system. The activities of the national FEPC during the war provide concrete proof. The breakdown of discrimination in one part of the labor market makes similar changes in all other parts of it easier.

Another practical plan would be to encourage the migration of Negroes into small but expanding towns of the North and West. Southern Negro migrants are usually less well suited for transplantation to small Northern cities than are Northern Negroes. Only individually picked, well-educated, and preferably, vocationally trained young Northern Negroes could ordinarily hope to get a permanent foothold in smaller communities. The attempt should be made at such times and in such localities as there is a labor shortage, so that employers would be interested and white workers not hurt by the new competition. Such an organized migration could obviously be carried out only by a federal agency with the support of an educational campaign and the help of local church, school, business, and labor leaders.

3. The Problem of Vocational Training

The fact that Negroes are excluded from so many jobs results in a lack of properly trained Negro workers. In the North, where the vocational branches of the public school system are open without discrimination, the teachers and vocational guidance agencies connected with the schools often advise Negro youths not to take courses in those fields where they will later encounter difficulties in getting apprenticeship and employment.

The advisers are in a difficult dilemma. It must seem unrealistic and even dangerous to the future of young Negroes to encourage them to take vocational training in fields where they will be barred later on. On the other hand, to avoid such training means to accept and strengthen the system of exclusion, since then no Negroes will ever be equipped to challenge it. If the white persons responsible for vocational guidance are themselves a little prejudiced, this will strengthen their inclination to discourage Negro youths from entering these vocations. At the same time they can have good consciences and tell themselves and others that they are absolutely unprejudiced and are acting solely in the best interests of Negro youths. It is not their task to reform American society but to give individual guidance.

4. THE SELF-PERPETUATING COLOR BAR

The vicious circle of job restrictions, poverty, and all that follows with it tends to fix the tradition that Negroes should be kept out of good jobs and held down in unskilled, dirty, or otherwise undesirable work. Residential segregation and segregation at places of work keep whites from having personal acquaintance with Negroes and from recognizing that Negroes are much like themselves. To white workers the Negroes easily come to appear "different," as "low-grade people," and it becomes a matter of social prestige not to work under conditions of equality with them. The fact that Negroes work almost only in menial tasks makes it more natural to look upon them in this way.

Once white workers look upon Negroes as different from themselves and, consequently, do not feel a common labor solidarity with them, "economic interests" will back up discrimination. By excluding Negroes from the competition for jobs, the white workers can decrease the supply of labor in the market, hold up wages, and secure employment for themselves. To give white workers a monopoly on all promotions is, of course, to give them a vested interest in job segregation.

Negroes, on their side, have to try to use every opening, even if it means working for lower wages or under inferior working conditions. The abundance of Negro labor kept idle because of exclusionist policies must always be feared by white workers. If given the chance, Negroes will accept positions as "sweatshop" competitors—something which cannot fail to increase the resentment of the white wage earners. They may even work as "scabs" and so white workers get additional justification for the feeling that Negroes represent danger of "unfair competition." The Negroes react by being suspicious of the white workers and their unions. For this reason, they are sometimes "poor union material" even if white workers choose to let them in on a basis of equality. White union members then resent the "ingratitude" of the Negroes.

The racial beliefs are conveniently at hand to rationalize prejudice and discrimination. With some difficulty white people can be taught that there are all kinds of Negroes as there are all kinds of whites, some good and some bad, and that many—not just a few—individual Negroes are better than many whites. But here the separation between the two groups works strongly against the Negroes. Anyone having to fill a position or a job, having to select a fellow worker at his bench, or a neighbor in the district where he lives, just by drawing a white or a Negro man without knowing anything in particular about him personally will feel that he has a better chance to get the more congenial and more capable man if he selects the white. Here the stereotype of the average Negro in the Northern white man's mind works as an economic bias against the Negro.

5. Getting Negroes into Industrial Jobs

There is great resistance to overcome when attempting to place even highly qualified Negro labor in a plant where Negroes did not work formerly. Negro labor is often, however, superior to the white man's expectation, partly because thinking in averages and stereotypes makes him underestimate the individual Negro. Moreover, the fact that Negroes have great difficulties in getting employment makes it probable that there is a greater proportion of capable workers in the Negro than in the white unemployed labor reserve. Employers who do employ Negroes, therefore, often get a higher appreciation of them as workers than employers who do not. The same seems to be true of white workers. If they work with Negro workers, they come to like them better, or to dislike them less, than they expected to. Under these circumstances we can expect that if Negroes do get into factories where they have not been before, there is a good chance of their staying, because of their own merits.

This has been true in the past. During the First World War the Negro had a chance in the North to enter new fields of employment. During the twenties he fortified his position in these new fields. During the Great Depression, of course, he could not make any further gains, but the remarkable thing is that he kept as well as he did the new positions he had won. During the Second World War the Negro made similar gains.

When, during the recent labor shortage, Negroes were introduced into industries where they had never worked before, a certain amount of friction was expected. Workers are usually conservative and resent competition from new groups, especially in skilled jobs. Yet, experience in World War II proved that it is not impossible to overcome such difficulties. Much depends upon the firmness of the decision of the employers and upon the manner of introducing Negroes. If Negro workers are introduced a few at a time, if they are carefully picked, if the leaders of the white workers are taken into confidence, and if the reasons for the action are explained, then the trouble can be minimized. Now that Negroes have become established in new industries, much depends upon the attitudes both of employers and of unions as to whether they are allowed to keep these gains. We shall discuss this in detail later.

6. In the South

These observations have all referred to the North. The situation in the South is not entirely different, but there are differences. The factors of ignorance and lack of concern are important in the South too. Many white Southerners would back positive measures to create some opportunity for the Negro if they knew more accurately about his plight and the unfavorable trends. But there is in the South a widespread and strong popular theory that the Negro should be kept in his "place." Discrimination in justice, politics, education, and public service creates an atmosphere in which economic discrimination becomes natural or even necessary in order to prevent "social equality."

There are many unfavorable factors for the future of Negro employment in the South, most of which we have mentioned: the pressure of whites on traditional "Negro jobs"; the increase in this pressure due to the high natural increase of the white population in the South and the pushing of white farmers out of Southern agriculture; the concentration of Negroes in unskilled jobs which are subject to mechanization and changes in techniques which make them "suitable" for white workers. In view of all this and the resistance against keeping Negro labor in skilled work or "nice" unskilled work, it is difficult to see much hope for the Negro in Southern industry.

7. The Wages and Hours Law and the Dilemma of the Marginal[2] Worker

During the thirties the danger of being a marginal worker became increased by social legislation intended to improve labor conditions. This legislation included, among other laws, the Wages and Hours Law, the National Labor Relations Act, and the Social Security laws. The dilemma, as viewed from the Negro angle, is this: on the one hand, Negroes, much more than whites, work under imperfect safety

---

[2] "Marginal" is a technical economic term, applied to workers or businesses which are the least demanded by the economy; consequently, the first to be unemployed or to fail.

rules, in unclean and unhealthy shops, for long hours, and for sweat-shop wages; on the other hand, it has largely been the availability of such jobs that has given Negroes any employment at all.

As low wages and substandard labor conditions are most prevalent in the South, this danger is mainly restricted to Negro labor in that region. When jobs are made better, employers become less eager to hire Negroes and white workers become more eager to take the jobs from the Negroes. There is, in addition, the possibility that the policy of setting minimum standards might cause some jobs to disappear altogether or to become greatly decreased. When labor is no longer cheap, mechanization will come in and wipe out many types of jobs. While the great demand for all kinds of labor during the war and the shortage of goods, which enabled even marginal firms to show a profit, have prevented these effects from becoming serious, they are likely to show up in the next few years. This is especially true of mechanization which has been held back by the impossibility of buying new machines during the war years.

Not only were these reform laws necessary, but it is to be expected that there will be more in the future and that present minimum standards will be raised. This means that, if we are not to work hardships on the Negroes in our population, strong countermeasures must be taken to improve employment opportunities for Negroes in the better industrial jobs. Because of the institution of large-scale public assistance in times of need, the government has in addition a fiscal interest in the welfare of the Negro. It seems unlikely that the alternative of letting most Negroes become habitual relief recipients will be permanently accepted.

8. LABOR UNIONS AND THE NEGRO

The increased power of labor unions, and particularly their rising importance for unskilled and semiskilled workers, is to the Negroes a most important recent change in the American economy. Their past experiences with trade unions have been none too good. Recent developments, especially during the war, seem to offer some hope. There is now an increased number of strong unions in which Negroes are included on a basis of equality or near-equality. These more liberal unions have usually tried to break occupational barriers against Negroes and to see that they were promoted on merit.

There is no doubt that the rise in industrial unionism has increased the number of unions which do not discriminate against Negroes. The old unions of this group, like the United Mine Workers' Union and the International Ladies' Garment Workers' Union, have grown stronger, and new ones, like the United Steel Workers' Union and the United Automobile, Aircraft, and Agricultural Implement Workers' Union, have been added. When the C.I.O. organized the mass production industries, it followed the principle that Negroes should be organized together with whites wherever Negroes were working before unionization. They have even followed this principle in their recent organizational campaigns in the South.

There are grave risks, however, in increased union power. A strong union movement holding power over employment might, if dominated by monopolistic and prejudiced workers, be able to keep Negroes completely out of industrial employment. The Negro is a precarious issue for American trade unions. If the unions take Negroes in and treat them as equals, employers often find it advantageous to appeal to the race prejudice of the general public and of the white workers themselves; particularly is this possible in the South. On the other hand, if unions exclude Negroes or otherwise discriminate against them, it may be hard to convince the American public, particularly in the North, of their belief in democracy. It is not that Americans, even outside the South, are so much concerned about the welfare of the Negro; but they are concerned about the integrity and honesty of those who claim to be in favor of social and economic equality. As we have pointed out, the Northern whites are "against" economic discrimination as a general proposition. Even if the general public failed to react this way on its own account, the enemies of trade unionism could always publicize the racial discrimination in trade unions.

Weighing the various factors, however, we are inclined to believe that the growth of unionism will in the long run favor the Negro. Two main reasons for this belief are: (1) that to exclude one group from full participation in the union movement is to put a weapon into the hands of the enemies of trade unionism, which they will know how to use; (2) that the labor market will in all probability be subject to more government control and the national administration will be forced to attempt to defend the Negro's place in the labor market.

9. A WEAK MOVEMENT GETTING STRONG POWERS

All these difficulties must be seen against the background of the fact that American trade unionism, in spite of its age and recent progress, is still a comparatively weak movement. Basically, it is this weakness that endangers the Negro's position.

In 1947 labor unions had only about 15,000,000 members, yet the total labor force outside of agriculture must have amounted to at least 50,000,000. In 1939, just before the beginning of the war boom, there were only about 8,500,000 union members in a total nonagricultural labor force of 44,500,000. A common explanation of why the American labor movement has not developed more strength is that there has been strong resistance from the employers. The resistance from the side of employers, however, is not only a cause of the weakness in the American trade-union movement. To some extent it is also an effect of it. Employers in all countries have initially been hostile to unions, yet other countries have developed strong labor movements.

The readiness shown by some American unions to use violence and other extralegal measures also is a sign of weakness. Strong and well-established unions do not need to condone illegal methods and still less to resort to such methods themselves. All those other excellent reasons with which some American unions, particularly those organized along craft lines, provide the labor-baiters—job monopolism and nepotism, exploitative entrance fees, "closed unions," petty jurisdictional fights, boss rule, even corruption and racketeering—also are nothing more than signs of organizational weakness.

While all young labor movements have had to cope with similar irregularities, it is difficult to understand why they should persist in the American labor movement. They are sometimes said to be "growing pains" or "child diseases" of unionism, but—contrary to the general impression—the American labor movement is one of the oldest in the world and should no longer be having growing pains.

The basic weakness of many labor unions in America has always been their lack of democracy. The rank and file have been allowed too little influence; they have also cared too little about controlling their leaders. As a result, the American labor movement is actually provoking government control. Aside from the irregular practices, the labor movement, because of this weakness, is forced to press for union shops. But such power can be tolerated in a democratic country *only* if the doors to the unions are kept open and if democratic procedures within the unions are amply protected. Congress has recently passed the Taft-Hartley Bill which sets up various types of controls. The only way by which the unions will be able to protect their independence will be to reform themselves quickly.

Either government control or independent democratic control will benefit the Negroes. Another help for the Negro, less harmful to the independence of unions, is prohibition of discrimination by a national or state FEPC. The Negroes themselves are demanding more strongly than ever their share in all sorts of jobs, including those in skilled, clerical, and professional occupations. Much depends on how well they are able to consolidate and improve the gains made during World War II, and this will be considered in the next chapter.

10. The Negro Wage Earner and the War Boom

The Negro has seen his position strengthened since World War II, not only because of the scarcity of labor but also because of a revitalization of the democratic creed. The Negro, however, did not share in the employment gains made by white workers until after 1942. Nor did he make the tremendous gains of the First World War. For several reasons there was no northward migration comparable in size with that of the First World War. Moreover, there was no new industry or previously all-white industry where Negroes made gains of the same importance as they made during the First World War in Northern iron and steel plants, shipyards, automobile factories, and slaughtering and meat-packing houses.

There are several reasons for this:

(1) When the war boom started, there was still widespread unemployment. In the early stages of war production, therefore, there were large numbers of white workers available.

(2) There is now in the North a much better organized resistance to accepting Negroes than there was during the First World War.

(3) Since employers today have to a great extent accepted trade unions as bargaining agents, their need of the Negro as an ally in the fight against unions is much smaller than it was formerly.

(4) The need for unskilled labor is much smaller than it was during the First World War, and most Negroes were unskilled.

It must be considered, further, that the South, as was true during the First World War, received less than its proportionate share of war contracts. The reason, of course, is that heavy industries are less well represented below the Mason and Dixon line than they are in other parts of the country.

11. A Closer View

In spite of all these limitations, Negroes made considerable gains during the war, especially after 1942. By the end of the war, for one thing, anybody who wanted a job could get one of some kind. In addition, for the first time, Negroes made real inroads into skilled and semiskilled jobs. Weaver gives the following figures:

In 1940 . . . only 4.4 per cent of all male Negro workers were in skilled industrial jobs; in 1944, the figure was 7.3 per cent. In 1940, about

13 per cent of the same group was in semi-skilled industrial work; by 1944, the figure was 22.4 per cent . . . . Really significant gains occurred in single-skilled and semi-skilled occupations. In 1940, for example, Negro males were 5.9 per cent of all male operatives; four years later, they were 10.1 per cent. Negro women constituted 4.7 per cent of all female operatives; in 1944, they were 8.3 per cent of the total.[3]

One of the most important gains Negroes (especially Negro women) made was in government service.

In Washington in 1938 less than 8.5 per cent of the federal employees were colored and 90 per cent of the Negroes were in subclerical capacities. By November, 1942, about 17 per cent of the federal workers in Washington were Negroes, and almost half of the colored employees were in clerical and professional capacities. (These figures must be considered in light of the fact that over 20 per cent of Washington's population is Negro.) [4]

Weaver points out, however, that over 98 per cent of the clerical and sales force in the country remained white; about 95 per cent of the professional and managerial jobs are still held by whites.[5]

As in the past, the industries that delayed employing Negroes longest were light and clean manufacturing, which employed mainly white women.[6] As was to be expected, the Negroes made far greater gains in the North than in the South. While there was plenty of employment at relatively high wages, especially in the shipyards of the South, for the most part Negroes were confined to unskilled jobs, except those jobs which had traditionally been held by Negroes. One important thing to notice about the wartime employment of Negroes is that they were much more concentrated in areas of critical labor shortage than were whites. This means that they probably suffered more unemployment during the short period of reconversion in those areas than did whites; also, their future chances in such surplus labor areas are not likely to be very good.

Although the Negro did not make permanent inroads into the new industries he entered, such as the aircraft and ordnance industries, he did succeed in getting into semiskilled and skilled jobs in industries where he already had a foothold, such as the steel and automobile industries. Since he has traditionally been in these industries and since the unions in these industries have an excellent record of helping the Negro, it is likely he will keep these gains.

[3] Robert C. Weaver, *Negro Labor, A National Problem* (New York: Harcourt Brace & Company, 1946), pp. 79–81.
[4] *Ibid.*, p. 137.
[5] *Ibid.*, p. 81.
[6] *Ibid.*

Perhaps the most important single change for the Negro is that a large percentage of Northern industrial workers have acquired some skill, through defense training, through upgrading and on-the-job training in industry, and to some slight extent in the Army and Navy. For the first time, too, Negro women have moved out of domestic service into other jobs, clerical jobs in Washington, and positions of waitress, cook, hairdresser, and similar jobs. Although these last listed are low-paid service jobs, they can still be considered superior to domestic service in salary, dignity, and job requirements.

These real and important gains made by Negroes were due partly to the great need for labor in the last two years of the war. Even so, it took action by the federal government to bring about employment of Negroes in many cases. Whether the Negro will be able to hold his recently acquired position now that the federal government has withdrawn is a moot question.

12. GOVERNMENT POLICY IN REGARD TO THE NEGRO IN WAR PRODUCTION

The failure to let the Negro participate fully in war production during the first years of the war did not go unnoticed. The Negroes were embittered and, being better organized than ever before, protested strongly. In addition, well-known public leaders, like Wendell Willkie, Pearl Buck, and Eleanor Roosevelt, dealt with the problem repeatedly.

The government made various attempts to straighten out the matter, most of them ineffectual; some were just gestures, which could not possibly appease the Negro leadership. In January, 1941, A. Philip Randolph, president of the Brotherhood of Sleeping Car Porters, started organizing his famous "March-on-Washington Movement." President Roosevelt, for reasons of both internal and external policy, did not want any such protest march and talked to Randolph in June, 1941, in order to prevent it. Randolph, however, failed to come around until the President agreed to sign an executive order "with teeth in it" abolishing discrimination in defense industries as well as in the federal government itself.

Executive Order 8802, of June 25, 1941, started with a general statement to the effect that there shall be no discrimination in the employment of workers in defense industries or in government because of "race, creed, color, or national origin." There was a clause to this effect in all defense contracts. The order contained, further, a confirmation of previous orders about nondiscrimination in defense training programs. Finally, a President's Committee on Fair Employment

Practice (FEPC) was set up for the purpose of receiving and investigating complaints of discrimination in violation of the order. In addition, certain Northern states took similar measures against racial discrimination, supplementing those of the federal government. Frequently state agencies went even further than the federal agencies, since they dealt not only with war industries but also with the policies of the public employment services, with private employment agencies, and with advertisements for workers in newspapers.

Although the powers of the FEPC were limited (it could hold public hearings, remind government services of their duty, and cite offenders to the President) and its personnel and funds even more so, it did much to stop economic discrimination. Several thousand cases were successfully resolved, almost all by committee field representatives in unpublicized negotiations.

The FEPC was killed by Congress in the spring of 1946, and a permanent FEPC has not as yet been enacted although both parties were pledged to it in 1944. There is some scattered evidence to show that in 1946, after the FEPC was closed, Negroes were generally being dropped from government service, that white workers were disproportionately being retained at higher paid jobs, and that the United States Employment Service consistently referred Negroes to low-paid jobs only.[7] Fortunately, some of the states have taken over the problem by passing state FEPC laws; six states—Massachusetts, Connecticut, New York, New Jersey, Indiana, and Wisconsin—have already passed such laws and there are bills pending in many more, although undoubtedly all of them will not pass. Some cities, for example Minneapolis, also have local FEPC laws.

13. The Negro in the Armed Forces

Experience in the armed forces during World War II meant a great deal to Negroes. Probably over a million young Negroes were "employed" in the armed forces, where they found food and clothing good, and the pay higher than that available to them in most civilian occupations. The travel and the diverse social conditions which Negroes experienced in the armed forces was broadening for most of them. Some were able to better their formal education.

But there is also a dark side to their wartime experiences. There was a definite reluctance to utilize Negroes in all branches of the service, and they were concentrated in the dirty and hard service jobs

[7] The material in the last two paragraphs has been taken from Malcolm Ross, "The Outlook for a New FEPC: The 80th Congress and Job Discrimination," *Commentary*, 3 (April, 1947), 301–308.

(road building, supply distribution, ship loading, and so on). While in the States, they were—like white soldiers—concentrated largely in the South, where they usually met hostile community attitudes. The armed services have practiced segregation, except in nonoperating outfits like officers' training camps, hospitals, and replacement depots, and except for the experimental employment of mixed combat outfits during the last three months of the war in Europe. In great measure, the Negro was kept out of combat, even to the extent of giving combat-trained outfits service jobs. Inferior white officers were often foisted on Negro outfits, and for a while Negroes who tried to become officers were strongly discouraged. In Europe there were some efforts made to keep Negroes from fraternizing with the civilian population, when no such bar was set up against the white troops. All this helped to embitter the Negro. He felt that he was not wholeheartedly wanted by white America even when he offered to fight for it.

From every war there are numerous records of Negroes who have distinguished themselves for bravery and gallantry. Negroes cherish these memories. An outsider occasionally gets the impression that they sometimes exaggerate their significance; but this is very likely just a natural human reaction in view of all the contempt Negroes have experienced from most whites. Deliberate attempts have been made to minimize the Negro's military record.

After the First World War the Negro became an insignificant element in the armed forces. There were no Negroes in the Marines, and the Navy took them only as stewards. Negroes were allowed representation in the Army, but less well, proportionately, than whites. In 1940 there were only two Negro combat officers in the Regular Army and none in the Navy.

In October, 1940, the War Department announced that Negro personnel should be increased in such a way that Negroes would constitute the same proportion in the Army as in the general population of the country; and, further, that Negroes would be represented in all major branches of the Army. While Southern draft boards held down the induction rate for a while, and more Negroes than whites were found to be disqualified for military service, Negroes gradually did form a proportionate share of the Army. In both Army and Navy they did get into combat branches of service, but not in proportion to their population or to their qualifications. On September 30, 1944, there were close to 800,000 Negroes in the Army (including the Air Forces) and more than 5,000 commissioned officers. As of September, 1945, the Navy had 165,000 Negroes and 52 commissioned officers. A few Negroes were in the Coast Guard and the Marines. Negro women were allowed into the women's branches of the Army, Navy and Coast Guard, but not in that of the Marines.[8]

The two chief problems of Negroes in the Army during the later years of the war were incidents of friction and segregation. It is frequently hard to allocate blame when Negro and white troops clash, but there are numerous instances where white officers have been able to eliminate racial friction by impartial treatment and enforcement of the rules. The majority of white soldiers wanted segregation, but, besides being an affront to Negroes, the armed services often found it extremely inefficient to maintain. During the late months of the war in Europe, when the need for combat troops was great and there were no Negro combat units to which newly trained Negro combat soldiers could be attached, the Army experimented with putting Negro platoons in otherwise white companies, with white officers and even white noncoms. The experiment was successful, in terms of the praise received from the white leaders and other white soldiers in the mixed companies.

The War Department, through its Gillem Board (formed after the war to set future policy on Negroes), was forced to take cognizance of this success, and lip service was given to the principle of nonsegregation. However, the Army retains segregation, although it now allows no separate Negro unit larger than a regiment. The Navy, which had always been more backward in its treatment of Negroes, suddenly became liberal toward them in 1945. The Navy even approved a congressional bill in 1947 to abolish segregation in the armed forces, while the Army opposed it.

14. The Postwar Period

What will be the Negro's economic lot in postwar America? There is no definite answer to the question, of course, but we can list some of the main factors entering into the problem.

The more the Negroes gained during the war the more will they have advanced themselves permanently; and even if, during a later development, they have to give up some ground, they are not likely to be driven back as far as they would have been had their previous gains been smaller. Conversely, the more they lose during the next unemployment crisis the smaller chance will they have of reaching anything near full employment during a subsequent period of labor shortage. In regard to the Negro's economic status, we need to em-

[8] Florence Murray (editor), *Negro Handbook 1946–1947* (New York: Current Books, Inc., A. A. Wyn, Publisher, 1947), pp. 325–326.

phasize the significance of what happens during the short-term development. The Negro's position in the American economic system depends in a large measure on traditions which have actually become settled because of rather accidental happenings.

Of paramount importance will be the general level of employment. The Negroes' hope of becoming integrated into American industry is much greater if the American economy is geared to a full utilization of its productive forces. Should there be widespread unemployment for a long period, it may be concentrated on the Negro. On the other hand, a severe economic depression will certainly be fought by the government. The Negro will have to be considered in this. As always, he will be unemployed much more often than the white worker. As time goes on, it will become more apparent that either the Negro will have to be cared for as a more or less permanent relief client or positive measures must be taken for his integration into the regular economy.

Another important factor is the position of the labor unions. The attempt by Congress to weaken the national power of unions may have unhappy results for the Negro. Many times in the past, it has been the strong and more liberal national union officers who have enforced the no-discrimination policy. If unions are weakened, especially the national unions, there will be one less among the few forces working to integrate Negroes into American industry. Too, some of the most potent anti-Negro forces in the American community are, at the same time, antilabor, and a decrease in labor's power will strengthen the anti-Negro forces. In politics, white industrial workers will have more to gain by siding with the Negro.

Much more generally, the Negroes' economic fate will depend upon the popular attitudes toward race in America. There are two favorable developments in this respect: (1) Negroes today are strongly organized and are pressing hard for economic equality; (2) the ideological shake-up of the war has convinced many white groups which were formerly indifferent that democracy in America must be made to work and that removing the obstacles to equal economic opportunity for Negroes is a good place to start. In addition, on the favorable side, can be listed the fact that the Negro is better qualified in training and experience than ever before; that during the war both white employers and white workers had favorable experience with Negroes as employees and fellow workers; and finally, that, in the South, there is a political upheaval, centered about the position of the Negro, greater than anything since the Civil War. The outcome, of course, can go either way, but there is a 50-50 chance for the Negro's economic opportunities, at least, to be improved.

CHAPTER IX

The Basic Political Factors

1. THE NEGRO IN AMERICAN POLITICS AND AS A POLITICAL ISSUE

This chapter is confined to politics in the narrow sense, that is, the vote, political parties, and political rewards. We concentrate on the South, not only because most of the Negro people live there but because the South is the only region where Negro suffrage is a problem.

The value premise in this chapter is the doctrine of political equality among all citizens of the United States. This is prominent in both the American Creed and the American Constitution. By political discrimination and, specifically, disfranchisement we mean withholding the vote from citizens merely because they are Negroes.

In early colonial times, free Negroes apparently enjoyed the same civic rights and duties as poor white people, but by the time of the Civil War, Negroes were disfranchised until they could vote only in five New England states and, in some cases, in New York. As a result of the Civil War and the Reconstruction Amendments, Negro men were given the vote throughout the United States. In the North this change became permanent. In the South, where most Negroes lived and still live, it was rapidly undone.

While the Negroes have been kept out of politics in the sense that they have been kept from voting, in another sense, namely, as a political issue, they have been an important factor in the very region where they cannot vote, the South.

The issue of "white supremacy versus Negro domination," as it is called in the South, has for more than a hundred years stifled freedom of thought and speech and affected all other civic rights and liberties of both Negroes and whites in the South. It has retarded the South's economic, social, and cultural advance. On this point there is virtual agreement among all competent observers.

In the North, on the contrary, the Negro has nowhere and never been a political issue of primary and lasting importance—except in so far as he has been an issue in national politics. The issue has, then, always been the Negro's status in the South or, earlier, the South's struggle to widen the area over which its concept of the Negro would prevail.

2. The North

In the North, Negroes have the vote like other people and there is nowhere a significant attempt to deprive them of the franchise. Although Negroes were not allowed to vote in many places in the North until after the Civil War, once the franchise was granted, it seems to have become rooted in the order of things. The Northerner's attitudes toward suffrage and equality in justice are two areas in Negro-white relations where he acts absolutely according to the American Creed.

In explaining this we have to consider that voting is a formal relationship between a citizen and the officials representing society. The Northerner, as has been mentioned, tends to adhere to the American Creed in impersonal things and to slip away from it when it involves personal relationships.

Another relevant fact is that the Negroes in the North—as well as unpopular immigrant groups—are clustered mostly in the big cities where people are conditioned not to be concerned much about one another. These cities have often been dominated by political machines. The machines find the Negroes and the immigrant groups easy to handle. The politicians, therefore, have no reason to try to eliminate the Negro vote.

Whether or not these explanations are adequate, it seems to be a fact that Negroes can feel sure that, unless this country undergoes a revolution, their right to vote will remain unquestioned in the North, regardless of any migration from the South. Without doubt, this is one of the best protections of the Negro people in American society. The Negro vote in the North is already of considerable importance. It could become of much greater importance were it more wisely used. As the educational level of the Negro people is being raised and as the northward migration is continuing, it might become powerful enough within the next couple of decades to demand some real reward, not only in local Northern politics but also in national politics. The Northern vote might become the instrument by which the Negroes can increasingly use the machinery of federal legislation and administration to tear down the walls of discrimination.

3. THE SOUTH

The white people's attitude in regard to Negro suffrage in the South is complicated. Before the Civil War the South developed an elaborate theory to justify slavery. In this theory all whites, independent of their rank in society, were superior to the slaves. Politically whites were all equals, since they were free citizens. The poorer classes of whites were generally ignorant, dependent, and living in deep poverty. The only thing they did have was "white supremacy." When they heard that the North wanted to free the Negro slaves, and when they sensed the danger of being thrown into competition with the black masses, the great majority of poor whites felt a sense of solidarity with the slaveholders.

The defeat in the Civil War did not break the general direction of Southern political thinking. The strong measures taken by the victorious North to reform the South quickly favored the consolidation of reactionary forces. This consolidation became particularly effective in disfranchising the Negroes when the North no longer wished to bear the costs and the inconveniences of upholding its military regime indefinitely.

The former Negro slaves, therefore, started their new life as free citizens with solid mistrust against them. The very idea of giving the vote to Negroes was, to the average Southerner, preposterous. The white South wanted the Negroes to fail as freedmen and saw in their failure a confirmation of their own wisdom and the Northerners' folly.

But the North was in power and the right of the Negro to vote was included in the Constitution. Thus Southern conservatism started with the law against it. As the Southern conservatives did not have the power to overthrow the fundamental laws of the land, they had through generations, and have today, to oppose law and order. The American South is the only place in the world today where one can get a reputation for being a liberal simply by urging obedience to law, and where conservatives regularly violate the law.

The abolition of slavery had to be accepted as an accomplished fact throughout the South. The Fourteenth and Fifteenth Amendments, which granted the Negroes civil rights and suffrage, were not so readily accepted by Southern opinion. They were looked upon as the supreme foolishness of the North and, worse still, as an expression of ill-will of the Yankees toward the defeated South. The Negro vote became the symbol of humiliation of the South.

But it was not until the 1890's that the Negroes were disfranchised

by new laws requiring property, poll tax payments, literacy, understanding of the Constitution, good character, and so on, before being
allowed to vote. These were openly declared to aim at getting around
the new amendments to the Constitution.[1] But keeping the Negroes
disfranchised in the face of the clear-cut constitutional amendments
allows Southern conservatism nothing more than a pretense of respect
for the law. On this most crucial point it is doomed to insincerity.

4. MEMORIES OF RECONSTRUCTION

A view of the various devices by which the Negroes are kept from
voting in the South today shows a shocking picture of legal trickery,
unfair administration, intimidation, and outright violence. In explanation of this the Southerner will regularly bring forward the horrors
of the Reconstruction governments and "black domination." These
memories are cherished.

The Southerner's picture of the period following the Civil War,
which is popularly shared by Northerners, does not square with the
facts. The "carpetbaggers" were not Northerners who came down to
prey on the devastated South. The great majority of them were either
agents sent out by the federal government to try to help the South to
its feet under the principles of the Constitution and its amendments
or they were New England Abolitionists, often spinsters, who came
to educate the Negroes. The federal government did not send its
agents to the South until 1867 after the South had demonstrated for
over two years that it was determined to retain slavery in fact if not
in name. It is true that these carpetbaggers did some stupid things,
that their plans were vague and inconsistent, and that the federal government failed to give them adequate backing.

[1] James Weldon Johnson makes the following statements:

"Not so long ago, in a widely circulated weekly magazine, Senator George, formerly
a member of the Supreme Court of Georgia, was quoted as saying in the course of an
interview:

" 'Why apologize or evade? We have been very careful to obey the letter of the
Federal Constitution—but we have been very diligent and astute in violating the
spirit of such amendments and such statutes as would lead the Negro to believe himself the equal of a white man. And we shall continue to conduct ourselves in that
way.'

"Senator Glass was quoted by the same interviewer as saying:

" 'The people of the original thirteen Southern States curse and spit upon the
Fifteenth Amendment—and have no intention of letting the Negro vote. We obey the
letter of the amendments and the Federal Statutes, but we frankly evade the spirit
thereof—and purpose to continue doing so. White supremacy is too precious a thing
to surrender for the sake of a theoretical justice that would let a brutish African deem
himself the equal of white men and women in Dixie.' " ("A Negro Looks at Politics,"
The American Mercury, 18 [September, 1929], 92.)

The "scalawags" were mainly poor and ignorant native Southerners who saw a chance—in the South's defeat—to effect something of a revolution against the relatively few wealthy aristocrats. But many of them had honestly and consistently wanted the abolition of slavery. Some of them had favored the Union cause throughout the Civil War when it was extremely unpopular to do so. Not a few of them were backwoodsmen who followed the Jacksonian tradition.

The masses of Negroes were, of course, uneducated, and a number of them were resentful. But they never engaged in organized violence against the whites. They were led by the educated carpetbaggers and by the free Southern and Northern Negroes who had quite often attained a high level of education. Actually, there were only 22 Negro members of Congress from 1870 to 1901; 10 of these had gone to college. The Northern Republicans came in for their share of hatred. For example, few names in American history have come down with such an evil reputation as that of Thaddeus Stevens, the leader of the Republican party in the House of Representatives until his early death in 1868. There is evidence that Stevens had an enlightened plan of social reform far in advance of his time and that he was not at all violent in inciting Negroes to reform the South.

The myths about the Reconstruction period are found in most school textbooks, and to a lesser extent in scholarly histories. They still give undue emphasis to the sordid details of the Reconstruction governments but avoid mentioning their accomplishments. They exaggerate the extent of "black domination," while they give subtle excuses for the cruelty and fraud employed in the restoration of white supremacy.

There is a purpose in this distortion of the facts. The Southerner resents the thought of Negroes voting on a par with white men. Yet the Constitution is clear in specifying that no one is to be kept from voting for reasons of "race, color, or previous condition of servitude." Thus the Southerner is forced to circumvent the Constitution if he is to keep the Negro from voting. But the Constitution and its principles have a grip on the Southerner's own soul. He, therefore, needs to believe that when the Negro voted life was unbearable. The myth of the horrors of Reconstruction thus permits the Southerner to reconcile two conflicting desires within himself. This we call a false belief with a purpose.

5. The Tradition of Illegality

While, as we said, the Northerner is likely to be less inclined to discriminate against the Negro the more formal and impersonal the relationship, the white Southerner is inclined to react in nearly the opposite way. From Reconstruction on, voting was to the white Southerner more than a mere action; it was, and still is, a symbol of superiority. Partly because it is a public activity and does not lend itself to privacy or segregation, it becomes hard for the white Southerner to admit the Negro to full participation in it. This is one side of the general difference between the two regions: the white Northerners may dislike and ignore the Negro but are prepared to give him his formal rights, while in the South even individual whites who like and care for Negroes will not give them their rights because this would imply equality.

In order to understand Southern conservative illegality fully, we must remember that the actual trickery, cheating, and intimidation necessary for the smooth operation of disfranchisement need be engaged in by only a small number of people. Most people can avoid it. All they need do is preserve public sentiment upholding and supporting the illegal system. In most cases, a resolute election registrar can himself take care of the matter. And he does not need to act openly when it has once become generally known among Negroes in a community that they had better keep away from all political matters.

The illegal practices also have a long tradition behind them: vigilante organizations such as the Ku Klux Klan and a great number of "protective" leagues and secret terror organizations, which grew up in the Reconstruction period, successfully used violence in preventing Negroes from voting. After the overthrow of the Reconstruction governments in all Southern states, which was accomplished by 1877, a tendency to abstain from violence and threats of violence, as a means of keeping the Negroes away from the polls, gradually developed. The dominant white Southerner found it easier to buy, steal, or fail to count the Negro vote or to block the Negroes' voting by intricate election laws and manipulation of the election machinery. The Reconstruction governments, themselves, had done much of this, and the conservatives of the seventies took over and perfected the existing techniques. But already before the Civil War the white South had gradually been conditioned for at least thirty years to increased suppression of freedom of speech and all other civil liberties in the service of upholding its solidarity.

Thus, disrespect for law, order, and public morals has complicated causes and a deep-rooted history in the South. It is certainly one of the worst heritages of the region. It spells danger for a democratic society and involves serious maladjustments.

6. The "Solid South"

Except for a short period after the Civil War, the South has always deprived the Negro of the vote and has had to cling to the Democratic party to do so. The suppression of the normal two-party system has given the region the name "Solid South." In spite of state provisions for disfranchising the Negro and, in addition, the illegal social pressures, the greater part of the white South still does not dare to have political division lest the white factions be tempted to seek Negro support. The irony of the situation is that the disfranchisement of the Negro had been argued as the only means of preventing corruption at the polls and of allowing the whites to divide along natural political lines. The second goal is obviously not reached, as the one-party system is still retained. Since the one-party system is the only guarantee against Negro voting, the elimination of it would be the basis for freedom of the whites to split. To prevent corruption under a one-party system in a region with the unfortunate traditions of the South—when it is so difficult everywhere in America even when an opposition party is present—is practically impossible. In this vicious circle Southern politics is caught.

The one-party system in the South, its supporting election machinery with its restrictions, intricacies, and manipulations, its vast allowances for arbitrary administration, and the low political participation of even white people favor rule by a few people. This is broken here and there, now and then, by demagogues, from Tom Watson to Huey Long, who appeal to the lower classes among the whites. The ruling class consists of the big landowners, the industrialists, the bankers, and the merchants. Northern corporate business with big investments in the region has lately been sharing in political control.

There is an amazing avoidance of issues in Southern politics. The chief direct reason for this is, of course, the one-party system, which normally keeps politics within a single political machine and restricts political struggle to personalities and offices. The Southern conservatives argue that unless the whites sink their differences on social and moral issues and present a united front against the Negro, the days of Reconstruction will be repeated. It is not the Negro himself who is feared, but white politicians who might be tempted to use the Negro vote. Even more important, the whites must keep political control because they are the superior race and cannot submit to domination by an inferior one.

Southern liberals hammer away against these arguments. They

point out that the one-party system fosters mediocrity, demagoguery, political apathy, and irrationality. They point out that the fear of the Negro shadows every political discussion and prevents the whites from doing anything to improve themselves. The conservatives answer that the Southern system does allow for political division—in the primaries, though not in the general elections. This, however, is a myth which Southerners have carefully fostered: in 1940 only 36 of the 78 Democratic primaries—less than half—were contested in the eight poll tax states.

But undoubtedly there are sometimes real divisions in the South on interests and issues: poor people against rich, the hill country against the plantation lands, the coast against the inland. But the fact that the issues have to be fought out under cover of personalities and within a one-party machine must, particularly in a region of inadequate political education, confuse those issues. It has, indeed, been the tradition and the spirit of the Solid South to have such confusion. The newspapers usually respect this tradition. They publish the generalities contained in the various candidates' platforms and speeches but usually abstain from giving information on any real issues that might be involved.

Even admitting, therefore, that the one-party system allows for a certain number of issues and divisions, it must be maintained that, to a considerable degree, the one-party rule of the South destroys healthy democratic politics, both in national and in local affairs.

7. Southern Conservatism

Democratically organized people's movements, giving voice to the needs of the simple citizen and a power basis for his full participation in the control of society, do not thrive in this political atmosphere. There have been few spontaneous movements to improve the well-being of the masses of people, such as trade unions or adult education. Even farmers' co-operatives have been lagging in the South. All modern reform movements which have penetrated the rest of the country and gradually changed American society—woman suffrage and economic equality, collective bargaining, labor legislation, progressive education, child welfare, civil service reform, police and court reform, prison reform—have until recently hardly touched the greater part of the South except in so far as the federal government has imposed them from the outside. In particular, there has been no active participation of the masses.

This political conservatism is directly tied up with the Negro problem in several ways. The devices used to deprive the Negro of the vote, the one-party system, low political participation of the white masses, and other peculiarities of Southern politics, all give a large share of power to classes, groups, and individuals who feel their interests tied up with conservatism in social issues. But there is a more direct connection between Southern conservatism and the Negro problem. For constitutional and other reasons, social reform measures have to include Negroes, and this is resented. The conservative opponents of reform proposals can usually discredit them by pointing out that they will improve the status of Negroes and that they prepare for social equality. The poor white Southerners have been prepared to pay the price of their own distress in order to keep the Negro still lower.

In addition to technical factors and the constitutional barriers of making social legislation openly discriminatory, there is also the sense of rationality and fairness in the minds of the Southerners themselves. As the South is now gradually accepting social reform, it will also have to give up a considerable part of its discrimination against the Negroes both in principle and in practice.

8. Is the South Fascist?

On account of the one-party system and the weak condition of civil liberties, the South is sometimes referred to as fascist. This is, however, wrong. The South entirely lacks the centralized organization of a fascist state. Southern politics is decentralized and often chaotic. The "regimentation" that keeps the South politically solid is not an organization *for* anything; it is a regimentation *against* the Negro.

Fundamentally the white Southerner is—like the Negro, who is molded in the same civilization—even more of an individualist and a romantic than the Northerner. There is "an intense distrust of, and, indeed, downright aversion to, any actual exercise of authority beyond the barest minimum essential to the existence of the social organism," according to W. J. Cash.[2] The Southerner wants and expects a personal touch, a measure of arbitrariness and, indeed, of adventure in all his relations with public authorities. He wants them to be informal, considerate, and personalized.

The South has not yet reached the objectivity and legality of the mature democracy. But still less does it resemble the tight, totalitarian regimentation of the fascist state. Fundamentally, the South is a stubbornly lagging American frontier society with a strong paternalistic

[2] *The Mind of the South* (New York: Alfred A. Knopf, 1941), p. 33.

tinge inherited from the old plantation and slavery system. Paternalism is cherished particularly as the ideal relation between whites and Negroes. The Southerner is proud of his benevolence toward Negro dependents but would resent vigorously their demanding this aid as a right.

Registrars and other country officials in the South show surprising indifference to, and sometimes brazen ignorance of, the laws and formal procedures. They are systematically careless, and are proud of it. Even political discrimination against the Negro is haphazard and accidental in this romantic and individualistic region. Most of the time the Negro is not allowed to register or to vote, and he might risk anything up to his life in attempting to do it. But sometimes he is allowed: because he is a "good nigger," because "he has the right," because his voting "proves" that there is no discrimination, or for no particular reason at all, or just for the fun of doing the opposite of what is expected.

Related to the South's individualism and frontier heritage is its strong democratic temper—except toward the Negro. Even if the South until this day is under the political control of a ruling class, this group always has to appeal to the common white man as an equal in order to remain in power.

Religion also tends to create a feeling of equality among human beings in the South—not even excluding the Negroes. An even stronger influence has been created by the American Creed. Despite all professions to the contrary, the acceptance in principle, even by the conservative white Southerners, of the American Creed explains why so many exceptions are made to the rule of excluding Negroes from voting. It opens many possibilities for the Negro people to increase their political participation. It makes it possible that the barrier against them might, in the future, fall altogether. Because of the Creed, the Negroes in the South are getting some education, and are gradually getting more. Because of the Creed, Southern discrimination against the Negroes in the local application of New Deal measures was not extreme. Without the Creed, it would be inexplicable why the South, with all its traditions of inequality and illegality, is on the way toward social democracy and law observance and why it is not headed the other way. The conservative Southerner is not so certain as he sometimes sounds. He is a split personality. Part of his heart belongs to the American Creed. The Southern conservative white man's faith in American democracy and the Constitution, which he is not living up to, is a living force of great importance for the future.

9. THE CHANGING SOUTH

The South is changing rapidly. During the thirties the changes went into high speed and the effect of the war was to increase this speed. It is easy to give the false impression that the South is static. There are two main causes of this illusion. One is the extremely low starting point in all respects—general education, political culture, economic standards—of the South at the end of the Civil War. The second cause is a curious tendency of Southerners to stress in conversation and literature that customs are strong and that there is much resistance to change. Things are actually changing in the South, but the average Southerner does not seem to believe in the changes that are going on right before his own eyes.

Industrialization and urbanization are proceeding at a greater speed in the South than in other parts of the country. Agriculture in the South is facing a more thoroughgoing adjustment to world market conditions than is the case elsewhere, and this change means more to the South because its economy is based on agriculture to a great extent. Unionization is proceeding in spite of all impediments.

The economic depression of the thirties meant distress everywhere, and particularly in the poor backward South. The South accepted the New Deal partly because it was sponsored by the traditional party of the Solid South, and even more so because the South was too poor to scorn systematically the gifts of national charity. Not overlooking the discrimination against Negroes in the local administration of New Deal and wartime measures in the South, we must see that a lasting break in Southern racial practices was made.

The whole nation has become somewhat aware that the Negro problem in the South affects other regions. Southern congressmen—because of their longer tenure in office and consequent importance in committee assignments—exert a disproportionate influence on legislation. The North is beginning to feel that it can no longer ignore what goes on in the South.

If we note further that the long-run trend in the South toward a higher general level of education and cultural participation of both Negroes and whites is steadily proceeding, we have accounted for the main reasons for change in the Southern political situation. No Yankee will be tactless enough to mention it, in so many words, and no Southerner can afford to admit it, but the main thing happening to the South is that it is gradually becoming Americanized.

10. SOUTHERN LIBERALISM

Southern liberalism is not liberalism as it is found elsewhere in America. For one thing, it gets its power from outside the South. For decades Southern liberals have been acting as the trusted advisers and executors of the Northern philanthropists who wanted to do something for the region. During the thirties they were entrusted to bring the New Deal into effect in the South. The power and prestige of this function and, even more, the recent changes in the South have given them high political importance.

As social change increases in the South, the future of Southern liberalism might become great. But it must be recognized that, outside the sphere dominated by Washington, its actual influence today on Southern politics is still minor. It has as yet little organized support among the broad masses of workers, farmers, and the lower middle class. The liberals are the intellectuals of the region and are responsible for a large part of the high-grade literary, journalistic, and scientific output of the region. Here and there they have influenced state and local affairs to a limited extent. But nowhere in the South are they in power. A few, however, have reached out into national politics, where distance apparently makes them more acceptable to the Southern electorate. But for the most part Southern liberalism has its main stronghold in a few universities and among newspaper editors, both found most often in the Upper South. Other liberal groups—some book writers, some professionals, such organizations as the League of Women Voters, union officials, interracial commissions—may have limited local influence in a liberal direction. The Southern Conference on Human Welfare and the Southern Regional Council are trying to draw these liberal forces together and strengthen their influence.

When attempting to map the political opinions of white Southern liberalism, it must first be recalled that the region is exceptional in Western civilization since the Enlightenment in that it lacks nearly every trace of radical thought. The second main consideration when judging Southern liberalism is that the liberals are definitely a political minority. This accounts for the rather academic nature of liberal thinking in the South. Until recently Southern liberals planned their programs without thinking in terms of pressure politics and without taking account of practical details. For the same reason—lack of expectation of being in power—the Southern liberal has become inclined to stress the need for patience, to exalt the cautious approach, the slow change, the organic nature of social growth. In their activities, Southern liberals have developed the tactics of evading principles, of being very indirect in attacking problems, of cajoling and coaxing the public into giving in on minor issues.

The Southern liberal, having to be critical of the South, has to emphasize strongly his local and regional patriotism. He has also, if he wants to keep respectability and the possibility of accomplishing something, to tread most cautiously around the Negro problem. Many Southern liberals, for example, feel it is important to keep the Negro out of sight in the fight for the abolition of the poll tax. On the other hand, the liberals will be found to stand for the most advanced policies in the Negro problem that are possible in the Southern communities where they are active. Southern liberals have been standing up for equal justice to the Negroes and have fought lynching. They have often declared themselves against the disfranchisement of the Negroes. They have been active in helping the Negroes get a fairer share of education, housing, and employment. They do not, however, go so far as to demand "social" equality for Negroes and they declare against "intermarriage."

The central concern of the Southern liberals is always the South. They feel themselves as belonging together in a fighting unity. The acute awareness of the pressing problems of the region is likely to make the Southern liberals more definitely practical in their interests even if this has not until recently brought them to think constructively along power lines and in terms of social engineering. As a movement, Southern liberalism's main weakness lies in its lack of mass support. It wants to see its ideals realized, it simply must get its message out from the conference rooms and college lecture halls to the people on the farms and in the shops.[3] Under the pressure of the accumulating changes, the Solid South might sometime be broken and a two-party system develop. Southern liberalism will then face a political task for which it must be prepared. The leaders for a truly progressive political movement in the South are there; the staff work for the battle is largely done. If Southern liberalism can recruit an army to lead, it will become one of the major factors of change in the South and in the nation.

[3] Many Southern newspapers are liberal in their politics and are making a definite effort to reach the masses, especially in the cities. Noteworthy is *The Southern Farmer*, published in Montgomery, Ala., which reaches farmers throughout the South and is written with a content and in a style that appeal to them.

CHAPTER X

Political Practices Today

and in the Future

1. THE SOUTHERN POLITICAL SCENE

The future may belong to liberalism, but the South of today is ruled mainly by its conservatives. Although the South, as part of the United States, has, in the main, the same political forms as the North, the activity that goes on within these forms is strikingly different. The difference not only makes internal politics in the South distinctive, but it also influences the activities of the federal government. Although there are local exceptions, the South differs from the rest of the nation in the following ways:

(1) For all practical purposes, the South[1] has only one political party. In the 1944 election, for example, 72 per cent of all votes were cast for the Democratic candidate for president. In the extreme cases of Mississippi and South Carolina, 98 per cent and 95 per cent of the votes, respectively, went to the Democratic candidate. This causes the primary to be far more important than the general election. In fact, the general election is usually a formal ritual to satisfy the demand of the federal Constitution.

(2) A much smaller proportion of the population participates in the elections in the South than in the North. In 1940 only 28 per cent

[1] In this chapter we are including in the South only the Upper and Lower South (Alabama, Arkansas, Georgia, Florida, Louisiana, Mississippi, Oklahoma, South Carolina, Texas, North Carolina, Tennessee and Virginia). The Border States (Delaware, Kentucky, Maryland, Missouri and West Virginia) have two-party systems (Oklahoma does also, but we shall consider it as in the South because it disfranchises Negroes). The people living in the District of Columbia have no vote.

of the adult population voted in 12 Southern states, as compared to 53 per cent in the North and West. In the extreme case of South Carolina, only 10 per cent voted. Most of this voting is carried on with a corruption and a disrespect for law that is found in only a few areas of the North and West.

(3) Until now, Negroes have been disfranchised in the South. Out of a total Negro adult population of 3,651,256 in the 8 Deep Southern states (excluding Oklahoma) of Alabama, Georgia, Mississippi, Louisiana, Florida, Texas, South Carolina, and Arkansas, Bunche estimates that only 80,000 to 90,000 Negroes voted in the general election of 1940. Practically none voted in the primary.

These three major political facts about the South are really part of one single problem, and—as we shall find—this problem is the Negro problem. In keeping Negroes from the polls by such devices as the poll tax, white men have been disfranchised. In preventing a two-party system from arising—which might let in the Negro vote—white men have been kept politically apathetic. White Southerners stay away from the polls for the most part. Another large proportion come to the polls solely because they are given a dollar or two apiece for their vote by the local political machine. As few people vote, relatively little money can often control elections in the South. Investigations show that corruption and illegal practices at the polls are the rule—not the exception. The election machinery is in most parts of the region far behind that in the North and in the other democratic countries of the world. For example, the secret, printed, uniform ballot (the so-called "Australian ballot") is still not used in South Carolina, and five years ago it was not used in many other areas of the South.

The difference between politics in the South and in the rest of the nation is so great that it visibly affects the personality of Southern members of Congress. The typical Southern members of Congress are so far away from national norms that, in spite of all accommodations, they remain a distinctive force in Washington. This fact becomes all the more important as they have a disproportionate influence in national politics.

Seats in the House of Representatives are apportioned according to population, and the nine million Negroes in the South give the South a good share of its seats, although few Negroes are permitted to vote. The large amount of nonvoting among Southern whites similarly makes each vote count more. The small electorate, the one-party system, and the well-organized local machines create a near-permanency of tenure for the average Southern member of Congress which is seldom paralleled in the North. With seniority as a basis for holding important committee posts in Congress, and with acquaintance as an almost necessary means of participating effectively in congressional activities, the Southerner's permanency of tenure gives him a decided advantage in Washington. This is especially true when the Democratic party is in power.

There are two important limitations to the South's influence on the Democratic party and thereby on the nation. First, it can practically never hope to control the Presidency, since the Democratic candidate for president is almost sure of the South, but must be especially attractive to the North. Second, the Democratic party is solicitous of the Northern Negro and has been successfully weaning his vote away from the Republican party.

To the national Republican party, the South has for a long time been a place from which practically no support could be expected, and Southern Republicans have for the most part been persons whose votes for nomination had to be bought up at the national conventions. To the Southern Republicans, the national Republican party has been a source of federal patronage. To Negro Republicans it has also been a traditional but failing hope. In most places and at most times in the South, white persons consider it a disgrace to vote Republican. White Republicans have traditionally been labeled "scalawags" and "nigger lovers"—epithets which express the most extreme form of disfavor and reveal the heart of the political situation in the South.

At the time the Republican party was declining in the South (1880–1890), the whites within it were splitting off from the Negroes to form what has been commonly called the "lily-white movement." The aim of the lily-white leaders was to build up a Republican party in the South by dissociating the party from Negroes. It is not completely anti-Negro, however; lily-white Republicans want Negro votes but do not want to recognize Negro influence or claims. As yet the movement has had no great success. It has led to no mass defection of whites from the Democratic party. Many Negroes in the South feel that the old rump Republican party never did any good for the Negroes. They felt hurt by the Republican party's defection when it went lily-white. It cannot be proved, but it seems likely that there was a landslide away from the Republican party in the South as well as in the North during the New Deal. Still, many Negroes are shrewd enough to calculate that if the lily-white movement should be successful, there could develop a two-party system in the South which would give the Negro a chance to become a voter again.

2. SOUTHERN TECHNIQUES FOR DISFRANCHISING THE NEGROES

Three principles seem to govern the extension of the franchise to Negroes in the South. In the first place, there is the Constitution of the United States, which states:

The right of citizens of the United States to vote shall not be denied or abridged by the United States or by any State on account of race, color, or previous condition of servitude.

In perfect opposition to this is the Southern caste principle that no Negro should be allowed to vote. State laws setting the qualifications for voting have usually been the result of an attempt to get the caste principle around the Constitution. A third principle is this: Negroes may be allowed to vote according to the discretion or need of those whites who exercise influence over the conduct of the election. This third principle is the cause of the variation in Negro voting in different parts of the South.

Until 1944 the most efficient device in use to keep Negroes from voting where the vote would count most in the South was the "white primary." The Democratic party prohibited Negroes from participating in its primary (also conventions, caucuses of voters, mass meetings, party offices, and candidacies) by means of state-wide rule in nine Southern states: Mississippi, Alabama, Georgia, Florida, South Carolina, Louisiana, Arkansas, Virginia, and Texas. In 1944 the Supreme Court held that the white primary was illegal as it was part of governmental election machinery. Some Southern states then tried to turn the primaries completely over to the Democratic party; but in 1947 in a United States district court it was ruled that the purely "private" white primary in South Carolina was illegal, thus apparently knocking the last legal prop from any kind of white primary.

Probably the best known—though not the most efficient—device for keeping the Negro from voting in the South is the poll tax. The poll tax is one of the oldest forms of direct taxation, but it was usually *compulsory* and, therefore, had little effect in restricting the vote. Seven Southern states have a *voluntary* poll tax and have it for the express purpose of restricting the vote.

In many states the poll tax is cumulative and the payment of more than one year's poll tax is required for the right to vote (in some states back to the time the individual became 21 years of age). While the poll tax is low, except where and when it is applied cumulatively, it means quite a bit to those Negroes and whites who work for a dollar or two a day. It means more for Negroes because more of them are poor. But its greatest restrictiveness against Negroes results from discrimination in its application; election officials practically always demand to see the poll tax receipts of Negroes and seldom those of whites. Too, it is common for politicians to pay the poll tax for whites in return for voting for the benefactor; but in only a handful of Southern cities is the Negro vote so bought.

Because the poll tax hurts poor whites as well as Negroes, there is a growing movement in the South to abolish it. Some liberals even claim that the main purpose of the tax is to disfranchise poor whites, since Negroes can be kept from the polls in many other ways. Still, if poor whites are encouraged to vote, they may stir up issues and put through legislation that will have the ultimate effect of helping all poor people, including Negroes.

The poll tax disfranchises and is subject to political manipulation, not only because it costs the voter a dollar or two but because it must be paid by a certain date (which is often long before anyone knows who the candidates will be), because officials often misdate the receipt to violate the date provisions and pay the tax themselves, and because employers force their employees to pay the tax. The importance of the poll tax in keeping even whites from voting is suggested by the following figures: in 1940 Oklahoma (without a poll tax) had 60 per cent of its adult citizenry voting as compared to 18 per cent in Arkansas (with a poll tax); North Carolina had 43 per cent as compared to 22 per cent in Virginia; and Louisiana, which has been without the poll tax only since 1934, had 27 per cent compared to 14 per cent in Mississippi.

Similar to the poll tax, in that they restrict Negroes because they are poor, are property, educational, and "character" requirements for voting. These, too, are seldom applied to whites but almost always to Negroes. Seldom is a white man "insulted" by being given an educational test; yet many cases have been recorded where a Negro "failed" a test when he mispronounced a single word. Even professors at Tuskegee and other Negro universities have been disfranchised by failing to pass these tests.

In addition to the better known legal requirements for voting, there are several others, which have been employed in one or more Southern states to disfranchise Negroes. A tricky registration blank must be filled out: whites will be given assistance, and their errors adjusted or overlooked; Negroes will not be allowed even the most trivial incompleteness or error, and are given no assistance. Certain of the previously discussed requirements are waived for war veterans or for the aged in certain states; in practice, whites are informed of such privileges but Negroes who qualify are not expected to ask for them. Some Southern states withhold the vote from anyone convicted of a crime; this is overlooked for most of the whites but applied rigorously to the Negro.

More important than the legal requirements in disfranchising Negroes in the South are extralegal practices. Violence, terror, and intimidation have been, and still are, effectively used to disfranchise Negroes in the South. Physical coercion is not so often practiced against the Negro, but the fact that it can be used freely and devastatingly creates a mental coercion that exists nearly everywhere in the South. A Negro can seldom claim the protection of the police and the courts if a white man knocks him down, or if a mob burns his house or inflicts bodily injuries on him or on members of his family. Besides violence, illegal "tricks" will be played on Negroes to prevent them from voting: Negroes will be told that there are no registration cards, that they should go somewhere else, that their names were "forgotten" when the voting lists were made up, and so on. In such circumstances it is no wonder that the great majority of Negroes in the South make no attempt to vote and—if they make attempts which are rebuffed—seldom demand their full rights under the federal Constitution.

3. THE NEGRO VOTE IN THE SOUTH

As has been observed, the general pattern in the Southern states since their constitutions were changed (1890–1910) has been to deny the vote to Negroes. Still a small proportion of Negroes do vote.

As we have noticed, the most important voting in the South is in the Democratic primaries, and these are restricted to whites. Here and there a small community will let one or two "good" Negroes vote in the primary. In some of the cities, especially where political machines can control the Negro vote—such as in San Antonio and Memphis—Negroes vote in the primaries in restricted numbers. Since the war there has been something of a break in this pattern, but it is too early to estimate the size or permanency of this break.

While the Democratic primary is the most important election in the South, there are other elections. First, there is the general election, conducted under the Constitution and laws of the United States and administered by the state government. Besides the primary and the general election there are two types of so-called "nonpartisan" elections. Both of these are in large measure restricted to cities. One type of nonpartisan election occurs in those cities which operate under a city manager or commission form of government. The second type is that involving initiative and referendum. Referenda concerning bond issues, tax rates, amendments, city extensions, and so on are not at all uncommon in Southern cities.

In general and nonpartisan elections, Negroes vote to a greater extent than in primary elections, since there is no uniform rule barring them. All the other devices outside of the formal no-Negro rule may be applied to keep them from voting, however, and in the 11 states south of the Border states there are probably less than 250,000 Negroes who voted between 1936 and 1942.

Southerners often explain that Negroes can vote in the South but that they just do not care to. This is, of course, a rationalization justifying white policy. In one sense it is true that the Negro is politically apathetic. Like many a white man, he is uneducated and ignorant of the significance of the vote. But it should not be denied that a large proportion of poor Southern Negroes feel that "politics is white folks' business." Some of the apathy is peculiar to the Negroes because some Negroes have been so frightened by experiences when attempting to vote that they swear never to try again.

Another charge levied against the political activity of the Negro is that he is frequently the pawn of the political machine. This is true, especially in the South, but it must be seen in the light of other facts. In the first place, it is often a political machine that makes it possible for Negroes to vote at all. Too, the machine gives them something for their vote—not only do they often get dollars for their individual vote, but they get paved streets and schools as a group. In the third place, Southern Negroes have been able to vote only in cities, and cities are the places where political machines are most powerful. Finally, it should be remembered that there are places—even Southern cities—where Negroes have voted in significant numbers without machine backing and control. Since the white primary is no longer legal, and the poll tax is under heavy attack, only violence and trickery on the white side and ignorance and apathy on the Negro side remain as barriers to Negro suffrage. During the next ten to fifteen years we can, therefore, expect a heavy increase in Negro voting in the South, especially in the cities.

4. THE NEGRO IN NORTHERN POLITICS

The Negro coming from the South to the North was as politically innocent and ignorant as the immigrant from a country like Italy, where democratic politics was not well developed. It was quite natural, therefore, for Negro politics in the North to take forms similar to Italo-American politics. For example, ignorance and poverty caused a disproportionate amount of nonvoting among Negroes. Like other immigrants, since young adults migrate to a greater extent than other age groups, Negroes formed a larger proportion of the adult population than of the total population; therefore, they had a potential voting strength greater than their total numbers would indicate. Like other immigrants, they continually got into minor legal difficulties and sought the friendly services of petty politicians. Like other immigrants, they often traded their votes for these favors. Like other ignorant immigrants, they followed the narrow political leadership of those of their own group who sought political plums for themselves. Still they were not unified partly because of the rivalry between the recent migrants of the South and those longer established in the North.

There were some peculiarities about the political behavior of Negroes in the North that differentiated it from that of the foreign-born whites as well as from that of the native whites. In the first place, it was strongly attached to the Republican party because of gratitude to the symbol of Lincoln, the example of early leaders like Frederick Douglass and Booker T. Washington, and the continuous spectacle of what the name "Democratic party" meant in the South. Another trait of the Negro vote was that it was, on the whole, passionately aware of the relation of a candidate or issue to the Negro problem.

Although individual Negroes are not restricted from voting in the North, there may be one condition which limits the influence of the Negro's vote once it is cast. We refer to the practice of gerrymandering—that is, of so setting the boundaries of election districts that the vote of a minority group is cut up and overwhelmed by the vote of the majority group. There is evidence that gerrymandering of the Negro vote exists in some Northern cities. Besides gerrymandering, there is another way in which the Negro vote is kept from having its proper weight. This is by neglecting to redistrict as population grows or declines at different rates in different districts. The neglect to redistrict also creates a form of "natural" gerrymandering that hurts the Negroes.

No comprehensive study has yet been made on the extent of nonvoting among Negroes in the North. The general impression is that Negroes—like whites with the same average educational and economic status—are somewhat apathetic. Negro apathy, however, as some studies show, varies with local conditions. In Chicago, for instance, 77 per cent of the adults of a Negro ward registered as compared to 68 per cent for the entire city (1930).

Although the Negroes were strongly attached to the Republican party, when the New Deal relieved the economic plight of the Negroes during the depression and—in the North—treated them almost without discrimination, and appointed Negro advisers for many phases of the government's activities, Negroes began to shift to the Democratic party in large numbers. It is not certain whether the Northern Negro vote will remain Democratic, but it is certain that it has become flexible and will respond more readily to the policies of the two parties toward the Negro. This will probably bring more political advances to Negroes, since their vote will take on more strategic significance in the close elections often occurring in the North. It is also a sign that politically Negroes are becoming more like other Americans.

On the whole, Negroes have come to be rather like whites in their political behavior in the North. They vote in about the same proportion as whites; they are no longer tied to the Republican party; they avoid third parties; they have manifested a class differential in their adherence to the Democratic party. On the other hand, most Negro voters are more keenly aware of a candidate's attitude toward their group than are most other Americans—perhaps only because they are one of the few ethnic groups against whom politicians ever discriminate. Even though Negroes are seeking only their rights as citizens and a proportionate share of the political spoils, they find they have to be choosy about parties and candidates to get these.

5. WHAT THE NEGRO GETS OUT OF POLITICS

Although there are as many Negroes voting today in the United States as there are whites voting in the seven Southern states of Mississippi, Louisiana, Alabama, South Carolina, Arkansas, Georgia, and Florida, yet Southern whites get incomparably more benefits from politics than do Negroes. Negroes are grossly discriminated against in what they get from politics just as they are in their exercise of the right to vote. A striking measure of this fact is that the seven Deep Southern states have 52 members of the House of Representatives and 14 members of the Senate, whereas the Negroes, with the same number of actual votes, have only 2 members of the House of Representatives and no senators. There are many other ways in which the Negroes are deprived of the benefits of politics.

Unquestionably, the most important thing that Negroes get out of politics where they vote is legal justice—justice in the courts; police protection and protection against the persecution of the police; ability to get administrative jobs through civil service; and a fair share in such public facilities as schools, hospitals, public housing, playgrounds, libraries, sewers, and street lights. The Negroes' votes in some parts of the country buy them their rights as citizens to a large extent, while their lack of votes in others causes them to be discriminated against all around. Political spoils, favors, and "protection" also are given to Negroes for their votes. In getting illegal and extralegal returns from their votes, Negroes are like whites, except that they probably do not get so much on the average. As Gosnell and Bunche point out, Negroes seldom get the really big graft.

Just as they are practically voteless in the South, Negroes there have a minimum of what we have called "legal justice." But even where Negroes have only a few votes in the South they have at least some opportunity to bargain for police and court protection. Wherever Negroes vote in the South white politicians who gain from their votes "repay" them with a few minor administrative or menial jobs, a few streets paved or lighted, and occasionally a school building or community center.

Negroes have been elected to office in the North, but not nearly in proportion to their numbers. Even in the Border states of Kentucky, West Virginia, and Missouri there have been a few Negroes in the state legislatures. Most of the large cities in the North containing a significant proportion of Negroes have one or two Negro aldermen or councilmen each. There are more Negroes appointed to public office than elected, relative to the total number of offices available, but even these are nowhere near the proportion of the Negro vote.

Because voting Negroes are concentrated in a half dozen Northern cities, they can exert little influence on the federal government. This is more than balanced, however, by the federal government's greater conformity to the principles of the American Creed. The federal courts, especially the United States Supreme Court, have been traditional guardians of the Negro's rights. Congress and the presidents have usually sought to be fair to the Negroes.

As we had occasion to mention, the only elected Negro representatives in Washington are a congressman from Chicago and one from New York. Few Negroes hold top-rank appointive positions, and these few are usually in positions that have "traditionally" been held by Negroes since Reconstruction days. Once in a while a new "traditional" Negro job is created: when William Hastie, the Roosevelt-appointed federal judge in the Virgin Islands, resigned, another Negro was appointed in his place. There are only about a dozen of these traditional top-rank Negro positions in the federal government.

More important, during the Roosevelt administration, were the positions created in various governmental bureaus to advise or direct the application of federal policies to Negroes. The Negroes selected to fill these positions usually had a superior educational background and only one or two have participated in party politics. Although many Negroes have condemned the appointments to these positions as representing an effort to keep Negroes satisfied, there are important achievements to their credit, and they are the first significant step, in recent years, toward the participation of Negroes in federal government activity. Unfortunately, with the abolishing of many of these New Deal and wartime agencies, the positions were abolished too.

6. THE NEGRO'S POLITICAL BARGAINING POWER

To make political forecasts is hazardous; however, in the Negro problem certain dominating factors make a forecast considerably simpler than for the American nation at large.

If we focus our attention on Negro voting in those parts of the country where Negroes have, or will have, the unhampered right to the ballot, it can, with reasonable security, be foretold that there is not going to be a "Negro party" in American politics. It is true that there are strong ties of common interest in the Negro group. But Negroes know from bitter experience that there is nothing which can so frustrate their hope of having a voice in public affairs as arousing fear of "Negro domination." Negroes in America are, further, bent on cultural assimilation to the fullest degree allowed by the white majority. In addition, Negroes are in a minority in all but a few parts of the country. Finally, the peculiar American political system is strongly against small parties.

The Negro voter will, therefore, have to exert his influence through one of the two dominant political parties. Since the Negroes broke their traditional allegiance to the Republican party, the Negro vote has been fluid. It is likely to remain fluid. The Democratic and Republican parties, therefore, will increasingly compete for the Negro vote. The question arises whether, in this haggling and bargaining, the Negroes will be able to extract the maximum advantage by acting as a political unit, nationally and locally.

One prerequisite for such a tactic is present to a greater degree than in any other American group of voters. Negroes, as a consequence of the bonds of caste in which they are enclosed, have a strong in-group feeling. There are certain concrete demands—all centering around the insistence that Negroes should be treated like other citizens—about which there is almost universal agreement among Negroes.

In the sphere of national politics, however, the attempt to bargain with the two political parties on behalf of the Negro voters has not been effective. Since the Negro vote became fluid in the 1930's and both parties now recognize this fact, it would be natural for a national Negro political leadership to form and start negotiations with the two parties in advance of each national election. This has not happened. The "bidding for the Negro vote" has been left almost entirely to the two parties themselves and has been directed principally to the individual Negro voter, through party-appointed Negro leaders. The situation has not been utilized to any extent approaching the political possibilities. Negro communities everywhere display, in the most glaring manner, clear-cut problems of housing, employment, education, health, and so on, calling not only for expert planning but for formulation of Negro political programs. Why has Negro pressure in these communities, at least in the North, been so politically ineffective?

Part of the explanation is undoubtedly the poverty and the inherited psychology of dependence and apathy among the Negro masses, their low educational and cultural level, and the lack of political tradition and experience both in the masses and in the upper levels of the Negro community. All this is bound to change in time. Apart from this, however, the Negro leader is in a dilemma. If he pleads allegiance to a political party he will lose in bargaining power. If, on the other hand, he keeps outside the parties he loses some of the direct influence he could exert by being in the inner circle of one of them. Out of this dilemma, there is only one possible and rational escape: a division of labor and responsibility among Negro leaders so that the Negro politicians proper and the party workers identify themselves with political parties and work with them and for them, while other Negro representatives, invested with superior prestige among their people, remain independent of close party ties and do the important bargaining. The former group represents the Negro people's allegiance to the American party system, the latter group their separate interests as an independent unit.

7. THE NEGRO'S PARTY ALLEGIANCE

Our assumption has been that the Negro vote will remain fluid but will keep conservatively to the two big parties. One thing seems certain: Negroes will not go fascist. All their interests are against right-wing radicalism. More problematic are Negro attitudes toward communism. It is true that the majority of Negro people are in economic distress. It is also true that they are increasingly becoming conscious of being severely maltreated in America and that they sense social exclusion. It is further true that the Communists have seen their chance and have been devoting much zealous work to cultivating the Negroes. They are the only American political group that has in practice offered Negroes full social equality, and this is highly valued not only among Negro intellectuals but much deeper down in the Negro community, particularly in the North.

Still the Communists have not succeeded in getting any appreciable following among Negroes in America, especially among the masses. During the depression and again since the war, a number of leaders and intellectuals have become Communists or "fellow travelers." But it does not seem likely that many Negroes will turn communist. To begin with, poor, uneducated, and socially disadvantaged groups have never been particularly susceptible to radical propaganda. It is usually the intellectuals and higher strata of the working class that have been reached first. The strong impact of church and religion in the Negro community should not be forgotten. Most important, many Negro leaders, both in the past and at present, are constantly warning of the dangers of communism, not only to democracy but to the particular interests of the Negroes. As one Negro explained, "It is bad enough being black without being black and red."

If we thus conclude that—for the near future at least—communism or any similar movement will not be able to muster any numerical support from the Negro voters, we must, on the other hand, be aware that Negroes as a group will from now on be in strong favor of a political party which stands for social reform and civic equality. In this respect, the New Deal promises to have permanent effects. Negroes, in both the higher and the lower classes, seem to understand pretty well that a liberal attitude in questions of economic relief and social reform is generally connected with a more equalitarian attitude in racial matters.

8. Negro Suffrage in the South

The concern of the Southern Negroes is not how they shall use their votes but how to get their constitutional right to vote respected at all. Indeed, no single one of the Southern Negroes' deprivations and sufferings is unconnected with their disfranchisement. The Negroes' interests in politics in the South are primarily concerned with the handling of local matters. Negroes need, in order to protect themselves, a voice in deciding who will be the judges of the courts, the public attorneys, the sheriffs and the chiefs of police, the members of the school board and other agencies deciding upon their share of public services. As national politics is increasingly important for all questions of social and economic welfare, they are also interested in who represents their districts in Congress. On this point of suffrage, there has *in principle* never been any great difference of opinion among Negro leaders although some of the early leaders thought other things more important at a particular moment.

While, with a few local and regional exceptions, the Southern Negroes remain disfranchised, we have noted recently increased political participation. This is due to a number of reasons: For one thing, the legal foundations of Negro disfranchisement are gradually being repealed under various pressures—four states have abolished the poll tax; increased education of Negroes is rendering ineffective the literacy and understanding clauses; the white primary, as we mentioned before, is under heavy attack. For another thing, the South is on the defensive in regard to the Negro. Congress has attempted to abolish the poll tax nationally, to enact an antilynching bill, and to create a national FEPC. It failed to do all three, but it cannot escape the South that the antilynching bill and the attempt to abolish the poll tax were directed against the South alone.

It is certain that the South is in a political ferment at present, under the influence both of the structural changes taking place in the South's economy and of the emphasis on democratic ideals during the war; white liberals and Negro leaders are pressing hard for reform; the Negro veteran is pressing for his rights; some, at least, of the white veterans are helping him; the recent increase of unionization and the activities during the last two elections of the C.I.O.-P.A.C. have also increased political participation of the Negroes and paved the way for even more in the near future.

9. The Stake of the North

This is perhaps the point at which to take up for consideration the stake of the North in the Southern suffrage problem. It is apparent, and rather surprising, that the liberal forces in the North have not until recently given this problem more attention.

There is actually a provision in the Fourteenth Amendment requiring a reduction in representation in Congress as a punishment for disfranchisement. But this provision has never been applied. The conservatives had, of course, no interest in doing it, and it could not be attractive to liberals either, as it would imply a formal sanction of disfranchisement. Further, the Southern conservatives' position became stronger when it gradually became clear that they were assisted by the Supreme Court decisions that gave a twisted construction to the Reconstruction Amendments and read into them a meaning never intended by their authors. It is generally held that the Supreme Court acted in agreement with and expressed what was then the general sentiment even in the North. The North had got tired of the Negro problem. But it must not be forgotten that the decisions of the court had themselves a substantial share in solidifying Northern apathy.

The Supreme Court is, however, seemingly changing its attitude and is again looking more to the spirit of the Reconstruction Amendments. Meanwhile, the forces for social reform in Congress are feeling the opposition from Southern conservative members more and more cumbersome. They are increasingly irritated when they remember that congressmen from the South are not truly representative of the region. "In the 1940 election about 10 per cent of the voting population of the United States . . . was able to elect . . . one-fourth of the members of Congress,"[2] writes a Southern liberal, and this truth is dawning upon many Northerners too. Both the labor vote and the Negro vote in the North will in all probability exert a considerable pressure toward increasing Southern political participation in at least the national elections.

Northerners far to the right of labor also have cause to feel increasingly uneasy about Southern disfranchisement of Negroes as well as about judicial and economic discrimination. There was a disturbing racial angle to World War II and there is also one in the building of a postwar world order.

Southern conservatives dislike nothing more than the threat of federal interference in their "states' rights." But the South's strategic position is weakening every day. There are reasons to anticipate that both the Negro and the labor bloc will exert increasing political power and that liberalism generally will become stronger in both the South and the North. The Supreme Court is likely to continue in its new trend. The only means of escaping federal interference might be for the South to start to carry out reforms on its own initiative.

10. Practical Conclusions

In the South the whole unique political system is becoming increasingly shaky. This is realized by those Southerners who have any insight into politics, even if they do not admit it publicly. Our conclusion is thus that the Southern conservative position on Negro franchise is politically untenable for any length of time. Any change, of course, should not be made by sudden upheavals but in gradual

[2] Marian D. Irish, "The Southern One-Party System and National Politics," *The Journal of Politics*, IV (February, 1942), p. 82.

steps; therefore, it is an urgent interest and a truly conservative one for the South to start enfranchising its Negro citizens as soon as possible. This is also seen by a small group of Southern liberals. Since in many areas of the South the Negroes are extremely ignorant, ill educated, and isolated from American institutions, it is urgent, from a conservative point of view, to begin allowing the higher strata of the Negro population to participate in the political process as soon as possible, and to push the movement down to the lowest groups gradually. It is also urgent to speed up the civic education of these masses who are bound to have votes in the future.

But the great majority of Southern conservative white people do not see the handwriting on the wall. They do not study the impending changes; they live in the pathetic illusion that the matter is settled. They do not care to have any constructive policies to meet the trends. They think no adjustments are called for. The chances that the future development will be planned and led intelligently—and that, consequently, it will take the form of cautious, foresighted reforms instead of unexpected, tumultuous, haphazard breaks, with mounting discords and anxieties in its wake—are indeed small. But we want to keep this last question open. Man is a free agent, and there are no inevitabilities. All will depend upon the thinking done and the action taken in the region during the next decade or so. History can be made. It is not necessary to receive it as mere destiny.

CHAPTER XI

The Unequal Administration

of Justice

1. DEMOCRACY AND JUSTICE

The American tradition of electing, rather than appointing, minor public officials is serious in regard to the judiciary branch of the government. The immediate dependence of court and public officials upon popular election—that is, upon local public opinion and political machines—instead of upon appointment strictly according to merit, and the uncertainty of tenure implied in this system, decreases the attractiveness of these important positions to many of the best persons who would otherwise be available. Professional standards are thus kept lower than those which could be attained under a system of permanent appointment.

Apart from such general effects, the fact that the administration of justice is dependent upon the local voters is likely to imply discrimination against an unpopular minority group, particularly when this group is disfranchised as Negroes are in the South. The elected judge knows that sooner or later he must come back to the polls and that a decision running counter to local opinion may cost him his position. The dependence of judges on local prejudices strikes at the very root of orderly government. It endangers the law in its primary function of protecting the minority against the majority, the individual against society, indeed, of democracy itself against the danger of nullifying in practice the settled principles of law and impartiality of justice. The American jury system, too, while it has many merits, is likely to strengthen this dependence of justice upon local popular opinion. If, as in the South, Negroes are kept out of jury service, the democratic safeguard of the jury system is easily turned into a means of minority subjugation.

The popular election of the officers of law and the jury system are expressions of extreme democracy in American handling of justice; this extreme democracy, however, turns out to be a menace to legal democracy when it is based on restricted political participation and on an ingrained tradition of caste suppression. Such conditions occur in the South with respect to Negroes.

If there is a deficiency of legal protection for Negroes, white people will be tempted to deal unfairly with them in everyday affairs. They will be tempted to use irregular methods to safeguard what they feel to be their interests against Negroes. They will be inclined to use intimidation and even violence against Negroes if they can count on going unpunished. When such patterns become established, the law itself and its processes are brought into contempt, and a general feeling of uncertainty, arbitrariness, and inequality will spread.

The Negroes, on their side, are hurt in their trust that the law is impartial, that the court and the police are their protection, and indeed, that they belong to an orderly society which has set up this machinery for common security and welfare. They will not feel confidence in, and loyalty toward, a legal order which is entirely out of their control and which they sense to be inequitable and merely part of the system of caste suppression.

Having accepted the American Creed as our value premise in this study, we must also accept a consequence of this creed; namely, that Negroes are entitled to justice equally with all other people. This principle is upheld by the Constitution and is held supreme in the legislation of all states. In this chapter we do not discuss inequalities *in law,* or the results of inequitable administration. The subject of the discussion here is the actual handling of justice.

2. RELATIVE EQUALITY IN THE NORTH

There are deficiencies in the working of the machinery of the law in the North too. American justice is everywhere expensive and depends too much upon the skill of the attorney. Not only does the Negro suffer from the usual difficulties of the poor man, but there have been occasional instances of lack of serious treatment of Negroes in court.

A most important matter is the treatment of Negroes by the police. In most Northern communities Negroes are more likely than whites to be arrested under any suspicious circumstances. They are more likely to be accorded discourteous or brutal treatment at the hands of police than are whites. The rate of killing of Negroes by the police is high in many Northern cities. Negroes have a high crime rate, but the average white policeman is inclined to exaggerate it.

In some Northern cities I have heard complaints that the police will sometimes restrict Negroes to the Negro districts, particularly at night. There have been bombings against Negroes who tried to move into "white territory," and even race riots. The police have not always been strictly impartial during such incidents, but the courts have usually not shielded the white transgressors afterward in the way that has become a pattern in the South. Vigilantism occasionally occurs in the North. In many Northern cities Negroes relate that they find it difficult to get the courts to punish violations of the civil rights laws; for example, when Negroes are not permitted in certain restaurants and hotels. But these occurrences are relatively rare.

There are, in many Northern places, Negro judges, Negro court officers, and Negro policemen. Commonly there are Negroes on the jury list. The majority of all Negro lawyers practice in the North. Negro lawyers in the North do not generally complain of being treated differently in court from their white colleagues or of meeting prejudice from the juries.

Since, on the whole, Negroes do not meet much more discrimination from officers of the law than do white persons of the same economic and cultural level, there is in the North no special problem of getting justice for Negroes, outside the general one of improving the working of the machinery of the law for the equal protection of the rights of poor and uneducated people.

Part of the explanation of why the Negro gets more legal justice in the North is the fact that Negroes can vote in the North and, consequently, have a share in the ultimate control of the legal system. In addition, there is the general inclination of white people in the North to regard Negroes as full citizens in their formal relations with public authority. This is one point where the ordinary Northerner is almost unfailingly faithful to the American Creed. He wants justice to be impartial, regardless of race, creed, or color. Whatever the reasons, it seems to be a fact that there is a sharp division between North and South in the granting of legal justice to Negroes. In the North, for the most part, Negroes enjoy equitable justice.

3. The Southern Heritage

Because the main problems of justice for the Negro are found in the South, this chapter will deal almost exclusively with the

South. The difference in feeling of personal security between Negroes in the two regions is most striking to an observer. The Southern Negro seems to suspect a possible danger to himself or to other Negroes whenever a white stranger approaches him. The Northern Negro, in general, appears different in this respect. His self-assurance in behavior often seems preposterous or obstreperous to the Southern white man, who has become accustomed to the submissive and guarded manners of the Southern Negro.

The reason for this, as we shall see, is that in the South the Negro's person and property are practically subject to the whim of any white person who wishes to take advantage of him or to punish him for any real or fancied wrongdoing or "insult." The large element of chance and arbitrariness should be emphasized in a discussion of lawlessness in the South. Physical violence and threats against personal security do not, of course, occur to every Negro every day. But violence *may* occur at any time and it is the fear of it as much as the violence itself that creates the injustice and the insecurity.

When trying to understand the Southern situation as to law enforcement and the Negro's personal security, it is necessary to examine the historical heritage of the region. Under slavery the Negro was owned, bought, and sold as property. In general the Negro slave had no "rights" which his owner was bound to respect. While most states inaugurated statutes to protect the slave from unnecessary sufferings, to the extent that these regulations were not sanctioned by the master's own economic interests and his feelings for his human property or by community sentiment, they seem not to have been enforced.

The psychic pressure upon white society of the slavery system and of the various devices necessary to uphold it against rebellious Negroes, envious poor whites, Northern Abolitionists, and world opinion, must have been intense. In addition, the slavery system itself —and particularly the right it gave and the custom it nurtured to punish bodily other adult human beings—must have conditioned people to violent and arbitrary behavior patterns.

After the Civil War the Negroes—having lost the protection for life and personal security which their property value had provided them, and also, frequently, the personal relationship to their old masters—became the subjects of much greater violence. The Reconstruction Amendments, however, gave civil rights to Negroes for the first time. Even after the restoration of white supremacy was accomplished, all state legislation in the South had to be written upon the fictitious assumption that Negroes enjoyed full and equal protection under the law. The administration of justice had to proceed upon the same imaginary principle. In reality, legislation, courts, and police were used to keep the Negroes "in their place." This intention had to be kept hidden, so as not to come into conflict with the Constitution. On the other hand, the belief in legal inequality could never again be wholehearted. The upstanding Southern white men were compelled by their allegiance to their nation and its Constitution to observe a degree of both the form and the content of equality in justice. The present writer has met few Southern white people— above the lowest level of education and culture—who have not declared themselves prepared *in principle* to abstain from illegality in the sphere of personal security and private property.

It may, therefore, be expected that there will be a rapid development in the field of justice in the near future; there is some tendency in this direction at the present time. The lingering inequality in justice in the South is probably due more to low and lagging professional standards—certainly among the police, and in many regions even among the lawyers who are willing to enter into court service—than it is to opinion in favor of legal inequality.

While lack of legal justice can be considered in itself as crucial to the peace and sanity of the South, this problem is interrelated with many others. When the Negro is discriminated against by the police, in court, and in private dealings with whites, this is made more possible by his poverty, his lack of political influence, and his social abasement. An improvement in any of these fields will reflect itself in a greater security before the law. On the other hand, inequality in justice is undoubtedly responsible for no small part of the Negro's difficulties in rising economically and socially.

4. LOCAL PETTY OFFICIALS

Practically all public officials in the South are whites. The principle is upheld that Negroes should not be given positions of public authority even on a low level. This situation is, of course, closely related to their disfranchisement. Even in the South, however, Negroes are sometimes appointed to minor offices in the localities where they are permitted to vote. Since World War II many Southern towns have started to use Negro policemen; this is a new and important development; it will undoubtedly mean a greater amount of equal-handed justice for Negroes.

The Negro's most important public contact is with the policeman. He is the personification of white authority in the Negro community.

In the policeman's relation to the Negro population there are several peculiarities. One is that he stands not only for civic order as defined in formal laws and regulations, but also for "white supremacy" and the whole set of social customs associated with this concept. It is demanded that even minor transgressions of caste etiquette should be punished, and the policeman is delegated to carry out this function.

To enable the policeman to carry out this function, the courts are supposed to back him even when he proceeds far outside normal police activities. His word must be taken against Negroes without regard for formal legal rules of evidence, even when there are facts supporting the Negro. Negroes are arrested and sentenced for all sorts of actual or alleged breaks of the caste rules, sometimes even when it is clear that their only offense was to resist a white person's unlawful aggression.[1] Other peculiarities in the activity of the Southern police system are, on the one hand, the availability of the police for sanctioning private white interests against Negroes and, on the other, the indulgence of private white persons in taking the law into their own hands.

The philosophies and tradition of the police have been borrowed, and a similar status and function have been assumed, by a large number of other functionaries; for instance, the operators and conductors on public carriers. The Jim Crow regulations vary from city to city, or from state to state; they are complicated and technically impractical, and a constant source of tension and friction. The operators and conductors—like the police officers—feel themselves obliged to sanction and enforce rules of racial etiquette and custom. They also are the watchdogs against "social equality."

Under these conditions it is no wonder that these functionaries often feel themselves—and white authority—challenged. As weak men (their economic and social status is low) with strong powers, they can seldom afford to take back a charge or an order. Numerous Southern Negroes have complained about the arbitrary and high-handed manner in which the Jim Crow regulations in transportation are often handled.

These contacts are of paramount practical importance: they represent the major part of all official relations of Negroes with organized

[1] A great many of these arrests occur on streetcars and buses. A Negro may be arrested for demanding the right change from the conductor or for refusing to give up his seat in the colored section of the car to a white person; he may be arrested for being in the white section of town after dark. (Arthur Raper, "Race and Class Pressures," unpublished manuscript prepared for *An American Dilemma* [1940], pp. 6–7, 56–57.)

society in which they live, and they determine largely their attitudes to this society. A change to easier, friendlier, and more impartial public contacts would improve race relations immensely.

5. THE SOUTHERN POLICEMAN

The central relation in this system is that between Negroes and the local police. In purely rural districts, the police consist of the sheriff and his deputies. Usually they are petty politicians with no police training at all except the experience they get in their work. In the rural South, the caste rules are so fixed that the peace officers' police duties are intermittent and restricted to occasional incidents. In the Southern cities where the two racial groups are more separated, the duty of policing the population becomes continuous and specialized.

It is of great interest to study the qualifications and personality types of the Southern policeman who has been awarded this crucial position in the caste society. A special investigation was undertaken for this study by Dr. Arthur Raper, who made inquiry as of 1940 into the personnel of the police force in 112 towns and cities in 14 Southern states. He found the level of general education among policemen to be low. In many small cities "almost anyone on the outside of the penitentiary who weighs enough and is not blind or crippled can be considered as a police candidate."[2] Even the formal police training is usually very deficient.

Slightly over half the police systems studied were using some form of civil service. But in Southern cities, elected officials still run the civil service and select among the many who meet the formal requirements. This means a low degree of personal and professional independence. Salaries of policemen rank somewhere between those of unskilled and skilled workers. Less than half the police systems studied have worked out some sort of retirement fund. In the typical Southern police force the turnover is small and the average age high. Even when the police force is replaced for political reasons this does not generally mean a rejuvenation, "for older men can commonly deliver more votes."[3]

The typical Southern policeman is thus a low-paid and dependent man, with little general education or special police schooling. His social prestige is low. But he is the local representative of the law; he has authority and may at any time resort to the use of his gun. It is not difficult to understand that this economically and socially in-

[2] *Ibid.*, p. 14.
[3] *Ibid.*

secure man, given this tremendous and dangerous authority, continually feels himself on the defensive.

He usually expects to be challenged when about routine duties. . . . This defensive attitude makes the policeman's job tedious and nerve-racking and leaves the public feeling that policemen are crude and hard-boiled.[4]

He is a frustrated man, and, with the opportunity given him, it is to be expected that he becomes aggressive. There are practically no curbs to the policeman's aggressiveness when he is dealing with Negroes whom he conceives of as dangerous or as "getting out of hand."

6. THE POLICEMAN IN THE NEGRO NEIGHBORHOOD

This weak man with his strong weapons—backed by all the authority of white society—is now sent to be the white law in the Negro neighborhood. His social heritage has taught him to despise Negroes, and he has had little education which could have changed him. His professional experiences with criminals, prostitutes, and loiterers in Negro joints are strongly selective and only magnify his prejudices. The result is that probably no group of whites in America has a lower opinion of the Negro people and is more fixed in its views than Southern policemen.

In many, but not all, Southern communities, Negroes complain indignantly about police brutality. It is apparent that the beating of arrested Negroes often serves as vengeance for the fears and perils the policemen are subjected to while pursuing their duties in the Negro community. When once the beating habit has developed in a police department, it is, according to all experience, difficult to stop. The most publicized type of police brutality is the extreme case of Negroes being killed by policemen. This phenomenon is important in itself, but it constitutes only a minor portion of all police brutality, and the information available on Negro killings by the police does not give a reliable index of the wider phenomenon. A perhaps untypical example for the Border states, but not unusual for many areas in the Deep South, comes from Baltimore between 1938 and 1942, when nine Negroes were killed by police officers.[5] The majority of police killings of Negroes must be deemed unnecessary when measured by a decent standard of policemanship.

The main reasons why Negroes want to have Negro officers appointed to police departments are to have a more understanding,

[4] *Ibid.*, pp. 19, 20.

[5] Charles S. Johnson and Associates, *Into the Main Stream* (Chapel Hill: University of North Carolina Press, 1947), p. 23.

less brutal police supervision in the Negro community and to have an effective supervision of Negro offenders against other Negroes. The second reason is not unimportant. Everywhere in Southern Negro communities comes the complaint from law-abiding Negroes that they are left practically without police protection.

There are some encouraging signs of change in the police systems of the South. The civil service system seems to be on the increase. The general influences of education, urbanization, and industrialization also are tending to modernize the administration of local governments in the South. Finally, the new functions of the policemen —answering questions for tourists, helping school children cross the streets, and so on—may serve as a humanizing force tending to counteract the stultifying effects of catching and beating criminals.

Most important of all is the growing use of Negro policemen. A recent newspaper report states that there are now 42 cities and towns in ten Southern states having an estimated 230 Negro policemen patrolling Negro sections. Five Negro policewomen are on duty in three cities. Alabama, Mississippi, and Louisiana are the three Southern states in which no Negro policemen are employed.[6]

The Southern police system represents a crucial and strategic factor in race relations. Could standards be raised—of education, specialized police training, independence of local politics, salary, and social prestige—some of the most morbid tensions in the South could be lessened. Ideally the policeman should be something of an educator and a social worker at the same time that he is the arm of the law. The South, particularly, needs to stress the preventive aims and the peacemaking functions of the police.

7. ANOTHER TYPE OF PUBLIC CONTACT

Besides the police and other functionaries who regard their chief function with respect to Negroes to be restraint and suppression, there are public officials in the South, as elsewhere, who regard their function to be service. Longest established among these are the postal officials, who are unique because they are under federal control and have to meet civil service standards.[7]

[6] Statistics compiled by the Southern Regional Council in Atlanta. Reported in the New York *Times* (July 13, 1947), p. 6E.

[7] Even here Negroes sometimes meet discrimination. Reports in the New York *Times* (June 2, and 3, 1947) state that many Negro veterans in the South were unable to take advantage of the GI Bill of Rights because post offices would not give them the necessary application blanks. For a further account of discriminations against Negro veterans, see Charles G. Bolté and Louis Harris, *Our Negro Veterans* (New York: Public Affairs Committee, Inc., 1947).

Other people who are building up a tradition of equal and just treatment of Negroes in public contacts are those concerned with social adjustment and social reform. They became especially numerous and important under the New Deal. To this new group of officials belong the relief administrator, the county farm agent, the Farm Security supervisor, the home demonstration agent, and the doctors and nurses of local health programs.

These functionaries have given the Negroes a new type of contact with public authority: educated and trained white men and women whose primary interest is not simply to keep them in their place, but to advise them and help them to a better life.

8. THE SOUTHERN COURTS

Apart from the basic weakness already referred to, that the courts are too directly controlled by local public opinion where the Negroes are without a voice, there are other characteristics of Southern courts which operate against all poor and uneducated groups. The great number of courts, with higher or lower rank and with complicated jurisdictional boundaries between them, are likely to bewilder the unsophisticated citizen who attempts to protect his rights. Technicalities and legal fictions are allowed to play a great role, to the sacrifice of justice. This is true of American justice in other parts of the country also, but the fact that the South after Reconstruction had to build up large parts of its legal system of discrimination against Negroes in evasion of the Constitution has particularly stamped Southern justice with these traits.

Under such circumstances a clever lawyer can work wonders, particularly in those rural districts where the judge feels that the attorney knows more about law than he does himself. The strength of the counsel a man can provide depends upon his wealth, and Negroes, as a poor group, suffer together with lower-class whites. The American bond and bail system, too, works automatically against the poor classes. The poor man generally cannot raise bail or bond himself to secure his release from jail pending trial. As the privilege of bail is discretionary, it is often refused or made prohibitively high to accused Negroes, particularly when the alleged crime is against whites. Then there is the fee system. Under this system—still in use in more than half the South—all the minor court officials get their pay out of fines.

Not only are all the court officials white, but the jury, too, is usually composed of whites only, except for cases in the federal courts and in some of the large cities. (Yet to prohibit Negroes from jury lists is clearly unconstitutional.) To this should be added that Negro lawyers are scarce in the South. In some places Negro lawyers are not allowed to appear in courts, and even where they are allowed, they tend to stay away. Negro clients know that a Negro lawyer is not much use in a Southern courtroom. There are other handicaps for Negro lawyers: their clients are usually poor; they cannot afford a well-equipped office; they have not had experience in handling important cases; they cannot specialize.

9. DISCRIMINATION IN COURT

In a court system of this structure, operating within a deeply prejudiced region, discrimination is to be expected. The danger is especially strong in lower courts, where the pressure of local public opinion is most strongly felt and where the judges are often men of limited education and provincial background.

In civil cases the average Negro will not only be unable to meet the costs involved, but when his adversary is a white man he also encounters white solidarity. Greater reliance is ordinarily given a white man's testimony than a Negro's. This fits into the pattern of thinking that it is dangerous to allow Negroes to vindicate their rights against white people. It is becoming more common nowadays, however, to give the Negroes what is due them as long as it concerns merely their property rights.

In criminal cases the discrimination does not always run against a Negro defendant. As long as only Negroes are concerned and no whites are disturbed, great leniency will be shown in most cases. This is particularly true in minor cases. The sentences for even major crimes are ordinarily reduced when the victim is another Negro.[8] The Southern Negro community is not at all happy about this

---

[8] A white lawyer from the Upper South writes in a letter (June 19, 1940):

"When the cases involve no such issues [on the race question] but are merely cases, I have noted that cases between Negro and Negro are handled somewhat differently than cases between white and white. I mean a spirit of levity, an expectation of something 'comical' appears to exist. The seriousness in the white vs. Negro case is decidedly lacking. As you know it is a rare case indeed in which a Negro who has murdered a Negro receives the extreme penalty, either death or life imprisonment here, regardless of the facts. Only the other day in a local case a Negro who murdered another with robbery as a motive, a charge that would have been as between white and white, or Negro and white victim, good for the electric chair, was disposed of by a jury with a 15 year sentence. The punishment as between Negro and Negro, as distinguished from white vs. white, or Negro vs. white victim, is decidedly different and clearly shows the racial approach to the question. In short the court-room feeling is that the Negro is entirely inferior, with punishment for crimes by him against his own kind punished with less punishment than when the white man is involved."

double standard of justice in favor of Negro offenders. Law-abiding Negroes point out that there are criminal and treacherous Negroes who secure immunity from punishment because they are fawning and submissive toward whites. Such persons are a danger to the Negro community. Leniency toward Negro defendants in cases involving crimes against other Negroes is thus actually a form of discrimination.

For offenses which involve any danger to whites, however, Negroes are punished more severely than whites. The courts, particularly the lower courts, often seem to take for granted the guilt of the accused Negro. Negro defendants are sentenced upon scanty evidence. There is an astonishing atmosphere of informality and lack of dignity in the courtroom, and speed seems to be the main goal. It should be emphasized, however, that there are great differences between different courts, due partly to the differences in the personalities of the judges. The higher state courts and the federal courts observe much more of judicial decorum and are, for this reason, less likely to discriminate against Negroes.

The jury, for the most part, is more guilty of obvious partiality than the judge and the public prosecutor. When the offender is a white man and the victim a Negro, a grand jury will often refuse to indict. It is notorious that practically never have white lynching mobs been brought to court in the South, even when the killers are known to all in the community and are mentioned by name in the local press.[9] When the offender is a Negro, indictment is easily obtained. The petit jury is even less impartial than the grand jury, since its range of powers is greater.

Public tension and community pressure increase with the seriousness of the alleged crime. If a lynching is threatened, the court makes no pretense at justice; the Negro must be condemned before the crowd gets him. On the other hand, it is quite common for a white criminal to be set free if his crime was against a Negro.

10. Sentences and Prisons

The South has the highest crime rates in the country. Not only Negroes but whites in the South, too, have a higher crime rate than the average for the nation. *Within* the South the number of convictions of Negroes is not much greater, on the average, than their proportion in the population. Not only do Negro criminals serve

[9] Witness the nation-wide publicity given to one of the few really serious attempts to convict the participants in the lynching of the Negro, Willie Earle, in Greenville, S.C., in the spring of 1947.

longer terms for crimes against whites, but they are pardoned and paroled much less frequently than white criminals in comparable circumstances.

America is famous for the high aims and accomplishments of many of its progressive penal institutions in the North and West, but America is famous also for the convict camps in the South. The low level of Southern penal institutions is well known. There is no doubt that the average Southern prison is likely to make hardened criminals of all who fall into its clutches. This inexpensive penal system in the South—from the point of view of budgetary income and outgo—is tremendously expensive from the point of view of real social costs.

Conditions are generally so bad in Southern prisons that it would be difficult to say whether Negro prisoners receive poorer treatment than white prisoners. The penal institutions in the South are usually segregated for whites and Negroes. There is some opportunity, therefore, for state officials to purchase less food and equipment for Negroes than for whites and to discriminate in other ways. The wardens and guards are, in all cases, Southern poor whites. Probably the most harmful form of discrimination occurs because several states do not provide separate reformatories for Negro juvenile offenders as they do for white juvenile offenders, and the Negro youth must live with the hardened older criminal.

11. Trends and Outlook on the Southern Legal System

This whole system of courts, sentences, and prisons in the South is overripe for fundamental reforms. It represents a tremendous lag in progressive, twentieth century America. There are, however, signs of change. The United States Supreme Court is increasingly active in censuring the state courts when they transgress the principles of legal procedure: it is pressing the courts to include Negroes on the jury lists, to curb appeals to race prejudice on the part of public prosecutors and private attorneys, to reject evidence obtained by third-degree methods, and so on. The attorneys of the federal government and the federal courts in the states have become more diligent in pursuing such offenses against civil liberties of Negroes as fall under their jurisdiction, thereby setting a pattern for the state courts also. Under these influences, the higher courts of the Southern states are increasingly condemning the more blatant forms of deviation from fair trial in the lower courts.

A new generation of lawyers with a better general education and professional training is coming forward; many of them will defend Negroes. The difficulty now is that most Negroes cannot afford good lawyers. Probably the most effective means of raising the standards of Southern courts would be the setting up of legal aid agencies everywhere in the South solely to assist poor whites and Negroes to enforce their rights under existing laws.

The growth of the educated class of Negroes in the South and the rising educational level of whites; the decreasing provincialism of the region, as a result of this and of industrialization, urbanization, and migration; the increasing importance of Southern liberalism; the activity of such organizations as the National Association for the Advancement of Colored People and the Southern Regional Council—all these are factors working toward the raising of Southern judicial standards. The continuous influence of public opinion and of the press of the North also is a major factor in reform. Another factor which is bound to have great influence in the future is the developing Negro vote.

Moreover, in principle, the average white Southerner is no longer prepared to defend racial inequality of justice. Much of the judicial discrimination against Negroes in the South seems to be tolerated by public opinion because of carelessness and ignorance in regard to the Negro rather than by an intentional and considered aim to discriminate. As far as public opinion is part of the problem, the task is, therefore, mainly one of adult education. White people must be taught to understand the damaging effects upon the whole society of a system of justice which is not equitable. Means must be found to bring the pressing problems of crime prevention and of punishment and prison reform into the awareness of the general public.

It is astonishing how far to the background these problems are pushed in America and how deep ignorance of them is even in the upper classes. Southern whites exaggerate the extent of Negro crime and underestimate the extent of white crime. Rape and sexual crimes play a great role in Southern thinking on the problem, but the idea that such crimes, when they occur, are probably symptoms of mental abnormality seems to be entirely absent. In the South, even educated people, when they think of punishment for crime, have their minds fixed on vengeance and on the isolation or eradication of the criminal. Seldom do they discuss punishment as a means of crime prevention. Other techniques of prevention—by rebuilding the criminal himself —are usually entirely ignored. It is not, however, difficult to understand the reasons behind this astonishing blind spot in Southern culture. These problems are unpopular because their discussion is bound to result in the demonstration that it is in the interest of society to care for the Negro—even for the criminal Negro.

12. THE PATTERN OF VIOLENCE

It is the custom in the South to permit whites to resort to violence and threats of violence against the life, personal security, property, and freedom of movement of Negroes. There is a wide variety of behavior, ranging from mild admonition to murder, which the white man may exercise to control Negroes. While the practice has its origin in slavery, it continues to flourish because of the laxity and inequity of the administration of law and justice. Any white man can strike or beat a Negro, steal or destroy his property, cheat him, and even take his life without much fear of legal reprisal. The minor forms of violence—cheating and striking—are everyday occurrences, but the major ones are infrequent enough to be talked about.

Negroes, of course, try to avoid situations in which violence is likely to occur, and if Negroes do incur the displeasure of a white man, a mere command or threat is usually enough to control them without the use of actual violence. The Negro's economic dependence upon whites makes these verbal controls especially potent. But accidental insult and sometimes nothing at all except the insecurity or sadism of certain whites can serve as occasion for violence. Of course, there are certain checks on violence: most Southerners do not want to be mean or dishonest toward Negroes directly. But the general attitude is one of let well enough alone: if a plantation owner cheats or beats his Negro tenants, "that's his business"; if a Negro is the victim of a sudden outburst of violence, "he must have done something to deserve it." Above all, the Negro must be kept in his "place."

There is little that Negroes can do to protect themselves. They cannot secure the protection of police or court against white men. They cannot secure the protection of white employers against white men unless the latter are poor or have a bad reputation. They can, of course, strike back but they know that that means a more violent retaliation, often in an organized form and with danger to other Negroes.

The principle that the law and the law-enforcing agencies are supreme, impartial, and above all groups in society has never taken strong root. White people are accustomed—individually[10] and in

[10] To the average Northerner, who has little contact with poor white Southerners but some contact with Southern Negroes, the carrying of knives and other weapons is a "Negro custom." Actually, of course, it is a Southern custom.

groups—to take the law into their own hands and to expect the police and the courts to ignore this or sometimes even lend their active co-operation.

13. Lynching

Lynching is spectacular and has attracted a good deal of popular and scientific attention. It is one Southern pattern which arouses disgust and reaction in the North and has, therefore, been made much of by Negro publicists. It should not be forgotten, however, that lynching is just one type of illegal violence in a whole range of types that exist in the South. The other types, which have already been considered, are much more common than lynching and their bad effects on white morals and Negro security are greater.

Between 1882 and 1946, according to Tuskegee Institute figures, 4,715 people were lynched, about three-fourths of whom were Negroes. The Southern states account for nine-tenths of the lynching. Over the years lynching has become more and more a Southern phenomenon and a racial one. While there has been a steady decrease in the number of victims in late years, there has been a marked trend toward greatly aggravated brutality, extending to torture, mutilation, and other sadistic excesses.

Lynching is a rural and small-town custom and occurs most commonly in poor districts. There are some indications that lynchings go in waves and tend to recur in the same districts. The accusations against persons lynched during the period for which there are records were: in 38 per cent of the cases for homicide, 6 per cent for felonious assault, 16 per cent for rape, 7 per cent cent for attempted rape, 7 per cent for theft, 2 per cent for insult to white persons, and 24 per cent for miscellaneous offenses or no offense at all. In the last category are all sorts of irritations: testifying in court against a white man or bringing suit against him, refusal to pay a note, seeking employment out of place, offensive language or boastful remarks. The meaning of these facts is that, in principle, a lynching is not merely a punishment against an individual but a disciplinary device against the Negro group.

The Negroes' imputed desire to rape white women is the most frequent reason given in defense of lynching. Actually, only 23 per cent of the victims were accused of raping or attempting to rape. There is reason to believe that even this figure has been inflated by the fact that a mob which makes the accusation of rape is secure against any further investigation, by the broad Southern definition of rape to include all sex relations between Negro men and white women, and by the psychopathic fears of white women in their contacts with Negro men. The causes of lynching must, therefore, be found outside the Southern rationalization of "protecting white womanhood."

14. THE REAL CAUSES OF LYNCHING

The psychopathology of the lynching mob has been discussed intensively in recent years. Poverty and economic fear have been stressed as background factors. It is generally held that the rise of lynchings during and immediately after the First World War had much to do with the increased mobility of and competition from Negroes during this period. There is a substantial correlation from year to year between low cotton prices and a high number of lynchings. Economic fear is mixed with social fear: a feeling that the Negro is "getting out of his place" and that the white man's social status is being threatened and is in need of defense. ". . . Lynching is much more an expression of Southern fear of Negro progress than of Negro crime," writes Walter White.[11]

The low level of education and general culture in the white South is another important background factor. Allied with it is the prevalence of a narrow-minded and intolerant "fundamentalist" type of Protestant evangelical religion. Another important background factor is the isolation, the dullness, and the boredom of rural and small-town life in the South.

Thus far we have considered the background factors and underlying causes of lynching. The causation is such that, when the time is ripe, almost any incident may touch it off. The incident is usually some crime, real or suspected, by a Negro against a white, or merely a "racial insult," such as a Negro's buying an automobile or stepping beyond the etiquette of race relations in any way. Rumors will often start or quicken a lynching. The lynching itself may take one or two main forms: in a *mob* lynching the whole community will participate with a high degree of frenzy; in a *vigilante* lynching a restricted number of men, often disguised, will perform the deed with much ceremony. The actual participants usually belong to the frustrated lower classes of Southern whites. Occasionally, however, the people of the middle and upper classes take part, and generally they condone the deed. Women and children are not absent from lynching mobs; indeed, women sometimes incite the mobs to action.

Where a lynching has occurred, the relations between Negroes and whites deteriorate. The Negroes are terror-stricken and sullen.

[11] *Rope and Faggot* (New York: Alfred A. Knopf, 1929), p. 11.

The whites are anxious and are likely to show the assertiveness and suspicion of persons with bad, but hardened, consciences. The long-run effects of lynching also are bad. Crime is not hampered but stimulated by violence. Far outside the locality where the lynching has occurred, in fact, all over the nation, it brutalizes feeling. It must have a particularly bad influence upon interracial attitudes of young people in the two groups. Thus lynching has a psychological importance out of all proportion to the few times it occurs.

The rising standard of living and improved education have no doubt been of importance in the decline of lynching; the fundamentalism and emotionalism of Southern religion have been decreasing, and the radio, improved highways, and cheap motorcars have made life in a small town less drab and monotonous. The national agitation against lynching, especially the introduction of several antilynching bills in Congress, has undoubtedly been of tremendous importance in stopping lynching.

Southern organizations of whites—some religious denominations, the Commission for Interracial Cooperation (now the Southern Regional Council), and many women's organizations—have been active in fighting lynching. Southern newspapers today come out openly against lynching and state authorities usually try to prevent lynchings. Behind this movement is the growing strength of Southern liberalism.

It is often said that lynching is declining but that there are substitutes for it—the killing of Negro criminals by police officers, the quick and predetermined trial, or quiet murder without the formation of a mob.[12] The authors believe that the substitutes, too, have been declining, but all the forms of violence against Negroes—striking, beating, robbing, destroying property, exiling, threatening—still occur often in the South. In the last analysis, the true cause of lynching, as of these other forms of violence and intimidation, is that white society does not respect the rights of Negroes on equal terms.

15. Riots

In one sense, the riot is the most extreme form of mob violence used to prevent Negroes from getting justice. In another sense, however, the riot is quite different from all other forms of mob violence: it is not a one-way punishment, but a two-way battle. The Negroes may be hopelessly outnumbered and beaten, but they

[12] For example, Tuskegee Institute reports only 1 lynching for 1945, but the Pittsburgh *Courier* reports 5 additional murders. Tuskegee reports 6 lynchings for 1946, the *Courier* adds 11 murders. (Pittsburgh *Courier*, June 14, 1947, p. 5.)

fight back. There is danger to the white man participating in the riot as there usually is not when he engages in other forms of violence against Negroes. The riot is as much, or more, characteristic of the North than it is of the South. The riot is primarily an urban phenomenon, as lynching is primarily a rural one.

It is impossible to say whether there is a trend in the number of riots. A great number of riots occurred during and just after the First World War, when the North was concerned with the tremendous migration of Negroes from the South and the South was concerned about the possible demands of returning Negro soldiers. Recent years have seen few race riots. They have become as unpopular as lynchings. There was a major riot in Detroit in 1942, arising out of the wartime migration of Negroes and Southern whites to that city. Throughout the country, cities and states took immediate steps to prevent anything like this from happening again during the war.

The causation of riots would seem to be much like that of lynching. There is a background of mounting tension, caused by economic insecurity of whites, belief that the Negro is rising, sex jealousy, boredom on the part of the lower classes of the white population. The local police are often known to be on the side of the whites. The breaking point is caused by a crime or rumor of crime by a Negro against a white person, or by the attempt of a Negro to claim a legal right. The effects of riots may be even more harmful to amicable race relations than those of lynching. Whites do not feel the twinge of bad conscience and their feelings of fear and insecurity are increased when some of their own number have been killed or injured.

That there have been no large-scale riots since 1942 is due to two things: the new consciousness of the American Creed and of its significance for Negroes; and, in some of the large and congested cities of the North, intelligent and foresighted plans to scotch rumors as they occur, to liquidate acute racial tensions to some extent, and to some training of the police in handling dangerous incidents. During the war, official committees were appointed by city mayors to do these things to prevent riots, but the end of the war has seen some tendency for these committees to become inactive.

The Basis of Social Inequality

1. THE VALUE PREMISE FOR THE STUDY OF SOCIAL INEQUALITY

The word "social" has two distinct meanings. There is the scientific usage of the term to refer to the whole range of relations between men. There is also the popular usage that refers to personal relations, particularly those of an intimate sort. It is in the latter sense that the term "social" is here used. Equality in "social relations" is commonly denied American Negroes. An elaborate system separates the two groups and prevents the building up of intimate relations on the plane of equality. Some of these segregation measures have a spatial or institutional character, others are embodied in an etiquette of racial behavior.

Our main value premise here is again the idea of equality of opportunity in the American Creed. Race and color are not accepted as grounds for discrimination according to the Creed. Social discrimination is defined from this value premise as an arrangement which restricts opportunities for some individuals more than for others. Judged by the norm of equality in the American Creed, such practices are unfair and wrong. As far as public services and state regulations are concerned, the Constitution requires that the Creed be adhered to.

But when segregation and discrimination are the outcome of individual action, the second main norm of the American Creed, namely, liberty, can be invoked in their defense. It must be left to the individual white man's own discretion whether or not he wants to receive Negroes in his home, shake hands with them, and eat with them. When, however, legal, economic, or social sanctions are applied to enforce conformity from *other* whites and when Negroes are made to adjust their behavior in response to *organized* white demands, this violates the norm of personal liberty. There is a certain amount of conflict between the demand for personal liberty, on the one hand, and the need for equality, on the other. But there is hardly any doubt that the major portion of the system of social segregation and discrimination against Negroes is a challenge to the American Creed. As this system is administered in practice, most of it is unconstitutional and even contrary to the state laws which, in the South as in the North, are framed in terms of equality.

We shall here attempt to study the mechanism of social segregation and discrimination as it operates today in various regions of the country. We shall again have to devote the major part of our inquiry to conditions in the South, where more than three-fourths of the Negro people live and where segregation and discrimination are most prevalent.

2. THE ONE-SIDEDNESS OF THE SYSTEM OF SEGREGATION

We shall start from the fact that social segregation and discrimination are a system of deprivations forced upon the Negro group by the white group. This becomes apparent in the one-sidedness of the system. Negroes are not admitted to white churches in the South, but if a strange white man enters a Negro church the visit is received as a great honor. Likewise, a white stranger will be received with utmost respect and cordiality in any Negro school.

The rules are understood to be for the protection of whites and directed against Negroes. The white man may waive most of the customs, as long as he does not demonstrate such friendliness that he becomes known as a "nigger lover"; the reaction then comes, however, from white society. A white man can recognize a Negro on the street and stop for a chat, or he can ignore him. He can offer his hand to shake, or he can keep it back. Negroes often complain about the uncertainty they experience because the initiative always belongs to the white man. When the white man takes certain freedoms, he usually gives the Negro to understand that he, the Negro, cannot claim them as a right. In so far as there is any restriction on the white man's freedom, this is made to appear as a privilege, whereas each restriction on the Negro's freedom is culturally defined as an insult or a discrimination. The one-sidedness of the system is apparent also in the fact that the better accommodations are always reserved for white people.

3. THE JIM CROW LAWS

There is no doubt that, after the Civil War, Congress intended to give the Negroes "social equality" in public life to a substantial degree. Besides the Thirteenth, Fourteenth, and Fifteenth Amendments to the Constitution (known as the Reconstruction Amendments), there was the Civil Rights Bill of 1875, which was explicit in declaring that all persons within the jurisdiction of the United States should be entitled to the full and equal enjoyment of inns, public conveyances, theaters, and other places of public amusement. Negroes, however, met considerable segregation and discrimination even during these few years of legal equality.

When, however, in 1883 the Supreme Court declared the Civil Rights Bill of 1875 unconstitutional in so far as it referred to acts of social discrimination by individuals, the way was left open for the Jim Crow legislation of the Southern states and municipalities. For a quarter of a century this system of statutes and regulations—separating the two groups in schools, on railroad cars and streetcars, in hotels and restaurants, in parks and playgrounds, in theaters and public meeting places—continued to grow, with the explicit purpose of diminishing, as far as was practicable and possible, the social contacts between whites and Negroes in the South.

The effect of this legislation was to push Negroes continuously backward. Before the Jim Crow legislation, white people tended to treat Negroes somewhat differently depending upon their class and education. This tendency was broken by the laws that applied to *all* Negroes. As we shall find, there is a tendency recently to apply the segregation rules with some discretion to Negroes of different class status.

The Southern whites in passing their various segregation laws to legalize social discrimination had to manufacture a legal fiction to get around the constitutional provision that Negroes are to enjoy full citizenship in the United States, that they are entitled to the "equal benefit of all laws," and that "no state shall make or enforce any law which shall abridge the privileges and immunities of citizens of the United States." The legal term for this trick in the social field is "separate but equal." That is, Negroes were to get equal accommodations, but separate from the whites. It is evident, however, and rarely denied that there is practically no single instance of segregation in the South which has not been utilized for discrimination. Again the Southern white man is in the moral dilemma of having to frame his laws in terms of equality and to defend them before the Supreme Court—and before his own better conscience, which is tied to the American Creed—while knowing all the time that in reality his laws do not give equality to Negroes and that he does not want them to do so.

4. BELIEFS SUPPORTING SOCIAL INEQUALITY

Of course, many Negroes, particularly in the South, are poor, un-educated, and deficient in health, morals, and manners and thus not very agreeable as social companions. In the South the importance of this is enhanced by the great proportion of Negroes in the total population.

This point is, however, more complicated. For one thing, there is a great class of Southern whites who are also poor and uneducated or who are coarse and dirty. Their presence in the South does not help the Negroes, however. It is, rather, the very thing that raises the need for a sky-high color bar. This class of whites knows that other whites are disposed to regard them as "just as bad as niggers," and they know, too, that they have always been despised by the Negroes, who call them "poor white trash." It is in their interest, on the one hand, to stress equality among all white people and, on the other hand, the gulf between the whites and Negroes. The rising Negroes became a threat to the status of these poor whites.

Most middle- and upper-class whites also get satisfaction out of the subserviency and humbleness of lower-class Negroes. The ordinary vicious circle—that the actual inferiority of the Negro masses gives reason for discrimination against them, while at the same time discrimination makes it difficult to improve themselves—is, in the social sphere, loaded with the desire on the part of lower-class whites, and also perhaps of the majority of middle- and upper-class whites, that Negroes remain inferior. This fact that a large class of whites is not much better off than the masses of Negroes, while whole groups of Negroes are decidedly on a higher level—in this situation when a general segregation policy protecting *all* whites against *all* Negroes has to be justified—makes the beliefs in the racial inferiority of Negroes a much-needed rationalization.

A tendency to exaggerate the lower-class traits of Negroes is apparent. One is told constantly that all Negroes are dirty, immoral, and unreliable. The fact that the average white man seldom sees an educated Negro makes it easier to believe in this stereotype. The feeling may be that Negroes have capacity but that it needs to be developed, and that takes a long time—"several centuries," it is usually said. Often it is argued that the low morals and the ignorance of Negroes are so prevalent that Negroes must be separated. It is also pointed out that Negroes are different in physical appearance even if they have the same basic mental and moral capacities. These differences are claimed to be repugnant to the white man.

Besides these beliefs centering around Negro inferiority, there are a great number of other popular thoughts justifying social segregation. One is that Negroes like to be separated, that they are happy in their humble status and would not like to be treated as equals. Another is that separation is necessary in order to prevent friction between the two groups. This thought is usually supported by the reflection that the whites "would not stand for" another social order. Segregation thus becomes motivated directly by the whites' will to segregate and by certain untested assumptions regarding the state of public opinion. Segregation and subordination of Negroes are also commonly supported by the consideration that these things have "always been" and are part of the mores and the social structure. Earlier, and to some extent even today, this direct application of the conservative principle was bolstered by religion. Race prejudice is presented as a "deep-rooted, God-implanted instinct." This thought that Negro subordination is part of God's plan for the world has, however, never been uncontested. The Bible, especially the New Testament, is filled with passages supporting equality, and the heart of Christian teaching is to "love thy neighbor as thyself."

Two points need to be made about the beliefs mentioned thus far: first—with the exception of the racial and theological beliefs, both of which are gradually losing out—they support segregation but not discrimination, not even that discrimination which arises out of segregation. Second, they do not support a wholesale segregation, for *some* Negroes are not educationally, morally, or occupationally inferior; *some* Negroes do not want to be segregated; and *some* whites feel no repugnance to the physical appearance of the Negro. If a man held these beliefs alone, therefore, and were willing to act upon them, and if he were provided with relevant facts, he would not advocate complete segregation and would permit immediate social equality to some Negroes in their relations with whites (at the same time he would want to restrict equality for some whites). As this is not the attitude of most whites, we have an indication that these beliefs are fundamentally rationalizations and not the real reasons for segregation and discrimination.

It would, indeed, be possible to defend the caste order simply by arguing that it is in the white people's interests to keep the Negroes subordinate. The remarkable thing, however, is that, in America, social segregation and discrimination are practically never motivated in this straightforward way. The motivation is usually suppressed, as being in flagrant conflict with the American Creed and the Christian religion. But it is equally clear that most white people take good care of their interests and practice discrimination even when it is not required for segregation, and that segregation most often has the function of allowing discrimination advantageous to whites.

5. The Theory of "No Social Equality"

The kernel of the popular theory of "no social equality" is a firm determination on the part of the whites to block amalgamation and preserve "the purity of the white race." The white man identifies himself with "the white race"; important in this identification is the notion of "the absolute and unchangeable superiority of the white race." From this racial dogma will often be drawn the *direct* inference that the white man shall dominate in all spheres. But when the logic of this inference is inquired about, the inference will be made *indirect* and to lead over to the danger of amalgamation, or, as it is popularly expressed, "intermarriage."

It is further found that the ban on intermarriage is focused on white women. For them it covers both formal marriage and illicit intercourse. It is more or less taken for granted that white men would not stoop to marry Negro women, and illicit intercourse does not fall under the same intense taboo, since offspring of illicit intercourse become Negroes anyway.[1] To prevent "intermarriage" in this specific sense of sex relations between white women and Negro men, it is not enough to apply legal and social sanctions against it—so the popular theory runs. In using the danger of intermarriage as a defense for the whole caste system, it is assumed both that Negro men have a strong desire for "intermarriage" and that white women would be open to proposals from Negro men *if* they were not guarded from even meeting them on an equal plane. This is not openly expressed, but is implicit in the popular theory. The conclusion follows that the whole system of segregation and discrimination is justified. Every single measure is defended as necessary to block "social equality," which in turn is held necessary to prevent "intermarriage."

The measures of segregation and discrimination are often of the type found in the true taboos and in the notion "not to be touched" of primitive religion. The specific taboos are characterized, further, by a different degree of excitement which attends their violation and

[1] James Weldon Johnson observes that in the South ". . . a white gentleman may not eat with a colored person without the danger of serious loss of social prestige; yet he may sleep with a colored person without incurring the risk of any appreciable damage to his reputation," and concludes, "Social equality signifies a series of far-flung barriers against amalgamation of the two races; except so far as it may come about by white men with colored women." (*Along This Way* [New York: The Viking Press, 1933], pp. 312–313.)

a different degree of punishment to the violator: the closer the act to sexual association the more furious is the public reaction. Sexual association itself is punished by death and is accompanied by tremendous public excitement; the other social relations meet decreasing degrees of public fury.

Sex becomes, in this popular theory, the principle around which the whole structure of segregation of Negroes—down to disfranchisement and denial of equal opportunities on the labor market—is organized. The reasoning is this: "May not all equalities be ultimately based on potential social equality, and that in turn on intermarriage?" In cruder language, the Southern man on the street responds to any plea for social equality: "Would you like to have your daughter marry a Negro?"

This theory of color caste centering around the aversion to intermarriage determines the white man's rather definite rank order of the various measures of segregation and discrimination against Negroes. In this rank order (1), the ban on intermarriage and other sex relations involving white women and colored men, takes precedence before everything else. It is the end for which the other restrictions are arranged as means. Thereafter follow: (2) all sorts of taboos and etiquettes in personal contacts; (3) segregation in schools and churches; (4) segregation in hotels, restaurants, theaters, and other public places where people meet socially; (5) segregation in public conveyances; (6) discrimination in public services; and finally, inequality in (7) politics, (8) justice, and (9) breadwinning and relief.

The degree of liberalism on racial matters in the white South can be designated mainly by the point on this rank order where a man stops because he believes further segregation and discrimination are not necessary to prevent "intermarriage." White liberals in the South today rather unanimously stand up against inequality in breadwinning, relief, justice, and politics. Hardly anybody in the South, however, is prepared to go the whole way and argue that the ban on intermarriage should be lifted.

6. CRITICAL EVALUATION OF THE "NO SOCIAL EQUALITY" THEORY

The sincerity of the average white person's psychological identification with the "white race" and his aversion to amalgamation should not be doubted; neither should his attitude that the upholding of the caste system is necessary to prevent amalgamation. But the way in which he constantly interchanges the concepts "amalgamation" and "intermarriage"—meaning a white woman's marriage to, or sex relations with, a Negro man—is bewildering. Amalgamation both in the

South and in the North is, and has always been, mainly a result not of marriage but of illicit sex relations. And these illicit sex relations have in the main been confined to white men and colored women.

However, since all mixed bloods are classified as Negroes, sex relations between white men and colored women affect only the Negro race. Sex relations between Negro men and white women, on the other hand, would be like an *attempt* to pour Negro blood into the white race. It cannot succeed, of course, as the child would be considered a Negro. But the white woman would be absolutely degraded. She must be protected and this type of amalgamation prevented by all available means.

The statement frequently made by whites in the South that there is an instinctive sexual repulsion between the two groups is doubtful, in view of the amount of white blood in the Negro people. Besides, if it were true, the insistence upon the measures for racial separation for preventing intermarriage would be unnecessary. Even the more general statement that there is an inherent repulsion to personal intimacies and physical contact between the two groups is unfounded. The acceptability of physical contact with favorite servants and the playing together of small children of both races are cases in point. This brings us to a consideration of the extent to which the anti-amalgamation doctrine is merely a rationalization of purely social demands, particularly those concerning social status.

We have already observed that the license of white men to have illicit intercourse with Negro women does not extend to formal marriage. The reason is that the latter but not the former relation gives social status to the Negro woman and takes status away from the white man. For a white woman both legal marriage and illicit relations with Negroes cause her to lose caste. The status concerns are obvious and they are serious enough both in the North and in the South to prevent intermarriage. But as they are functions of the caste apparatus, which, in this popular theory, is itself explained as a means of preventing intermarriage, the whole theory becomes largely a logical circle.

The circular character of this reasoning is enhanced when we realize that the great majority of nonliberal white Southerners use the dread of "intermarriage" and the theory of "no social equality" to justify discriminations which have quite other and wider goals than the purity of the white race. Things are defended in the South as means of preserving racial purity which cannot possibly be defended in this way. To this extent we cannot avoid observing that *what white people really want is to keep Negroes in a lower status.* "Intermarriage" itself is resented because it would be the supreme indication of "social equality," while the rationalization is that "social equality" is opposed because it would bring "intermarriage."

The persistent preoccupation with sex and marriage in the rationalization of social segregation and discrimination against Negroes is, to this extent, an irrational escape on the part of the whites from voicing an open demand for difference in social status between the two groups for its own sake. This has been particularly needed because of the strength of the American Creed. A people with less emphatic democratic beliefs would be more able to uphold a caste system without this tense belief in sex and race dangers.

The fixation on the purity of white womanhood and also part of the intensity of emotion surrounding the whole sphere of segregation and discrimination are to be understood partly as the results of the sore conscience on the part of white men for their own or other whites' relations with, or desires for, Negro women.

Our practical conclusion is that it would have cleansing effects on race relations in America, and particularly in the South, to have an open and sober discussion in rational terms of this ever-present theory of "intermarriage" and "social equality," giving matters their factual ground, true proportions, and logical relations. Great inhibitions have been built up against such a detached and critical discussion of this theory. There are reasons to believe, however, that a slow but steady cleansing of the American mind is proceeding as the cultural level is raised. The basic racial inferiority doctrine is being undermined by research and education. For a white man to have illicit relations with Negro women is increasingly meeting disapproval. Negroes themselves are more and more frowning upon such relations. This all must tend to dampen the emotional fires around "social equality." Sex and race fears are, however, even today the main defense for segregation and the whole caste order.

7. Attitudes among Different Classes of Whites in the South

Certain attitudes common in the South become more understandable when we recognize that, behind all rationalizing stereotyped beliefs and popular theories, a main concern of the white man is to preserve social inequality for its own sake. One such attitude is the great sympathy so often displayed in the upper classes of Southern whites toward the "old-time darky" who adheres to the patterns of slavery. The "unreconstructed aristocrat" after the Civil War believed with Carlyle that "[the Negro] is useful in God's creation only as a servant";[2] he remained paternalistic; he wanted to keep the Negroes dependent and resented their attempts to rise through education; he mistrusted the younger generation of Negroes; but he liked the individual Negro whom he knew personally and who conformed to the old relation of master and servant—who "stayed in his place."

Even today this attitude helps to determine the relations between the two groups in rural districts. It forms the pattern of the relationship between employer and employee on the plantation and in household service. This is a survival of slavery society where friendliness is restricted to the individual and not extended to the group, and is based on a clear and unchallenged recognition from both sides of an insurmountable social inequality. The paternalistic pattern becomes particularly cherished by the white men as it so openly denotes an aristocratic origin. This gives it its strength to survive. It is a sign of social distinction to a white man to stand in this paternalistic relation to Negroes. This explains why so much of the conversation in the Southern upper and middle classes turns around the follies of Negro servants. Their Negro dependents and their own relations to them play a significant role for white people's status in society.

To receive this traditional friendliness on the part of Southern white upper-class persons, a Negro has to be a lower-class Negro and to behave as a humble servant. When the Negro rises socially and is no longer a servant, he becomes a stranger to the white upper class. His ambition is suspected. He is disliked. The exceptions are when he, in spite of not being a servant, can establish a relationship of personal dependence and when he, in this relationship, can act out a role of deference and humility. He is then able to confer even more status to the white partner, and he is also rewarded by more protection and favors. Upper-class white men frequently praise Negro college presidents and other white-appointed Negro leaders quite beyond any reasonable deserts, merely for their humble demeanor.

Generally speaking, this attitude on the part of upper-class whites has demoralizing effects on Negroes. In employment relations the paternalistic pattern tends to diminish the Negroes' formal responsibilities. The Negro worker has less definite obligations as well as more uncertain rights. He comes to be paid, not only for his work, but also for his humility, for being satisfied with his "place," and for his cunning in cajoling and flattering his master. He has ready excuses for not becoming a really good worker. He is discouraged when

[2] Thomas Carlyle, *Occasional Discourse on the Nigger Question* (London: T. Bosworth, 1853; first printed in *Fraser's Magazine* [December, 1849]), p. 28.

he tries "to work his way up." Upper-class Negroes often find it advantageous to pretend dependence in order to avert hostility from the whites. This is one of the main roots of Negro "laziness and shiftlessness." And there are circular effects back on the whites—on their own standards and on the standards they expect from their servants. Deference is bought for lowered demands of efficiency.

There is in the South, however, another type of aristocratic attitude toward the Negroes, which is equally reluctant to modify the color bar but is prepared to allow the Negro people a maximum of possibilities for cultural growth and economic advancement behind the bar. The difference in attitude will show up significantly in relation to the upper- and middle-class Negroes. The ordinary white upper-class people will "have no use" for such Negroes. They need cheap labor—faithful, obedient, unambitious labor. But the white liberals are doing what they can to give the Negro a chance to rise behind the color bar.

So far we have considered only white upper-class people. It is the ambition of the white middle-class people in the South to identify themselves with the aristocratic traditions of the region, and, for reasons already mentioned, their relation to the Negroes is crucial to the achievement of their ambition. They will hasten to inform even the casual acquaintance of their relationship to slaveowners and of any old Negro servants—particularly if by any stretch of the definition a servant can be called "mammy." In their public contacts many middle-class whites try to manifest benevolent condescension toward Negroes. On the other hand, some of them are in competition with Negroes and many of them are able to rise economically only by exploiting Negroes. The attitudes of this white middle class toward the rising Negroes are decidedly less friendly than are those of the white upper class, and their attitudes toward even the subservient lower-class Negroes are decidedly conflicting.

Lower-class whites in the South have no Negro servants in whose humble demeanors they can reflect their own superiority. Instead, they feel actual economic competition or fear of potential competition from the Negroes. They need the caste line for much more substantial reasons than do the middle and upper classes. They are the people likely to stress aggressively that *no* Negro can *ever* attain the status of even the *lowest* white. The educated Negro, the Negro professional or businessman, the Negro landowner, will appear to them "uppity," "smart," and "out of place." They look on the formation behind the color line of a Negro upper and middle class as a challenge to their own status. They want all Negroes kept down "in

their place"—this place is to them defined realistically as under them-
selves. They are jealous of every dollar that goes to Negro education.
They will insist that the caste etiquette be enforced upon the rising
Negroes as well as upon lower-class Negroes.

The lower-class whites have been the popular strength behind
Negro disfranchisement and are the audience to which the "nigger-
baiting" political demagogue of the South appeals. They create the
popular pressure upon Southern courts to deny Negroes equal justice.
They form the active lynching mobs; they are responsible also for
most of the petty outrages practiced on the Negro group. They are
the interested party in economic discrimination against Negroes,
keeping Negroes out of jobs which they want themselves.

The unfriendly attitudes on the part of the lower-class whites become especially detrimental to the Negroes since upper- and middle-
class whites are inclined to let them have their way. Plantation owners and employers, who use Negro labor as cheaper and more docile,
have at times been observed to tolerate, or even co-operate in, the
periodic aggressions of poor whites against Negroes. It is a plausible
thesis that they do so in the interest of upholding the caste system
that is so effective in keeping the Negro docile. It is also probable
that the hatred of lower-class whites toward Negroes is partly dis-
located aggression arising from their own social and economic frustrations in white society.

The bitterness of racial feelings on the part of whites seems to be
slowly declining, and the lower classes are following the trend. There
is, moreover, one big factor of change which works directly on the
lower classes of whites. This is the growth of unionism in the South,
which has been especially important in the past half dozen years.
Many of the new unions have a policy of "no discrimination against
Negroes" and they have not only followed this policy strictly but
have undertaken to educate their white members to both the morality
and the necessity of such measures. In addition, business meetings
and in some cases social affairs are unsegregated; this, together with
working together on the job, has increased friendly personal contacts
and built up a feeling of class as opposed to racial solidarity. Since
unionism is increasing and will undoubtedly continue to do so in the
South, it is probable that caste antagonisms on the lower economic
levels will break down much faster in the future.

8. Social Segregation and Discrimination in the North

In the social field—as in breadwinning, but not as in politics and
justice—the North has kept much segregation and discrimination. In

some respects, the social bars were raised considerably on account of the mass immigration of poor and ignorant Negroes during and immediately after the First World War. Even so, it is a gross exaggeration when it is asserted that the North is getting to be "like the South." Even in the realm of social relations the average Northerner does not think of the Negroes as former slaves. He has not the possessive feeling for them and he does not regard their subservience as a mark of his own social status. He is, therefore, likely to let the Negroes alone. The ordinary Northerner is, further, conscious that social discrimination is wrong and against the American Creed, while the average Southerner tries to convince himself and the nation that it is right, or, in any case, necessary.

Moreover, in the North there is unawareness on the part of white people of the extent of social discrimination against Negroes. White Northerners are frequently surprised and shocked when they hear about such things and sometimes feel that something ought to be done to stop it. In this situation one of the difficulties for the Negroes in the North is simply lack of publicity. It is convenient for the Northerners' conscience to forget about the Negro. In so far as the Negroes can get their claims voiced in the press and in the legislatures, and are able to put political strength behind them, they are free to press for state action against social discrimination. The chances are that they will meet little *open* opposition.

Moreover, social segregation and discrimination have not acquired the strength, persuasiveness, or institutional fixity found in the South. Actual discrimination varies a good deal in the North: in several minor cities with a small, stable Negro population, social discrimination is hardly noticeable. In the bigger cities, the conditions of life for the Negroes have not been so good. In the Northern cities nearer the Mason and Dixon line there has always been more social segregation and discrimination than farther North.

One factor which in every Northern city of any size has contributed to form patterns of segregation and discrimination against Negroes has been residential segregation, which acts as a cause as well as an effect of social distance. Residential segregation followed the pattern for ethnic groups to live together in Northern cities. But while Swedes, Italians, and Jews could become Americanized in a generation or two and disperse themselves into other parts of the city, Negroes were caught in their "quarters" because of their inescapable social visibility; and real estate interests kept watch to enforce residential segregation. With residential segregation naturally comes a certain amount of segregation in schools, in hospitals, and in other public places even when it is not intended. Personal contacts become, as a matter of course, more or less restricted to Negro neighborhoods.

In this process white Southerners who also moved northward have played a crucial role. To make a manager of a hotel, a restaurant, or a theater keep Negroes out of his establishment, it is not necessary that more than a tiny minority of customers object, particularly if they make a scene.

The migrating Negroes have probably been even more influential in spreading Southern patterns in the North than the Southern whites. The low cultural level and poverty of the average Southern Negro stand out even more when he comes north, where general standards are higher. If he comes without any other education, he is at least thoroughly trained in scraping his foot, tipping his hat, and generally being subservient and unobtrusive in the company of whites. The submissive behavior of lower-class Southern Negroes is usually not at all appealing to the white Northerner, who has not been brought up to have a patronizing attitude and who does not need it for his own self-elevation. The white Northerner also dislikes the slovenliness and ignorance of the Southern Negro. Thus the Negro often seems only strange, funny, or repulsive to the white Northerner.

The resentment against Negroes in the North is different from that in the South, not only in intensity but also in its class direction. It does not seem to be directed against the rising Negroes. In the Yankee outlook on life, climbing and social success are given a higher value than in Southern society, and the ambitious Negro will often be rewarded with approval and even admiration.

Otherwise, the North is not original in its prejudice. When there is segregation and discrimination to be justified, the rationalization is sometimes a vague and simplified version of the "no social equality" theory of the South. More often the rationalizations run in terms of the alleged racial inferiority of the Negro, his animal-like nature, his unreliability, his low morals, dirtiness, and unpleasant manners. The references and associations to amalgamation and intermarriage are much less frequent and direct. This does not mean that the Northerner approves of intermarriage. But he is less emotional in his disapproval.

Not only is intermarriage frowned upon, but in high schools and colleges there will often be attempts to exclude Negroes from dances and social affairs. Social segregation is likely to appear in all sorts of social relations. But there is much less social segregation and discrimination than in the South. There is no segregation on street cars, trains, and so on, and above all, there is no rigid ceremonial governing Negro-white relations and no laws holding the Negro down. Since Negroes in the North may have the vote and a reasonable amount of justice in court, and since they can go to good schools and are, in fact, forced to get at least an elementary education, they can struggle for fuller social equality with some hope.

CHAPTER XIII

Social Segregation and

Its Effects

1. Segregation and Discrimination in Interpersonal Relations

In the preceding chapter the primary interest was in the attitudes displayed in connection with segregation and discrimination and the popular theories advanced as reasons for segregation. This chapter describes the actual patterns of social segregation.

The ban on intermarriage has the highest place in the white man's rank order of segregation and discrimination. Intermarriage is prohibited by law in all the Southern states, in all but five of the non-Southern states west of the Mississippi River, but only in Indiana among the Northern states east of the Mississippi. In practice there is little intermarriage even where it is not prohibited, since the social isolation from the white world that the white partner must undergo is generally intolerable even to those few white people who have enough social contact and are unprejudiced enough to consider marriage with Negroes. It is said that—as a reaction to the white attitude and as a matter of "race pride"—the Negro community is increasingly likely to ostracize mixed couples. This reaction is, however, much more pronounced toward illicit relations involving Negro women, and it has there the good reason that such relations are mostly of an exploitative type.

Extramarital relations between Negro men and white women are all but nonexistent in the South. There seems to be a small amount of interracial sexual experimentation in the North in bohemian and radical circles involving Negro men and white women. There are also some white prostitutes catering to Negro men. Although it is difficult to get accurate information, there is no doubt that extra-marital relations between white men and Negro women are fairly common throughout both the South[1] and the North. Though tolerated, it is not favored by public opinion and is usually secret. The old custom of white men keeping Negro concubines is disappearing in the South and is rare in the North.

Perhaps the most important thing in the South is the regulation of all the contacts between adult members of the two races so that these contacts will be as impersonal as possible. This is commonly called "the etiquette of race relations." This ceremonious attitude in race relations is especially striking when we consider that the American tends to be unceremonious in all his other relations.

The relations that, outside of the purely sexual, are most intimate and are never tolerated between Negroes and whites in the South are those which imply erotic advances or associations if the male partner is a Negro. Any attempt at flirtatious behavior in words or deeds will put him in danger of his life. Negro-white dancing is forbidden in the South whether the Negro partner be male or female. Even in the North interracial dancing seldom occurs. The taboo against swimming together in the South is equally absolute, apparently for the reason that it involves the exposure of large parts of the body. In the North the taboo against using the same beaches or swimming pools also is strong.

The main symbol of social inequality between the two groups has traditionally been the taboo against eating together. The taking of meals in America has little social importance and is almost barren of all the rituals of the older countries. In spite of frequent assertions to the contrary, eating in the South when only white people are present is generally an even simpler affair than in the North. But in interracial relations eating together has tremendous social significance. For whites and Negroes to eat together would call forth serious condemnation in the South. If a Negro man and a white woman should eat together, the matter would be even more serious. At interracial conferences where eating takes place, Negro participants are sometimes served in separate rooms or at separate tables in the same room. In factory lunchrooms, Negroes eat in separate rooms

---

[1] The toleration in the South is abetted by prohibiting Negro men from protecting their women against the white man's advances. In the city studied by Allison Davis and John Dollard (*Children of Bondage* [Washington, D.C.: American Council on Education, 1940], pp. 234–246), a Negro minister who protested in his pulpit against interracial liaisons was warned by a group of white businessmen.

or have to wait until the whites finish. Drinking is apparently less of an issue than eating. It is not considered quite so intimate since it requires less time and does not demand that the participants sit down. For a white woman to take part in an interracial drinking party would, however, be as bad as eating with Negroes, and it practically never occurs.

In the North the taboo against interracial eating and drinking is weak. Negroes and whites will often be found eating together in restaurants, conferences, and factory lunchrooms. Sometimes it is considered objectionable for whites to invite Negroes to their homes for social gatherings, but the few occurrences seldom result in any reaction more violent than gossip.

Next in order of degree of intimacy and in degree of reaction aroused by violation is a series of relations which, like eating, involve satisfying physiological needs, sitting down together, and engaging in sociable conversation. In public places there are separate rest rooms, toilets, and drinking fountains all over the South. Separate rest rooms, toilets, and drinking fountains are not maintained in the North.

Perhaps allied with the prohibition against the use of the same facilities for the satisfaction of physiological needs is the prohibition against the participation of Negroes where the human body is used. Dancing and swimming together are taboo, as we have mentioned, but the prohibition extends to other sports and games.[2] The prohibition does not extend to children. There is no general prohibition against Negroes taking part in sports and games in the North, although individual whites often refuse to play with Negroes.

[2] Sometimes the prohibition against mixed sports is extended to mixed equipment. Charles S. Johnson (*Patterns of Negro Segregation* [New York: Harper & Brothers, 1943], p. 274) records the case of a principal of a white high school refusing to accept a basketball belonging to his school after the team of a Negro high school had borrowed it.

The principle of "not to be touched" extends in many directions. In a county in Georgia, where the Negro schoolhouses were dilapidated, it was observed that there were good schoolhouses near by which had earlier been used for white children but had been left vacant as a result of the recent centralization of the white school system. Upon inquiring why they were not used for the Negro children, he was informed that this was impossible, for these reasons: in one case, there was a near-by old white graveyard and white people in the community would not like to think of the barefoot Negro children passing by the graves and perhaps even treading upon them, and in the other case, the schoolhouse was used for occasional elections and the white voters could not possibly be asked to enter a house used as a Negro school for casting their votes.

The conversation between whites and Negroes in the South is heavily regimented by etiquette. *In content* a serious conversation should be about those business interests which are shared (as when a white employer instructs his Negro employee), or it should be a polite but formal inquiry into personal affairs (either a white or Negro person may inquire as to the state of the other's health or business). There can generally be no serious discussion about local or national politics, international relations, or "news," on the one hand, or about items connected with the course of daily life, such as the struggle for existence or the search for pleasure, on the other hand. There are exceptions, of course. Some white women use their Negro servants as sources of gossip and local news.

The conversation is even more regimented in *form* than in content. The Negro is expected to address the white person by the title of "Mr.," "Mrs.," or "Miss." The white man addresses the Negro by his first name, even if they hardly know each other, or by the epithets "boy," "uncle," "elder," "aunty," or the like, which are applied without regard to age. If he wishes to show a little respect without going beyond the etiquette, he uses the exaggerated titles of "doctor," "lawyer," "professor," or other occupational titles, even though the terms are not properly applicable. The epithets "nigger" and "darky" are used even in the presence of Negroes, though it is well known that Negroes find them insulting. Recently there has been a slight tendency for this pattern to break down and some Southern newspapers have used the titles "Mr." and "Mrs." in reporting news of veterans.

Another aspect of the form of conversation between Negroes and whites is the rule that a Negro must never contradict the white man or mention a delicate subject directly. The apparent purpose of this etiquette of conversation is to provide a continual demonstration that the Negro is inferior to the white man and "recognizes" his inferiority. In the North the caste etiquette of conversation does not exist. That is, whites do not expect it. When Southern Negroes act it out they usually embarrass the average Northerner more than they please him. Where Negroes and Whites meet socially on the same class level in the North (which is rare) they may come to understand one another. Southern whites have a myth that they "know" their Negroes. This is largely incorrect, and in their franker moments white Southerners will admit that they feel that Negroes are hiding something from them. They cannot know Negroes as they know other human beings because in all their contacts Negroes must, or feel they must, pose in a framework of etiquette. "What the Southern people see who 'know their Negroes' is the role that they have forced the Negro to accept, his caste role."[3]

Closely allied to the forms of speech are the forms of bodily action when whites and Negroes appear before one another. For a Negro to sit down in the same room with a white person is not taboo, but it may be done usually only at the request of a white person. Since the invitation is often not extended, it frequently happens that Negroes must stand in the presence of whites. In conferences and public places, Negroes sit down without invitation, but there is usually segregation. In the North, Negroes, when they are allowed to enter, take seats much in the same manner that whites do. Whatever segregation in seating there is in the North would seem to have a voluntary or class basis rather than a strict caste basis as in the South. Many theaters in the North, however, refuse to let a Negro enter, or, if they are in a state with a civil rights law, they try to find some excuse to make Negroes stay away voluntarily. Where seats are reserved, the management will often try to sell seats to Negroes in a special section. Changing seats on the part of individual whites will sometimes isolate Negroes in a Northern theater.

In general, the American is a great and indiscriminate handshaker. The ceremony is to him a symbol of friendliness and basic human equality. The partial taboo against shaking hands with Negroes is, therefore, significant. The white man in the South may offer to shake hands with the Negro, but the Negro may not offer his hand to the white man. A white woman practically never shakes hands with a Negro man.

In coming into a white man's house, the rule was, and still is in most parts of the South, that the Negro must enter by the rear door. When a white man enters a Negro's house he cannot be expected to show any signs of respect. He will enter without knocking; he will not remove his hat; he will not stand up when a Negro woman enters the room; he may even insist that the Negro occupants stand in his presence. There is little occasion for a white man to enter a Negro's house: if he wants to see a Negro he will send for him, call him on the telephone, or drive in his car to his house and blow the horn. Practically nothing of any phase of the etiquette of bodily action exists in the North.

In an essential and factual sense the cumbersome racial etiquette is "un-American." When democratic European countries have be-

[3] John Dollard, *Class and Caste in a Southern Town* (New Haven: Yale University Press, 1937), p. 257.

come "Americanized," one of the positive elements in this change has been the throwing off of the inherited class etiquette and the breaking up of class isolation. In America the caste etiquette stands out as a glaring contradiction to usual ideals and customs. It indicates the split in the American's moral personality.

The entire etiquette of interpersonal relations between Negroes and whites in the South serves to isolate the two groups from each other and to place the Negro group in an inferior social status. It is, however, breaking down to a certain extent—especially in those relations which are least intimate and most removed from the sexual. It is also less rigidly applied to upper-class than to lower-class Negroes. However, while in everyday practice the upper-class Negro need not abase himself in accordance with the full requirements of the etiquette, he must never be allowed to consider his privilege as a right. Even so, the very existence of the privilege is a sign of change.

Conditions are sufficiently different in the North to lead us to regard the pattern of segregation and discrimination in interpersonal relations as having a different basis. The Northern pattern could hardly be called an etiquette because it does not require that Negroes act in a special way toward whites or that whites act in a special way toward Negroes. Rather it takes the form of institutionalizing and rendering impersonal a limited number of types of segregation. For the most part, the etiquette of interpersonal relations between the races does not exist in law.

2. HOUSING SEGREGATION

Residential segregation is extremely important because if Negro people do not live near white people they cannot associate with each other in the many activities founded on common neighborhood. Residential segregation often becomes reflected in uniracial schools, hospitals, and other institutions. It is relatively more important in the North than in the South, and for this reason we shall emphasize the Northern situation in this section.

Housing segregation necessarily involves discrimination, if not supplemented by large-scale intelligent planning in the housing field, of which America has as yet seen practically nothing. Housing segregation represents a deviation from free competition in the market for apartments and houses and curtails the supply available for Negroes. In Southern cities, when Negroes live in only a few sections, they receive fewer paved streets and street lights, less adequate sewage disposal, and so on. Rapid increases in the Negro population are typical of Northern cities, and residential segregation—by its curtailment of housing available for Negroes—prevents a proportional rise in housing facilities. In some neighborhoods of Northern cities housing conditions for Negroes are as bad as, or worse than, Southern ones.

Residential concentration is usually determined by three main factors: poverty preventing individuals from paying for anything more than the cheapest housing accommodations; a desire to live in an area where others of the same race live; segregation enforced by white people. Other poor or immigrant groups have been able to move to better neighborhoods as they became less poor and more Americanized, but the Negro, even when he has improved his economic condition, has been forced to remain in the ghettos.

Southern whites often do not want Negroes to be completely isolated from them. In some Southern cities, especially in the older ones, Negroes live on side streets or along alleys back of the residences of whites and sometimes in rear rooms of the whites' homes. If, however, a Southern city received most of its Negro population after the Civil War, and if a Northern city has a large number of Negroes, such a city will tend to have large areas in which Negroes live separated in space from the whites.

One force maintaining residential segregation of Negroes has been *informal* social pressure from the whites. Some white property owners in white neighborhoods would never consider selling or renting to Negroes; and even if a few Negro families did succeed in getting a foothold, they would be made to feel the hatred of the whites both socially and physically. The main reason why informal social pressure has not always been effective in preventing Negroes from moving into a white neighborhood has been the tremendous need of Negroes to move out of their intensely overcrowded ghettos and their willingness to bear a great deal of physical and mental punishment to satisfy that need.

When a few Negro families do come into a white neighborhood, some more white families move away. Other Negroes hasten to take their places, because the existing Negro neighborhoods are overcrowded due to segregation. This constant movement of Negroes into white neighborhoods makes the bulk of the white residents feel that their neighborhood is doomed to be predominantly Negro and they move out—with their attitudes against the Negro reinforced. Yet, if there were no segregation, this wholesale invasion would not have occurred. But because it does occur, segregational attitudes are increased and the vigilant pressure to stop the Negroes at the borderline is kept up. Such a situation creates a vicious circle, in which race prejudice, economic interest, and residential segregation mutually reinforce one another.

Various organized techniques have been used to reinforce spontaneous segregational attitudes and practices. These include local zoning ordinances, restrictive covenants, and terrorism.

The Supreme Court has repeatedly held that it is unconstitutional for a state or city to pass a law requiring residential segregation. When the court's opposition to such laws became clear, the restrictive covenant—an agreement by property owners in a neighborhood not to sell or rent their property to colored people for a definite period[4]—became popular, especially in the North. The exact extent of the use of the restrictive covenant has not been ascertained, but certainly most strategic areas in Northern cities are covered. The Supreme Court has as yet avoided the principal issue of the legal status of the covenants.

In addition to restrictive covenants, neighborhood associations have served as organized illegal agencies to keep Negro and white residences separated. The devices employed by them range all the way from persuasion to bombing.

One effect of segregation is to keep the few educated upper- and middle-class Negroes out of white neighborhoods. Whites ignore the fact that there exist Negro upper- and middle-class people who are searching for decent homes and who, if not shunned by the whites, would contribute to property values in a neighborhood rather than cause them to deteriorate. The presence of a small scattering of upper- and middle-class Negroes in a white neighborhood might serve to better race relations. Segregation has little effect on the great bulk of poor Negroes except to overcrowd them and increase housing costs, since their poverty would separate them voluntarily from the whites.

As pointed out in an earlier chapter, recent government policies have, on the whole, served to strengthen and widen rather than to mitigate residential segregation. Until 1947, the Federal Housing Administration, in effect, extended credit to Negroes only if they built or bought in Negro neighborhoods and to whites only if they built in white areas which were under covenant not to rent or sell to Negroes. The policy of the FHA is important since it has been the ambition and accomplishment of this agency to make housing credit available to low-income groups. The effect has probably been to bring about an extension of restrictive covenants to areas and groups of

---

[4] In the future, whites may themselves become trapped by the use of restrictive covenants, since they are now being used to exclude not only racial but also national and religious minorities from residential areas. A large percentage of white Americans belong to one or more of these nonracial minority groups.

white people who were earlier without it. The United States Housing Authority and its local affiliates are not so restrictive. Frequently they have been forced by public opinion to build separate housing projects for whites and Negroes, or to keep whites at one end and Negroes at the other end of mixed projects. However, Abrams reports:

There are 134 projects in the United States where Negroes and whites are already mixed. . . . In many, the races were mixed for the first time, Negro occupancy ranging from a small fraction to as high as 70 per cent of total project population. . . . Reports from the housing authorities speak glowingly of the success of the effort to mix Negroes and whites, considered the most difficult human-relations problem in projects. The experience has gone on successfully for more than a decade. Initial tensions have disappeared between Negro and white, difficulties have been adjusted, and an atmosphere of harmony has been created. . . . The projects, some of them higher-rental war undertakings, have shown that where Negroes live with whites in self-contained communities that create their own environment, are given the same privileges and share the same concerns and responsibilities, distinctions disappear, and a setting for the functioning of inter-racial harmony is soon created. Few tenants moved out even where comparable dwellings in unmixed projects were offered them.[5]

Negroes have reasons to be grateful to the USHA, not only for conducting such experiments in mixed projects but also for giving them a relatively large share of low-cost housing.

In practice and often in discussion about housing, the only alternatives have been segregation and free competition. It must be emphasized that segregation *can* be "positive" or "negative." The average individual white's attitude is, of course, only negative: he wants to be "protected" from Negro neighbors. But as long as the Negro population in a city is increasing, it is an irrational and, indeed, impossible policy in the long run to "protect" white areas against Negro intrusion. The result will be "doubling up," scandalous housing conditions for Negroes, destroyed home life, mounting juvenile delinquency, and other indications of social pathology which are bound to have their contagious influence upon adjoining white areas. And inevitably the Negroes will finally break through somehow and in some degree. It must be stressed that if white people insist on segregation —and if society is assumed not socially to tolerate costly substandard housing for Negroes—the logical conclusion is that in a planned and orderly way, either areas of old housing now inhabited by whites or vacant land must be made available for Negroes.

[5] Charles Abrams, "Homes for Aryans Only," *Commentary,* 3 (May, 1947), 426.

3. THE GENERAL CHARACTER OF INSTITUTIONAL SEGREGATION

While there is much segregation of Negroes in the North in public facilities and private commercial establishments—a segregation which we term "institutional," to distinguish it from both personal and residential segregation—there is a tremendous difference between the North and South in this form of segregation. The difference arises out of two facts.

One is that institutional segregation in the South is supported by an elaborate racial etiquette and a clearly perceived popular theory of "no social equality." The etiquette is almost entirely lacking in the North, while the theory of "no social equality" is perceived only vaguely and not taken very seriously. For this reason institutional segregation fits in more "naturally" in the South, while in the North it is constantly challenging other elements of popular thinking and customs. The second great cause of difference is that in the South institutional segregation is in the laws of the states and local communities, while in the North institutional segregation, arising out of personal distaste for Negroes and as a consequence of residential segregation, is entirely extralegal and often illegal.

Every Southern state and most Border states have state and city laws which prohibit Negroes from using the same schools, libraries, parks, playgrounds, railroad cars, railroad stations, sections of streetcars and buses, hotels, restaurants, and other facilities as do whites. In addition, officials frequently take it upon themselves to force Negroes into a certain action when they have no authority to do so. The inability of Negroes to get justice in the courts extends the powers of the police and other white officials. In addition, the Negro's reliance on the tolerance of the white community for his economic livelihood and physical security makes segregation easy to enforce, legally or illegally.

At present the Jim Crow laws are considered constitutional by the United States Supreme Court. However, institutional segregation as actually practiced is the basis for gross discrimination, and this *is* unconstitutional. It is noticeable that even the threat of legal action puts a certain restraint on institutional discrimination in the South. The dilemma of Southern whites in this field is increased by the fact that segregation without discrimination, which is the proclaimed purpose of the Jim Crow legislation, is financially impossible. As the Supreme Court has recently been agreeing with Negroes that the segregated facilities for them are not equal, the Southern states have been straining themselves financially to provide equal facilities.

In the North the Jim Crow laws are completely absent. In addition, eighteen states[6] have civil rights acts, which prevent any privately owned establishment open to the public from refusing to serve Negroes. These laws are not rigidly enforced, and there are all sorts of ways of getting around them. But their very existence makes institutional segregation more difficult in the North. Also, Negroes are protected in the courts and by the police to a much greater extent than in the South. Yet there is institutional segregation in the North, and its effects are important. Many institutions—such as schools, parks, playgrounds, stores, theaters, and other places of amusement—have a community basis, and residential segregation is, therefore, an effective means of getting separate units for Negroes. Sometimes school boundaries are set at the boundary of the white and Negro neighborhoods: if a white child lives in a "Negro school district," he is readily given a permit to go to another school; if a Negro child lives in a "white school district," he is encouraged and sometimes coerced into going to a Negro school.

In states where there is no civil rights law, the manager of any private organization, commercial or noncommercial, can refuse to serve Negroes and may even put up a sign to that effect. In states where there are civil rights laws, no manager or employee may refuse to Negroes, theoretically, the service that he would offer to white persons. Actually, many establishments refuse service to Negroes. Even when the police and courts take action, the practice may be kept up, since the fine is usually small and the probability of being called before the law a second time is small. Much more frequently the Negro is effectively discouraged from seeking service in these establishments: by letting him wait indefinitely for service, by telling him that there is no food left in the restaurant or rooms in the hotel, by giving him dirty or inedible food, by charging him unconscionable prices, and so on.

A voluntary organization, whether for civic, religious, political, economic, or associational purposes, will most often simply not invite Negroes to membership, even though they meet all other requirements. Even semipublic associations, such as the American Red Cross, the United Service Organizations, charities, and universities, grossly discriminate against Negroes.

This all leads to a fifth, and equally important, cause of segregation: voluntary withdrawal of Negroes into their own group. The

[6] These states are California, Colorado, Connecticut, Illinois, Indiana, Iowa, Kansas, Massachusetts, Michigan, Minnesota, Nebraska, New Jersey, New York, Ohio, Pennsylvania, Rhode Island, Washington, and Wisconsin.

effects—in terms of cultural isolation and lack of equality of opportunity—are the same. Many Negroes in the upper and middle classes make it a policy to abstain as far as possible from utilizing the Southern Jim Crow setups in theaters, transportation, and the like, or from entering places in the North where they know they are not welcome.

4. SEGREGATION IN SPECIFIC TYPES OF INSTITUTIONS

It is in government-owned institutions that legal segregation is most complete in the South. Seventeen states and the District of Columbia have two complete sets of elementary and secondary schools as part of state law. In nearly every community in these states there is a substantial amount of discrimination in the provision of education for Negroes. For higher education, Negroes are still worse off. Some of the Southern states support small Negro colleges—never comparable in facilities and personnel with even the average Southern state university. In December, 1938, the Supreme Court decided that a Negro could insist upon entrance into a regular state university if no separate but equal university was provided for Negroes by that state. With the exception of Maryland, West Virginia, and Delaware, which now admit qualified Negroes to their graduate schools, the other states planned to set up separate graduate schools, which will obviously be inferior in equipment and personnel. Texas has just appropriated $3,000,000 for a law school for Negroes, but how long the Southern states will be willing and able to pay for completely equal segregated facilities is a question.

In only one Northern or Western state (Arizona) is school segregation required by law; a few additional states make it permissible. No Northern state university prohibits the enrollment of Negroes although a few practice minor forms of discrimination once they are enrolled. This is often a matter of individual prejudice rather than of official policy. Private universities in the North restrict Negroes in rough inverse relation to their excellence: the great universities—Harvard, Chicago, Columbia, and so on—restrict Negroes to no significant extent, if at all. A few exceptions to this rule exist.

Most other public facilities—such as libraries, parks, playgrounds—are available to Negroes with about the same amount of discrimination and segregation, in the various regions of the country, as in schools. Negroes are not permitted to use these in the South and if there are segregated facilities, they are poor in quality and few in number.

Segregation of Negroes in jails, penitentiaries, reformatories, and insane asylums follows the same pattern found for schools and other public facilities. When the institution has as its primary importance not to protect white society, but to be of service to the Negro individual or community—as asylums for the insane and feeble-minded or specialized institutions for juvenile delinquents—many Southern states do not have a Negro unit at all.

The pattern of segregation found in privately run public services in the South is often less rigid than in those operated by government. This differential—not great—occurs because businessmen are more solicitous about Negro customers than local governments are about Negro citizens. The law compels the transportation companies to bear the extra costs of maintaining two sets of facilities. On the other hand, the companies—with a few exceptions—save money by giving Negroes inferior service for equal charge. It is a common observation that the Jim Crow car on railroads or streetcars is resented more bitterly among Negroes than most other forms of segregation. In the North there is no segregation in public carriers.

Segregation is practically complete in the South for hotels and restaurants, places of amusement and cemeteries. The same is true for churches. Many hospitals in the South receive Negro as well as white patients, but they are segregated; the Negro wards are mostly inadequate and inferior, and Negro doctors are usually not allowed to treat their patients there. In the North the patterns vary a great deal, depending upon the presence or absence of a civil rights law, the exclusiveness and expensiveness of the establishment, and tradition.

In factories segregation is usual throughout the South, by industry, job, or department. In the ordinary commercial establishments, such as department stores, the variation is tremendous. We may generalize thus far, however: for each community there would seem to be less discrimination and segregation where the service is less personal. Barbershops and beauty parlors are, both in the North and in the South, the most completely segregated while clothing stores allow Negroes to buy but discriminate more than do hardware stores.

The services of white professional men have always been available to Negroes. Some white professionals refuse to serve Negroes, but probably the majority will service Negroes who can afford to pay their fee. There is one service which is unique in that only Negroes serve Negroes: this is the undertaking service. The live Negro body may be handled by the white physician, but the dead one is handled only by the Negro undertaker. This is as much, or more, in accordance with the desires of Negroes as of whites. Undertaking is consequently one of the most lucrative businesses open to Negroes.

Because of their exclusion from the various associations, Negroes have formed their own. Every Negro community is abundantly supplied with social and fraternal organizations and nearly every city has its Negro businessmen's group. Negro professionals have formed national associations which usually take the name *National* (Medical, Bar) Association in contradistinction to the white *American* (Medical, Bar) Association. While white groups lose a little of the strength they might get by admitting all qualified persons, regardless of race, Negroes are materially hurt by not getting the advantages of membership in these bodies.

5. THE EFFECT OF SOCIAL INEQUALITY

The purpose—and the effect—of the social mechanism here discussed is to isolate Negroes and place them in a lower social class. Being a Negro involves—everywhere in America, and independent of social class—having an inferior status. This lower social status represents a gain to the whites. Besides the direct deprivation it imposes on the Negro, it indirectly hampers his ambitions in spheres of life other than the purely "social." Whereas it was appropriate to center the discussion of the causes of segregation and discrimination around the attitudes of the whites, who enforce the system, it is expedient, when we investigate the results of it, to view them as they affect the Negro people.

No responsible Negro leader ever accepted social discrimination or gave up the demand for *ultimate* full equality. The reason is clear. Social discrimination is powerful as a means of keeping the Negroes down in all other respects. It is not possible to isolate a sphere of life and call it "social." There is a social angle to all relations.

The interrelations between social status and economic activity are particularly important. Occupations have numerous social connotations. In the first place, they help to give social status. As long as Negroes, solely because of their color, are forcibly held in a lower social status, they will be shut out from all middle-class occupations, except in their own segregated social world. White nurses, stenographers, bank clerks, and store attendants will decline to work with Negroes, especially when the white person is a woman and the Negro a man. If social segregation is carried out in the factories, it will be expensive to the employer since he will have to provide special coordinating facilities and separate toilets, washrooms, and lunchrooms. The vicious circle works here too: the very fact that the masses of Negroes, because of economic discrimination—partly caused by social inequality—are prevented from entering even the lowest occupations, are paid low wages, and consequently are poor, gives in its turn motivation for continued social discrimination.

The fact that social segregation involves a substantial amount of discrimination adds its influence to this vicious circle. Negroes are given inadequate education, health protection, and hospitalization; they are segregated into districts where sewage and garbage removal, street cleaning, street lighting, street paving, police protection, and everything else is neglected or withheld while vice is often allowed. All this keeps the Negro masses inferior and provides reasons for further discrimination in politics, justice, and breadwinning.

Under these circumstances there develops a double standard of efficiency which puts the Negro in a still more inferior social position. The ambition of the Negro youth is cramped not only by the severe restrictions placed in his way by segregation and discrimination but also by the low expectation from both white and Negro society. He is not expected to make good in the same way as the white youth. And if he is not extraordinary he will not expect it of himself and will not really put his shoulder to the wheel.

Segregation and discrimination have had material and moral effects on whites too. Booker T. Washington's famous remark, that the white man could not hold the Negro in the gutter without getting in there himself, has been corroborated by many white Southern and Northern observers. Throughout this book we have noticed the low economic, political, legal, and moral standards of Southern whites—kept low because of discrimination against Negroes and because of obsession with the Negro problem. Even the ambition of Southern whites is stifled partly because, without rising far, it is so easy to remain "superior" to the held-down Negroes.

6. Increasing Isolation

One of the effects of social segregation is the isolation of Negroes and whites. The major effects of isolation are, of course, on Negroes. Contrary to popular opinion, however, there are bad effects on whites also. Whether they know it or not, white people are dwarfing their minds by avoiding contacts with colored people.

Against all the obstacles of segregation and discrimination, the Negroes are rising. Besides, education, industrialization, and urbanization are having an impact on the Negro. Migration, occupational changes, the Negro press, the growth of Negro organizations, the radio, the motion pictures, are working upon the minds of Southern Negroes introducing new thoughts and ideas, dissatisfaction and unrest. One result of these changes is increasing isolation. The spiritual effects of segregation are accumulating with each new generation, continuously estranging the two groups.

One phase of the rise of the Negroes is the formation of a Negro middle and upper class. Not only have their economic contacts with whites been reduced but, because they know they are not liked by whites and are likely to feel humiliated in all contacts with them, they avoid whites in all other spheres of life. This tiny upper group of the Negro community often lives in a seclusion from white society which is extraordinary and seldom realized by white people. This means that white men in all classes usually have few occasions ever to meet a Negro outside the servant class.[7]

Parallel to this tendency is the habit of Southern whites of ostracizing those white persons who work with Negroes in the field of education or who in other ways devote themselves to Negro welfare. More important is the related trend for Negro colleges to be manned by an all-Negro staff, which again means a growing separation between the two groups on the middle- and upper-class level.

The Southern Regional Council, various universities, and religious bodies have attempted to counteract this tendency by arranging interracial meetings for representatives of the "best people" of both groups. But it is doubtful whether these efforts outweigh the tendency of the segregation system, which drives toward greater spiritual isolation between the two groups. This is a heavy cost for Southern society and might create great dangers in the future.

The behavior and attitudes of the small Negro middle- and upper-class groups are of great importance for the whole Negro people, as they set the standards that are spread to the rest. Racial pride and voluntary isolation are increasingly becoming the pattern for the whole Negro people. Lower-class Negro parents now teach their children to keep away from white people. Meanwhile the old bonds of intimacy between upper-class white families and their Negro servants have been breaking down. There are fewer servant-employer rela-

[7] "Beyond that there is a type of Negro already referred to, whom the majority of whites never see and consequently do not know. They own their own homes, so the white landlord does not see them; they carry insurance with a Negro insurance company, so no white collector comes to their door; their groceryman is a coloured man; they travel by auto rather than by street car or train; as a rule they live in the segregated residence districts; their physician, lawyer, dentist, and often their banker is a Negro. As a result of all this, there is a constantly diminishing contact between the corresponding classes of the two races, which for the whites as a whole is fast approaching the zero point." (Robert R. Moton, *What the Negro Thinks* [Garden City, N.Y.: Doubleday, Doran & Company, Inc., 1929], pp. 17–18.)

tionships. Even the children keep apart. The only exception in the South to the general trend of increasing separation is the recent coming together of Negro and white workers in the new labor unions.

In the North the Negroes have always been more isolated from whites. With the formation of Black Belts in the metropolitan cities, isolation grew. In this particular respect the conditions of the Negro population in the two regions are approaching each other.

7. INTERRACIAL CONTACTS

It is useful here to put the reverse question: What contacts do remain and what is their significance for interracial relations? Actually, the patterns of segregation and withdrawal are so effective that even where Negroes are a common sight there is actual contact with them in practically only three spheres of life: the casual, the economic, and the criminal.

Casual contacts include passing on the street, passing or remaining briefly in the presence of each other in public buildings or public vehicles, and so on. Since the casual contact is one in which the participants have no occasion to regard each other as individuals but only as members of a group, the main effect of the casual contact is the strengthening of stereotypes. All Negroes come to look alike to the average white person.

Unlike casual contacts, economic contacts are important enough for the whites and Negroes to see one another as individuals. In the great majority of economic contacts, whites see Negroes as economic inferiors, as when they are servants or other types of menial workers. More rarely they meet as economic equals, as when Negro and white workers work on the same level or when businessman meets businessman or salesman meets customer. Practically never do whites see Negroes as their economic superiors. Most whites are vaguely aware that there are Negroes in high economic positions. But it is probable that they underestimate the number of such Negroes, and it is certain that they rarely have enough contact with them to know them as individuals. From their side, Negroes have economic contacts with whites mainly as superiors and only occasionally as equals. Thus they tend to have their attitudes of inferiority and dependence reinforced. The same can be said of their attitudes of resentment.

There is one sphere of economic relationship which is extremely important—personal and domestic service. The social importance of this relationship derives mainly from the fact that it is intensive on one side. The Negro maid knows the life of her white employer as few white persons know it; and the Negro janitor or elevator operator knows a great deal of what goes on in his building. The white employer, on the other hand, does not know the Negro's world even though he has Negro servants. In the South there are barriers of etiquette and segregation. What may happen in the employer-servant relationship is that the white man or woman makes an exception of his or her servant to the stereotyped conception of the "Negro in general." Or, the lower and dependent position of the Negro servant enhances the white person's belief that "the Negro is all right in his place."

One sort of economic relationship in which Negroes have a measure of near-equality with whites is that in which the Negro is an entertainer or artist. This is true also of athletics, in which Negroes have achieved notable successes. Besides the respectable entertainment fields, in which Negroes excel, there are the shady ones—"black-and-tan" cabarets, burlesques, and so on. Probably such contacts serve only to strengthen the stereotype that Negroes have wilder passions and that their excellence is limited to emotional activities.

Ordinarily in American society criminal relationships are minor. It is important in Negro-white relations because whites believe the Negro to be addicted to crime. Also, Negro crime gets great publicity. To many white Northerners, this crime news is the most important source of information they get about Negroes. To white Southerners, the crime news reinforces the stereotypes and sometimes serves to unite the white community for collective violence against Negroes. The crime news is unfair to Negroes because, on the one hand, it emphasizes individual cases instead of statistical proportions and, on the other hand, all other aspects of Negro life are neglected in the white press that gives the unfavorable crime news undue weight. Sometimes the white press "creates" a Negro crime wave where none exists. In the latter part of the summer of 1941, Washington, D.C., was disturbed by a Negro "rape-and-murder wave," according to white newspapers throughout the country. Actually only one Negro was found to be responsible for the crimes. Crimes against Negroes, outside of lynching, receive no publicity in the white press.

8. The Factor of Ignorance

White Southerners are still proud of insisting that they "know the Negro," but the observer easily finds that ignorance about the other group is often astonishingly great. Their lack of knowledge is of the Negro himself as an individual human being—of his ambitions and hopes, of his capacities and achievements. Because of this ignorance, and because of the etiquette, the white Southerner cannot talk to a

Negro as man to man and understand him. On their side, Negroes in the South instantaneously become reserved and secretive when they are in company with "their own whites."

The Northerner also is ignorant about the Negro, but his ignorance is less systematic and, therefore, less deep. As he is ordinarily less inhibited from looking upon the Negro as a normal human being, and as his observation of the Negro is not blinded by the etiquette, he is usually more cognizant of Negro attitudes and capacities and is more willing to lend a sympathetic ear to the Negro's plight. But he is much more ignorant of the conditions which the Negro faces. The Northerner is likely to insult Negroes out of sheer ignorance. The average Northerner does not realize that to call a Negro woman a "Negress" is taken as an insult, and he does not understand in what high esteem the Negro holds the title "Mr." Not knowing the patterns of violence and of laxness of law in the South, the Northerner does not comprehend the full reason for the Negroes' bitterness and fear.

On his side, the Negro is inclined to be suspicious of the Northerner's good intentions and to retain in the North the cynical attitude and secretive manners he has developed in the South. Seldom does a Negro know how white people on his own level live and think.

9. Changes Now Taking Place

Negroes have had to adjust to patterns of behavior which not only permit but call for discrimination by whites. The Negroes, however, can consider the system unjust and can explain it in terms of white people's prejudices, material interest, moral wrongness, and social power. But the unfortunate whites have to believe in the system of segregation and discrimination and to justify it to themselves. It cannot be made intelligible and defensible except by false assumptions which the whites force themselves to believe. While the lower caste may release itself intellectually, the higher caste, on the contrary, is enslaved in its prejudices by its short-range interests.

But the system *is* changing, though slowly. Modern knowledge and modern industrial conditions make it cumbersome. The Southerner is beginning to take on an apologetic tone when he speaks of his attitude toward the Negro. Southerners travel and migrate and are visited by Northerners and Europeans. They listen to the radio and read papers, magazines, and books directed to the wider national audience. The thesis that the region is poor and culturally backward, and that this is due largely to the South's Negro policy, has been for a long time developed by Southern authors. The average Southerner is beginning to feel the need for fundamental reforms. Many Southern newspapers have become liberal. Interracial work is beginning to be recognized as socially respectable. Social classes among Negroes are becoming recognized. Titles of respect, the offer to shake hands, permission to use the front door, and other symbols of politeness are more and more presented to certain Negroes who have attained social success.

These signs of wear and tear on the Southern color bar must not be exaggerated, however. "Social equality" is still a terribly important matter in the region. But it is less important than it was a generation ago. World War II, as we have pointed out, has accelerated these changes and made them more widespread throughout the region.

But the changes themselves elicit race prejudice. The white South was—and is—annoyed whenever the Negro shows signs of moving out of his "place." And the white North became more prejudiced when hundreds of thousands of crude Southern Negroes moved in. However, conditions for Negroes are improving, Southerners are being jolted out of their racial beliefs, and the group of white people interested in doing something positive for the Negro has grown.

CHAPTER XIV

Caste and Class

1. The Terms "Caste" and "Class"

The Emancipation of 1863 stopped the practice of calling Negroes "slaves." For a while "freedmen" and "ex-slaves" were popular terms, but it soon became evident that the nation wished to forget the issue that tore the country apart. Yet some term had to be found to describe the inferior status of the Negro, especially in scientific and literary circles. In the literature the term "caste," which was already in use before the Civil War, was increasingly employed.

As alternatives—often as synonyms—the term "race" and sometimes the term "class" have been used. The term "race" is, as we have shown in Chapter 2, inappropriate, since it has biological connotations which are incorrect and are even dangerous, as they support widely spread false racial beliefs. The term "class" is impractical, since it refers to a group from which an individual member can rise or fall. There are classes within each of the two groups, but the Negro and white groups cannot themselves be called classes. The term "minority group" also is impractical, since it fails to distinguish between the temporary social disabilities of recent white immigrants and the permanent disabilities of Negroes and other colored peoples.

The important difference between the terms "caste" and "class" as we are using them is the difference in freedom of movement between groups. In the entire United States, without any exception, a man born a Negro or a white is not allowed to pass from the one status to the other as he can pass from one class to another (unless he misrepresents his origin). In this important respect the caste system of America is closed and rigid, while the class system is usually open and mobile.

However, social relations across the caste line vary considerably from region to region within the country and from class to class within the Negro group. They also show considerable change over time.

Our value premise for this chapter will be based on that part of the American Creed which demands equality of opportunity. While Americans do not condemn differences in economic and social rewards, they do believe that people should be allowed to rise according to their ability through the process of free competition.

Caste, as distinguished from class, consists of drastic restrictions of free competition in the various spheres of life so that the individual in a lower caste cannot change his status except by secret and illegitimate "passing," which is possible only to the few who have the physical appearance of members of the upper caste. *Within* each caste, people also feel social distance and restrict free competition so that each caste has its own class system. The dividing line between the two castes is clear cut, consciously felt by every member of each caste, and easily observable. The class lines, on the other hand, are blurred and flexible, and one can rise from a lower to a higher class.

In the North, a proportion of the white population never discriminates against Negroes, and there is a small number who stand up against violation of the Negro's rights even if the matter does not concern them personally. Since such friends of the Negroes are not ostracized, and are in fact looked up to as "fighters," the color line may be said to be broken at spots in the North. Further, the color line is not a part of the law or of the structure of the buildings and so does not have the concreteness that it has in the South. When a white person in the South breaks caste solidarity, however, the white community puts him outside the caste system and calls him a "nigger lover." This means social and economic death, as such a person is allowed to associate neither with whites nor with Negroes, unless he can live completely within an isolated Negro community.

The counterpart to white solidarity on the Negro side of the caste gulf is the "protective community." That is, Negroes try to protect their own against the assaults or interests of whites.

An interesting aspect of the American caste system is the phenomenon called "passing." Passing requires anonymity and is, therefore, restricted to the large cities where everyone does not know everyone else. While we do not know how much permanent passing there is, we do know that a great many Negroes who look "white" do not pass. There are a number of reasons for this: loyalty to the Negro group; the assurance of obtaining a higher status in the Negro than in the white community; feelings of tension and strain in the passing

laborers, tenants, and household servants in the Southern rural districts. During the thirties a large portion of this group was on relief. Incomes are low and uncertain; levels of living do not include most of what is considered necessary according to the "American standard." Lower-class Negroes generally have little education. The older generation is often illiterate or practically so. Books, periodicals, and newspapers, social movements and ideas (except for the Negro problem), play insignificant roles in their lives.

The class is Southern in origin and character. Even in the Northern cities the lower class of Negroes is largely made up of recent migrants from the South and of their children. Both economically and culturally the Southern origin, to a great extent, projects into the present time the attitude and behavior patterns from slavery. Lower-class Negroes have kept more of the mental servility and dependence of the slave population and developed less resourcefulness, self-reliance, and sense of individual dignity. Their situation is not favorable for developing strong incentives to personal accomplishment and improvements. Standards of industry and honesty are low. Judged by American standards, their family life is disorganized and their sexual morals are lax. Aggression and violence are neither rare nor censured much by community disapproval. They are the group most subject to lack of legal protection in the South, and they probably have least respect for law and justice as it is applied in that region.

To a section of the lower class belong the chronic relief cases, the habitual criminals, prostitutes, gamblers, and vagabonds. In the upper levels of the lower class there are many persons who have definite ambitions to better their own, or at least their children's, status. These people will take care not to let their insurance lapse; they will have permanent affiliation with churches and lodges; they will try to keep their children in school.

At the other end of the social scale is the small Negro upper class. In rural districts the ownership and successful management of a sizable farm may give a person upper-class status. All over the country training for a profession or the carrying on of a substantial business, particularly in the field of banking or insurance, but also in contracting, real estate, and personal service, is the basis for an upper-class position. In smaller communities even today, and previously also in big cities, every steady employment where some training or skill was required, and the income was substantially above the average among Negroes, conferred upper-class status. Employment by public agencies, particularly federal agencies like the United States postal service, has always carried high social esteem in the Negro community and, if coupled with home ownership and education, usually puts the person in the upper class. Generally, in the relative absence of wealth, higher education is becoming almost an essential to an upper-class position. Light skin color and other white features also are associated with upper-class status, especially among Negro women. This basis of distinction grew up in slavery times, when the white master's slave children had a better chance of gaining freedom and getting an education and when house servants—often selected because of their "nice" appearance—had more privileges than the field slaves.

Often family background is stressed in the upper class. The family is organized upon the paternalistic principle, legal marriage is an accepted form, and illegitimacy and desertion are not condoned. Children are shielded as far as possible both from influences of the lower-class Negroes and from humiliating experiences of the caste system. They are ordinarily given a higher education and professional training. As Negroes are commonly believed to be loud, ignorant, dirty, and lax in sexual and all other morals, good manners and respectability become nearly an obsession in the Negro upper class. If the community offers a choice, they will tend to belong to Episcopal, Congregational, or Presbyterian churches, or, in any case, to those churches where there is less "shouting" and where the preacher has education and refinement.

The Negro upper class is most thoroughly assimilated into the national culture, but it is also most isolated from the whites. Its members are the most race conscious. They provide the leadership and a large part of the membership of the nationally established Negro defense organizations, such as the local branches of the N.A.A.C.P. But they sometimes feel great difficulty in identifying themselves with the Negro masses whose spokesmen they are, although certainly no more than the white upper class with the white lower class. The Negro upper class is characterized by many of the traits that are in complete contrast to those of the masses of Negroes in the lower class. Their social ambition is to keep up this distinction. In private they are often the severest critics of the Negro masses.

The Negro middle class is usually assumed to be larger than the upper class but smaller than the lower class. Members of the middle class have achieved a small but, in comparison with the lower class, less insecure occupational position. However, they are characterized even more by a striving toward a better economic position. They have typically had primary education and, not infrequently, secondary education, but few have been to college except the school teachers.

Education has a high ranking in their scale of values, and they want to give their children this means of fuller cultural emancipation. They also look down on the lower-class Negroes and attempt to be respectable. Thrift, independence, honesty, and industriousness are included in their standards. In the middle class it becomes a proud boast never to have been in trouble with the law. Family life is rather stabilized. Extramarital relations are not uncommon, at least for the men, but it is expected that affairs shall be carried on in decent secrecy. They are ordinarily energetic and loyal members of lodges and of churches—usually Baptist or Methodist.

In the bigger cities where prostitution, gambling, and other types of "protected" business have considerable importance, there is, parallel to the ordinary "respectable" class structure, a "shady" class structure. Its upper class consists of the successful racketeers. The middle class may be said to consist of their lieutenants and the less successful independents. The lower class consists of hangers-on and petty criminals. The upper and middle classes of this shady society have prestige with the lower classes of the general Negro society in the cities. For this reason, vice and crime can appear as a desirable career to almost any lower-class urban youth, who is shut out from respectable occupations. This shady Negro society has a parallel in the white world, but the shady white society has less prestige.

The foregoing picture of the Negro class structure is, like most other descriptions, static. Actually, the Negro class structure is dynamic: not only is there movement between the classes and changes within each of the classes, but also the entire class system is moving upward.

CHAPTER XV

Negro Leadership and the

Negro Protest

1. "Intelligent Leadership" in America

Despite the democratic organization of American society with its emphasis upon liberty, equality of opportunity (with a strong leaning in favor of the underdog), and individualism, the idea of leadership pervades American thought and collective action. The demand for "intelligent leadership" is raised in all political camps, social and professional groups, and indeed, in every collective activity.

If an ordinary American faces a situation which he recognizes as a "problem" without having any specific views as to how to "solve" it, he tends to resort to two recommendations: one traditionally is "education"; the other is "leadership." The belief in education is part of, or a conclusion from, the American Creed. The demand for leadership is a result of a practical approach to those activities which require the co-operation of many individuals. It is much less a part of Americans' knowledge about themselves than is the belief in education. Americans in general are quite unaware that the leadership idea is a particular characteristic of their culture.

The ordinary American has a liking for the personal and the dynamic in collective activity, a longing for the human, the unexpected, the adventurous. He wants changes, and he likes to associate them with new faces. He hopes for individuals to step out of the mass, to find formulas for directing the course of events, to take the lead. And he is prepared to create room for the exceptional individual's initiative. The American identifies himself with those who succeed. Of course there is personal envy in America. But there has been decidedly less of it than in the more static, less "boundless" civilizations of the Old World. Luck, ability, and drive in others are more tolerated and honored in America. Climbing is more generally acclaimed. Leadership is more readily accepted.

So it becomes natural and possible in America to associate the dynamic forces of society with individuals instead of with the masses. In the Negro problem "community leaders" are given an astonishingly important role. When the white people want to influence Negro attitudes or behavior in one direction or another, the natural device (besides the long-range one of education) is to appeal to the "community leaders." These leaders are expected to get it over to the Negro masses.

There are special reasons in the caste situation for this practice. But fundamentally this is a common American culture pattern. In all America it is assumed that every group contains leaders who control the attitudes of the group.

2. MASS PASSIVITY

The other side of this picture is, of course, the relative inertia and inarticulateness of the masses in America. The remarkable lack of self-generating, self-disciplined, organized people's movements in America is a significant historical fact usually overlooked by American historians and social scientists. The American trade-union movement, for example, is one of the oldest in the world, but it has always been comparatively inconsequential. Even with the active support of the federal government for over a decade, it has now only about 15,000,000 members. The observer is struck by the importance played by salaried "organizers" and the unimportance of, or often the lack of, spontaneous drive from the workers themselves.

The passivity of the public in America is, of course, a product of the nation's history. The huge and constant immigration from countries with different languages and different cultures prevented the lower classes from developing class solidarity and effective mass organization. The open frontier and the relatively good prospects for every able and energetic individual to rise out of the lower classes kept down social discontent. Perhaps even more important, this social mobility drained the masses in every generation of their potential "leaders."

Now the era of mass immigration has ended. The other main factors behind the political inertia of the American masses—the open frontier and the easy escape out of the lower classes—also are disappearing. The class barriers are thus becoming higher at the same time that the cultural differences within those barriers are decreasing. The masses receive an improved general education and keep a greater number of their potential leaders. These trends might make them active and articulate.

3. Leadership and Mass Passivity in American Politics

The American patterns of individual leadership and mass passivity are apparent in the political life of the nation. In both local and national politics the individual officeholder is—for the period he is in office—awarded much more power than he would be in democratic European nations. He is allowed to and, indeed, *expected* to follow the inclinations of his personal drives and ideas much more unhampered by laws and regulations or by continuous and democratic participation from the people.

In local politics, America has, on the whole, not spread political responsibility upon countless citizens' boards, as have, for example, the Northern European countries. (The draft and price control boards were successful exceptions.) Political participation of the ordinary citizen in America is pretty much restricted to elections. Politics is not organized to be a daily concern and responsibility of the common citizen.

The basic democracy is, however, maintained. While American democracy is weak from the aspect of the citizens' sharing in political action and responsibility, it is strong in the ultimate electoral controls. Several elements of what, from the other side of the Atlantic, looks like "exaggerated democracy" may be explained as having their "function" in preserving for the common man the ultimate political power in this system of government where he participates so little in its daily duties. It is this trait which prevents the hero worship and the delegation of such tremendous power to leaders from degenerating into fascism. Americans have such democratic devices as frequent elections, long ballots (so that even minor officers can be elected), the initiative and referendum, short terms of office, prohibitions against running for a second or third term. The intensive and ruthless publicity focused upon all officeholders—which does not spare even their private lives—serves the same "function." Finally, the American system of "checks and balances" not only has gone into the federal and state constitutions but has become entrenched in the American attitude toward all power problems. Americans are inclined to give not only much power but overlapping power to two or more officials or agencies and then leave it up to them to work out an arrangement through co-operation, mutual hamperings, and occasional stalls.

The patterns of strong and competitive personal leadership and weak followership, which we have pointed out in politics, run through the entire social structure. In most of these other fields the popular check on the system—that is, the strong election system—is much weaker. This gives much greater power to leaders. In large sectors of the labor movement it is thus a problem of how to avoid complete boss rule. Co-operatives often degenerate into ordinary business partnerships. Universities in America have never been controlled by their professors but by their presidents—not elected by the professors—and their appointed deans, subject to the control of boards of trustees who are outside the university. In modern business corporations in America, shareholders have lost their power to directors and other "insiders." Even in small groups—civic communities, research projects, Sunday schools—the same pattern prevails: the leaders run the show, the masses are passive except for an occasional election.

Now we may go on to a consideration of the leadership traits of America as displayed in the Negro community.

4. Accommodating Leadership and Caste

The Negro world conforms closely to the American pattern just described. In fact, the caste situation—by holding down participation and integration of Negroes—exaggerates the pattern. Negro leaders follow two opposing policies on behalf of their Negro followers: *accommodation* and *protest*. In this chapter we shall study the attitude of accommodation.

Accommodation is probably stronger than protest in the South, where caste is more widespread and unyielding. But it is practically never wholehearted in any American Negro however well adjusted he seems to be. Every Negro has some feeling of protest against caste, and every Negro has some sort of conflict with the white world.

The white caste has an obvious interest in having accommodating Negro leaders to help them control the Negro group. In any community where the Negro forms a substantial portion of the total population, the attitudes and behavior of the Negroes are never a matter of indifference to the whites. It makes a great deal of difference to the whites how the Negroes—within the narrow margin of their freedom —feel, think, and act. The whites want to keep the Negroes in a mood of wanting to be faithful and fairly efficient workers. They have an interest in seeing to it that the Negroes preserve as decent standards of homemaking, education, health, and law observance as possible so that at least contagious diseases and crime will not react back too much upon the whites.

The whites in the South have also a strong interest that Negroes be willing, and not only forced, to observe the complicated system of racial etiquette. They also want to keep Negroes from "red agitators" and "outside meddlers." Sometimes they want to keep them from joining labor unions and from reading the Constitution and studying social subjects. Besides these and other interests of a clearly selfish type, many whites feel an altruistic interest in influencing Negroes to gain improved standards of knowledge, morals, and conduct.

As the contacts between the two groups are becoming fewer and more formalized, whites, when they want to influence the Negro masses, are compelled to do so indirectly through Negro "leaders." On the other side of the caste gulf, Negroes need persons to establish contact with the influential people in the white group. They need Negro leaders who can talk to, and get things from, the whites. The Negroes in the South are dependent upon the whites, not only for a share in the public services but individually for small favors and personal protection.

5. Negro Leadership in the North and on the National Scene

In the North few white people care much about how the Negroes fare or what they think and do. The Negroes, on their side, have the protection of fairly impartial justice and of the anonymity of large cities. They also have the vote and can press their needs in the usual fashion of American minority politics. But the pattern of pleading to the whites through their own leaders, who are trusted by the whites, is firmly rooted in the traditions of Southern-born Negroes, who make up the great majority of adult Negroes in the North. Northern Negroes, also, are a poor group who are frequently discriminated against. They live in segregated areas and have few contacts with white people. For these and other reasons many of the Southern attitudes and policies in regard to Negro leadership continue in the North.

The Northern situation, however, is different from the Southern situation in two ways: (1) the white majority has no interest solidarity against Negroes and (2) the Negro minority is not cramped by anything like the Southern caste system. One effect of this difference is that the Northern situation gives greater opportunity for the protest motive to come out in the open.

In national affairs relations between whites and Negroes conform more to Northern than to Southern patterns. But Negro leaders are needed. The Negro people are set apart; they have distinctive problems; and they are hardly represented at all in the policy-forming and policy-deciding private or public organizations. The federal government and its various agencies, the political parties, and the philanthropic organizations have difficulty in reaching Negroes through their normal means of public contact. They must seek to open up special channels to the Negro people by engaging Negroes as observers, advisers, and directors of Negro opinion. The Negroes feel the same need for "contact" persons of their own. The individual Negroes who are appealed to in the national field immediately win great prestige in the Negro world.

In the sphere of power and influence—in politics and outside it, locally, nationally, in the South and in the North—the population thus becomes split into a white majority and a Negro minority; this means that intercaste power relations have become indirect from both sides. Direct contacts are established only between the two groups of leaders, acting on behalf of the two blocs. Except for these leaders, whites and blacks see each other only as strange stereotypes.

6. Accommodating Leadership and Class

When whites deal with a Negro as though he were a leader of the Negro community, that actually gives him the position of leader and also gives him upper-class status. Correspondingly, an upper-class position in the Negro community nearly automatically gives a Negro the role of Negro leader. He is expected by both whites and Negroes to act according to this role.

However, in some communities in the Old South, the leading whites have insisted on giving their ear even in public affairs to some old, practically illiterate ex-servant while cold-shouldering the upper-class Negroes. In the dependent situation of Southern Negroes, the Negro community is then willy-nilly compelled to use these old "darkies" as pleaders whenever the influential whites have to be appealed to. Under such circumstances, tremendous internal friction is likely to develop in the Negro community. The contempt of the upper-class Negroes for the uneducated, white-appointed "leaders" is increased by resentment born of extreme humiliation. The "leaders," on their part, feeling the contempt and resentment of the "uppity" Negroes, often turn into thorough yes-men for the whites and into "stuck-up" petty tyrants toward the Negro community.

Another widespread custom in the South is to use servants, ex-servants, and other lower-class Negroes as reporters and stool pigeons in the Negro community. Their spy activity and their being known to be "in with" white people give them a sort of power among their own people. Often they are used by the whites to "let it be known" in an informal way what the whites want and expect. Spying is declining, however, as employment relations become more impersonal and race solidarity in the Negro group increases.

Sometimes, too, upper-class Negroes do not care for the leadership role. They may desire to isolate themselves from the Negro lower classes. Some have made themselves so personally unpopular with Negroes or whites that they cannot act as leaders. Many are so filled by the protest motive that they cannot take the role of accommodating Negro leaders. Sometimes lower-class Negroes distrust upper-class Negroes. "Too much" education often meets suspicion among lower-class Negroes.

The result of this class conflict is that the Negro masses in the South often become so passive that they do not care much for anything except their physical demands and personal security. It is difficult to reach the Negro masses at all, especially in rural districts. It is often said that the Negro church and the fraternal and burial lodges are the only ways by which these masses can be reached. However, the Negro school, the Negro press, and the Negro professions are becoming the organizations that have the most influence with the lower classes. But there is no doubt that the Negro preacher—and, to a lesser extent, the lodge official—has more influence with the Negro masses than a white lower-class preacher or lodge leader has with the white masses.

With these reservations—and keeping in mind that a large portion of the Negro masses is apathetic and not "led" much at all—it remains true that the upper-class Negroes are increasingly the leaders.

7. Accommodating Leaders in the North

In the North there has never been much love for the lowly "darkies" on the part of the whites. They have never felt an inclination to lift poor, uneducated servants as leaders over the Negro community. Almost from the beginning the Negro upper class was accepted by the whites, without resistance, as the source of leaders.

On the other hand, probably a greater proportion of upper-class Negroes in the North do not care for the responsibilities and rewards of being active Negro leaders. On the whole, the Negro masses are less passive. Their preachers have less prominence as leaders and are, on the average, somewhat better educated and have a higher social status.

Negro suffrage in the North, however, allows for the possibility of *political* leadership. A good many of the petty politicians in Northern cities are lower-class Negroes, and these may be accommodating leaders. The labor unions, too, are training a new type of lower- or middle-class Negro leaders of particular importance in politics, but these are protest leaders.

On the national scene, upper-class status and, particularly, considerable education and personal ability are necessary for Negro leaders.

8. The Glamour Personalities

One peculiarity of the relation between Negro leadership and social class is the popular glamour and potential power of Negroes who have accomplished or achieved something extraordinary, particularly in competition with whites. They have broken through the barriers, and their achievements offer every Negro a gloating consolation in his lowly status and a ray of hope.

Under this principle every Negro who rises to national prominence and acclaim is a race hero: he has symbolically fought the Negro struggle and won. Great singers like Roland Hayes, Marion Anderson, and Paul Robeson have their prestige increased by the eager pride and hope of the whole Negro people. So have successful Negro authors like Richard Wright and Langston Hughes; scientists like George Washington Carver and Ernest E. Just; athletes like Joe Louis and Jackie Robinson; entertainers like Bill ("Bojangles") Robinson and Duke Ellington. Any one of them could, if he chose, exert considerable power as an active Negro leader. Yet Negro celebrities generally show great restraint in stepping outside their field of competence, although there are exceptions.

The importance of the Negro glamour personality, however, is not different from what is ordinary in white America. The popularity of the "first" or the "oldest," the "biggest" or the "smallest," the "best" or the "worst," the "only," has always colored America's conception of things and persons. It is characteristic of a young culture. Negroes are following a common American pattern, which, as usual, their caste status leads them to exaggerate.

Negro women have a somewhat greater opportunity to reach active leadership than do white women. This fact corresponds well with the fact of Negro women's relatively greater economic and social independence.

9. Early History of the Negro Protest

There has always been another type of Negro leader than the "pussyfooting" Uncle Tom. This is the "protest" leader, who has served to express a major demand on the part of the Negro masses. The leaders of the numerous local slave insurrections—Gabriel Prosser, Denmark Vesey, Nat Turner, and others—represented early types of pure protest leaders. They rose against overwhelming odds and succumbed with their followers. The chief short-range result of these slave rebellions was an ever-closer regimentation of free and slave Negroes. Southern white liberals and the great majority of accommodating Southern Negroes base their theory of accommodation on these failures. The theory holds that everything which stirs up the resistance of the whites will deteriorate the Negroes' status.

The Negro fighters in the Abolitionist movement in the North—Harriet Tubman, John M. Langston, Frederick Douglass, and many others—represented a second early crop of Negro protest leaders. Unlike the slave insurgents, these leaders set the future pattern on which Negroes based their protest. The new pattern consisted of nonviolent legal activities in accord with the democratic principles of the American Creed and the Christian religion. Frederick Douglass, the outstanding Negro leader of this period, in 1852 in his 4th of July oration at Rochester, voiced the Negro protest thus:

What to the American slave is your 4th of July? I answer: a day that reveals to him, more than all other days in the year, the gross injustice and cruelty to which he is the constant victim. To him your celebration is a sham; your boasted liberty, an unholy license; your national greatness, swelling vanity; your sounds of rejoicing are empty and heartless; . . . your prayers and hymns, your sermons and thanksgivings, with all your religious parade and solemnity, are, to him, more bombast, fraud, deception, impiety and hypocrisy—a thin veil to cover up crimes which would disgrace a nation of savages. . . .

You boast of your love of liberty, your superior civilization, and your pure Christianity, while the whole political power of the nation (as embodied in the two great political parties) is solemnly pledged to support and perpetuate the enslavement of three millions of your countrymen. You hurl your anathemas at the crown-headed tyrants of Russia and Austria and pride yourselves on your democratic institutions, while you yourselves consent to be the mere *tools* and *bodyguards* of the tyrants of Virginia and Carolina . . . . The fugitives from your own land you advertise, hunt, arrest, shoot, and kill. You glory in your refinement and your universal education; yet you maintain a system as barbarous and dreadful as ever stained the character of a nation—a system begun in avarice, supported in pride, and perpetuated in cruelty. You shed tears over fallen Hungary, . . . but, in regard to the ten thousand wrongs of the American slave, you would enforce the strictest silence, and would hail him as an enemy of the nation who dares to make those wrongs the subject of public discourse.[1]

After the Compromise of 1876, when Negroes were robbed of suffrage and civil liberties in the South, and the North became indifferent to the fate of the Negro, these leaders carried on the Negro protest. During this period—the last decades of the nineteenth century—they fought a losing struggle and in the South went underground.

10. The Tuskegee Compromise

In this great calamity for the Negro cause, Booker T. Washington stepped forward and established himself as the national leader of a practical and conciliatory school of thought, to which a great number of Negro leaders, particularly in the South, adhered. It is wrong to characterize Washington as an all-out accommodating leader. He never relinquished the right to full equality in all respects as the ultimate goal. But for the time being he was prepared to give up social and political equality, even to soft-pedal the protest against inequalities in justice. He was also willing to flatter the Southern whites and be harsh toward the Negroes—if the Negroes were allowed to work undisturbed with their white friends for education and business. But neither in education nor in business did he assault inequalities. In both fields he accepted the white doctrine of the Negroes' "place." In education he pleaded mainly for vocational training. Through thrift, skill, and industry the Negroes were gradually to improve so much that later the discussion could again be taken up concerning their rights. This was Washington's philosophy.

With shrewd insight, Washington took exactly as much off the Negro protest—and it had to be a big reduction—as was needed to get the maximum co-operation from the only two white groups in America who in that era cared anything about the Negroes: the Northern humanitarians and philanthropists and the Southern upper-class school of "parallel civilizations." Both of these "liberal" groups demanded appeasement. And so the Southern conservatives were allowed to set the conditions upon which Washington and the Southern and Northern liberals could come to terms.

Washington's policy was realistic from the short-range point of view, but from the long-range perspective it is doubtful if it was all the statesmanship that was called for by the interests of the Negro

[1] Quoted from W. E. B. Du Bois, *Black Reconstruction* (New York: Harcourt, Brace & Company, 1935), pp. 14–15.

people. Washington held a virtual monopoly of national Negro leadership for several decades. If leadership had been divided among groups with different points of view, both long-range and short-range interests might have been voiced.

11. The Spirit of Niagara and Harpers Ferry

Among the Negro intellectuals, particularly in the North, Washington and the strong "Tuskegee Machine" met severe criticism. It became vocal in 1901 when two Negro intellectuals, Monroe Trotter and George Forbes, began the publication of the Boston *Guardian*. W. E. B. Du Bois was soon drawn more and more from his brilliant scientific pursuits, and became the leader of this protest group. Du Bois demanded full social and political equality for Negroes, according to the Constitution, and complete cultural assimilation. And he offered his demands not as ultimate goals but as a matter of practical policy of the day.

In the summer of 1905, twenty-nine Negro intellectuals met at Niagara Falls (on Canadian soil, since they met discrimination in the Buffalo hotel at which reservations had been made for the conference). They had high hopes of forming a national protest organization with branches in the several states to wage a battle against all forms of segregation and discrimination, and, incidentally, against Washington's gradualist and conciliatory policy. The latter, they felt, sold out Negroes' rights for a pittance and even broke their courage to protest. The Niagara movement held two more meetings—one at Harpers Ferry—and issued proclamations. But it was never anything more than a feeble group with no mass following. It had against it Booker T. Washington and all his Negro and white friends, and it was not discreet for ambitious young Negroes to belong to this movement.

The Niagara movement represented the first organized attempt to raise the Negro protest against the great reaction after Reconstruction. It brought to open conflict and wide public debate two types of Negro strategy, one stressing accommodation and the other the Negro protest. Booker T. Washington and W. E. B. Du Bois became national symbols for these two main streams of Negro thought. Two groups of followers assembled behind them.

The agitation did not, for a long time, seriously encroach upon Booker T. Washington's power position. But he had increasingly to concede a place before the Negro public to critics of his policy and to proponents of a more militant course of action. And he had to watch his own words and deeds carefully. He had, thereafter, to reckon not only with reactions from the whites but also with reactions from the Negroes. When he died in 1915 he had moved considerably toward his opponents, and he knew that he alone no longer spoke for the whole Negro people.

By the year 1909–1910 the Niagara movement had ceased to be an effective organization. At this time, however, the stage was already set for the National Association for the Advancement of Colored People. The N.A.A.C.P. has, since its foundation, been the central organization of Negro protest carried on in the spirit of the Abolitionists and in collaboration with Northern white liberals. But the protest motive has also spread—in varying degrees—into the policies of all other Negro betterment organizations. It has, in fact, become part of the ideology of the entire Negro people to an ever-increasing extent.

It cannot be doubted that the spirit of the American Negroes in all classes is different today from what it was a generation ago. The protest motive is still rising. The Negro press, reaching ever closer to the Negro masses, has, as one of its chief aims, to give a national account of the injustices against Negroes and of the accomplishments and aspirations of Negroes. Negro churches and lodges are vehicles for a teaching which is equalitarian. Christianity is a radical creed even if its radical possibilities are suppressed. The school, merely by raising the general educational level, tends to influence the Negroes in the same direction. Generally speaking, every agency working for assimilation of the Negro people into the broader American civilization, which is democratic in its fundamental values, is bound to strengthen the Negro protest against caste.

12. The Shock of the First World War and the Postwar Crisis

The upheaval in Southern agriculture prior to the First World War, the mass migration to cities and to the North, and the war itself, all acted as stimulants to the rising unrest of the American Negro people. The war, too, made the whites place a higher value on democracy as "the American way of life." There was a certain amount of talk about lack of democracy at home which must be eliminated. These developments raised vague hopes among Negroes, or at least tended to fix their attention on their subordinate position in American democracy.

The Negroes wanted to fight in that war too. And they were needed: 400,000 Negroes were drafted. But they often found themselves segregated in labor camps or as servants. They met discrimination everywhere. Some 200,000 Negroes went to France, and so got a vision of the larger world. Everything that happened was eagerly reported by the Negro press and was widely discussed.

After the war the homecoming Negro soldier met the suspicions and fears of the Southern whites. In the North their new footholds in industry were contested by anxious white job seekers in the postwar depression. A wave of lynchings swept the South, and even more bloody race riots swept the North. Without doubt the accumulated experiences during and immediately after the First World War were a severe shock to the American Negroes and had lasting effects.

After the end of the First World War, America witnessed the first and, as yet, the only real mass movement of Negroes—*The Universal Negro Improvement Association*—organized by a remarkable West Indian, full-blooded Negro, Marcus Garvey. Garvey understood how to capitalize upon the growing dissatisfaction among American Negroes. He renounced all hopes of any assistance or understanding from the American whites. He also denounced practically the whole Negro leadership. Over their heads he appealed to the common Negroes, and especially to the darker Negroes. He exalted everything black. He even declared God and Christ black to spare the Negroes the humiliation of worshiping the images of white men. The only hope for American Negroes was to flee this country of oppression and return to Africa.

Garvey set up his organization with local branches and a number of subsidiary organizations. He published *The Negro World* as the official newspaper of the movement. He organized co-operative enterprises—grocery stores, laundries, restaurants, hotels, printing plants. During 1920–1921 the movement reached its peak. It was strong in many parts of the country. Eventually his movement collapsed. His various business ventures failed or involved him in legal tangles. He was finally deported by federal authorities on the charge of using the mails to defraud, in connection with the sale of stock for his shipping business. In 1940 he died in London, poor and forgotten.

Fascinating as Marcus Garvey was as a political prophet and as a mass leader, the response from the Negro masses is even more interesting. For one thing, it proves that it *is* possible to reach the Negro masses. It testifies to the basic unrest in the Negro community. It tells of dissatisfaction so deep that it amounts to virtual hopelessness of gaining a full life in America.

13. POSTWAR RADICALISM AMONG NEGRO INTELLECTUALS

After 1917 an attempt was made to organize and release the Negro protest into a political movement allied to radical white labor. Such young Negro Socialists as Chandler Owen and A. Philip Randolph started left-wing newspapers and magazines. They preached labor solidarity across the race line. The Communists, to the left of this group, promised "self-determination for the Negro in the Black Belt," to be realized by the setting up of an independent Black Republic. This fanciful construction failed to strike the imagination of the Negro masses and is probably part of the reason why the Communist party did not catch more Negro intellectuals.

More to the right of the Socialist group was "the New Negro movement," a somewhat undefined term to describe an outburst of intellectual and artistic activity and a tendency to glorify things Negro in a creative way. Although it was somewhat nationalistically Negro and was nurtured by Negro intellectual leaders—especially by Du Bois as editor of *The Crisis,* Charles Johnson, as editor of *Opportunity,* and Alain Locke, editor of the volume *The New Negro* (1925)—it was primarily a white-sponsored movement. This white patronage—which brought money and fame to a relatively small number of Negroes—gave the Negro masses the beginnings of respect for their abilities and their heritage.

The twenties and thirties saw also the rapid growth of a movement to discover a cultural tradition for American Negroes. Much of this is fantastic nonsense, but a considerable part is based on sound scholarship. The movement was given impetus in 1915 by the organization of *The Association for the Study of Negro Life and History* and its chief publication, *The Journal of Negro History.* The moving spirit behind the organization, and the editor of the *Journal,* is Dr. Carter G. Woodson. The articles in the *Journal* meet the usual standards of historical scholarship.

In spite of all scholarly pretenses and accomplishments, this movement is basically an expression of the Negro protest. Its avowed purpose is to enhance self-respect and race-respect among Negroes. Various devices are used to bring the findings of historical research before the Negro public. Summaries of articles are furnished Negro newspapers. Popular pamphlets and books are sold by house-to-house agents in the Negro community. Contact is made with Negro clubs. During "Negro History Week" the written and spoken word is applied with concentrated effort, especially to Negro school children.

In one phase of their activities, Negro historians have the support of some white scientists. This is the field of African culture, in which anthropologists have recently shown interest and appreciation.

Aside from the question of admiring their past achievements, Negroes are faced with the question of whether they should attempt to

build morale by glorifying their present achievements or attempt to
raise standards by criticizing the present low ones. Almost all Negroes are agreed that some of the traits for which they are praised by
Southern whites (loyalty, tractability, happy-go-luckiness) are not the
traits of which they should be primarily proud. But there are other
alleged Negro traits that white men praise which present more of a
dilemma to Negroes. These are the so-called special Negro aptitudes
for music, art, poetry, and the dance. Some Negroes feel that it is unwise for Negroes to specialize in so few fields, but that they should
put more effort into breaking into new fields. They know that
achievements in some of these fields merely strengthen the harmful
stereotypes.

14. The Great Depression and the Second World War

The Great Depression struck the Negroes even harder than it did
the whites, as we reported in the economic chapter. Between 1930 and
1933 there was distress and pessimism among Negroes. Negroes were
skeptical of the new president, Franklin D. Roosevelt, because he was
a Democrat. Yet they swung rapidly around and became the strongest supporters of his politics. There had been no race riots for several
years; lynchings reached a new low; Southern liberalism—with federal government support—seemed to be growing. All these things
made the late 1930's a period of somewhat less despair and pessimism
for Negroes. But there was little long-range hope.

When the United States entered the Second World War in December, 1941, Negroes were not optimistic as to what its significance
for them would be. But, as we have pointed out, the rise of democratic ideals, the political necessity of winning the colored peoples of
the world to the Allied side, and the desperate need for labor in the
United States made it easier for Negroes to win better job opportunities and to make other gains. These gains were not freely given,
however. They were the result of widespread and organized Negro
protest made by the March-on-Washington Movement, the Urban
League, the National Association for the Advancement of Colored
People, the Negro press, and other smaller and local groups of the
same type.

The moral preparation, experience, and organization accumulated
through the past twenty years stood the Negroes in good stead at this
time. Since the end of the war, the protest has gone on, strong and
continuous. Its success depends on many things, most important,
perhaps, the economic situation of the United States in the next few
years and the strength of the democratic ideology.

15. The Struggle for Balance in Negro Personality

The Negro protest is shut in by caste. But there is no wholehearted acceptance of the present situation. Even in the most dependent and destitute classes of Negroes in the rural South, the individual Negro keeps a recess in his mind where he secretly harbors the Negro protest. In the upper strata, and everywhere in the North, the Negro protest is expressed in social, economic, and political terms.

But with the individual Negro there is always a tendency for the protest to be bent into defeatism. Negroes on all class levels give vent to this spirit of defeatism. This cannot be said publicly, though. The protest motive does not allow it. No Negro leader could ever preach it. No Negro newspaper could print it. It must be persistently denied. But privately it can be said, and it *is* said.

Sometimes—and this also in all classes—the blame will be put on Negro inferiority. This agrees with what most white people believe and want to believe. To Negroes it represents the old caste accommodation pattern. It kills ambition and makes low standards of morals and accomplishments seem natural for Negroes. But Negro inferiority cannot be publicly admitted. Not only Negro leaders and educators, but all whites who address Negroes in a spirit other than the oppressive one, find it of greatest importance to combat what has come to be known as the Negro "inferiority complex." The lives of Negroes are filled with disappointments. Equal accomplishment is rare. Even the most race-conscious Negroes have their moments of tiredness when they slip back into the inferiority doctrine. The inferiority doctrine remains, therefore, as an ever-present undercurrent in Negro consciousness which must be suppressed. It is no longer, however—and this is the result of the Negro protest—an attitude of carefree complacency, but a complacency tainted with much bitterness.

The standard explanation of Negro failures, and the only one publicly accepted, is to place the responsibility upon the caste system and the whites who uphold it. This theory preserves self-respect and does not necessarily damage ambition. Many Negroes succeed in holding to this theory without mental conflict. They are able to measure their failures and accomplishments in realistic terms. Such persons thus keep a balanced personality.

The temptations are great, however, to lose this precious balance, either by falling into the bitter complacency of the inferiority doctrine or by overdoing the equality doctrine and trying to build up a case that black is superior to white. A third temptation is to exaggerate the accusation against whites and so use caste disabilities to cover all personal failures.

16. Negro Sensitiveness

It requires hard and continuous struggle for Negroes to overcome the effects of the caste deprivations and humiliations. The intensity of this struggle is suggested by the fact that often a small personal incident has the power suddenly to infuriate even those Negroes who pretend that they are not "race men." They feel overwhelmed by the discriminations and the prejudice. This is what is called Negro "sensitiveness."

Some of the Negro sensitiveness is centered around the word "Negro" and its synonyms. Even the lower-class Negro in the rural South feels insulted when he is called "nigger" by a white man. The word is hated because it symbolizes what prejudiced white people think of Negroes. The large number of such words and special ways of addressing Negroes indicate why Negroes have much to be "sensitive" about.

Indeed, the entire racial "etiquette" and system of segregation in the South are taken as insults by the Negro. The mere assumption by the Southerner that his deprecation of the Negro is not taken as an insult helps to make the Negro sensitive. Ray Stannard Baker tells of the following occurrence:

I was lunching with several fine Southern men, and they talked, as usual, with the greatest freedom in the full hearing of the Negro waiters. Somehow, I could not help watching to see if the Negroes took any notice of what was said. I wondered if they were sensitive. Finally, I put the question to one of my friends: "Oh," he said, "we don't mind them, they don't care." One of the waiters instantly spoke up: "No, don't mind me; I'm only a block of wood."[2]

The constant insulting in the South has developed the trait of sensitiveness in some Negroes to an unusually high degree. There is much cause for sensitiveness in the North also, but sometimes certain actions of Northern whites are taken as insults by Negroes when no insult is intended. This is understandable in view of the mutual ignorance of the two races in the North, but it nevertheless makes for mental unhealthiness on the part of some Negroes.

In the lower classes the protest motive is weaker and the equality doctrine not practical. Frazier tells us that lower-class parents in Wash-

[2] Ray Stannard Baker, *Following the Color Line* (Garden City, N.Y.: Doubleday, Page & Company, 1908), p. 27.

ington "caution their children to avoid conflicts, to ignore insults, and to adopt techniques for 'getting by.' These include 'acting like a monkey,' 'jibbering,' flattery and plain lying."[3] Without doubt this pattern is less common in the Northern cities, and it is becoming less common everywhere. The pattern that is becoming generally approved is an attempt at voluntary withdrawal. This pattern has become perfected in the upper classes; it is spreading into the lower classes.

17. Negro Aggression

But some Negroes will openly tell the interviewer: "I just get mad when I think about it all." Some really "get mad" occasionally and hit at the whites in the fury of frustration. But physical attack upon the whites is suicidal. Aggression has to be kept suppressed and normally is suppressed. It creeps up, however, in thousands of ways. Not only occasional acts of violence but much laziness, carelessness, unreliability, petty stealing, and lying are undoubtedly to be explained as concealed aggression. The shielding of Negro criminals and suspects, the dislike of testifying against another Negro, and the defensive solidarity in the protective Negro community have a definite taint of hostility. The truth is that most Negroes do not feel they have unqualified moral obligations to white people.

A less dangerous outlet for aggression is to deflect it from the white caste and direct it upon other Negroes. The excess of physical assaults —and of quarreling—within the Negro community can be explained as misplaced aggression of a severely frustrated subordinate caste. This outlet is, however, prohibited in the Negro middle and upper class where respectability is a supreme norm and fighting and squabbling are severely censured. Hindered from taking out their aggression on either the whites or on other Negroes, they have to store up their aggression. This is probably another cause of their greater sensitivity. Some few find an outlet in organizational activity for the Negro cause.

18. Upper-class Reactions

Caste solidarity is founded upon the negative principle that all Negroes find themselves enclosed behind the same caste bar. Caste does not allow any Negro, when he has raised himself above the others in his group—and even if he then hates them—to leave the group.

There are some upper-class Negroes who try to escape from race

---

[3] E. Franklin Frazier, *Negro Youth at the Crossways* (Washington, D.C.: American Council on Education, 1940), pp. 44–51.

and caste. They have arranged a little isolated world for themselves and want to hear as little as possible about their being Negroes or of the existence of a Negro problem. They keep themselves and their children apart from "common Negroes."

The students at Negro colleges enjoy a particularly protected life for some years, and it will be found that often the entire campus, or at least the majority cliques, arrange their lives according to this pattern. They ordinarily meet difficulties in keeping it up in later life when they have left college. But many will try.

Most upper-class Negroes cannot sustain and cannot afford for economic reasons even to attempt the isolation from the Negro caste which this type of escape presupposes. They must identify themselves with "the race." But their class also is important to them. They then often try to take the whole "race" along in an imaginary escape into class. Many Negroes, who by individual ability, hard work, or luck have succeeded in climbing the social ladder in the Negro community, think of their own exceptional success as applicable to the whole race. They are then inclined to minimize the handicaps the Negro caste labors under. But there is little basis in reality for this attitude. It also is an escape. The boaster often reveals that he, himself, is not unaware of the self-deception that he has made into a "race philosophy" by showing in one way or another that he actually considers himself as a great exception while common Negroes are classed as inferior.

This last view is more consistently displayed by many upper-class Negroes in the South who build up their careers by pleasing white people. In private they are often as overbearing to common Negroes as they are weak and unassertive to the whites. But they, too, usually cannot stand absolute loneliness and have to keep their superiority feelings somewhat camouflaged. Between this last type, the "white man's nigger," and the Negro boaster fall most of the balanced and well-adjusted upper-class Negroes.

19. The "Function" of Racial Solidarity

All upper-class Negroes, except those who try to escape "the race," have their status defined in relation to the Negro masses and practically all depend upon the lower classes of Negroes for their living. The Negro masses are the only people they can influence, and to many upper-class Negroes this is important not only in itself but also as a basis for influence with white people. Upper-class Negroes, further, share some of the disabilities inflicted by caste, and they undoubtedly feel the humiliation of caste more strongly. Their formula for being accepted as "belonging" to the Negro caste is the appeal to "race." In order to gain their purpose, this appeal has to be invested with a certain amount of protest. It becomes an appeal to race solidarity. The feeling of racial solidarity and the work for Negro betterment fill many of them with an altruistic urge. Many succeed in building up a balanced personality in striving unselfishly for the Negro group. Of course, in their narrow shut-in world, there is much envy and personal strife too.

The Negro lower classes are likely to view the superior status and opportunities of upper-class Negroes with envy. It is natural that the Negro upper class gets the brunt of the antagonism from the lower class that arises out of the latter's poverty and dependence and rightly should be directed partly against the caste system and the whites. Therefore, upper-class Negroes find it necessary to protest against caste for all the Negro masses as a means of turning lower-class opposition from themselves toward the white caste. The protest motive also allows lower-class Negroes to take vicarious satisfaction in the attainments of the upper-class Negroes.

In this way, both upper-class and lower-class Negroes are likely to swing between, on the one side, desire for intense isolation and resentment against other Negro social classes and, on the other side, race solidarity based on the caste protest against white society. For all Negroes, the Negro protest fills a "function" of allowing a higher degree of caste solidarity.

20. THE DAILY COMPROMISE

As we have said, the protest motive is ever present and in some degree it has reached practically all American Negroes. But the protest motive is limited mainly to the spreading of certain ideas about how things *should* be. Few Negro individuals are in a position to do anything practical about it. Everyone has to get on with his own life from day to day. He has to accommodate. The Negro protest is thus mainly suppressed and turned inward. But it has effects upon Negro personality, upon the relations between the classes in the Negro community, and also upon caste relations.

The Southerner keeps watching all the time for germs of unrest and dissatisfaction in the Negro community. The caste controls are always prepared and occasionally applied as an exercise or a demonstration. In this system the Negroes *have* to accommodate, individually and as a group. This is the situation in the South. The Northern situation will be discussed later.

In the protective Negro community much goes on which the white man does not know about. But the Negro leader has stepped out of the community, and the eyes of influential white people are focused on him. He has to watch his moves carefully in order not to fall out with them. This would end his usefulness to the Negro community as a go-between, and it would spell his own ruin, as the whites have control over his income and his status.

In the South practically all Negro teachers—up to and including the presidents of Negro colleges—are appointed by white leaders and hold their positions under the threat of being dismissed if they become troublesome. Even in the Negro church—usually considered independent—there are ties of small mortgage loans and petty contributions from whites which restrict the freedom of the ministers. Negro professionals, Negro businessmen, and to an even greater extent, successful Negro landowners also are dependent on the good will, indulgence, and sometimes the assistance of whites. For all local Negro leaders, it is perhaps not the economic sanction that is most important, but the sanction of physical punishment, destruction of property, and banishment. There is much bitterness among Southern Negro leaders because they are criticized for being "Uncle Toms," especially by Northern Negro intellectuals. They will tell the observer that it takes little courage to stay in the safety of the North and protest against Negro sufferings in the South.

Accommodation can be and often is a sacrifice of personal dignity and conviction which is undergone to further the aspirations of the whole group. Too, the Southern Negro leader can point out, rightly, that reckless opposition on his part might endanger Negro welfare. On the white side, the motives may be neither base nor crude. But they operate within the framework of the Southern white philosophy of race relations. According to this philosophy, the whites should "look after their Negroes." Negroes should not protest, but accommodate. They should not demand their rights, but beg for help and assistance.

The selection and the behavior of Negro leaders in the South is an outcome of the fact that practically all the economic and political powers are concentrated in the white caste, while the small amount of influence, status, and wealth that there is in the Negro community is derivative and dependent. The Negro masses are well aware of this situation. They need Negro leaders who can get things from the whites. They know that a Negro leader who acts aggressively may not only lose his own power and often his livelihood, but might endanger the welfare of the whole Negro community. The Negro community itself will thus often, before there is any white interference, advise individual Negroes who show signs of aggression that they had better trim their sails.

21. The Protest Motive

Nevertheless, the protest motive is not without influence on Negro leadership in the South. For one thing, some protest is almost a necessity in the leadership appeal to Negroes. The Negro community enjoys the demonstration of the Negro protest—as long as it does not become too dangerous for racial harmony. Whenever a Negro leader can afford—without endangering his own status or the peace of the Negro community—to speak up against or behave slightingly toward members of the superior caste, this will increase his prestige.

Usually, the presence of the protest motive in the Negro community induces the Negro leader to take on two different appearances: one toward the whites and another toward his Negro followership. To the Negroes he will pretend that he has dared to say things and to take positions much in exaggeration of what actually has happened. There is a limit, though, to what an accommodating Negro leader can pretend. What he says to the Negroes, if it is really startling, will usually be reported by stool pigeons to the whites, and might make them suspicious of him.

The Negro community gets revenge against the whites not only out of the Negro leaders' cautious aggressions but also out of the whites' being deceived. If deception is achieved, the Negroes seem to enjoy their leaders' spreading the flattery thick when approaching the whites. This is the most concealed, the almost perverted, form of the Negro protest.

22. Negro Leadership Techniques

This situation is likely to make the Negro leader sophisticated and "wise." The successful Negro leader becomes a consummate manipulator. Getting the white man to do what he wants becomes a fine art. The Negro leader feels pride in his skill in flattering, beguiling, and outwitting the white man. The South is full of folklore and legend on this aspect of Negro leadership.

Every person in this game has a double standard of understanding and behavior. The white leaders know that they are supposed to be outwitted by the subservient but sly Negro leaders. In the Southern aristocratic tradition they are supposed not only to permit and to enjoy the flattering of the Negro leaders but also to let them get away with something for themselves and for their group. It is the price due the Negro leaders for their accommodating behavior and for not raising the Negro protest. The Negro leaders also know their double role.

The situation produces all sorts of double-dealing, cynicism, and low morals in the Negro community. The leaders are under constant suspicion from the Negro community. The Negro community in the South cannot expect—and does not want—its leaders to act out the protest the common Negroes actually feel. But the common Negroes do feel humiliated and frustrated. And they can afford to take it out on their leaders by defaming them for their "kowtowing," "pussy-footing," and "Uncle Tomming"; by calling them "handkerchief heads" and "hats in hand," and particularly by suspecting them of being prepared to barter away their own honor and the interests of the group for a job or a handout. The Negro hates the Negro role in American society, and the Negro leader, who acts out this role in public life, becomes the symbol of what the Negro hates.

The Southern Negro leader, being doomed to opportunism, having constantly to compromise with his pride and dignity, does not have the reasons usually operating to preserve the honor and loyalty of a representative leader. The temptation to sell out the group and to look out for his own petty interest is great. He thus easily comes to justify the common suspicions around him by becoming a self-seeker and opportunist.

23. Leadership Rivalry

Since power and prestige are scarce in the Negro community, the struggle for leadership often becomes ruthless. Since the leader derives his position more from the whites than from organized backing in the Negro community, rivalry is likely to be increased. For the same reasons, this rivalry does not provide a check on dishonesty. It also provides the influential whites with increased possibilities to "divide and rule."

These detrimental effects upon public confidence and morals in the Negro community are the result of the lack of democracy in the Southern caste situation and, further, they are increased by the rising Negro protest as long as it is denied free outlet. On the other hand, it must never be forgotten that there are in the South many honest and diligent Negro leaders who unselfishly forward Negro interests by slow, patient, but determined plodding along against odds and difficulties. And an important aspect of the changing South is that—as the educational level is raised, as racial liberalism progresses, and as federal agencies become more important—these are the Negro leaders who are becoming increasingly trusted by the whites in power.

24. Compromise Leadership in Southern Cities

In the rural South only accommodating Negro leadership is as yet possible. In Southern cities—except in the smaller ones—single individuals and small groups of followers around them use the protection of the greater anonymity of the segregated urban Negro community to raise cautiously the banner of Negro protest. For instance, they try to get the Negroes to attempt to register as voters; and they support local branches of the N.A.A.C.P., a national protest organization. The protest has little or no effect locally, but it has the symbolic function of keeping the flame of protest burning in the community. The president of the N.A.A.C.P. branch in one of the smaller capitals of the Deep South, a distinguished, elderly gentleman, a postal clerk who for many decades because of his economic independence as a federal employee had led a cautious fight for Negro interests in his community, during a conversation as to whether there were other similar organizations in the city, said:

"Yes, there is the League for Civic Improvement."

"Why do you bother to have two organizations with the same purpose of trying to improve the position of Negroes?"

"Sir, that is easily explainable. The N.A.A.C.P. stands firm on its principles and demands our rights as American citizens. But it accomplishes little or nothing in this town, and it arouses a good deal of anger in the whites. On the other hand, the League for Civic Improvement is humble and 'pussyfooting.' It begs for many favors from the whites, and succeeds quite often. The N.A.A.C.P. cannot be compromised in all the tricks that Negroes have to perform down here. But we pay our dues to it to keep it up as an organization. The League for Civic Improvement does all the dirty work."

"Would you please tell me who is president of this League for Civic Improvement? I should like to meet him."

"I am. We are all the same people in both organizations."

This story reveals much of the political shrewdness by which difficulties are sometimes met.

25. Compromise Leadership in the North

In the North the protest motive has a much freer scope and can come out in the open. The Negro community, therefore, demands a display of actual opposition from its leaders. The Negro leaders are also much freer in their actions. They do not fear violence, intimidation, and banishment. Even the white controls over their economic prospects are much less tight.

It is, thus, surprising that one meets in Northern Negro communities the same complaints about the incompetence and dishonesty of Negro leaders. One observes also much of the same keen and destructive personal rivalry of leaders. Part of this may be explained as a cultural heritage from the Southern situation. Another part may be due to the fact that the Negro protest is freer, more widespread, and more intensely felt in the North, but the results of this protest are not too great in the North either; consequently, it turns back on the Negro community and results in internal suspicion and vicious competition.

Most important in explaining dissatisfaction with leaders is that the share of power the Negroes hold in the North creates a much greater stimulus for various white interests to buy the Negro leaders. As the Negro people are poor and inexperienced in holding power, the temptations seem strong. It is possible that there is just as much or more outright corruption in Northern Negro leadership as in Southern. Nevertheless, the Negro community also gets something out of the greater freedom and out of its share in power. And the Northern situation is conducive to a gradual education of the Negro people to the opportunities and duties of free citizenship. The masses can demand that their leaders be protest leaders clarifying and defining Negro demands and making the necessary compromises in the full light of publicity.

26. COMPROMISE LEADERSHIP ON THE NATIONAL SCENE

The conspicuousness of Negro leadership on the national plane and the severe demands on competence and devotion have a cleansing effect. National Negro leadership is no more corrupt and no more ridden with personal envy and rivalry than other national leadership. The power situation will often induce national Negro leaders to be compromising and even accommodating. Considerations of personal advancement will sometimes make Negro advisers in government agencies more interested in calming down the Negro protest than in giving it force and expression. But they are persistently watched by the Negro press and by the national Negro protest and betterment organizations.

On the national scene—and also in the larger Northern cities—one often observes a phenomenon which has an exact parallel in the women's world, namely, that "one Negro" is put on boards, committees, and so on. The Negro, appointed for no other reason than that he is a Negro, often does not have the personal qualifications for holding a prominent position.

Popular Theories and Action

Organizations

1. INSTABILITY

Negro thinking is thinking under the pressure and conflicts to which the Negro is subjected. Frustration and defeatism, forced accommodation under concealed protest, vicious competition modified by caste solidarity, form the main tapestry into which the patterns of Negro political and social thinking are woven. Upon the personality basis we have sketched, these patterns cannot possibly be consistent and stable.

For one thing, Negro political and social thinking does not have much connection with broader American and world problems. To an American Negro there is little point in having definite opinions about the world. To an extent this is true of the little fellow everywhere in a big world. But Negroes are denied identification with the nation or with national groups to a much larger degree. To them social speculation, therefore, moves in a sphere of unreality and futility. Instead of organized popular theories or ideas, there is, in the Negro world, only a fluid mass of all sorts of beginnings of thoughts. Negroes seem to be held in a state of constant preparedness for a great number of contradictory opinions—ready to accept one type or another, depending on how they are driven by pressures or where they see an opportunity.

This is what white Americans perceive when they tell the observer that Negroes are "emotional" or "unstable." Most American whites believe that emotionalism and lack of rationality are inborn in the Negro race. But scientific studies have made such inherent temperamental differences between Negroes and whites seem improbable. The author is inclined, for these reasons, to view this characteristic of Negro thinking as a result of caste exclusion from participation in the larger American society.

2. NEGRO PROVINCIALISM

Another observable characteristic of the Negroes' thinking about social and political matters is its provincialism. Here also we see an effect of caste exclusion, and not a racial trait. Provincialism in social and political thinking is not restricted to Negroes. Everybody is inclined to consider national and international issues from the point of view of personal, group, class, or regional interests. Negroes face so many difficulties and suffer so many injustices that it is only natural that when they think at all about social and political problems they think nearly exclusively about their own problems. The Negro protest defines the ills of the Negro group ever more sharply in their minds and emotionalizes narrowness. Race consciousness and race pride give it glorification and systematization.

The Negroes are so destitute of power in American society that it would, indeed, be unrealistic for them to concern themselves with a wider range of problems. It seems functional and rational for them to restrict their efforts to what is nearest home. They are not expected to have worth-while judgments on national and international affairs, except in so far as Negro interests are concerned. To most white Americans it would be preposterous and impudent, or at least peculiar, if Negroes started to discuss general problems as ordinary Americans and human beings. So the Negro protest and white expectations work together to narrow the range of Negro thinking.

Negro thinking is almost completely determined by white opinions —negatively and positively. It develops as an answer to the popular theories supporting caste prevalent among whites. In this sense it is derivative thinking. The Negroes do not formulate the issues to be debated; these are set for them by the dominant group.

Restricted and focused in this way, the problem of housing becomes to Negroes a problem of residential segregation and their share in public housing projects. Education becomes Negro education; politics concerns Negro disfranchisement and what the Negroes will get out of it. The fight between the C.I.O. and the A.F. of L. is a question of whether Negroes will be allowed into labor unions.

The American caste situation being what it is, there should be nothing astonishing in the provincialism of the Negroes in their thinking. The Negroes can even be said to act in a practical and rational way when they concentrate their efforts on their own worries and press their own local and national interests. But all this does not wipe out the distorting effects of huge gaps in knowledge and interests. Negro provincialism damages the efficiency of the Negroes' own struggle for a larger share. A balanced and integrated world view is denied American Negroes, together with many other good things in our social life.

3. Courting the "Best People among the Whites"

The popular theories on Negro strategy all try to solve the fundamental problem of how to make a compromise between accommodation and protest. Any workable policy has to gain support from white groups. We shall first, therefore, study Negro ideologies from the point of view of what social class or group among the whites is chosen as a prospective ally.

Both lower-class Negroes and some upper-class Negro leaders feel that the "quality folks," the "best people among the whites," are friends of the Negroes. They are held to be "too big" for prejudice. They are secure and out of competition. The lower-class whites, on the other hand, have been considered by Negroes to be the Negroes' natural enemies.

The policy of "courting the best people" has been allied with Booker T. Washington's philosophy. This philosophy—that, as Negroes increased in thrift, education, and efficiency, whites would gradually give them equality—has been taken over without substantial change by the Negro leaders and organizations pursuing a policy of conciliation, expediency, gradualism, and realism. It is, naturally, not conductive to broadening Negro opinions on general issues. It ties Negro thought to what is narrowly opportune for "getting along with the white folks." By allying the Negro cause exclusively with upper-class white interests, it kept Negroes, for a long time, from considering labor solidarity across the caste line.

The trends of change in American society have made this optimistic, gradualist philosophy increasingly unrealistic even as a short-range strategy. The federal government, particularly, is becoming a decisive factor as far as Negroes' interests as workers or unemployed workers are concerned. Even Negro education is becoming dependent upon the federal government. At the same time the government is becoming less dependent upon the white upper classes. It depends upon the general electorate and, in labor issues, increasingly upon organized labor.

4. THE DOCTRINE OF LABOR SOLIDARITY

The wave of Socialist thought after the First World War brought to the fore the demand for labor solidarity across the caste line. But it was not until the New Deal that labor solidarity became a realistic basis for Negro policy.

The younger generation of Negro intellectuals, with few exceptions, supported by a growing number of Negro trade unionists, have since 1930 preached labor solidarity as the cure-all of Negro ills. White labor is explained to be the Negroes' "natural" ally. Negroes are advised to think less about race and more about class—that is, the working class. The caste disabilities are said to be due to the poverty and economic dependence of Negroes and not to their color.

The eager intent to explain away race prejudice and caste in the simple terms of economic competition, and the exaggerated notions about the relative unimportance of caste, are an attempt to escape from caste into class. As such, it is similar to the tendency of certain Negro upper-class persons, already described, who also want to forget about caste and want to ally themselves with the white upper class. The differences are, however, significant. In the theory of labor solidarity, the identification would include the whole Negro people. The aim of this theory is to unify the whole Negro people, not with the white upper class, but with the white working class.

The theory of labor solidarity has been taken up as a last "solution" of the Negro problem, and as such is escapist in nature; its escape character becomes obvious to every member of the school as soon as he leaves abstract reasoning and goes down to the labor market, because there he meets caste and has to talk race and even racial solidarity.

Not only the National Association for the Advancement of Colored People, but also such conservative agencies as the Negro church and the Southern Regional Council have been becoming friendly to unions—provided they let the Negroes in. In practically the whole Negro world the C.I.O. is looked upon as a great Negro hope because it has followed a more equalitarian policy than the A.F. of L. Practically all articulate voices among Negroes are coming out in favor of unionism—with this one condition that they do not discriminate against Negroes. This new policy preserves much of the Negro protest but attempts to merge it with a class protest as far as possible. If Negro workers should be accepted completely into the

American labor movement, one of the important consequences would be the widening of the horizons of Negro social and political thinking.

Granted that attempts toward an understanding with the white working class are of paramount importance, other sectors should not be forgotten. The Negroes' status in America is so precarious that they simply have to get the support of all possible allies in the white camp.

5. "THE ADVANTAGES OF THE DISADVANTAGES"

Repeatedly we have pointed out the fundamental dilemma of the Negro upper classes. On the one hand, upper-class Negroes are the ones who feel most intensely the humiliations of segregation and discrimination. On the other hand, segregation and discrimination create an economic shelter for them. They are exploiting "the advantages of the disadvantages."

When we remember that upper-class Negroes are responsible for the thinking on their group's problem, the question must be raised as to how this situation influences popular theories on the Negro problem. (Here the crucial matter is the attitude toward segregation rather than with what white group Negroes have sought allegiance.) It is the upper-class Negroes who have felt and expressed most clearly and persistently the Negro protest against segregation. They have manned the chief organization to defend the civil rights of Negroes, the N.A.A.C.P. They often complain that lower classes do not resent the Jim Crow restrictions strongly enough.

The sincerity of the upper-class Negroes' opposition to segregation cannot be doubted. Nevertheless, the opposition against segregation in upper-class circles is directed primarily against those sectors of the caste system where it functions least as a shelter to themselves. The protest is thus outspoken and unanimous in regard to exclusion from hotels, restaurants, theaters, concerts, and segregation in transportation facilities. It is ordinarily less unanimous with respect to segregation in education. Negro schools provide employment for Negro teachers who, with present prejudice, would have less chance in non-segregated school systems. In regard to segregation in hospitals there is the same ambivalence.

As Negro institutions are improved and increasingly manned exclusively by Negro professionals, segregation is undoubtedly becoming strengthened in America. Powerful Negro vested interests in segregation are thus created. The trend is also in line with the rise of the Negro protest, which, on the one hand, means intensified "race pride" and, on the other hand, voluntary withdrawal and increasing isolation of Negroes from the larger American scene. The Negro protest, primarily caused by and directed against segregation, thus comes to build up a new spiritual basis for segregation.

6. Boosting Negro Business

The idea that the development of a Negro middle class of land-owners, businessmen, and professionals would have importance in the fight for equality and opportunity is old with the Negro people. It played an important role in Booker T. Washington's philosophy. In 1900 he founded the National Negro Business League, which is still functioning.

The philosophy held that business will stimulate the Negro's initiative, give him valuable training and experience, increase his self-confidence, increase his wealth, create a relatively secure middle and upper class, give employment to Negroes in the lower classes, and provide a reservoir of resources which could be used in competition with the whites. "Business" in this popular theory includes all free professions. The scant success in building up a substantial Negro business and professional class and the explanations of this have been reviewed in Chapter 6. But the ideology is more alive than ever.

Aside from its capacity for maintaining itself, Negro business has been thought of as a means of improving the whole Negro people. It is obvious, however, that even if Negro business succeeds, in and of itself it will never be able to provide sufficient employment or goods for the great mass of the Negro people. The chief advantage of the movement is really the tiny Negro business and professional class that lives by providing goods and services to Negroes. It is this class which has the education and leisure necessary to articulate the Negro protest and to take up successful collective bargaining with white society. In the long run, this class can be depended upon to voice the interests of the broad masses of Negroes, simply because its own economic interests are convergent with those of the masses of Negroes.

7. "Back to Africa"

The idea of sending American Negroes to Africa or to some other place outside the United States has, in the main, been confined to the whites. *The American Colonization Society* was organized in 1817 to rid America of the free Negroes who were considered a danger to slavery in the Southern states. After the Civil War and Emancipation the movement gradually vanished.

The Garvey movement shows, however, that the Negro masses are not immune to the idea that colonization would be preferable to their hopeless position in America. There have also always been individual whites who have propagandized for it. Recently Senator Bilbo of Mississippi made himself the white spokesman for it. Negro intellectuals are practically united against the back-to-Africa proposal. This is understandable. They are entirely American in their culture; they want to stay in America and fight it out. At the present time so do the Negro masses.

8. AN AMERICAN PATTERN IN ORGANIZATIONS [1]

A profusion of associations and organizations for worth-while causes is an American characteristic. Americans are great "joiners," and they enjoy "campaigns" and "drives" for membership or contributions. Social clubs are plentiful, and even they are taken with a seriousness difficult for a stranger to understand. Enthusiasm is invested in committee work in churches, lodges, clubs, and civic organizations of all kinds.

This general American pattern will have to be kept in mind when we survey the Negro protest and improvement organizations. We shall find that, as usual, Negro culture follows the American pattern with some differences in details, explainable in terms of the singular circumstances in which the Negro people live. As in other instances, those differences make the Negro appear as an exaggerated American.

9. THE NATIONAL NEGRO CONGRESS MOVEMENT

The Joint Committee on National Recovery was formed in the early days of the New Deal to watch out for Negro rights in the policy making at Washington. *The National Negro Congress* grew out of a conference in the spring of 1935 held at Howard University under the joint auspices of its Division of Social Sciences and of the Joint Committee on National Recovery. The idea behind the Congress was that a national Negro agency embracing the existing Negro trade unions, and all the religious, fraternal, and civic bodies, could give more strength and unity to all those organizations and, particularly, help awaken a response from the Negro masses. Stress

---

[1] In this and the following sections we shall not deal with white-dominated organizations which demand better conditions for Negroes but whose primary purpose is something else. Nor do we deal with the minor nationalist organizations in the Garvey tradition or the primarily business and professional organizations. We are also omitting organizations discussed elsewhere in the book such as *The-March-on-Washington Movement* and *The National Negro Business League*.

was laid upon economic and social betterment as well as upon justice and citizens' rights.

A. Philip Randolph—the head of the Brotherhood of Sleeping Car Porters, who is not only the most prominent Negro trade unionist but one of the wisest Negro statesmen in the present generation— undertook the presidency. Local councils were established in many cities and seemed, in the beginning, to have been quite active. For a time the National Negro Congress showed prospects of becoming a strong Negro movement.

At the third congress meeting, held in Washington, D.C., in April, 1940, the congress became simply a front organization for the Communist party. Randolph left the presidency and the congress sank into unimportance. During the war it lost membership heavily and devoted its relatively meager efforts to urging Negroes to support the war effort. After the end of the war, still a Communist-front organization, it renewed its original purpose of voicing vigorously the Negro protest. It gained membership significantly and secured a good deal of publicity among Negroes.

10. The National Association for the Advancement of Colored People

The National Association for the Advancement of Colored People (N.A.A.C.P.) is without question the most important agency for the Negroes in their struggle against caste. In the summer of 1908 there occurred a severe race riot in Springfield, Ill., the home of Abraham Lincoln. Scores of Negroes were killed or wounded and many driven out of the city. Wide publicity was given the affair in the press, and one writer, William English Walling, threw a challenge to the nation: there was need for a revival of the spirit of the Abolitionists to win liberty and justice for the Negro in America. The appeal was answered by Mary White Ovington. In January, 1909, Miss Ovington met with Mr. Walling and Dr. Henry Moskowitz in New York, and plans were laid for a new organization.

A conference which included many prominent white liberals was called on February 12, 1909. The following year, at a second conference, these white liberals of Abolitionist traditions and the Negro liberals of the Niagara Movement joined forces. Out of these two groups the N.A.A.C.P. was formed. Moorfield Storey of Boston was elected the first president. He and all other officers of the new organization were white, except Du Bois, who became the salaried director of publicity and research. The platform adopted was practically indentical with that of the Niagara Movement. From the beginning Du Bois gave the tone to the new organization's activity. By 1914 there were thirteen Negro members on the Board of Directors, most of whom were veterans of the Niagara Movement. In 1910 the publication of the organization's journal, *The Crisis,* began and it soon became popular.

The long-run objective of the organization has always been to win full equality for the Negro as an American citizen. The specific objectives can be seen from the program as announced in 1947:

1. Abolish injustices in legal procedure based solely on race or color.
2. Banish lynching and mob violence.
3. Secure passage of liberal legislation.
4. Secure passage of a federal civil rights bill and civil rights legislation for all states.
5. Secure the right of franchise for all American citizens.
6. Abolish discrimination and segregation in education, transportation, employment and housing.
7. Secure recognition of worth and dignity of the Negro members of the Armed Forces.
8. Secure freedom from insult and discrimination for colonial peoples in other countries.[2]

The N.A.A.C.P. works through the National Office in New York City and through branches or local associations in cities everywhere in the country. The National Office determines the policy of the organization and supervises the work of the branches. The National Office, including *The Crisis,* employs a staff of 91 people of whom all but 5 are Negroes. The president of the association has always been a white man; at present he is Arthur B. Spingarn. The Board of Directors has members of both races; at present it is composed of 28 Negroes and 20 whites. There are 15 vice-presidents, 8 of whom are Negroes. The main executive officer and the responsible head of the association is the secretary. This office is now held by Walter White. Few branch officers are white, although some whites serve on executive committees of branches. It is estimated that about 10 per cent of the total membership of the association is white. The association is interracial at the top, practically all Negro at the base.

During the past few years there has been a remarkable increase in the number of local branches and in membership rolls. As of January, 1947, there were 1,195 branches of the association and, in addition, 254 youth councils and 48 college chapters. As of January,

[2] National Association for the Advancement of Colored People, "The NAACP: Goals and Achievements, 1946–1947" (Jan. 30, 1947), mimeographed.

1947, the total membership of the association was estimated to be between 550,000 and 600,000. The 1947 membership drive hopes to make this at least 1,000,000. *The Crisis* has a circulation of about 50,000 copies. The National Office operates on a budget of around $396,000. Much of the larger part of the budget is derived from membership fees, but a smaller part is raised by contributions from individuals and from a few foundations, most often given for specific purposes.[3]

The activity of the association depends largely upon the effective organization of its branches. They provide it with membership, the larger part of its financial support, and information from and contacts with its field of work. The National Office advises its branches on tactics as well as aims. The branches are advised "that injury to one Negro on racial grounds affects the status of the whole group, and hence, the health and happiness of our American civilization."[4]

When these things are considered: the immensity of the task set for the branches; the high demands made upon the time, interest, intelligence, and tact of the branch officers; the fact that these officers work on a voluntary basis in their free time; the power situation in the South; the fact that few local white people are prepared to give assistance or even sympathy to the work; while poverty, ignorance, and defeatism are widespread among the Negro masses—when all these adverse factors are considered, it should not be a surprise that hardly any branch approaches the ideals envisaged for its active working.

In many Southern communities, conservative or dependent upper- and middle-class Negroes share the common white opinion in the region that the N.A.A.C.P. is a "foreign" or "radical" organization, that its policy is "tactless" and "tends to stir up undue hostility between the races." Another difficulty of the typical N.A.A.C.P. branch is the competition for interest, time, and money from churches, lodges, social clubs, and independent local civic organizations. Frequently the main function of the branch is to scare the white man. White Southerners will help more conservative organizations in order to keep the N.A.A.C.P. branch inactive.

The N.A.A.C.P. branches in the Northern cities usually have

[3] The material in this and the above paragraph has been taken from a letter from Julia E. Baxter, Division of Research and Information, N.A.A.C.P., July 21, 1947.

[4] *Program Book for N.A.A.C.P. Branches* (1939), p. 1. Quoted in Ralph Bunche, "The Programs, Ideologies, Tactics and Achievements of Negro Betterment and Interracial Organizations," unpublished manuscript prepared for *An American Dilemma* (1940), Vol. 1, p. 45.

larger membership rolls than those in Southern cities. They are free to carry out campaigns and to take cases into court. The Negro vote gives them backing for their demands.

The major part of the work carried on by the association is performed by its National Office. The National Office acts as a "watchdog" over Negro rights. When anything important develops on the national or on some local scene which is adverse to Negro interests, the association promptly intervenes. Systematic lobbying, primarily in Washington, but also in state capitals, is kept up.

The association puts its trust in publicity. A large part of the work of the National Office is in the nature of educational propaganda. It not only publishes *The Crisis* and the *N.A.A.C.P. Bulletin,* but also a great many pamphlets, brochures, and books on various aspects of the Negro problem. The officers of the National Office also try to present their case to the white public through articles in outstanding national periodicals. The National Office provides data for research work on the Negro problem; it furnishes speakers for important meetings. In its publicity the National Office has a militant and challenging tone but is ordinarily scrupulously correct in statements of fact.

From the beginning, the association has laid stress on its legal redress work. In hundreds of cases, the lawyers of the N.A.A.C.P. have been instrumental in saving Negroes from unequal treatment in the courts, sometimes getting them acquitted when they were sentenced or in danger of being sentenced on flimsy evidence, sometimes getting death penalties or other severe penalties reduced. In numerous cases the exclusion of Negroes from juries has been challenged. Police brutality, third-degree methods, and peonage have been fought.

The association has likewise been active in defending the Negroes' right to vote. One of its first successes was to get the "grandfather clauses" declared unconstitutional and recently it has got the courts to outlaw the white primary. Challenging the legality of residential segregation has been one of the main efforts of the association. The association has also been vigilant, although with caution, against the Jim Crow laws and, particularly, against inferior facilities for Negroes in segregated setups of various sorts. In recent years it has concentrated its attack on the barriers against Negro students and on the unequal salaries of Negro teachers.

Some conservative Negroes and most conservative and liberal whites in the South accuse the N.A.A.C.P. of being "reckless" in striking out in all directions against the caste order of the region.

Yet, the association has avoided launching a wholesale legal campaign against the Southern segregation system, as this would have provoked a general reaction. It has selected its points of attack with care and has pushed ahead with caution.

On the other side, Northern sociologists and Negro Marxists have criticized the N.A.A.C.P. for concentrating on publicity, suffrage, and civil liberties instead of on the economic problem. To this criticism the N.A.A.C.P. answers that it considers its work in the civil liberties sphere important enough not to be lightheartedly jeopardized by radical ventures in other directions. It has machinery set up for this work, and three decades of experience have gone into perfecting it. For a Negro protest or betterment organization to adopt a revolutionary program would be suicidal for the organization and damaging to the Negro cause.

To the outside observer the reasons are strongly on the side of the N.A.A.C.P. The American Constitution and the entire legal system of the land give the Negro a strategic strength in his fight against caste which it would be senseless not to utilize to the utmost. In addition, the N.A.A.C.P. has been successful in accomplishing each task it has set for itself.

While there are many issues, especially in the economic sphere, which need to be tackled, it is not necessarily wise for the N.A.A.C.P. to take on these extra burdens. It does not have the finances, the staff, or the experience. There is thus room for other agencies working in other fields than those chosen by the N.A.A.C.P.

11. The Urban League

Like the N.A.A.C.P., the *Urban League* is an interracial movement started on white initiative. In 1911 three groups interested in improving the economic conditions among urban Negroes united to form the National Urban League. The philanthropists, social workers, and professionals who made up the nucleus of the new organization "held that the Negro needed not alms but opportunity —opportunity to work at the job for which the Negro was best fitted, with equal pay for equal work, and equal opportunity for advancement."[5] Edwin R. A. Seligman became the first president of the organization.

The National Urban League, with its central office in New York, is the parent organization. In order to expand the work of the league in Southern communities, it has a Southern Field Branch Office in Atlanta, Ga. The National Urban League is governed by an Execu-

[5] Bunche, *op. cit.,* Vol. 2, pp. 218 ff.

tive Board of 21 persons of whom 8 are Negroes and 13 are whites, and a National Committee of 39 members, 23 white and 16 Negro. Members of the National Committee are called on for advice and help in the communities where they live and have influence. The president of the organization is Lloyd K. Garrison, the executive secretary, Lester Granger. There is a staff of 38, two of whom are white; all the rest are Negroes. The league publishes *Opportunity* and *The Secretariat,* the one directed to the general public, the other serving as house organ. The National League operated in 1947 upon a budget of approximately $184,000 (including *Opportunity*). It is raised by contributions from foundations and from individuals. Local branches are established in 56 cities.[6] The local Urban Leagues are governed by interracial boards. Sometimes there are other committees, usually interracial in composition. Many local leagues, for example, have a committee on industrial relations. Many of the local Urban Leagues are members of city-wide Community Chests. For much of their work the local leagues are able to solicit voluntary services from ministers, teachers, doctors, and other public-spirited citizens in the Negro community in addition to the trained secretary and specialized social workers and office workers in each local office.

The local leagues carry on a multitude of activities: day nurseries, sometimes with baby clinics and child placement agencies, and occasionally schools for Negro girls who have become pregnant; clubs for boys, girls, mothers, neighborhood and other groups; training schools for janitors or domestics; parent-teacher associations; study groups in trade unionism; health weeks, and so on. To mitigate delinquency among Negroes they offer to co-operate with the law-enforcement agencies and to perform such tasks as furnishing supplementary parole supervisors, safeguarding the interest of girls appearing in court, and, in some cases, finding homes for them. Fights are waged against commercial prostitution in the vicinity of Negro homes, schools, and churches.

None of the local leagues can afford to become active in all these fields, but a primary task of all leagues is to find jobs, more jobs, better jobs for Negroes. They all function as employment agencies. They try to "sell" Negro labor—impressing upon the employers that Negro labor is efficient and satisfactory, and upon the unionists that the Negro is a good and faithful fellow worker. The possibilities

[6] This material was obtained from a letter from Guichard Parris, promotion and publicity director of the National Urban League (July 16, 1947), and from *National Urban League, Thirty-Sixth Annual Report, 1946* (New York: National Urban League, 1947).

of vocational training have to be kept open to Negro youth, and the youths themselves have to be encouraged to be ambitious. The civil service boards have to be watched so that they do not discriminate against Negroes, and Negroes must be encouraged to take civil service examinations.

The National Urban League is the general staff for all this work. It directs and inspires it, co-ordinates and evaluates the experiments made in one place or another. It conducts community surveys and other research work. It educates and sometimes agitates: among the Negroes to improve themselves and among the whites to reduce prejudice and to give the Negroes a fair chance. It uses its own publication, *Opportunity,* pamphlets and books, the radio, the pulpit, and the lecture platform.

In many communities white people often look upon the league as "dangerous," "radical," and "too friendly to labor." Among the younger Negro intellectuals, on the contrary, the league is commonly accused of being too "timid." Against these charges the league retorts that "it is a social service organization attempting to perform a helpful task in a limited field." The dispute has come to center about the league's attitude toward trade unionism. The National Urban League stated long ago that its official policy is in favor of collective bargaining and against strikebreaking, provided the unions are kept open to Negro workers. Generally speaking, local Urban Leagues change with the community, and, in most cities, change as much in advance of the community as is possible while maintaining community good will and financial support for their program. Much the same is true about the National Urban League. As the trade-union movement and collective bargaining are gradually becoming normal and appreciated factors in American society, the Urban League is increasingly holding the lead as a pro-union force working among the Negro people.

12. The Commission on Interracial Cooperation and the Southern Regional Council

The Southern Regional Council grew out of two organizations, the Commission on Interracial Cooperation, and the Durham-Atlanta-Richmond series of conferences. The council was formally established in February, 1944. Charles S. Johnson and his associates give the following report of its founding and functions:

The Council's area was defined as the states of Alabama, Arkansas, Florida, Georgia, Kentucky, Louisiana, Mississippi, North Carolina, Oklahoma, South Carolina, Tennessee, Texas, and Virginia. The first officers were: Dr. Howard Odum of the University of North Carolina, president; P. B. Young of Norfolk, Virginia; Homer P. Rainey of Austin, Texas; and Carter Wesley of Houston, Texas, vice-presidents; Miss Emily H. Clay, Secretary-treasurer. The executive director is Dr. Guy B. Johnson of the University of North Carolina. . . .

To quote from its own statement of programs and methods, issued in June, 1944, the Council "represents the combined efforts of liberal and progressive people of both races to give democracy a chance in the South. Its long-time goal is the improvement of social, civic, economic, and racial conditions in the South.

"The Council's functions may be summarized as follows: (1) clearing house and coordinating work with numerous agencies working on Southern problems; (2) research and survey to determine the facts and the state of public opinion as a basis for sound social action; (3) educational activities through a monthly paper, *The Southern Frontier,* and through pamphlets, press, radio, conferences, and personal contacts; (4) consultative services to private or official agencies; (5) constructive action at every possible point on the social, economic, political and racial problems of the South."[7]

The council may be considered a revitalization of the former Commission on Interracial Cooperation in that its members are tackling the South's problems with renewed vigor and idealism. But its basic work, ideals, and personnel are essentially the same as that of the commission.

The Commission on Interracial Cooperation, like the N.A.A.C.P. and the Urban League, was not a Negro movement but a joint effort by whites and Negroes. While the first two organizations have a national scope, the Interracial Commission worked in the South only.

The Commission on Interracial Cooperation was organized in 1919 as an effort to meet the great uncertainty and strain in the relations between whites and Negroes after the First World War. The leading spirit of the movement and, later, the director of the work was W. W. Alexander. The purpose of the new organization was:

. . . to quench, if possible, the fires of racial antagonism which were flaming at that time with such deadly menace in all sections of the country.[8]

Local interracial committees were started, and a series of ten-day schools for whites and Negroes, respectively, were held for the pur-

[7] Reprinted from *Into the Main Stream* (pp. 6, 8), by Charles S. Johnson and Associates. By permission of the University of North Carolina Press. Copyright, 1947, by University of North Carolina Press.

[8] *A Practical Approach to the Race Problem,* leaflet published by the Commission on Interracial Cooperation (October, 1939).

pose of training leaders of both races to promote the interracial work. The school concentrated upon community readjustment and care for the returning troops. Started for the purpose of meeting a temporary emergency, the commission's work was so successful and was deemed so important that it was decided to transform it into a permanent institution.

The Commission on Interracial Cooperation became the organization of Southern liberalism in its activity on the Negro issue. In its publications it demanded a fair opportunity for the Negro as a breadwinner; equal participation in government welfare programs; equal justice under the law; suffrage and other civil liberties. It did not attack segregation but stood against discrimination. The South was and is so far from having achieved the commission's aims and the liberal forces of the region are so weak that the commission was compelled to adopt a gradualistic approach. The chief political means of approaching the goal set up by the commission were conciliation, moral persuasion, and education. Its practical task was formulated as the attempt to promote:

. . . the creation of a better spirit, the correction of grievances, and the promotion of interracial understanding and sympathy.[9]

In this spirit the commission sponsored and carried out important research on various phases of the Negro problem such as cotton tenancy and lynching. It published monthly *The Southern Frontier* and a great number of pamphlets and educational material. It tried to influence the white press to give more favorable publicity to Negroes and to suppress such material as was likely to inflame white opinion. The commission encouraged the introduction of courses on race relations in hundreds of colleges and high schools throughout the South. Sometimes the commission entered legal redress work in selected cases which had broader applications. From the beginning a main interest of the commission was that of stamping out lynching. The commission had a share in the achievement of the dramatic decrease in lynching, and generally in the greater enforcement of law in the South during the past two decades.

The commission did not escape criticism from conservative Southerners. But one of the important accomplishments of the commission is to have made interracial work socially respectable in the conservative South. Liberal white Southerners on their part usually backed the commission. Negroes, on the other hand, tended to be critical of the commission—even the older and most conservative

[9] *Ibid.*

Negro leaders. Few Negroes in the South wholeheartedly praised its work. This criticism seems too strong. It overlooked the power situation in the South. A movement which sets out to change public opinion and social institutions in the South must make opportunism its principle. It must develop an indirect approach instead of a direct attack. The commission was a useful agency. This, of course, should not exclude other and more radical efforts at the same time. Also it does not exclude a criticism that the commission could work more effectively. But its main tactics must be condoned. These tactics *are* radical in the South, and among white people they can secure the backing of only the small group of Southern liberals. The need for a more active policy, better financial support, and greater participation by Negroes led the commission to reorganize itself into the Southern Regional Council. The same criticisms have been leveled at the council, and the same rebuttals can be made.

What the council needs is a broader appeal in order to reach directly the middle and lower classes of whites. Until recently the council has been working mainly with the "intelligent leadership" of the South and has not touched the "mass mind."

13. Negro Strategy

Certain general observations and conclusions on Negro strategy should now be brought together. But first, the value premises that have been applied in the foregoing sections should be made explicit. They are only an adaptation of the values contained in the American Creed:

1. It is neither practical nor desirable for American citizens of Negro descent to be deported from this country. The problem is how to adjust race relations in America.

2. All concerted action by, or on behalf of, American Negroes should be judged by how effectively it contributes to the ultimate destruction of caste in America. The interest of the Negro people in winning complete citizenship in American society is taken for granted in the American Creed. The power situation in America makes it an obvious Negro interest and, consequently, a general American interest to engage as many white groups as possible as allies in the struggle against caste.

It is a peculiar trait of much of the discussion of Negro concerted action in America that it assumes that one unified Negro movement is desirable. This is unrealistic and impractical for several reasons. For one thing, a unified Negro movement would not gain the support of the Negro masses except by an emotional, nationalistic, race-protest appeal of the Garvey type. Such a movement would probably estrange most of the Negro upper class and practically all white groups. By this we do not mean that the racial appeal should not be used. It has to be used with caution. Still less do we mean that the Negro masses should not be appealed to. They should, but by movements with specific and limited aims.

When we look over the field of Negro protest and betterment organizations, we find that only when Negroes have worked with whites have organizations been built up which have any strength and which have been able to do something practical. There are several explanations of this. One is that Negroes on the whole are poor. Another is the lack of political culture in the traditions of the Negro people, because they have been subdued for generations. A third is the existence of the interracial organizations. They have drawn to themselves much of the individual talent for political leadership in the Negro people. A fourth and basic explanation is the fact in the power situation that it is advantageous and, indeed, necessary to have white allies in order to accomplish anything.

The interest in keeping as allies as many white groups as possible, and the interest in maintaining a high effectiveness in the work being done, speak for having not one Negro organization, but a whole set of organizations specializing on different tasks and applying different degrees of opportunism or radicalism.

There is need for a militant organization like the N.A.A.C.P. to uphold the great Abolitionist tradition, taking its stand on the American Constitution. There is also need for a social service organization like the Urban League, doing its work among the victims of caste, educating and protecting Negroes, and exerting its pressure against the dominant white society from the welfare point of view. In America there will always be white supporters for such work. In addition, there is in the South a pressing need for an interracial movement, with limited immediate objectives, such as the Southern Regional Council.

There is little "overlapping" or "duplication" among the various existing Negro organizations, and there is little friction and rivalry among the three main organizations. Instead of unification there is need for further specialization.

For example, Negroes need an agency to carry on—locally and nationally—political collective bargaining with the political parties. This organization should preferably be an all-Negro organization and should be narrowly specialized to play the political game. There is also need for a legal aid agency concentrating its work on improving law enforcement in individual cases in the South. To the degree that the N.A.A.C.P. does this it weakens itself by drawing too heavily on its financial and personnel resources. Such an agency preferably should not be set up separately for Negroes but should be an agency to defend the rights of all poor and disadvantaged people. Finally, there is need for an organization to integrate Negroes into the labor movement and work as a pressure group on the trade unions.

Negroes should attempt to develop that type of political culture which is ideal in any democratic nation. There must be radicals, liberals, and conservatives. An American Negro should select the front where he wants to take his stand. But he should keep his eyes wide open to the desirability that other Negroes have other stands. The militant Negro should be able to see the usefulness—in some situations—of some Negro leaders who "pussyfoot," and contrariwise. The Negro labor organizer should be grateful that there are others who fight for his civil liberties, and still others who do the welfare work for his potential members.

A word must be added on the moral aspect of Negro leadership. To the Negro people dishonest leadership is an important cause of weakness in concerted action. It should be preached against and fought against. It should be a main topic in the teaching in Negro universities, in the Negro journals, in Negro adult education. If a generation of young Negroes could be brought up to understand how scrupulous honesty could tremendously advance the Negro cause, this would mean a great deal for Negro progress. This has been largely achieved on the national level, but is still a need on the local level.

Basic Protest Institutions:

Church, School, Press

1. NONPOLITICAL AGENCIES FOR NEGRO CONCERTED ACTION

The primary functions of the Negro church, school, and press
are not, of course, to be agencies of power for the Negro caste. Nevertheless, they are of importance in the power relations within the
Negro community and between Negroes and whites. They bring
Negroes together for a common cause. They train them for concerted
action. They provide an organized followership for Negro leaders.
In these institutions, theories of accommodation and protest become
formulated and spread. The institutions sometimes take action themselves in the power field, attempting to improve the Negro's lot or
voicing the Negro protest. Even more often they provide the means
by which Negro leaders and organizations, which are more directly
concerned with power problems, can reach the Negro people.

The Negro churches and the press are manned almost exclusively
by Negroes. None of these organizations is, however, outside the
control of the whites. The Negro press is the freest, the Negro school
the most tightly controlled. But in all these institutions Negroes are
usually away from the presence of whites, and this creates a feeling
of freedom, in smaller matters if not in major policies.

The very existence of Negro institutions is, of course, due to caste.
Under the caste system they all take on a defensive function for the
Negroes, and sometimes they take on militant function. The Negro
press is, in this sense, more radical than the other nonpolitical agen-

cies. However, all these agencies, in the long run, tend to build up the Negro protest.

2. Historical Background of the Negro Church

With few exceptions the Negro slaves brought to America had not been converted to Christianity. After 1700, when it was legally decided that one could be both Christian and a slave, many slave-holders provided religious teaching and a place of worship for their slaves, or at least did nothing to hinder missionary work among them. On many plantations the slaves were allowed to attend the same churches as did the whites, although they were seated separately. Later there were Negro ministers and separate worship became common. After the slave rebellion in 1831, many masters tried to stop separate religious meetings, but there was never a complete stoppage of religion among Negroes. The advantage of having a slave work off his frustration in religion was too strong. Slaves were allowed to meet by themselves if a white minister led them or if any white man observed them. Practically the only religious meetings completely free of whites were secret ones.

In the North the few Negro churches before the Civil War served much the same functions as they do today. Many of them were also "stations" in the "underground railroad," and centers of Negro Abolitionist activities.

At the time of Emancipation probably only a minority of the Negro slaves were nominal Christians. At the end of the Civil War there was, on the one hand, an almost complete and permanent exclusion of Negroes from the white churches of the South and, on the other hand, a general movement among Negroes to build up their own denominations. This period witnessed a wave of conversion to Christianity of the Negroes and the firm establishment of the independent Negro church.

Many Negro political leaders during Reconstruction were recruited from among the preachers. After Reconstruction many of them returned to the pulpit. While there was little real chance, during this period, of rebellion against caste, there was opened a new possibility for the Negro church to serve as a power agency for Negroes; the white preachers and white observers disappeared. There remained only the Negro stool pigeon to report to the whites.

In practically all the rural areas, and in many of the urban ones, the preacher stood as the acknowledged local leader of the Negroes. He became the typical accommodating Negro leader. The Negro church in the South, due to its accommodating role, has earned considerable good will among the whites. It is also taken for granted that the Negroes should be left considerable freedom to develop their religious life as they want to. The Negro churches are, therefore, not closely controlled. The Negro preacher is trusted. Thus, while the Negro church in the South did not lead the opposition to the caste system, it was sometimes able to modify the harshness of the system and helped maintain the solidarity of Negroes in their cautious pressure to better their position.

In the North the Negro church has, of course, remained far more independent. But even the Northern Negro church has remained conservative and has largely ignored the practical problems of the Negroes' fate in this world.[1]

3. The Negro Church and the American Pattern of Religious Activity

The Negro church and Negro religious life adhere closely to the common American pattern. Americans are a religious people; Southerners are more religious than the rest of the nation, and the Negroes, perhaps, still a little more religious than the white Southerners. According to the United States Census of Religious Bodies, which is inaccurate but has the best data available, Negro churches claimed 5,660,618 members in 1936 and white churches 50,146,748. That is, 44.0 per cent of the Negro population are members of Negro churches as compared to 42.4 per cent of the white population in white churches. This is an underestimation, because there are many Negroes who belong to white churches and many of the small denominations to which Negroes belong have been overlooked.

Negroes, like the majority of Americans, are Protestant; and, again, like the majority of Americans, the majority of Negroes belong to the churches with less formal rituals, the Baptist and Methodist, and the small sects that have split off from these. As in the white American population, among the Negroes the upper class tends, more than the lower classes, to belong to the Episcopalian, Congregational, and Presbyterian churches. There has been a recent movement, however, into the Catholic Church on the part of Negroes of all classes—due largely to the welfare activities sponsored in the Catholic Church among Negroes and to the recent Catholic stand

[1] There are many exceptions—for example, the Abyssinian Baptist Church in the Harlem section of New York City, led by A. Clayton Powell, Jr., and the Good Shepherd Church of Chicago, which sponsors a community center.

against discrimination and segregation in many areas of life. Protestant religion in America has always had relatively more emotionalism than in other countries: revival meetings and evangelists have
played a greater role and the church services have exhibited more
emotional traits. The South displays these traits to a marked degree,
and the Negroes still more so. As in the white population, there
is a class differential as well as a geographical one in regard to degree
of emotionalism in religious services. Upper- and middle-class Negroes are likely to frown upon the old practices that still prevail in
the lower classes. Americans are divided into a great number of denominations. The split into miniature congregations is driven nearly
to its limit in the Negro world.

In other respects than its emotionalism, the Negro church is quite
like any lower-class white Protestant church. The visitor to an average Negro church will see much the same type of service—with
choir singing, hymns by the congregation, organ music (in the larger
churches), prayer, sermon, collection—and hear the same theological
terms that he hears in the average white Protestant church.

4. A Segregated Church

Both the strength and the weakness of the Negro church as a
power agency for the Negro people is related to the facts that the
Negro church is a segregated church and that there is little interracial co-operation between white and Negro churches. Church segregation must be a great moral dilemma to many earnest Christians
among the whites. Among Negroes all over the country the fact of
segregation is constantly used to prove the insincerity of white people.

If this moral problem of organized American Christianity has
not become more conspicuous and troublesome to the white people's
conscience, the explanation is that probably most Negroes—the caste
situation being what it is—prefer to worship in Negro churches, even
if they are against church segregation in principle. Negro preachers
suspect many of the projects of interracial co-operation in church
activities as attempts to deprive them of influence. They feel, often
with some justification, that interracial religious activities would
mean having white men as church leaders for Negroes but not Negroes as church leaders for whites. In the South there is practically
no contact at all between Negroes and whites for religious purposes.
In the North there are more interracial contacts but not enough to
modify the basic fact of church separation. What little there is probably tends to improve race relations, to bring the Negro church

closer to white norms of religious behavior, and to get money from the whites for the Negro church.

5. THE WEAKNESS OF THE CHURCHES

The Negro church is the oldest and—in membership—by far the strongest of all Negro organizations. Potentially the Negro church is a power institution. It has the Negro masses organized and could line up the Negroes behind a program. Actually, the Negro church is, on the whole, passive in the field of intercaste power relations. In the South it has not led in attacking the caste system or even in bringing about minor reforms; in the North it has only occasionally been a strong force for social action. Of 100 sermons delivered in urban Negro churches, and analyzed by Mays and Nicholson, only 26 touched upon practical problems. The rural Negro church makes an even poorer showing. Too, the Negro church is out of touch with current social life in the field of morals; the teaching of traditional puritanical morals has little effect on the bulk of the Negro population, and the real moral problems of the people are seldom considered in the church. Ignorance, poverty, cultural isolation, and the tradition of dependence are responsible for this situation.

The frequent schisms in Negro churches weaken their institutional strength. New Negro churches and sects seldom begin because of theological differences, but because a preacher wants to get a congregation, because some members of a church feel that the minister is too emotional or not emotional enough, because some members feel that they have little in common with other members of the church, as well as because of outside missionary influences. The competition between the preachers is intense and most churches are small. There is little collaboration between the churches; overhead expenses tend to be high. Since, in addition, the membership is usually composed of poor people, the economic basis of the churches is weak. Poverty often makes the Negro church dependent upon white benefactors. It also prevents paying salaries that could tempt ambitious young men to educate themselves properly for the ministry. The chief prerequisite for becoming a minister in most of the denominations to which Negroes belong is traditionally not education but a "call." Such preachers tend to retain the emotionalism that has traditionally been identified with the Negro's religion.

As a class Negro preachers are losing influence, because they are not changing as fast as the rest of the Negro community. Young people have begun to look down on the old-fashioned Negro preacher. Few college students are going into the ministry. If this development goes on, it will spell the further decline of the Negro church as an active influence in the Negro community.

6. TRENDS AND OUTLOOK FOR THE CHURCHES

The Negro church has been lagging ideologically too. While for a long time the protest has been rising in the Negro community, the church has, on the whole, remained conservative and accommodating. Its otherworldly outlook is itself an expression of political fatalism. Although one does meet Negro preachers who are active in the work for protest and betterment, progressive ministers are still exceptions. Their existence might, however, signify a trend.

It must never be forgotten that the Negro church is fundamentally an expression of the Negro community itself. If the church has been otherworldly in outlook and has indulged in emotional ecstasy, it is primarily because the downtrodden common Negroes have craved religious escape from poverty and other troubles. The rivalry and factionalism, the organizational weakness and economic dependency, the often faltering economic and sexual morals of the preachers and their suspicion of higher education—all these reflect life as it is lived in the subordinate caste of American Negroes.

When the Negro community changes, the church also will change. The Negro church is part of the circular process that is moving the American Negroes onward in their struggle against caste. The increasing education of the Negro masses is either making them demand something more of their church or causing them to stand aloof from the institutionalized form of religion. With some lag, the Negro clergymen, too, are acquiring a better education, which is reflected in their work. The movement to the North and to the Southern cities also tends to free the Negro preacher from white pressure. These trends are making the Negro church a more efficient instrument for betterment of the Negro's position at the same time as they are reducing the relative importance of the church in the Negro community.

7. NEGRO EDUCATION AS CONCERTED ACTION

The trend toward a rising educational level of the Negro population is of tremendous importance for relations between Negroes and whites. Education means an assimilation of white American culture. It decreases the dissimilarity of Negroes from other Americans. Since American education is permeated by democratic values, and since the caste relation is anything but democratic, education is likely to increase dissatisfaction among Negroes. Increasing education provides theories and tools for the rising Negro protest against caste. It also trains and helps to give an economic livelihood to Negro leaders.

In the Negro community education is the main factor dividing the Negro people into social classes. The professionals who have acquired a higher education form a substantial part of the Negro upper classes. In the middle and lower classes, also, educational levels signify class differences. In addition, education has symbolic significance in the Negro world:[2] the educated Negro has, in one important respect, become equal to the better class of whites.

The tendencies are most unhampered in the North. There Negroes have the entire educational system open to them without much discrimination. The American Creed permeates instruction, and Negro as well as white youths are encouraged in the traditional American virtues of efficiency, thrift, and ambition. The American dream of individual success is held out to the Negroes as to other students. But employment opportunities—and, to a lesser extent, some other good things of life—are closed to them so that severe conflicts in their minds are bound to appear. Often they become cynical in regard to the official democratic ideals taught by the school. But more fundamentally they will be found to have drunk of them deeply. The American Creed and the American virtues mean much more to Negroes than to whites. They are all turned into the rising Negro protest.

The situation is more complicated in the South. The Negro schools are segregated and the Negro school system is controlled by different groups with different interests and opinions concerning the desirability of preserving or changing the caste status of Negroes. White liberals in the region and Northern philanthropists have given powerful assistance in building up Negro education in the South. They have thereby taken and kept some of the controls. In the main, however, the control over Negro education has been preserved by other whites representing the political power of the region. On the other hand, the salaried officers—the college presidents, the school principals, the professors, and the teachers—are now practically all Negroes.

---

[2] Between 1913 and 1932, there were constructed some 5,357 Negro school buildings in 15 Southern states. "The total cost of these buildings was $28,408,520, of which . . . $4,725,871 (17%) [came] in a flood of small contributions from Negroes themselves—striking evidence of the desire of members of this race for schooling for their children." (Edwin R. Embree, *Julius Rosenwald Fund: Review of Two Decades, 1917–1936* [1936], p. 23.)

With this setup it is natural that the Negro school adheres rather closely to the accommodating pattern.

Negro teachers on all levels are dependent on white community leaders. This dependence is particularly strong in the case of elementary school teachers in rural districts. Their salaries are low and their security almost nothing. They can be used to spread the whites' expectations and demands through the Negro community. But their extreme dependence and poverty, and the existence of better-off and more independent Negroes, excludes them from having any leadership status in the Negro community. In so far as their teaching is concerned, they are more independent than it appears simply because the white superintendent and the white school board ordinarily care little about what goes on in the Negro school. As long as Negro stool pigeons do not report that she puts wrong ideas into the children's heads, the rural Negro school teacher is usually ignored.

In cities the situation is different. Negro elementary and high schools are better; teachers are better trained and better paid; they have a higher social status in the Negro community. While city teachers have a measure of independence due to the anonymity of a city, the Negro principal in a city school, who is directly responsible to white officials, watches his teachers closely. In state colleges the situation is similar, except that the professors have a still higher social status in the Negro community.

In the private colleges there is much more independence from local white opinion within the limits of the campus. The influence exerted by the Northern philanthropists and church bodies who have contributed to the colleges is, to a great extent, effective in upholding the independence of Negro college presidents and professors.

In spite of the local controls, strongest at the bottom of the educational system but strong also in the higher institutions, there is no doubt that the long-range effect of the rising level of education among the Negro people is to nourish and strengthen the Negro protest.

8. EDUCATION IN AMERICAN THOUGHT AND LIFE

Even where the Negro school exists as a separate institution it is, like all other Negro institutions, patterned on the white American school. It is different only for reasons connected with the caste situation. Education has always been the great hope for both individual and society. In the American Creed it has been the main ground upon which "equality of opportunity for the individual" and "free outlet for ability" could be based. Education has also been considered as the best way—and the way most compatible with American individualistic ideals—to improve society.

American Negroes have taken over the American faith in education. As self-improvement through business or social improvement through government appeared so much less possible for them, Negroes have come to affix an even stronger trust in the magic of education. To an extent, this faith was misplaced: many Negroes hoped to escape drudgery through education alone. But it is also true that this faith has been justified to a large extent: education is one of the things that have given the Negroes something of a permanent advance in their condition.

In education, as in many other fields of culture, America shows great differences: there are at once many model schools and a considerable amount of illiteracy and semi-illiteracy. There is no doubt that a change of American attitudes in this respect is under way and that an increasing stress is placed upon the desirability of raising the educational level in the substandard regions to greater equality. This change—which is part of a much more general tendency of the American Creed to include ideals of greater economic equality—has taken form in the proposals for greater federal aid to education. The Negroes' chance of getting more equality in education is bound up with this movement.

Considering the importance attached to education in America, it is surprising that the teacher has not been awarded a higher status in American society. The Negro community, in this respect, is more like Northern European societies. The teacher generally has a symbolic prestige from his calling. Because of the scarcity of business opportunities, the teacher is also freer from competition for prestige. However, the great personal dependency of the teacher, particularly in the rural South, and her low income tend to deflate her position in the Negro community.

While there is not much of an adult education movement in America, there is a great deal of passive mass education through the radio, press, popular magazines, and movies. The rise of the Negro population to literacy must have a strong influence in raising the cultural level of Negroes. Through these means they are made more American.

9. The Development of Negro Education in the South

The history of Negro education in the South is one of heroic deeds as well as of patient, high-minded, and self-sacrificing toil.

One of the differences between the North and the South at the outbreak of the Civil War was that the Northern states had established tax-supported public schools, while the public school movement in the South was just beginning. The few Negroes in the North shared in the educational facilities there. In the South most white people had little or no formal schooling. In all Southern states (except a few Border states and the District of Columbia) it was forbidden to teach slaves how to read and write, and several states extended the prohibition to free Negroes. Still, a few of the slaveowners or their wives and daughters considered it a Christian duty to teach slaves to read, and, by 1860, perhaps as much as 5 per cent of the slaves could read and write. A larger proportion of the free Negroes had acquired some schooling.

After the Civil War there was a tremendous demand for education in the South. A number of Union soldiers stayed in the South to teach the freedmen the "three R's." They were immediately assisted by better trained idealists—largely Abolitionists from the North, especially from New England. Northern Negroes also came down to swell the number. The Freedmen's Bureau did some of its most important work in establishing and supporting schools for Negroes. Missionary and church organizations in the North contributed both teachers and money. Fisk, Atlanta, Howard, and Hampton were founded between 1865 and 1880. The Negro communities themselves collected much money for their schools, particularly on the elementary level.

But during the Restoration, Negroes were severely discriminated against; in many parts of the South Negro education deteriorated for decades. The great wonder is that the principle of the Negroes' right to public education was not renounced altogether. But it did not happen. One explanation is the persistency and generosity of Northern philanthropy. It is to be noted that the South allowed this. The American Creed, backed by the Constitution, showed itself strong enough not to allow the sacred principle of public education to succumb. Even in the South—as it came out of the Civil War and Reconstruction—the caste interest could never be pursued wholeheartedly.

Almost as soon as the movement for the education of Negro youth began, the quarrel started as to whether Negro education should be "classical" or "industrial." If the white Southerners had to permit the Negroes to get any education at all, they wanted it to be the sort that would make the Negro a better servant and laborer, not that which would teach him to rise out of his "place." The New England school teachers wanted to train the Negroes as they themselves had been trained in the North: the three R's at the elementary level, with such subjects as Latin, Greek, geometry, and rhetoric at the secondary and college levels.

The struggle between the conservative and radical groups of Negro leaders became focused on this issue. Booker T. Washington became the champion of "industrial" education. Du Bois headed the group of Negro intellectuals who feared that most often the intention, and in any case the result, of strictly vocational education would be to keep Negroes out of the higher and more general culture of America.

From the Civil War until today there has been a steady stream of money going from Northern philanthropy to Southern education. While a large part of it has gone to white education, a considerable portion has gone to Negro education. In the first two decades of the twentieth century Negro education received a great boost when the Northern philanthropic foundations stepped into the picture on a really large scale. One important effect of this Northern support of Negro education has been to spur the Southern state and municipal authorities to improve facilities for Negroes.

At the college level, Hampton and Tuskegee continue with their vocational emphasis but have recently tended to give a good basic education of the academic type. Most of the Negro liberal arts and teachers' colleges of the South are inadequate. The best Negro *universities* in the South—Howard (in Washington, D.C., supported by the federal government), Fisk (in Nashville, Tenn., privately supported), Atlanta (in Atlanta, Ga., privately supported)—are as adequate in many ways as the better Southern white universities. There are also one or two Negro *colleges*—for example, Talladega (in Alabama, privately supported)—that rank with the better white colleges. Only a half dozen of the Southern Negro universities offer any training on the graduate or professional levels and, with the exception of Howard University, graduate training is restricted to a few fields.

10. The Whites' Attitudes toward Negro Education

There are conflicts between whites and Negroes in regard to Negro education. The situation is complicated by the fact that both whites and Negroes are divided in their own minds.

The American Creed definitely prescribes that the Negro child or youth should have just as much educational opportunity as is offered anyone else in the same community. This equalitarian ideal is strong enough to dominate public policy in the North. In the South the great discrimination in education indicates that another value is dominating white people's actions. But it is a mistake to believe that the

American Creed is not also present and active. Negroes would not be getting as much education as they are getting in the South if the equalitarian Creed were not also active.

By itself the caste system would motivate Southern whites to give Negroes no education or restrict it only to training in such lowly skills as would make Negroes better servants and farm hands. The poorer classes of whites in this respect have interests similar to those of the planters. They are in competition with Negroes for jobs and for social status. In addition, the segregated school system of the South allows a substantial saving by keeping Negro education low.

The caste interest is not merely economic. The whites believe that education will make the Negro conscious of "rights" which he should not know about. It will make him dissatisfied. It will raise some Negroes above many whites in culture. The supremacy of individual whites is bound up with Negro ignorance.

The white people have all the power and so their interests have molded Negro education in rural districts. The low standard of Negro schools is the result. But even in the rural South the observer sees the impact of the American Creed. Often it is revealed only in a bad conscience. In most localities there also seems to be a gradual improvement of Negro schools. In practically all places no obstacles are placed in the way of outside help if it observes the proper Southern forms.

In the urban South, whites of the employing class do not have the same interests in keeping Negroes ignorant. They gain if their Negro servants and laborers have at least some education. The poorer classes of whites, however, are interested in keeping Negroes as much as possible out of competition in the labor market. The interest in preserving the caste order is shared by all classes but felt most strongly by the poorer whites. City populations are, however, more closely integrated into the life of the nation: Southern traditions are somewhat weaker, the cultural level among whites is higher, the American Creed is stronger. So we find that Southern cities offer the Negroes a substantially better education than do the rural areas.

11. "Industrial" versus "Classical" Education among Negroes

Quite independent of the value of "vocational" or "industrial" education as compared with a more liberal education, there is no doubt that the popularity among whites, now as earlier, of the former type of Negro education is motivated by the interests of preserving the caste order. Industrial education for Negroes is the formula upon which Southern whites have been able to strike a compromise between their belief in education, which stems from the American Creed, and their interests as white Southerners in preserving the caste order of the region. In the South the problem of industrial versus classical education for Negroes is not, and never has been, discussed merely in terms of pedagogical advantages and disadvantages.

Two factors complicate the issue even more: the relatively high costs of modern vocational education and the white laborers' fear of the Negroes as competitors. As a result, no effective industrial education has ever been given the Negroes in the Southern public schools, except training for cooking and menial service. The discussion of whether Negroes should have a vocational or a liberal schooling is thus only in part a real issue. Partly it is a cover for the more general problem as to what extent Negroes should have much education at all. The main conflict is between the ever-present equalitarian American Creed, on the one hand, and the caste interest, on the other.

12. NEGRO ATTITUDES TOWARD EDUCATION

The attitudes of the whites are of the greatest importance for the growth of Negro education, as they have all the power. The Negroes are, however, not without influence, partly because the whites are divided in their own conscience. The remarkable thing is that Negroes are split in much the same way and on the same issues.

The major split in the Negro world is as to what kind of education is desirable. On the one hand, they sense the caste motivation behind most whites' interest in industrial education for Negroes. They know also that they can hope to win the respect of whites and take their place as equal citizens in American democracy only if they are educated in the cultural values of the broader American society. On the other hand, they know how many lines of work are closed to them. In order to utilize fully what openings there are, and in order to open up new roads into industrial employment, they often conclude that Negroes are in particular need of vocational training.

Negroes are divided, too, on the issues of segregated schools. In so far as segregation means discrimination and is a badge of Negro inferiority, they are against it, although many Southern Negroes would not take an open stand that would anger Southern whites. Some Negroes, however, prefer the segregated school, even for the North, when the mixed school involves humiliation for Negro students and discrimination against Negro teachers. Other Negroes prefer the mixed schools at any cost, since for them it is a matter of principle or they believe that it is a means of improving race relations.

13. Trends and Problems for the Schools

The major problem is, of course, that the educational facilities for Negroes in the South, particularly in many rural areas, are scandalously poor. But it is equally important to recognize that there are differences in the level of educational facilities offered Negroes and there is a definite trend upward. In spite of much discussion regarding the type of Negro education, its actual development has never followed any plan or theory. The main problem has always been not what sort but how much education the Negro should have and how much he gets. The truth is that any type of improved education for Negroes is healthful.

There is an immense need for new school buildings for Negroes, particularly in rural districts but also in most Southern cities. There is also need for new equipment of all sorts, for consolidated schools and for school buses.

A second most important condition for progress is to improve the standards of Negro teachers. Negro teachers need not only better training and higher salaries; they also need more security of tenure. The present drive to equalize salaries between white and Negro teachers, which is occurring in almost every Southern state, will undoubtedly tend to raise standards as well as salaries.

If the federal government undertakes further financial responsibility for education, it will be up against a difficult problem. How is it possible to aid without decreasing local responsibility? In our judgment, Northern philanthropy has probably had a certain demoralizing influence on the South. The South has become accustomed to taking it for granted that not only rich people in the North but also poor church boards should send money south. Thus far, rich people in the South have been less inclined to give away their money for philanthropic purposes. For these moral reasons it is important, when the federal government steps in, that local financial responsibility be preserved as much as possible. The ideal solution would be that the federal government pay certain basic costs all over the country, such as original building costs and basic teachers' salaries. It is, of course, of special importance that absence of discrimination be made a condition for aid. Otherwise the idea will become established that Negro education is the business of the federal government and less a concern of the state and the municipalities. In this sense there is a danger that the Negro people might become "the ward of the nation."

One emphasis of Negro education in the past has frequently been upon maintaining the relations of the student to his community. This is a good idea in many respects, but one main point has been forgotten. With the present trends in Southern agriculture, it is fairly certain that many of the children born in a cotton county today are going to live and work in Northern and Southern cities. What, therefore, is primarily needed is an education which makes the Negro child adaptable to and movable in the American culture at large. Above all, he needs not to be specialized, but to be changeable, "educable." And he needs it more than the white child, because life will be more difficult for him.

Meanwhile, Southern Negro schools are going to remain inadequate. The North will continue for many decades to get untutored and crude Negro immigrants from the South. These uneducated masses of Southern-born Negroes will be a heavy burden on the social and economic order in the North. It is, therefore, an interest for Northern cities, and not only for the migratory Negroes, that a program of adult education be instituted to teach the migrating Negro masses the elements of American culture and also, perhaps, elements of vocational skills.

14. The Press as an Organ for the Negro Protest

Most white people in America are unaware of the Negro press's bitter and relentless criticism of them; of their policies in domestic and international affairs; their legal and political practices; their business enterprises; their churches, schools, and other institutions; their social customs; their opinions and prejudices; and almost everything else in white American civilization. Week in and week out these are presented to the Negro people in their own press. It is a fighting press.

In 1945 there were 155 Negro weekly, semiweekly, or biweekly newspapers.[3] Some of these are for the general Negro public; others are organs of Negro religious denominations and labor organizations. Most of the general newspapers have a circulation limited to the locality where they are published. But ten to twenty Negro papers have large circulations extending to whole regions and sometimes to all of Negro America. In 1945 the circulation of the 155 Negro papers reached 1,809,000. In addition, there are some 105 monthly, bimonthly,

[3] U.S. Bureau of the Census, "Negro Newspapers and Periodicals in the United States." (Washington: Government Printing Office, 1946), Negro Statistical Bulletin No. 1.

[4] Ibid.

and quarterly magazines.[5] Two of these have national importance: *The Crisis,* published by the N.A.A.C.P., and *Opportunity,* published by the National Urban League. The former reaches over fifty thousand people.

Practically all Negroes who can read are exposed to the influence of the Negro press at least some of the time. The subscribers to the Negro press are the most alert and articulate individuals who form Negro opinion. In addition, newspapers are passed from family to family, and they are sometimes read aloud in informal gatherings. They are available in barbershops, and sometimes in churches, lodges, and pool parlors. Their contents are passed by word of mouth among those who cannot read. Indirectly, therefore, this press influences a large proportion of the Negro population.

15. Characteristics of the Negro Press

Negro newspapers are similar to other American newspapers, particularly those circulating among the lower classes. Many of the differences are exaggerations of common American traits, called forth by the caste situation. On broader political issues unconnected directly with the Negro problem, Negro newspapers have the fullest range between radical and conservative. It is only on the Negro problem that the press is "radical."

The Negro newspaper is typically an "additional paper." More white papers than Negro papers are probably bought and read by Negroes, who read the local news and the local ads daily. The Negro papers, therefore, largely supplement the ordinary papers with Negro news and opinions.

As the Negro newspaper is a weekly paper, as Negro news is not too plentiful because of the scarcity of agencies and reporters to communicate it, and as much of the news is several days old when it appears in the weekly press, it is natural that editorials, columns, and other non-news items are given a proportionally larger space than in an ordinary daily newspaper, and that the news itself is more "edited." This is true of all weeklies. In the Negro weekly it is further motivated by the strong propaganda purpose: the news is presented mainly to support the Negro protest.

The Negro weekly is ordinarily a "sensational" paper. Sensational journalism is, however, not an un-American trait. The Negro press has merely adopted a technique from the white press with which it

[5] Florence Murray (editor), *The Negro Handbook, 1946–1947.* (New York: Current Books, A. A. Wyn, Publisher, 1947), p. 237. These figures are from a 1943 census report and refer to the period between July 1, 1942, and June 30, 1943.

is in competition. The most sensational white newspapers are found in the big cities, and there they appeal to the masses. Negro editors and publishers, too, seek to reach a mass audience. Thus the explanation of why the Negro press exaggerates the American pattern of sensational journalism is, of course, that the Negro community, compared with the white world, is predominantly lower class. Sensationalism also occurs in the Negro press because it is an "additional" Negro paper. Its excuse for existing is to select those items with a race angle and to "play them up" as they are "played down" in the ordinary white press. In hammering the Negro protest week after week, the press is constantly in danger of becoming boring. It must, therefore, attempt to "personalize" the news as much as possible. It must accentuate the human-interest angle and create a feeling that people are fighting and that big things are happening.

Much space is thus devoted to crime. This might seem surprising, since Negroes rightly accuse white newspapers of giving too much space to Negro crime and too little to all other Negro activities. But most Negroes, like other lower-class persons, want to read about crimes.[6] Furthermore, the white papers write little about crimes in the Negro community and about crimes committed by white persons against Negroes. The last item, particularly, is important to the Negro newspaper seeking to combat the white stereotype of "the criminal Negro." Crimes against Negroes by whites are always "played up" greatly. Lynchings are, of course, a specialty of the Negro press. In the other direction, the Negro press is likely to treat as sensational, individual accomplishments of Negroes and public statements by whites for or against the caste system. It also dramatizes the society news.

The "society" page of the Negro newspaper is a direct copy of that of the white paper. It is certainly no more exaggerated than the gossip pages of the small-town American newspaper. Whites are amused by it partly because of their belief in the inferiority of the Negro, but also partly because they are seldom aware of the existence of a Negro upper class, especially one so attentive to the social niceties.

Most upper- and middle-class Negroes "overdo" their social activity because they are struggling for status as individuals. Negroes stress "society" because whites deny them social prestige. But apart from this, Negroes, like other Americans, enjoy reading about themselves in pleasant situations. The Negro paper gives almost every

---

[6] It is interesting to observe, on the other hand, that "sex" is played up less in the Negro press than in the white tabloids appealing to lower-class people.

upper- or middle-class Negro family a chance now and then to see one of the family displayed, with name and picture, at least as a member of a club, a church, a committee, a high school class, or as attending a tea, a dance, a bridge party, or a sports event.

The sports columns record and exalt Negro performances. Even the comics usually have, in addition to their usual purpose, a race message to tell. The Negro newspapers do what the national press in every country does; they flatter the group and appeal to group pride even when admonishing; they help to make it feel self-confident and superior.

16. Outlook for the Press

The importance of the Negro press for the formation of Negro opinion, for the functioning of all other Negro institutions, for Negro leadership and concerted action, is enormous. The Negro press is an educational agency and a power agency. Together with the church and the school, it determines the direction of the process through which the Negroes are becoming more a part of American culture. The Negro press causes, on the one hand, an intense realization of American ideals on the part of the Negroes. On the other hand, it makes them realize to how small a degree white Americans live up to them.

As the educational level of the Negro masses rises, as those masses become less dissimilar in culture to other Americans, as the isolation between the two groups increases under voluntary withdrawal on the part of the Negroes, as race consciousness and race solidarity are intensified, as the Negro protest is spread among the lower classes, the Negro press will continue to grow. With larger circulation, there will be increased possibilities of getting advertising. With increased income, the Negro press will be able to buy better equipment, to engage better trained journalists, and to organize a better national news service. When the Negro press can produce a better product than now, it will sell more. Whether or not this forecast of an increasing circulation for Negro papers becomes true, the Negro press is of tremendous importance. It has rightly been characterized as "the greatest single power in the Negro race."[7]

[7] Edwin Mims, *The Advancing South* (Garden City, N.Y.: Doubleday, Page & Company, 1926), p. 268.

CHAPTER XVIII

The Negro Community

1. THE NEGRO COMMUNITY AS AN UNHEALTHY FORM OF AN AMERICAN COMMUNITY

Until now the Negro community has not been the primary object of our study, although we have touched upon various aspects of it. There are a number of problems, however, such as those of the Negro family, crime, insanity, and cultural accomplishments which we need to deal with in more detail.

The value premise for this chapter comes from the American Creed. America was settled by people who, for one reason or another, were dissatisfied with conditions in their homelands and sought new opportunities. Until 1921 the nation welcomed immigrants. They came from everywhere and brought with them their institutions and cultural patterns. It was natural that the "melting pot," "Americanization"—or, to use a more technical term, "assimilation"—became a central element in the American Creed. To make a unified nation out of different ethnic groups, the immigrants were to abandon their cultural "peculiarities" and to take on the cultural forms of America.

Negroes have been living here for over three hundred years, and practically all the ancestors of present-day Negroes came to this country a hundred years ago. It is probable that, on the average, Negroes have been Americans longer than any other immigrant group except the British. They should be well assimilated by now. Negroes, however, together with the Orientals and, to some extent, Indians and Mexicans, have not been allowed to assimilate as have European immigrants.

Negro institutions are, nevertheless, similar to those of the white man. They show little similarity to African institutions. Some peculiarities can be characterized as "exaggerations" of American traits.

In his allegiances the Negro is characteristically an American. He believes in the American Creed and in other ideals held by most Americans, such as getting ahead in the world, individualism, and the importance of education and wealth. For the most part he is not proud of those things in which he differs from the white American. Moreover, in practically all its differences, American Negro culture is not something independent of general American culture. It is a distorted development, or an unhealthy condition, of American culture. The instability of the Negro family, the inadequacy of educational facilities for Negroes, the emotionalism in the Negro church, the insufficiency and unwholesomeness of Negro recreational activity, the excess of Negro sociable organizations, the narrowness of interest of the average Negro, the provincialism of his political thinking, the high Negro crime rate, the cultivation of the arts to the neglect of other fields, superstition, personality difficulties, and other "characteristic" traits are mainly forms of social ill-health, which, for the most part, are created by caste pressures.

This can be said positively: it is to the advantage of American Negroes as individuals and as a group to become assimilated into American culture, to acquire the traits held in esteem by the dominant white Americans. We do not here imply that white American culture is "higher" than other cultures, but *here, in America,* American culture is "highest" in the sense that holding to it is practical for any individual or group which is not strong enough to change it.

2. THE NEGRO FAMILY

The book by E. Franklin Frazier, *The Negro Family in the United States* (1939), is such an excellent description and analysis of the American Negro family that it is necessary only to relate its conclusions to our context and refer the reader to it for details.

The uniqueness of the Negro family is a product of slavery. Most slaveowners either did not care about the marital state of their slaves or were interested in seeing to it that they did not form strong marital bonds. Certain practices grew up in slavery which retain their influence today in rural Southern areas: marriages sometimes occur by simple public declaration or with a ceremony conducted by a minister but without a marriage license. Coupled with this was the popular belief that divorce could occur by public declaration or simply by crossing state or county lines. At the close of the Civil War the slave states legalized existing common-law marriages and, with the disappearance of the master's interests and of forced sale, there was a great increase in family stability. But the starting point was so low that

Negroes never caught up. Isolation, poverty, and ignorance were again the obstacles to raising standards.

There are two outstanding types of exceptions to the observation that the average Negro family is more disorganized than the white family. In rural areas of the South, especially in isolated areas, there is a large class of Negro families which is so like the ideal of the monogamous patriarchal Christian family that Frazier calls them "Black Puritans." Much more significant is the upper- and middle-class Negro family in the towns and cities. Upper- and middle-class Negroes probably have fewer extramarital relations and less divorce than upper-class whites. They have reacted against the reputation of lower-class Negroes and have not permitted themselves the marital laxness of some upper-class whites.

Perhaps the best index of family stability that is available is that of illegitimacy. For the United States as a whole, the figures indicate that in 1944 Negroes (nonwhites) had about eight and a half times as much illegitimacy as whites.[1]

There are no nation-wide statistics on divorce by race and the scattered statistics available are of limited significance because most Negro couples who separate do so without divorce. Lodgers and "one-person" families constituted about 10 per cent of the Negro population in 1940, whereas the corresponding figure for the white population was 5 per cent.[2] Broken families were 28 per cent of all Negro families, but only 12 per cent among white families, despite the greater concentration of Negroes in rural-farm areas where broken families are least frequent.[3]

In addition to the direct evidence of family disorganization, there are several other signs that Negroes have a larger share of the factors contributing to family disorganization. Lodgers, for example, are often a disturbing factor in family life. In Northern urban areas 29 per cent of the Negro families reported lodgers in their homes in 1930 as compared to 10 per cent of the native white families. In South-

[1] U.S. Department of Commerce, *Vital Statistics of the United States: 1944.* Pt. II, *Natality and Mortality Data for the United States. Tabulated by Place of Residence.* (Washington: Government Printing Office, 1946) Table T, p. xvii.

[2] U.S. Bureau of the Census, *Sixteenth Census of the United States: 1940. Population, Families, Size of Family and Age of Head* (Washington: Government Printing Office, 1943), p. 122; and United States Bureau of the Census, *Sixteenth Census of the United States: 1940. Population,* Vol. IV. *Characteristics by Age. United States Summary.* (Washington: Government Printing Office, 1943), Table 10.

[3] U.S. Bureau of the Census, *Sixteenth Census of the United States: 1940. Population, Families, Types of Families* (Washington: Government Printing Office, 1943), calculated from Table 7.

ern urban areas the proportions were 20 per cent for Negroes and 11 per cent for whites. "Doubling up" of families in a single household is another factor contributing to family disorganization, and Negroes have more of it. Similarly, as we have noted, Negroes have more overcrowding and less homeownership.

While the Negro masses undoubtedly have more of all those characteristics which define family disorganization in the traditional American sense, they have certain other cultural traits which tend to reduce the disorganizing effect of those characteristics. One is marriage for almost all, and a high rate of remarriage for divorcees and widowed persons. Further, common law marriage and illegitimacy are not seriously condemned within the Negro community—except among the upper classes—and they have, therefore, fewer disorganizing effects on the individual. The Negro community also has the healthy social custom of attaching no stigma to the illegitimate child and of freely adopting illegitimate children and orphans into established families. A high value is placed on children generally, and those who mate outside of marriage do not usually prevent the coming of children. There are few unwanted children.

The existence of these practices does not mean that the Negro community has no moral standards, even in the traditional American sense. "Fast women," philandering men, and "fly-by-night" affairs are condemned. In the rural South, the rule is that a person may cohabit with only one person during a given period; there is little promiscuity. But the important thing is that the Negro lower classes, especially in the rural South, have built up a type of family organization conducive to social health, even though the practices are outside the American tradition. When the practices are brought into closer contact with white norms, as occurs when Negroes go to cities, they tend to break down and to cause the demoralization of some individuals.

3. The Negro Church in the Negro Community

Probably the chief "function" of the Negro church has been to buoy up the hopes of its members in the face of adversity and to give them a sense of community. Negroes, more than whites, have had to place their hopes for a better life in religion. As a Negro poet puts it, "Our churches are where we dip our tired bodies in cool springs of hope, where we retain our wholeness and humanity despite the blows of death from the Bosses . . ."[4]

The religious service in Negro churches is often characterized by

[4] Richard Wright, *12 Million Black Voices* (New York: Viking Press, 1941), p. 131.

extreme emotionalism. Whites, in trying to justify the subordination of the Negroes, have seized upon the fact of religious emotionalism and ascribed it to "animal nature" and even to "excessive sexuality." Two things are important in attempting to explain emotionalism. In the first place, it has been exaggerated by the whites. A large minority of Negroes do not attend church and another large minority do not have emotionalism in their church. Negro youth tend to avoid the emotional type of church and the same is true of the social "climbers" of all ages and occupations. Even in the churches of the rural South emotionalism is declining. The second point is that the great periods of Negro conversion to Christianity were periods when the emotional forms of religion were taking hold of the whites too. Negroes—and lower-class whites in isolated communities in the South—have retained these religious practices to a certain extent. Negroes have been losing them, but not so rapidly as have whites. Another explanation may be that emotionalism in religion is more helpful in taking the Negro's mind off his degradation and frustration.

The Negro church is frequently the only community center, especially in the South. It is owned by the Negroes themselves and they can feel free to do what they please in it. The school is often located in a church in the rural South. Lodges and clubs frequently hold their meetings in the church. Lectures and meetings for discussion of civic problems—including political meetings in the North—are probably most often held in churches. In fact, the Negro church is such a good community center that it might be said that anyone who does not belong to a church in the rural South does not belong to the community.

In its relation to the Negro community, the Negro church tends to be different from the white church. The Negro preacher must, on the one hand, preach "race solidarity" because his congregation demands it and frequently because he believes in it too. On the other hand, he is not only a focus of caste pressure, but his position of leadership depends upon the monopoly given him by segregation. Negro preachers usually support Negro business. Where Negroes vote, preachers frequently take a stand and use their influence and their pulpit to swing Negro votes. A minister who has a political connection gains in power since he can "fix" minor difficulties with the law for members of his congregation and he sometimes has control over a few jobs, political or otherwise. The church, as the community's most central public institution, seems to many Negroes to take on political and other nonreligious functions quite naturally.

The Negro community is so poor and the number of Negro churches so large in relation to the number of churchgoers that the upkeep of the church is a financial drain. The Negro church is more expensive to the average Negro than the white man's church is to him. Most Negroes are aware of this fact and are not happy over it.

4. THE NEGRO SCHOOL AND NEGRO EDUCATION

Since the Civil War the proportion of Negro children attending school has gone up so rapidly that now it is not far behind the also increasing proportion of white children attending school. These figures are deceptive, however, since the bulk of Negro children live in the South and education for Negroes in the South is inferior to that for whites. The main reason for the discrepancy still existing is that Negroes do not attend high school and college to the same extent as do whites.

It is unnecessary to take up the Negro school in the North, since it hardly exists as a separate unit. The main reason why the average Negro gets an education inferior to the average white in the North is that poverty and disease keep him out of school more and force him to leave school at an earlier age. ·

The situation in the South, however, is different. In the rural South the one-room schoolhouse for Negroes is fairly typical, with all the elementary grades taught by a single teacher in a single room. Negro schoolhouses may be far apart. School buses are generally provided for rural whites, but are rarely provided for Negroes. The Negro school in the rural South is kept open only about seven months a year; Negro children must work in the fields in planting and harvesting seasons, and the white planters give the signal for the Negro school to close or to open. Another handicap is that Negro children must sometimes provide all their own books and other school supplies; white children get these things free. The content of the elementary education in the rural South is almost unbelievably poor; a poorly trained and poorly paid Negro woman must control and teach a group of children from poor and uncultured homes in an overcrowded, dilapidated, one-room schoolhouse where she must perform at least some of the janitorial and administrative duties. She is also subject to unusual outside pressure.

There is a clear tendency to avoid civics and other social sciences in the Southern Negro public schools. In some places there are different schoolbooks for Negroes and whites, especially in those fields that border on the social. Where white students are taught the Constitution and the structure of the governments, Negroes are given courses in "character building" by which is meant courtesy, humility, self-control, satisfaction with the poorer things of life, and all the traits that mark a "good nigger" in the eyes of the Southern whites.

While the quality and quantity of education in the city schools is better than in the country schools, the subjects taught and their content are about the same. High schools for Negroes in the South have existed in significant numbers for only about thirty years and are still inadequate. The Negro public junior college is practically nonexistent in the South. Of 76 Negro institutions of higher learning in the United States (1944–1945) only 22 were public. Of the 54 private colleges, all but 12 were church affiliated. There were, in addition, 12 four-year teachers' colleges and 19 junior colleges and two-year normal schools. Even some of these were privately supported.[5] Most of the colleges did not have the teachers and school facilities to provide an adequate education.

5. VOLUNTARY ASSOCIATIONS

America has an unusual number of social clubs, recreational organizations, lodges, fraternities and sororities, civic improvement societies, self-improvement societies, occupational associations, and other organizations which may be called "voluntary associations." While this is true of Americans generally, Negroes seem to have an even larger relative number of associations. This is the more striking when it is realized that upper- and middle-class people usually belong to more associations than do lower-class people. Thus, although they are predominantly lower class, Negroes are more inclined to join associations than are whites; in this respect, again, Negroes are "exaggerated" Americans. Only a small number of the Negro associations have as their primary purpose to protest against caste or to improve the Negro community in some way, and these we studied in Chapter 16.

Here we shall try to understand the reasons for the many associations which have a "sociable" or "expressive" function. The situation is basically an unhealthy one: Negroes are active in associations because they are not allowed to be active in much of the other organized life of American society.

A second reason is that Negroes seem to follow a pattern which is about a generation behind the general American pattern. Whereas in white America the lodges—with their secret rites and elaborate ritual —began to become unpopular at least thirty years ago, the decline

[5] Florence Murray (editor), *The Negro Handbook, 1946–1947* (New York: Current Books, Inc., A. A. Wyn, Publisher, 1947), pp. 139–143.

of Negro lodges occurred not because they became unpopular but because they failed to pay insurance premiums. The content of the meetings of the Negro sociable groups, even outside the old-fashioned lodges, also reveals the lag in their adaptation to modern American standards. The meetings are often heavily formalized, in the manner of white upper-class clubs of a generation or two ago. Strict rules of parliamentary procedure are followed in the "business" meetings; a complete set of officers is elected even if there are less than a dozen members in the entire club; in upper-class clubs formal dress is required at certain meetings.

Another reason why we regard the great number of Negro voluntary associations as a sign of social ill-health is that they accomplish so little of what they set out to achieve. They collect money and hold dances or card parties for civic or race causes, yet frequently, because of the heavy expenses of the entertainment, the net proceeds are extremely small in relation to the time involved. In addition, these clubs drain off a large part of the Negroes' spare time.

Aside from the above-mentioned differences between Negro and white associations they are much alike. Negro associations are apparently modeled after white associations, even if the white models are remnants of a past generation and so appear ludicrous to some white people today.

The distinctive thing about Negro associations has been the death benefit and sickness insurance feature of some Negro lodges and benevolent societies. Although white lodges frequently had that too, it was much more developed among Negroes. The insurance features of many lodges elicit the only serious praise that has been bestowed upon Negro sociable organizations.

Aside from the fact that all Negro groups are inevitably forced to be "race conscious" and that most of them at least pretend to improve the position of the "race," most associations become purely recreational. To determine whether their recreational function deserves a high evaluation, we shall have to consider the general character of recreation and amusement in the Negro community. This we shall do in Section 8 of this chapter.

6. "Peculiarities" of Negro Culture and Personality

The increasing isolation between Negroes and whites has increased the mutual ignorance of the two groups. Because of their lack of intimate contact with Negroes, whites create and maintain stereotypes about them. Most of the stereotypes have no basis in fact, but even those which are superficially true are not understood by whites. Even when they do not mean to be unfriendly to Negroes, whites observe that certain aspects of Negro life are "different" or "peculiar," and some of these peculiarities bother whites. Here we shall attempt to describe those differences in Negro culture which whites find most unusual or disturbing. We shall start from our conclusion in Chapter 2 that these differences have no basis in biological heredity, that they are of a purely cultural nature.

In this section, we shall sometimes be writing about Negro culture traits as though they applied to all Negroes. This is, of course, incorrect, and it disturbs many Negroes. There is a diversity of behavior patterns among Negroes, perhaps as great as in white American society. Negro communities range from the folk societies of isolated rural Southern areas to the highly sophisticated, wealthy, night-club groups of Harlem. We shall try to take account of the diversity, but we feel we are justified in writing of Negro culture traits because *average* Negro behavior differs from *average* white behavior.

The trait that the whites perhaps associate most with Negroes is aggressiveness. This is remarked about whenever Negroes commit crimes, whenever they are insulting, and even whenever they try to rise out of their "place." The tendency is not only exaggerated in the minds of whites, but whites at the same time frequently speak of the Negroes as docile, subservient, and dull. The tendency is exaggerated partly because white newspapers give relatively little news about Negroes other than crime news, partly because of the traditional racial stereotypes, and partly because many whites do not attribute to Negroes the natural human reactions to insult and deprivation.

Except for the sullen criminal youths found mainly in Northern cities, Negroes seem to be no more aggressive than whites. In view of the fact that they are so frequently discriminated against and insulted, Negroes are remarkably passive and polite toward whites. It is probable that when noncriminal Negroes are called "bumptious," especially in the South, they are merely trying to get their rights as citizens. Sometimes Northern whites unwittingly insult Negroes and are then surprised at the violent reaction. In the North, too, Negroes may do unpleasant things out of ignorance or because they are glad to be free of Southern restrictions.

Next to aggressiveness, probably the most striking trait of Negroes noticed by whites is emotionality and spontaneous good humor. This is given both a high and a low evaluation. On the one hand, the ability to enjoy life is recognized as desirable, but, on the other hand, lack of self-control and the tendency to act on impulse are deprecated. Because Negroes have no direct background in puritanism, they have taken sex more as it comes, without all the encumbrances and inhibitions. The relative economic independence of the Negro woman allows her to mate more in the spirit of equality and mutual enjoyment and less out of a sense of duty or to get economic advantages. Because they have so little money to spend on entertainment, Negroes have learned to enjoy small and inexpensive things and to get as much pleasure as they can out of their free time.

On the other hand, Negroes know that all the striving they may do cannot carry them very high anyway. They often feel "Oh, you might as well make the most of it"; "what the hell difference does it make?" In this spirit, life becomes cheap and crime not so bad. Thus both the lack of a strong cultural tradition and the caste-fostered trait of cynical bitterness combine to make the Negro less inhibited in a way which may be dangerous to his fellows. They also make him more lazy, less punctual, less careful, and generally less efficient as a functioning member of society.

The good humor that is associated with the Negro's emotionalism is frequently the outcome of fear of the white man in the South. The loud high-pitched laugh was evolved in slavery as a means of appeasing the master by debasing oneself before him and making him think that one was contented. Negroes still "put it on" before whites in the South for a similar purpose.

In a similar manner, the Negro slave developed cleverness in language. Like the "Negro laugh," he found that a clever remark amused the white man and often staved off punishment or brought rewards.

The most important use of humor to the Negro . . . was in his personal relations with his white master. The master says to a young slave, "You scoundrel, you ate my turkey," and the slave replies, "Yes, suh, Massa, you got less turkey but you sho' got more nigger." The slave lives to eat another turkey and the master has another entertaining story.[6]

Like the Negro's cackling laugh and appeasing humor, his "dumbness" has been developed as an accommodation to caste. In addition to the real ignorance of the Negro community there is a good deal of pretended ignorance on the part of the Negro. To answer certain questions posed to them by white people in the South is a way of getting both themselves and their fellows in trouble. To volunteer information is often a sure way of being regarded as "uppity" by whites. In other cases Negroes may lie to whites in resentment of the caste system.

Another trait attributed to the Negro and connected with emo-

[6] W. D. Weatherford and C. S. Johnson, *Race Relations* (Boston: D. C. Heath and Company, 1934), p. 284.

tionalism is a love of the gaudy, the bizarre, the ostentatious. The Negro's reputation for conspicuous display is, of course, exaggerated; most Negroes do not have the money to be ostentatious. White people often generalize about the Negro race from a single observation: a Negro racketeer driving a gaudy, expensive car will cause thousands of white people to remark about the ostentatiousness of Negroes. Upper-class Negroes are conservative in their dress and public behavior. They avoid everything that is loud, gaudy, and cheap. They imitate the staid old-fashioned patterns of some upper-class white people. Their clothes are most "respectable" and expensive; their homes are furnished in "good taste"; their social gatherings are costly and ceremonial. They try to copy the "highest" standards of white people and yet get no recognition for doing so.

The eating of chicken, possum, watermelon, corn pone, pork chops is part of the stereotype of the Negro, at least in the North. These things are, of course, either common or delicate foods in the South for both whites and Negroes, and there is no reason why their consumption should be regarded as a "Negro trait."

The Negro's superstitiousness has been given much attention by whites. As among white people, superstition among Negroes is a survival of an earlier period and as such is disappearing as Negroes assimilate modern American culture traits. Upper-class Negroes are about as free from superstition and magical practices as upper-class whites, and Negro youth of the lower classes adhere to them only loosely. It is only in the rural areas of the South that these beliefs and practices have a strong hold on Negroes.

To the Northern white man, although seldom to the Southern white man, the speech of the Negro seems unusual. In fact, the "Negro dialect" is an important cause of the Northern whites' unconscious assumption that Negroes are of a different biological type from them. It is not realized that the so-called "Negro dialect" is simply a variation of the ordinary Southern accent that many Northerners like so well. There is no biological basis for it. Negroes are as capable of pronouncing English words perfectly as whites are.

7. Crime

Negro crime has periodically been the subject of serious debate in the United States and, at least since 1890, has often been the object of statistical measurement. At all times the stereotyped notion has prevailed that Negroes have a criminal tendency, which manifests itself in acts ranging all the way from petty thievery by household servants to razor-slashing homicide.

Statistics on Negro crime have not only all the weaknesses of crime statistics generally—such as incomplete and inaccurate reporting, variations between states as to definition and classification of crimes, changes in policy—but also special weaknesses due to the caste situation and to certain characteristics of the Negro population. Breaking the law is widespread in America, but only a small proportion of the population is arrested, convicted, and sent to prison. Only when official action is taken are there statistics. Some major crimes (such as violation of the Sherman Antitrust Act and avoidance of tax payments) are committed in the ordinary course of conducting a business; others (such as fraud and racketeering) are committed frequently and often go unpunished. It happens that Negroes are seldom in a position to commit these white-collar crimes; they commit those crimes which much more frequently result in apprehension and punishment. This is a chief source of error when attempting to compare statistics on Negro and white crimes.

In the South, inequality of justice seems to be the most important factor in making the statistics on Negro and white crime not comparable. Negroes are more likely to be arrested than are whites, more likely to be indicted after arrest, more likely to be convicted in court and punished more heavily. Some white criminals have made use of the popular belief that Negroes are inherently criminal, and by blackening their faces when committing crimes have diverted suspicion onto Negroes. Some of the crimes in the South usually *can* be committed only by Negroes; for example, the violation of the segregation laws. Again, when white lawyers, installment collectors, insurance agents, plantation owners, and others cheat Negroes, they are never regarded as criminals.

A third cause of distortion of the Negro's crime record is his poverty: he cannot bribe the policeman to let him off for a petty offense; he cannot have a competent lawyer to defend him in court; he usually cannot pay fines and must then serve a prison sentence. The Negro's ignorance acts in a similar fashion: he does not know his legal rights and he does not know how to present his case; he lacks influential connections. In the North the fact that an unusually large proportion of Negroes are in the age group 15–40, which is the age group to which most criminals belong, operates to make the Negro crime rate, based on total population figures, deceptively high. Negro concentration in the cities in the North, where the crime rate is higher than in rural areas, acts in the same manner.

In general, our attitude toward crime statistics must be that they do not provide a fair index of Negro crime. Even if they did, a higher crime rate would not mean that the Negro was more addicted to crime, either in his heredity or in his culture, for the Negro population has certain external characteristics (such as concentration in the South and in the young adult ages) which give it a spuriously high crime rate.

In 1939 there were about three times as many Negro males in prisons and reformatories as there were native white males, in proportion to the sizes of their respective populations; the rate for Negro women was more than four times as great as that for native white women. In the South the number of Negro male felony prisoners was only between two and two and a half times as great (in proportion to population) as the number of native white male felony prisoners. In the North, however, the Negro rate was almost five times as large as the white rate. This would seem to be due mainly to the fact that Northern Negroes are concentrated in cities, where social disorganization is greater and law enforcement is more efficient.

In view of the fact that whites generally believe that Negroes are especially responsible for rape and sex crimes, it is important to note that these offenses are relatively unimportant among Negroes (although the rate is higher among Negroes than among whites). Like other Negro crime rates, the Negro rape rate is fallaciously high: white women may try to extricate themselves from the consequences of sexual delinquency by blaming or framing Negro men; a white woman who has a Negro lover can get rid of him or avoid social ostracism by accusing him of rape; neurotic white women may hysterically interpret an innocent action as an "attack" by a Negro. Real cases of a Negro's raping a white woman probably involve only psychopathic Negroes, at least in the South, for punishment is certain and horrible.

The first group of "causes" of Negro crime to be considered is the discrimination in justice, already summarized. In the same way, poverty, ignorance of the law, lack of influential connections, Southern patterns of illegality and use of weapons in fights, concentration in the cities and in young adult ages in the North—operate to make the Negro crime rate higher than the white crime rate, and so may be thought of as another group of causes.

A third group of causes of Negro crime is connected with the slavery tradition and the caste situation. It has always been expected that Negro servants in the South should pilfer small things. In fact, their money wages are extremely low partly because white employers expect them to take part of their earnings in kind. Something of the same custom prevails between all white employers and Negro employees in the South. This custom operates to raise the Negro's criminal record in two ways: First, it has developed in the Negro a disrespect for the property of others. This feeling is strengthened by the fact that Negroes know their white employers are exploiting them. The second way in which this Southern custom gets the Negro in trouble is when he moves north. In the North any type of taking of property without express permission is regarded as stealing and it may sometimes lead to arrest: Negro servant women in the North have a bad reputation for petty pilfering, and this adds to bad interracial feeling.

Much more deeply based in the caste situation than this custom is the Negro's hatred of whites. A good many crimes of Negroes against whites are motivated by revenge for discriminatory or insulting treatment. Caste, especially when it causes legal injustice and insecurity of life and property, prevents the Negro from identifying himself with society and the law. Because the white man regards him as apart from society, it is natural for a Negro to regard himself as apart. The Negro community tends to be sympathetic toward an individual Negro who commits a crime against whites, since he is only expressing a hostility which is generally felt. The slavery tradition and the caste situation are reflected also in the low regard for human life that characterizes lower-class Southerners generally, and especially Negroes. The fact that the law is arbitrary in the South further depreciates the value of a Negro's life and property.

Certain traits, present everywhere, but more developed in the Negro as a consequence of his slavery background and his subordinate caste status, also have been conducive to a high Negro crime rate. Sexual looseness, weak family bonds, and poverty have made prostitution more common among Negro women than among white women. Carelessness and idleness have caused the Negro to be the source of a disproportionate number of accidental crimes and of vagrancy.

Social disorganization is generally high among Southern Negroes, but disorganization reaches its extreme when Negroes migrate to cities and to the North. The controls of the rural community are removed, and the ignorant Negro does not know how to adjust to a new type of life. Negroes are especially prone to take over the criminal patterns of the urban slums, since they have difficulty in getting regular and decent jobs. More Negro mothers than white mothers have to work for a living and so do not have time to take care of their children properly. Negro children, more than white children, are forced to engage in street trades where they easily pick up the arts of robbing and prostitution. The overcrowdedness of the homes and the consequent lack of privacy prevent the growth of ideals of chastity and are one element in encouraging girls to become prostitutes.

Partly because Negro neighborhoods are slum areas and partly because Negroes are supposed to be masters of sensuous pleasure, Negro neighborhoods are frequented by whites who wish to do something illicit or immoral. Gambling dens and cabarets, illegal selling of narcotics, white and Negro brothels are concentrated in Negro neighborhoods. The owners of these enterprises are practically all whites. The police do not enforce the law much in Negro neighborhoods; what goes on is too much for them to handle, and they come to expect graft for "protection." In such a neighborhood Negroes, especially children, develop a distorted sense of values.

We know that Negroes are not biologically more criminal than whites. We do not know definitely that Negroes are culturally more criminal than whites, although we do know that they come up against law-enforcement agencies more often. We suspect that the "true" crime rate—when outside influences are held constant—is higher among Negroes. This is true at least for such crimes as involve personal violence, petty robbery, and sexual delinquency, and because of the caste system and the slavery tradition. The upper and middle classes among Negroes are at least as law-abiding as the corresponding classes among whites; much of the differential in gross crime rate lies in the fact that the proportion of lower-class Negroes is so much greater.

8. RECREATION

Negro recreation is conditioned by three factors: First, Negroes are barred from using recreational and amusement facilities in many places, even in the North, and are inadequately supplied with private facilities. Second, their geographical concentration in the South means that many of their recreational patterns follow those of the rural South. These are carried over to the urban North by the migrants from the South and are further shaped by the fact that the great bulk of the Negro population is of low economic status and lives in slum areas. Third, because recreation and amusement must be carried on almost entirely within the isolated Negro community, Negro recreation has developed peculiar traits of its own, different from those which characterize recreation in the white community. One of the most striking characteristics of Negro amusements and recreation is their tendency to be informal, intimate, and sociable.

Recreation in rural areas tends to be informal and unorganized.

Besides swimming, hunting, and fishing, a considerable amount of time is spent in loafing, talking, boasting, telling tall stories, singing. One of the chief amusements in rural areas is "going to town," which may be to the nearest town, to the general store, or to the "ice-cream parlor." For the older women church activity is usually the only form of recreation. Limited use is made of radios, phonographs, and movies; what there is tends to break down the isolation of these communities.

The informal gatherings to talk, joke, and meet one's friends are carried over from the rural areas to the city. There the barbershop, the street corner, and the poolroom become the gathering places for the lower-class men and boys. The atmosphere is much less wholesome and innocent than that which surrounds the same sort of loafing and talking in the country. Y.M.C.A.'s, settlement houses, city playgrounds, and athletic clubs in the North do provide organized and wholesome recreation, although not enough of it.

Negro people in the city, even of the respectable middle class, spend much of their time on the streets, partly because of the crowdedness and unattractiveness of their homes. There is also much casual visiting back and forth in the respectable lower- and middle-class community, especially among the women.

Urban Negroes find most of their amusement and recreation in the social clubs, athletic clubs, churches and lodges. In the large Northern (but not the Southern) cities, movies, theaters, concert halls, night clubs, and restaurants are generally available to Negroes (if they can afford them), but there is always the possibility of insult or unpleasantness, and no Negro section, even in New York or Chicago, can support a complete set of recreational facilities. The voluntary organizations, therefore, continue to be a chief source of Negro recreational life.

Most Negroes do not follow the usual American pattern of taking a vacation. The great majority of them are too poor. The upper classes, who can afford to, are usually barred from those vacation resorts which meet their standards, and there are only a few Negro resorts.

One of the most wholesome aspects of Negro recreation and amusement is that it is not a separate part of their lives but is well integrated into the daily routine. Part of this seems to be that Negroes, having little time free from hard work, devised relaxing accompaniments to their work. Part of the reason for this is that so many of the usual recreational forms were denied them that they learned to enjoy the everyday things they did.

9. Negro Achievements

Opportunity is the most important prerequisite for achievement; and since the Negro's opportunities in America have been kept low, his achievements also are small. No Negro is outstanding in national, state, or local politics. Few Negroes have been outstanding in business. There have been but one or two outstanding Negro military leaders. There have been only half a dozen outstanding Negro natural scientists and perhaps a dozen or so outstanding Negro social scientists. The only esteemed fields in which Negroes have made many achievements are those of the theater, of sports, and of entertainment.

Before we go into these we call attention to the high performance of Negroes in a field that is often overlooked by whites—the field of race leadership. If we include this field with politics, we can honestly say that some of the most capable statesmen in the United States are Negroes. If these men, with their training in practical politics, were white, they would no doubt be national leaders, as they now are race leaders. This was almost recognized of Frederick Douglass and Booker T. Washington, but the two other Negro statesmen of equal stature—W. E. B. Du Bois and James Weldon Johnson—have been virtually ignored by whites. On a second level, still high when compared with most white national leaders, are such people as Elmer Carter, Lester Granger, Charles Johnson, A. Philip Randolph, Walter White, Mary McLeod Bethune, and Roy Wilkins. In addition, there are wise Negro politicians all over the country, in the national offices of the betterment and protest organizations, and in the federal government in Washington.

It is in the field of entertainment that the Negro's achievements are most widely recognized, and the opportunities made available to him there have made it possible for him to develop excellence in the lucrative fields of arts and sports. In sports we can list Joe Louis, Jackie Robinson, Jack Johnson, Henry Armstrong, John Henry Lewis, Jesse Owens, and Lany Doby. Among the concert artists are Marian Anderson, Dorothy Maynor, Paul Robeson, Roland Hayes, Carol Brice. The stage has long witnessed front-rank Negro actors and is now graced with such figures as Todd Duncan, Canada Lee, Paul Robeson, and Ethel Waters. On the dance stage there are such masters of their respective talents as Katherine Dunham and Bill Robinson. The screen and radio are practically closed to serious Negro actors—but some Negroes have achieved huge success in the role of buffoon, notably Hattie McDaniels and Rochester, or in limited roles, such as Lena Horne has portrayed. Negro jazz band leaders are among the most popular—Louis Armstrong, Count Basie, Cab Calloway, Duke Ellington, Fletcher Henderson, Jimmie Lunceford, King Oliver, and Fats Waller. Negroes have contributed such popular musical forms as ragtime, jazz, the blues, swing, and boogie-woogie.

Negroes have been greatly hampered in more serious music, but Dean Dixon has emerged as a symphony orchestra conductor. Negroes have achieved moderate success in composing serious music (for example, William Grant Still) and much greater success in composing lighter music (for example, Will Marion Cook, Duke Ellington, James Reese Europe, W. C. Handy, and Rosamund Johnson). There have been a few front-rank American Negro painters and sculptors: (Richmond Barthé, Aaron Douglas, Augusta Savage, Henry O. Tanner). In literature, Negroes have made outstanding achievements. The names of Countee Cullen, Langston Hughes, Claude McKay, Sterling Brown, Frank Yerby, Willard Motley, and Richard Wright (and, in the past, Paul Laurence Dunbar and James Weldon Johnson) are well known to the white reading public, and there are at least a score of other Negro writers of equal merit but little known to the white reading public.

Until recently, the puritanical spirit has been a powerful influence on entertainment and the arts in America. To a large degree, white Americans have considered it somewhat immoral to be an entertainer, and white American men have considered it beneath their dignity to cultivate artists. Since whites stereotype Negroes as immoral, they have been willing to let Negroes entertain them. They could enjoy the bawdy and frivolous songs, dances, and jokes without "sinning."

Negroes, on their side, have developed entertainment and the arts because they were relatively free of puritanical traditions and because they were offered relatively attractive economic opportunities. They have been so successful at this that they have taken over the whites' false racial belief that Negroes are innately superior in emotional expression. This has, however, helped to provide a tradition of success which has spurred them on. Further, novels, poetry, songs, even painting and sculpture, have proved excellent means for expressing the Negro protest. Even the spirituals often have these themes, sometimes under the guise of religious words to avoid censure from the whites ("Didn't my Lord deliver Daniel, and why not every man?" "Let My People Go").

Whatever the reason for the success of Negroes in the fields of entertainment and the arts, the success has had predominantly bene-

While the sudden influx of Southern Negroes of low educational and cultural attainments during and after World War I increased racial prejudice and social discrimination, Negroes have a measure of protection against social discrimination in the eighteen Northern and Western states with civil rights laws. The rising educational and cultural attainments of Northern Negroes plus the activities of the Negro betterment organizations have succeeded in enforcing many of these laws. At the same time it must be remembered that to an upper- or middle-class Negro, whose moral and living standards are at least equal to those of the white middle classes, the constant fear of social discrimination and the necessity of fighting for civil rights are sources of cynicism toward and hatred for whites.

The two areas in which Northern Negroes suffer most are housing and employment. While all America is today suffering from a housing shortage, the Negro is the worst sufferer. In every large Northern city, where most Northern Negroes live, they are restricted to certain areas which were run-down and overcrowded long before the war. Very few new areas are being made available to them in spite of their increased needs. Like social discrimination, the housing shortage bears most heavily on the upper- and middle-class Negroes, whose standards demand decent housing which they have never been able to get even though they are able and willing to pay for it. Among these are many veterans, who, like white veterans, feel that the least they are entitled to is decent housing for themselves and their families.

The employment situation is, at the present time, not clear. As we have pointed out, Negroes made tremendous gains during the last two years of the war. They were able to break into new industries, to enter skilled work, and to join unions. Unemployment, which, during the Great Depression had been disproportionately heavy among Negroes, had almost disappeared. Postwar prosperity enabled the Negroes to hold most of their gains, at least to the point of avoiding unemployment. Since Congress failed to pass a national FEPC law, however, Negroes have met with increasing discrimination both in hiring and in layoffs. Furthermore, Negroes in general have less seniority than whites do, and they are concentrated more in the over-expanded wartime industries. Six states, and several cities, however, have passed FEPC laws and in general the unions have protected their Negro members from discriminatory discharge. The real test of whether Negroes have been granted equal economic opportunity will come if and when America again faces mass unemployment. If we allow unemployment to be concentrated on the Negro masses, thus reducing them to a group unable to support themselves, we will have failed in one of the basic ideals of the American Creed—to allow each individual, regardless of race, creed, or color, the opportunity to raise himself as far as he is able.

3. IN THE SOUTH

The Negro's position reached its lowest level in the South around 1900. Since then it has been rising steadily. The increasing industrialization and urbanization of the South, rising educational and cultural standards among both Negroes and whites, and disapproval of the South's attitudes toward the Negroes on the part of the rest of the country are all factors in this rise.

In the field of social relations we traced a slow but visible decrease of discrimination in the South during recent decades up to the outbreak of World War II. The racial etiquette has been weakening, even if ever so little. White people are beginning to recognize distinctions in education and class within the Negro community and are becoming prepared to treat Negroes somewhat differently according to their individual worth. The "no social equality" theory is not quite so rigid as in earlier generations. The entire Jim Crow apparatus is maintained, but its motivation is no longer so unquestioned. Southern liberals have been demanding with increasing courage and determination that the "separate but equal" doctrine should be followed out in its "equality" aspect as well as in its "separateness" aspect.

The separation of the two groups in the South is, meanwhile, becoming more and more perfected. There seems to be a growing mental isolation between whites and Negroes. Behind this potentially dangerous development is not only the exclusionist policy of the whites but also the sullen dissatisfaction and bitter race pride of the Negroes themselves.

In the administration of justice there was a definite improvement, even if Negroes were still far from enjoying equality before the law. In the political sphere, the South continued up to the war to disfranchise the Negro contrary to the clear precept of the American Creed and the Constitution. The masses of whites also have been kept from political participation. Real issues are kept out of politics and there is a great amount of corruption. But these things prove increasingly difficult to keep up. In the enjoyment of public services the Negro has been discriminated against severely in the South in blunt repudiation of the Constitution and the state laws. But even in this sphere there has been a slow improvement of his status.

While in all these spheres the trends at the outbreak of the war were definitely in the direction of a rise in the status of the Negro, the same cannot be said about those relating to his occupational status. In Southern agriculture the Negro's plight has been becoming continually worse and shows no prospects for a brighter future. The new unions in the mass production industries gave Negro workers hope by organizing them together with whites in fields in which Negroes were already working. But with few exceptions they did not open up new industries for Negro employment during the thirties. Neither did they pave the way for Negroes to rise by promotion from the level of unskilled workers to that of the semiskilled and skilled. Negro business did not flourish either, and the small gains made in a few professions were insignificant.

The situation changed rapidly during and after the war. While some of the gains seem spectacular, it must be remembered that they were the result of decades of tedious and expensive litigation and propaganda. First was the revitalization of the democratic ideology, which quickened the consciences of the whites toward the Negroes. Coupled with this were the economic gains made by Negroes due to the tremendous need for manpower, the national FEPC, and the policies of the national unions. But as Negroes made economic gains and became more independent, white Southerners again began to fear the rising Negro. The increased activities of the Negro protest organizations in the South, demands for more equality from the returned veteran, and the generally increased hostility toward whites on the part of Southern Negroes added to this feeling. As a result, Negroes have had both gains and losses in the South. As in the North, they have made substantial gains in industry, many of which they have been able to hold. National policies and the attitudes of the unions will be important in deciding how long they will be able to hold these gains.

Great gains have been made in the educational system. The long-continued campaign of the N.A.A.C.P. to win equal facilities has at last borne fruit in the series of Supreme Court decisions requiring educational facilities, if separate, to be equal. Noteworthy also is the increased use of Negro police throughout the South, an important step in establishing fair and equal justice for the Negroes.

By far the most important gain in the sense that it has far-reaching effects on Southern politics and, consequently, national politics, is the extension of the franchise. This has been accomplished by the final outlawing of the "white primary." This has always been the most efficient barrier to Negro voting and, while there are other barriers, we can expect a gradually increasing number of Negroes to vote during the next decade. Several consequences can be expected from this: (1) increasing interest in voting on the part of the poor whites; (2)

growth of a two-party system; (3) end of a distinction between the South and the rest of the nation in federal politics.

On the other hand, there has been a sharp increase in antagonism and violence toward the Negroes manifested in lynchings, beatings, and killings of Negroes by sheriffs; agitation against veterans and sometimes refusal to grant them GI rights; the raising of the "white supremacy" demand in political campaigns; and a flood of apologetic literature from the South.

The truth is that the South is at present under terrific pressure to change her ways and, since her ways are bound up in all respects with the Negro problem, her attitudes toward the Negro are undergoing drastic changes. The pressures include the South's own needs for increased industrialization and economic efficiency, for more and better education, for incorporation into the rest of the nation both economically and culturally rather than remaining a backward region, and the general American need for vitalizing democracy, both at home and abroad, and for increasing the security of her citizens. Therefore, in so far and as quickly as the South succeeds in bringing her standards up to the rest of the nation's, to that extent will she succeed in solving the Negro problem in terms of the American Creed. Contrary to the opinion usually expressed by Southerners, disapproval on the part of the rest of the nation forces the South to conform more to Northern standards.[1] The more the North cleans its own house and the higher it raises its own standards of equality in regard to the Negro the clearer will its conscience be, the more indignant it can then be with the South, and the quicker will the South conform to the American Creed.

It is much easier now to make the South change than it used to be. For one thing, leading Southerners themselves now publicly state that the South ought to change. As Federal Judge J. Waties Waring of Charleston, S.C., said in his 1947 decision outlawing the white primary, "It is time for South Carolina to rejoin the Union. It is time to fall in step with the other States and to adopt the American way of conducting elections." For another thing, the popular theory behind

[1] A striking though minor example of this is shown in a recent incident in Ahoskie, N.C.: The local Kiwanis club held a drawing, offering a Cadillac as the winning prize. When a Negro won, the club refused to award him the car, gave him back the price of his ticket, and held a second drawing. A young singer from the North who drew the tickets was the first to protest, refusing to make the second drawing. The Kiwanis club attempted to suppress the whole incident (thereby revealing a guilty conscience), but news of it leaked out. Protests arose immediately from all over the country and the national Kiwanis organization ordered the local group to make proper restitution to the Negro, which it finally did. In all the subsequent publicity, the heads of the Ahoskie Kiwanis denied having any prejudice against Negroes.

race prejudice is breaking down. In the South three generations ago, white people had for their defense a consistent and respectable theory, endorsed by the church and by all sciences, printed in learned books and periodicals, and expounded by the South's great statesmen in the Capitol at Washington. The Negro was regarded as a completely different species of mankind: undeveloped, "childlike," amoral, and much less endowed with intellectual capacities than the white man; he was meant by the Creator to be a servant forever; if kept in his "place" he was tolerable, and there he was also happy; "social equality" was unthinkable as it implied intermarriage which would destroy the white race and Anglo-Saxon civilization. Most of this theory remained until a couple of decades ago. But now it is almost destroyed for upper-class and educated people. Its maintenance among lower-class and uneducated people meets increasing difficulties. It is significant that today even the white man who defends discrimination frequently describes his motive as "prejudice" and says that it is "irrational." The popular beliefs rationalizing caste in America are no longer intellectually respectable. This makes the prejudiced white man nearly as pathetic as his Negro victim. It also makes his attitudes more susceptible to change.

4. THE NEED FOR DOMESTIC UNITY

It may be thought that the changing situation in both North and South is proof that the Negro problem is well on its way to solution. And it is true that the whites have not been so consciously disturbed about the Negroes or the Negroes so successful in their protest for a long time. There are hundreds of white organizations and thousands of individuals holding discussions on the problem, arranging interracial meetings, making protests to Congress, writing books, and in many ways trying to promote better relations between the two groups. At the same time the Negroes are pressing their needs, with great success, through the government, local, state and national; through their press and the white press; and through the courts. All this activity, however, affects only a tiny portion of the deeply rooted prejudice and discrimination. It does not reach enough people; it does not move fast enough. The end result is that 14,000,000 Americans are not sharing fully in the rights and privileges guaranteed to every American. No country at a crucial moment in its history can stand to have such a substantial portion of its citizenry relegated to a second-class place. Especially is this true when the subordinate group is filled with the same ideals as the dominant group, when a substantial portion of its members have risen educationally and culturally to the standards of the dominant group, and when the rest are striving to raise their standards. Continual frustration is bound to make the subordinate group bitter, cynical, and eventually, disaffected. At the same time, since the dominant group's strongest ideals and traditions support equality, that group is bound to suffer from a guilty conscience and a weakening of morale.

America, in common with other mature, industrialized nations, is facing a series of problems that arise from the complexity, competitiveness, and urban character of her culture. One aspect of this, of which almost all Americans are well aware, is economic—there is a need to cushion a competitive system so that the weak or unfortunate need not suffer. Toward this end Americans have made much progress and have plans for more. Disregarding the moral problem, which we have already mentioned, it is obvious that a nation cannot afford such luxuries as social security, aid to its dependents, and relief grants, much less have a high general standard of living, if it is going to dispense with the full productive capacity of 10 per cent of its citizens. If, furthermore, Negroes are not allowed to rise economically to the full extent of their individual abilities, most of them will be in the dependent category during economic crises. This means that a disproportionately large share of relief will be spent on this portion of the population through no fault of their own—a highly inefficient and wasteful process and one bound to cause friction and hatred.

Another major problem America faces is that of integrating its citizens into its social and political life. The immense geographical spread of our country, the concentration of a large proportion of our population in large impersonal cities, and the highly specialized and increasingly centralized nature of our governments and our industries have resulted in people's feeling that they are no longer an important part of our government or of the businesses they work for, and hence in indifference toward government and business. Low productivity, poor quality work, labor strife, and corrupt and inefficient government are some of the many problems that result. A third result of both economic insecurity and inability to cope with the size and complexity of government and industry is a feeling of isolation, of insecurity, and of frustration.

It is in this situation of fear, bewilderment, and insecurity that internal disunity can arise. Instead of blaming the real causes, the white majority may put the blame for their difficulties on groups from whom they have traditionally been separated. This is all the easier if there are leaders who, for their own selfish reasons, encourage such splits. Such leaders can rise easily in a free democracy and only an alert and interested citizenry can choose between these and honest leaders. Much of European history shows us the internal quarreling, lack of progress, and general weakness that can result from having a sizable minority not integrated into the nation or not treated as equals. It is also of prime importance in America to remember that the Negroes are not her only minority group; while, at present, they are the group that suffers the greatest deprivations, it is conceivable that if America abandoned her principle of integrating minorities within the nation on terms of equality, a situation might result in which a third of her population would be separated from the rest. We need only look at the Nazi period in Germany to see how fast such a development can proceed once it is started.

The white man's guilty conscience toward his violations of the American Creed in regard to the Negro may make easier the process of blaming the Negro for personal insecurity feelings. It is always easier to blame the victim of one's evil deeds than one's self. If, on the other hand, America rights injustices done the Negro, she will gain not only the political strength that comes from unity but also the creative and productive values that a satisfied minority group will be able to contribute to the nation. There is no doubt that a large part of America's phenomenal growth and success in the past has been due to the high morale that comes from a sense of righteousness, the feeling of everybody's working together toward a common goal, and the great freedom of opportunity. When today we face new and serious problems we can do no better than to look to the American Creed for a moral guide and follow our traditional path of seeking unity within the nation.

5. The Effect of the Negro Problem on International Relations

International affairs today are confused and bewildering. All we hope to do here is to point out several ways in which the Negro problem in America has a direct effect upon America's relations to the rest of the world.

In all this confusion one fact is startlingly clear. America is now, for better or for worse, and despite her wishes, a world power. She shares this position with Russia, and she is a competitor with Russia for world leadership. Furthermore, in this day of movies, radio, and a mass press, every nation in the world is aware of what is going on in America, her black spots as well as her white ones. America's treatment of the Negro is rapidly becoming known throughout the entire world.

For a century America has stood to all the world as the most democratic nation, one to be admired and followed. When the late Wendell Willkie returned from his "One World" trip he reported that "America has a reservoir of good will" upon which to draw. Undoubtedly the war-torn nations of Europe desire to follow democratic ways. While they need our economic aid, they, like most people who have to accept help and are thereby indebted, do not love us for that. They love us because we have stood as the nation in which men were free, free to speak, think, and worship as they pleased and to rise economically according to their own efforts, unhandicapped by class or caste barriers. This is our strongest appeal against the Russians and one which we need to propagandize. The American Creed must, however, be lived up to if other nations are to believe what we say, and lived up to in regard to the Negroes as well as other groups. Europeans, after their recent experiences, well realize that failure to extend equality to one group may mean failure later to extend it to other groups.

Our handling of the Negro problem has much more effect on Asia and Africa than it does on Europe, however. Most of the inhabitants of these continents are colored (in appearance if not in race). Hatred of "white" people is intense in Asia and Africa, not only because the whites have set themselves up as racially superior but also because the whites are seen as conquerors and as tyrants. Hatred against whites is identified with the struggle for national freedom. The colored peoples of the world have always had divided feelings about America; they have admired our treatment of the Philippine Islands, our attitude after the Boxer Rebellion in China, our lack of imperialistic aims, and our democratic government at home. At the same time they have resented deeply our treatment of the Negroes and our theories of the racial inferiority of darker peoples.

Until recently, what the colored peoples thought of us did not make much difference. Now it has become of crucial importance to us. Whatever Russia's faults may be, she has no color prejudice. Again and again she has demonstrated that she does not regard colored people as inferior, that she respects their culture. Laws against discrimination or the manifestation of prejudice are strictly enforced. To the colored peoples of the world, suffering under the double yoke of prejudice and colonial exploitation from white people, this attitude of Russia's has strong appeal. It is doubtful, however, if it is as appealing as the promise of real democracy America can hold out—provided we can hold out also the promise of equality to the individual regardless of color.

Much of the future lies in Asia and Africa. These are new nations, whose period of greatest growth lies ahead of them. The white peoples of the earth began to reduce their death rate a century ago and, as a result, experienced a tremendous increase in population. They are now, with the discovery and widespread use of birth control, entering a period of population decline (except the Russians, whose population is still growing). The colored peoples, especially the Asiatics, starting with an even larger base population, are just now entering the period of a declining death rate. We can expect their populations to expand for a considerable time yet before they begin to use birth control widely. Moreover, since they are just beginning to build up their industrial plants, they will have the advantage of new equipment and methods and will be industrial competitors of the United States. In other words, the colored peoples of the world, because of their huge populations and the newness of their productive equipment, will be factors to be reckoned with in the next century.

It is to our own advantage both now and for the future to live on friendly terms with the rest of the world. At the moment we are the strongest economically, the most advanced technologically, and we own the atomic bomb. But these are temporary advantages. If we are to live at peace in the world (and peace may mean having these great colored nations as our allies), we will have to win them by ideas and not by force. Today, as always, the ideals of the American Creed, the ideals of freedom and equality, if lived up to, are our strongest tools in building the international future.

Index